D1555585

# Capital for Profit

# Capital for Profit

*The Triumph of Ricardian Political Economy
Over Marx and the Neoclassical*

## Paul Fabra

HB
75
.F313
1991
West

Rowman & Littlefield Publishers, Inc.

ROWMAN & LITTLEFIELD PUBLISHERS, INC.

Published in the United States of America
by Rowman & Littlefield Publishers, Inc.
8705 Bollman Place, Savage, Maryland 20763

Copyright © 1991 by Rowman & Littlefield Publishers, Inc.

*All rights reserved.* No part of this publication may
be reproduced, stored in a retrieval system, or transmitted
in any form or by any means, electronic, mechanical,
photocopying, recording, or otherwise, without the prior
permission of the publisher.

© 1979 Flammarion, Paris. Originally published as
*L'Anticapitalisme: Essai de réhabilitation de l'économie politique.*

ISBN 0–8476–7657–9 (cloth, alk. paper)

5    4    3    2    1

Printed in the United States of America

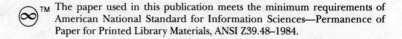
™ The paper used in this publication meets the minimum requirements of
American National Standard for Information Sciences—Permanence of
Paper for Printed Library Materials, ANSI Z39.48–1984.

# Contents

# Foreword

## Michael Novak

Since my university days, I have always been attracted to certain features of the intellectual life of France. In order to achieve eminence as a philosopher in France, it is not necessary to be an academic. In few other places in the world do intellectuals, as distinct from academics, play so large and popularly acclaimed a role. This is perhaps why for intellectuals, artists, journalists, and writers of every sort there is no city in the world like Paris. There, one way or another, such persons may find position, acclaim, and an appreciative community of peers.

Moreover, in France the best minds generally become accomplished in more than one field; it is not considered at all odd for the same person to write serious essays, topical journalism, philosophical reflections, treatises on some specific problem, a novel, or perhaps even a play or movie script—*pourquoi pas*? All the best people practice more than one such art in communicating with the public.

There is yet a third feature of intellectual life in France that I find attractive. In its concern for large and grave ideas, French journalism may perform at the highest level in the world—and here I do mean the journalism of the daily newspapers. The best papers in Paris convey the same large range of information, business notices, diversions, and titillation that newspapers everywhere convey; they carry the same amounts of fact and analysis as their rivals elsewhere in the world. In addition, however, they almost always carry essays of such unusual historical awareness and philosophical depth as one seldom finds in any daily paper in the United States. It is not so much that French intellects are deeper or that American papers are of a lower order; rather, French custom and French tradition have set expectations for journalists that invite them to become essayists of a very high philosophical order.

In what other culture, for example, could men like Jean-Paul Sartre, Albert Camus, François Mauriac, Raymond Aron, and many others move so easily from books to journalism, and back again? In France, it is expected that philosophers and novelists should from time to time conduct their most serious arguments in the daily papers and before the public; and that journalists, from time to time, should free themselves from the cramped restraints of space and time in newspaper work to conduct in public, through books or some other work of art, a sustained and imaginative argument, as if to reveal to the public the depths of the intellectual passion that impels their daily work.

In France today, Paul Fabra is a well-known public figure; his column on economics in *Le Monde* is widely regarded as one of the most significant for public debate in France. Like other journalists, Fabra enjoys reporting and commenting on the daily parade of events and personalities. Far more than most, however, he enjoys following with a keen mind, incisive logic, and intense passion the combat of ideas among scholars and theoreticians of the economy. As if from afar, he enjoys watching the clash of ideologies. Always holding something in reserve, he enjoys probing assumptions, accepted lines of thought, and points of intersection. In this respect, his work often mediates between the academy and the public. He stands outside the "schools" and is known to think deeply and seriously, without being an academic, but he makes it a matter of pride to be abreast of what is going on in the academy—and to comment on it incisively.

In this book, Fabra unveils a lifetime of reflections on the work of several among the classical economists. He does not idolize these classic figures; he questions them, often brusquely. He is rather quick—journalists learn they must be quick—to brand certain opinions as mistakes. He often turns thoughts over and over, in a fashion that few are used to seeing in a classroom, but that is fascinating to experience. Fabra makes one realize quite early that, to join him on this adventure, one will have to think outside familiar categories. The problem that grips him is how long a society can last that believes in the primacy of consumption rather than in the primacy of work.

Fabra is no supply-sider, but he is certainly critical of an excessive emphasis upon demand. He does not believe that such excessive emphasis upon demand is long sustainable.

So he has set out to rethink the basic dynamics of economic activity. He is not trying to write speculative economics, however; he is trying to make sense of the economic realities he sees around him today, and to question the great economists again in the light of new experiences. Some of the things the great ones said, he finds, don't hold up; or contradictions have appeared; or new perplexities have arisen.

One of Fabra's favorite interlocutors is Marx—France having been, during his lifetime, deeply in the grip of arguments with Marxists, whether dogmatic or merely (in Raymond Aron's phrase) followers of "the Marxist vulgate." But his real energy is directed at the neoclassicists.

It has been my experience that French writing in the genre that Fabra here pursues is intended largely as an *hypothèse*—a bold stab of light intended to illuminate dark neglected corners. In order to reap great benefits from each chapter, it is not necessary to hold that this hypothesis is true. One will collect quite enough treasure through catching glimpses of many things that one had never before seen quite so clearly. Reading this book, therefore, brings many pleasures. Not the least of those pleasures is prolonged conversation with a well-stocked mind, and another is a fresh way of thinking about the role of work in the economy. Finally, the book furnishes new arguments on the state of public economic thinking.

Michael Novak
April 1990

# Preface to the English Edition

Even though some progress has been made in recent years toward an understanding of the many conditions that have to be met in order to rejuvenate *capitalism*—a better and more comprehensive term would be the "exchange economy"—the capitalist world is still struggling to create the political, ethical, and monetary framework that the "system" needs in order to thrive and progress. Should it ultimately fail, there is no rational system of a different kind that will necessarily succeed it; it will be replaced by increasing disorder and by arbitrary regimes and policies endeavoring, if at all possible, to correct that disorder.

New approaches to the economic problems facing policymakers have been proposed by enthusiastic prophets of renewal; and new policies, inspired to differing extents by their ideas, have been announced and tried. All have ultimately led to frustration. Thus, in the case of supply-side economics, it appears—with the benefit of hindsight—that the most interesting thing about that brand of economics is its name. The reason why the outcome of the supply-side economic program still is a moot point is that no serious theoretical groundwork has been done to elucidate the far-reaching implications of a genuine shift from demand to supply. The supply-siders have debased their cause by reducing it to a few nostrums, like cuts in direct taxation, which are not so much different from the measures of a conventional demand management policy (that said, tax cutting can be a very useful measure, always provided that budgetary equilibrium permits). The analyses they have put forward have been pedestrian. They have proved unable to bring any fresh insight into either the intellectual vacuum or the material morass we are struggling through.

It is no exaggeration to say that economic thinking has been entrenched for more than three-quarters of a century in a conceptual system based, intrinsically, on demand. That system was constructed in the 1880s and 1890s by Léon Walras and the other founders (mostly Austrian) of the marginalist school. Their primary objective was to restore demand to the rank (which it held prior to the advent of Adam Smith and David Ricardo) of main determinant of value. Their new theory, in complete opposition to the classical labor theory of value, was, as I endeavor to show here, incompatible with any lucid analysis of the notions of labor (within the context of economics), capital, and profit. Nor can it provide any convincing explanation of why profit is necessarily included in the price (value) of any commodities—goods and services—exchanged in the marketplace. The fact is that, though the capitalist world has produced new generations of economists writing ever more sophisticated works, all of them—whether Keynesians, neo-Keynesians, neoclassicists, Friedmanites, or even socialists—are the spiritual descendants of the founders of the "new economics" in the last quarter of the nineteenth century. So modern capitalism, appearances notwithstanding, is in the unfortunate position of lacking any theory of capital (as evidenced yet again by the famous Cambridge controversies of the 1960s on the theory of capital) or profit, which is usually presented as a residual or as the "reward of risk." In other words, profit as viewed from the subjective standpoint of the entrepreneur—a remarkable illustration of the psychological nature of modern economics—is intrinsic to the marginalist construct. No wonder then that pseudo-theories with a semblance of scientific objectivity, like the Marxist one, have for long enjoyed prestige despite the absence of any empirical evidence to substantiate them. I shall return later to this aspect of the abdication of current economic thinking. In order to reconstruct a genuinely supply-based economic theory, a critical scrutiny of several of the key assumptions made by contemporary economists is essential, and this I attempt in my book through, first, a reappraisal of the history of economic thought regarding the concepts of value, labor, capital, and profit (and their relationship one to another) and, second, the formulation of a theory of profit within the framework of a generalized exchange mechanism that is apt to give to the Ricardian labor theory of value (not to the Marxist one) its full meaning.

In 1874 Léon Walras wrote: "In the phenomenon of exchange . . .

demand has to be regarded as the principal fact and supply as a subordinate fact," an assessment which contained in embryo all the future developments in twentieth-century economics, not least the so-called "Keynesian revolution." In spite of the efforts made subsequently by John Hicks and others to allow for the impossibility of quantifying the psychological notion of "want" (on which any theory of demand is based), the fact remains that modern theories of price formation, interest rates, inflation, and so on, have to give considerable weight to the psychology of economic agents. A high level of "real" (an ambiguous word, to say the least) interest rates is therefore explainable today by "expectations" of continuing inflation. One's lurking suspicion is that it would not be possible for "rational expectations" to have such a disproportionate weight if central government based its policies on more rational grounds (because really sound policies cannot be thwarted by "expectations"). Walras was right in thinking that supply and demand are not symmetrical. Either the one or the other is predominant or subordinate. So there are two kinds of market: the market where the competition is on the side of the demanders (or bidders, as in an auction) and the market where the competition is on the side of the suppliers—in other words, a buyer's market. Only a buyer's market can be called "competitive" from the strict economic standpoint. As I show (in Chapters 9 and 10), the Walrasian model, including the model of so-called "perfect competition" leading to "general market equilibrium," presupposes limited supply (scarcity is the assumption on which demand-based economics depends for its very existence). So it can rightly be argued that all modern theories of perfect competition are actually based on the assumption of absence of free entry into the market (this notion of free entry has happily been recently introduced in modern economic thinking). If the competitive market is given back its most important precondition, namely the indeterminacy of the quantity supplied (further supply forthcoming as long as the price is not on the same level as the cost of production, average profit included), it is not necessary to add the condition of multiplicity of suppliers in the market. The size and number of the firms competing with one another is not an essential condition for assuming a competitive market. Ricardo rightly puts supply first because there can be no demand if there is not already supply (supply is the "principal fact"), and because, in the economy as a whole, demand for product A is nothing other than products B, C, and so on, offered in exchange for A. The "law of markets," according to which "products are bought by products," is the cornerstone of classical economics, as Keynes so rightly noted. It is directly at variance with the so-called "law of supply and demand," the rationale of which is to assert the primacy of demand (because of the above-mentioned necessarily asymmetrical relationship between the two sides). We are living in a world in which this alleged "law" reigns supreme. This has tremendous consequences, both theoretical and practical. They stem from the economic system's being deprived of its most powerful regulator, the cost of production. The system's ultimate achievement (and the main instrument of its instability) is the so-called free rates monetary regime. There is no cost of production for the issue of money. The only pragmatic way to reintroduce the discipline of cost into the monetary system is to peg, by way of a convention, the value of the money unit to the value of a determinate weight of gold (or any other commodity chosen for its convenience), the place of that commodity in the scale of prices (value) being determined by its relative cost of production. Ultimately, the floating of currencies, far from being a manifestation of an enlarged free market, is the outcome of a restricted market: Our fiat money currencies must inevitably "float" each in terms of the others. With the abolition of convertibility, the central bank is freed from the discipline of the market through which any producer—here, the issuer of monetary unit—is constrained to exchange its product value for value.

The demand curves as conceived by the marginalists denote another abnormality in the demand-oriented economic construct. The demand curve plots the quantity demanded at different prices overshadowing the market logic according to which there is only one "rational price," the price corresponding to the cost of production (including the current rate of profit). It is only at that price that the principle of equivalence of exchange is respected. At a higher price, the demander will give a sum of money the value of which exceeds that of the good purchased. Will he accept that wittingly except under the pressures of dearth?

One hundred years or so separate the publication of Adam Smith's *The Wealth of Nations* from that of Léon Walras' *Eléments d'économie politique pure*. Another hundred years have gone by since this second book began to undermine the foundations of classical economics. The demand-oriented economy has outstayed its welcome. Theoreticians are uselessly expending much effort and talent in an endeavor to refine perfect equilibrium models or else to refute those artificial constructs. The key to a renewal, both theoretical and political, is a more objective approach to economic phenomena. To reintroduce supply as the sole determinant of value in the long run, it is not enough to expose the shortcomings of the theory of demand. We have to have a point of reference outside the economic system, *other than want,* or else we find that all prices in the market are determined by one another so that we are forced to reinstate demand as the ultimate determinant. For the classicists, this external point of reference was the quantity of labor bestowed on the production of the commodity exchanged (allowing for the phenomenon of accumulation and the profit attached to it). It is one of the purposes of this book to show that Marx completely misinterpreted the so-called "labor theory of value" and to propose a new interpretation that fits the facts and unlocks the door to the impressive but somewhat inadequately formulated Ricardian theory of value. The latter, as I endeavor to explain in this book, is quite different from (and in some respects quite the opposite to) Smith's—a very important fact, because Marx took over the theory (and interpreted it in his own fashion) not from Ricardo's hand, which would have been a blessing, but from Smith's, which has been a theoretical, and historical, disaster. It makes an enormous difference living in a world where the point of reference of the economic system is labor (Ricardian economics) instead of wants (our hedonistic system).

In his most important and enlightening booklet *The End of Laissez-faire,* Keynes questions "how a doctrine [Marxian socialism] so illogical and so dull can have exercised so powerful and enduring an influence on the minds of men and, through them, the events of history." To my mind, there could be two main reasons. The first is that, in our present age of "subjectivist" economics, Marxism has for long appeared as a more objective approach to sociological and even economic issues. The Marxist analysis of profit formation via surplus value might be at variance with observed facts, but first it has to be disproved on logical grounds, which I do in this book within the framework of a non-Marxist and, in my view, correct interpretation of the labor theory of value—a theory which would be better called "objective value theory" because value is proportional to the quantity of labor but labor as such has no value.

A second reason why Marxism has for long looked so attractive was its apparent vindication of modern pessimism and self-denigration (rooted in the Rousseauist view that society is "bad" and oppressive whereas men were born "good" and free). It provides arguments with which to "condemn" capitalism whatever the latter's achievements; it appeals to the modern relativism in showing that capitalism is an "historic" phase and not a permanent structure of any economy based on exchange (which is what it really is). As a matter of fact, Marxism is at the very root of modern "historicism," which holds history up as the supreme tribunal and denies the existence of any permanent principle or rules. A more optimistic view of the economic system would meet with considerable scepticism, because most people today instinctively prefer any theory that seems to explain why "the rich get richer and the poor get poorer"; a theory which conveys a less gloomy view is likely to be considered too complacent a justification for the world as it is. So the pessimistic view is more appealing, since, apparently implying no complacency, it seems more likely to be "scientific"; and, because it dooms the discredited system to failure, it ultimately commits science to the search for a better world. So the attraction of Marxism is a seeming objectivity which flatters modern subjectivism. The vogue of pessimist theory is not confined to Marxism. Malthusianism, which still yields considerable influence in the English-speaking world (and elsewhere), is another striking example. Malthus, whom Keynes considered his spiritual ancestor, and Ricardo were opponents. (Malthus argued the merits of a "passion for consumption" whereas Ricardo was the advocate of more saving and investment.) An academic tradition has made Ricardo another pessimist, because he is supposed to have "predicted" the fall of both wages and profits (in spite of the fact that in his theory a fall in wages necessarily entails a rise in profit, and vice versa) and the ultimate end of growth with the attainment of the "stationary state." These judgments are not borne out by a thorough scrutiny of Ricardo's writings. Ricardo refuted the Malthusian theory of overpopulation. In this book, first published in 1974, I argued that the all-too-famous Club of Rome's forecast of a Third World population "explosion" was probably not justified. Subsequent statistical evidence has lent support to this more sanguine view.

*Capital* has a subtitle, *A Critique of Political Economy*. Walras and the other marginalists explicitly criticized Ricardian economics. So the two main branches of economic thinking in modern times both stem from an endeavor to disprove Ricardo's arguments and Ricardo's approach to economic phenomena. I try here to confront the doctrines of the contradictors, whether Marxian or marginalist and "neoclassical," with the theory they contradict. No such systematic confrontation has been to my knowledge attempted so far. I use only arguments of logic (without mathematics) and I show that, even at the time they wrote, it would have been possible, on purely logical grounds, to show the inconsistency of both Marxian and marginalist theories and, conversely, the consistency of Ricardian analysis.

Marx announced the ultimate abolition of the state when socialism is established. Free-marketers, Friedmanites, and supply-siders, too, are not far removed from this utopian view, the sole difference being that for them the withering away of the state will be the outcome of an extended market economy. Ricardo, on the other hand, thought that the growth of the GNP share preempted by government was inevitable, in spite of the fact that he also favored the dismantling of controls and regulations.

Furthermore, a principle is to be found in the more objective approach to economics whereby, theoretically at least, the *scope* of the market can be defined and limited to products reproducible by standardized labor, whereas an economic system based on want assigns no limit to the market. But the very fact that it is the producers who are in competition means that they constantly seek an advantage over their competitors by quality improvements to the products they supply, the only way of rising above the world of purely interchangeable labor. That is one reason why a supply-oriented economic system is better able to satisfy the wants and tastes of the consumer than a demand-oriented system. Supply-side economics, in the full (and not yet accepted) sense of the term, requires that most of the concepts used by socialists, "liberals" (within the American meaning of that word), and free-marketers as well, be reassessed.

What is at stake today is not only the question of private versus public consumption but also the question of consumption versus investment. Humankind needs more capital than ever in order to embark on the new industrial revolution born of computers and robots, to conserve energy and to meet the pollution challenge. The real issue for capitalism is that it has ceased to be capitalist insofar as it does not accumulate sufficiently.[1] The ills of the so-called capitalist society we are supposed to be living in can be cured only by restoring capitalism— that is, an economic system which generates capital to meet the needs of the present and of the future, "In the long run we are all dead." This oft-quoted quip by Keynes is an outrageous assessment, indicative of the spirit of the day (see pp. 9–10). The triumph of subjective economics over objective economics means a shortening of our horizon. To restore capitalism is to give back to people a long-term perspective. Nothing is more important than to create new forms of saving. The resources are there. What is needed is to recreate the conditions for those resources to be invested productively in both the developed and the developing countries. In 1913, Great Britain invested roughly 10 percent of its GNP abroad, mainly in the poor countries.

With a stable system we could do as well—or better—in a non-colonialist framework.

This book deals with certain fundamentals. The monetary implications of the change of perspective which it proposes (the transition from subjective to objective economics) are set out in the most general terms. One of the implications meriting thorough and meticulous exposition would be the much-needed rehabilitation of the concept of the intrinsic value of money, disregarded (and ridiculed) by Keynes in his *Treatise on Money* and completely rejected by economists since the publication of that book, as important and as arguable a work as the *General Theory*. I hope to attempt such an exercise in the future.

In concluding this preface, I wish to extend my warm thanks to my friend Maurice Stroun, who made it possible for me to have this book translated. The translators, William Hall and Louis Janssens, have performed no light task and without their valuable help I could easily have been deterred from having this book put into English. I now consider the English version (which incorporates some changes) to be the more authoritative.

Paul Fabra

# Note

1. That was the reason why the original title of this book first published in 1974 was *L'anticapitalisme essai de réhabilitation de l'économie politique* (Essay on the rehabilitation of the political economy).

# Introduction

It requires a very unusual mind to
undertake the analysis of the obvious.

Alfred North Whitehead

Although it does propose answers, on a number of fundamental points,
to some questions that economists have long been asking themselves,
this is not a work on economics in the real sense. My starting point
was the idea that our society, as we still know it, resembles feature for
feature the model constructed of it in the last quarter of the last
century by the "hedonist" economists (Walras in France, Jevons in
Britain, and above all Böhm-Bawerk, Menger, etc., in Austria), so-
called because they placed the need or, alternatively, the desire for
consumption, or—putting it another way still—effective and potential
demand, at the center of economic life. In the main, modern economists, our contemporaries, have inherited what these men taught and,
all things considered, they have added nothing that breaks continuity
with their predecessors. From the fact that the latter were able to
foretell the coming of a new age, one might perhaps be tempted to
deduce that they had forged exactly the kind of analytical tool that was
needed—at least for their time—but there are grounds for doubt.
Careful scrutiny reveals the faulty logic of their arguments. Their
influence would seem to resemble that of a doctor mistaking ill health
for good health and unfailingly making all his patients sick.

The remedies administered today are becoming increasingly apparent for what they are. Just as the human system will reject drugs used to excess, so the economic system is rejecting these remedies, awakening to the realization that the real springs of its activity are elsewhere. Thus the premise upon which the doctrine officially taught as economics in the universities of the West and government "economic policy" are both based, namely that consumption is the motor of growth, full employment, and so on, is collapsing under the weight of events before the theorists have even had time to disprove it. Society is now throwing out its model and the abstract image it presents of society's defects. To advance along the path of economic progress we are discovering—or rediscovering—that we have to "conserve" energy and raw materials and, in general, reduce nonproductive consumption in order to create a bigger surplus (net product) from current production for application to the immense tasks still to be accomplished, namely launching the new technological revolution, completely reshaping the transport economy, increasing agricultural output and equipping the poor countries, whilst at the same time fashioning a less frantic way of life.

But the truth of the American economist's profound observation that "facts alone will not destroy a theory" is proved once again. Economic theory, in its more or less officially held version, is incapable of accounting for the facts but "it takes a new conceptual scheme to cause the abandonment of an old one."[1] No new one has yet emerged in spite of the efforts of some original thinkers, particularly in Great Britain—though it was there that the triumph of subjective and "utilitarian" (hedonist) economic policy was so sweeping. In 1926, Piero Sraffa, a Cambridge-based Italian economist, was already challenging the assumption on which the most important theory of "modern" economics is founded, namely marginalism, which states that price on a competitive market is determined by the production cost of the last unit produced. This theory implies that cost rises as production increases: It has to, for the price at the margin to be higher than average cost. It is this principle of diminishing returns, so contrary to experience in industry (firms' costs would not increase if they could afford to increase their output), that Sraffa contested, without, however, being able to assemble his criticisms into a rounded argument that would finally have disposed of marginalism. To reduce its scientific pretensions to nought it would first of all have been necessary to show that the only reason for the existence of the "diminishing returns" assumption was to justify the psychological conception of value that had been developed with fallacious logic, as we shall see, by the Vienna school, Walras, Jevons, and others.

Basing themselves on the "law" of the satiability of wants, they believed they had made a tremendous advance when they invented the concept of "marginal utility," their term to express the idea that if you already have a large amount of water, adding one last gallon will not greatly increase the utility of the total volume. With the aid of this "discovery" they were able to derive value from utility without running up against the classic objection: Water is more useful than diamonds but its *value* is infinitely lower. The reason it is low, the marginalists replied, is that value is a matter of the utility of the marginal unit.

This contrivance, pretentiously called a "theory of value," was nevertheless going to enchain the whole of modern economics in an unresolvable contradiction. If value is an inverse function of quantity available, *scarcity* is promoted to the level of universal cause of value; but scarcity is the characteristic of a monopoly situation. To be strictly logical, the "psychological" theory of value should have brought the marginalist economists to reject the competitive market assumption that they had inherited from the founders of political economy, Adam Smith (1723–1790), David Ricardo (1772–1823), and Thomas Robert Malthus (1766–1834).

Unaware that the assumption was incompatible with his idea of value (that is, of price formation), Walras (followed by the "neoclassical" school) brashly advanced his celebrated "general equilibrium" model, which he said was applicable to a market *assumed* to be one of perfect competition. A century later, this model is still puzzling economists. They are only just beginning to realize that it cannot possibly work, even theoretically. Learned mathematical demonstrations have been devised to prove its untruth but none has yet done so altogether and this has caused a kind of embarrassment among the best economists, vexed at not being able to rationalize an obviously sound intuition. Mathematics predictably is not to blame for this temporary failure. To find its cause, we have to go back to the starting point of all "formalization," namely the concept definition stage. The general equilibrium model represents *nothing,* in the full sense of the word; in other words, even as an abstract construction, it is faulty because it rests on a concept that fails to describe economic reality (the "scarcity" concept) and, what is more, that concept is incompatible with the competitive market assumption on which the model is based. Via this theoretical (mis)representation of reality, the auction, or the stock market, have become for a century or so the benchmark for a market economy. This analogy has been the source of many misunderstandings, economical, political, and theoretical.

For the British classical school, and Ricardo in particular, competition has a very different dimension—first, because the fact that it can exist only on a market supplied with goods reproducible at will is admitted in the most explicit terms from the outset (so the logical cohesion of the theory is based on the exclusion of scarcity); second, because not merely does Ricardian theory hold good in the absence of the perfect competition assumption, but—as I shall show from his own words—it postulates that absence; and last, because, unlike the neoclassical economists who based their reasoning on the (real or supposed) behavior of economic agents, Ricardo argues from the start by treating the market as a whole, before descending to the level of its individual components. Thus competition is perceived initially not in terms of *rivalry* among producers, but as a principle of social organization shorn, as to its nature, of all psychological connotations.

The economists of the classical period wondered whether the process of wealth accumulation would one day come to an end. Ricardo's answer was that *logically* one cause and one only could bring about the "stationary state" which today would be called zero growth, and that was the impossibility of further increasing agricultural production to feed a growing population. The halt to growth would be due to the fact that the intensive farming of all existing fertile land would have increased the cost of the most necessary foods to such an extent that, once wages were paid, no surplus (net product) would be left for new investment. For Ricardo, the end of economic growth is not marked by the advent of plenty on this earth (as Marxism and hedonism, with a kind of naive folk wisdom, believe), but by the increasing difficulty of meeting the basic needs of a world population that cannot grow any longer. Furthermore, for the classical economists (Smith and Ricardo) considering human wants as "unlimited" by nature, the very concept of plentifulness is elusive in their system.

The most important thing here is to remember that, in Ricardo's mind, an exchange economy forms what certain theorists of our day would term an "open system"—open, that is, to the surrounding environment. The economic system borrows energy—including man's labor—and raw materials from nature and restores them in the form of the products of "labor." Now it is well known that the state of equilibrium—a word that Ricardo *never* uses—is a characteristic of closed systems (a chemical compound, for example, enclosed in a test tube), but not of open systems. It can be shown that Ricardo, a contemporary of Goethe, saw political economy as a science of organization, a conception of which his successors failed to take advantage. In *Le Hasard et la Nécessité,* Jacques Monod writes:

> As we know, it was a return to the source—to the very source of knowledge—that was to provide the foundation for the second age of science, that of the 20th century. From the end of the 19th century, the absolute necessity for an epistemological critique becomes necessary *again* [my italics], as the essential conditions for scientific objectivity. From then on, it is not just philosophers who address themselves to this critique but men of science as well who find they have to include it in the theoretical fabric itself. It was on that condition that the theory of relativity and quantum mechanics could be developed.

The central thesis of this book is that economics will not get out of the blind alley into which it has led itself, and economic policymakers along with it, until it too, with a lag of seventy-five years behind the physical sciences, undertakes this epistemological enquiry. About three decades ago there was the famous controversy, still remembered in university circles, between the neo-Keynesians and the neoclassicists over the theory of capital. One of the main protagonists admitted that the participants in this debate—which is, after all, regarded as a milestone in the economic thinking of our time—did not really communicate because they could not agree on what they were supposed to be debating.

This book is concerned only with the most general problems that confront the economist. I will therefore deal at length with the theory of value, not because value exists, per se, but because without such a theory the workings of the price mechanism are left to the so-called "law" of supply and demand (see Chapter 9). Modern economists have thought that they can forget about the concept of value, but that, by implication, is to subscribe to a certain theory of value. They argue that there is no need to enquire into the cause of value: It is sufficient that a commodity be traded on the market. This reasoning seems at first sight to be the only one tenable from the scientist's standpoint. The scientist has to work from observed data—in this case, prices as he sees them. He then must try to explain how they are determined. Discoursing on the origin of value would be tantamount to asking why there are prices, a question appropriate to scholasticism but not to modern science.

But the question is really a different one. It is one of defining the scope of economic science, if a science it is. Chemistry, biology, physics, all the traditional scientific disciplines, define what their subject matter is. Economics, at least in its present version, is the one exception. If it is enough for the economist that a commodity should have *a price* on the market, what are the limits of the market? Is it true that, for the economist, you can buy an automobile which is a product of labor, or you can buy the labor itself (the "labor market")? This heterogeneity does not seem to bother the economist. And the reason is that the psychological theory of value, despite all its subtleties regarding marginal utility, relieves him of the need to clarify the concepts he uses. His sole criterion is want—in other words, the necessary and sufficient condition for something to have a price is that there should be a *demand* for it. The market is therefore by nature infinitely expandable, and "economic goods" form a set that is limitless. In the marketplace of modern economics everything becomes a commodity. This is why the "cost of production" takes second place as a determinant of prices, since there are commodities that cost nothing to produce but are worth a great deal, like a site in the center of Paris. Hence the importance given to "marginal utility" as an explanatory principle.

To demarcate the field of his researches Ricardo, in the opening pages of his *Principles of Political Economy and Taxation,* first published in 1817, expressly states that the laws governing price formation apply solely to the products of human labor. This initial stance caused him to take over the labor theory of value formulated by his predecessor, Adam Smith. Take any economics textbook written for students at American or European universities and you will read something like this: The labor theory of value on which the classical English school built the edifice of political economy served as the point of departure for Marx, and then was discarded by all other economists. You will not find a single non-Marxist who refers to that theory.

Is there any justification for this? Is it possible to construct scientifically an economic doctrine without the starting premise that the scale of prices, if it is to be "rational," has to reflect production costs assumed proportional to the quantity of labor, allowing—as we shall see later—for the rate of profit, that is, for the phenomenon of accumulation? This book has two aims which, I admit, are ambitious. First, I set out to prove that, if it is to lay any claim to objectivity, economics will have to go back to the labor theory of value. The fact that quantity and intensiveness of labor are magnitudes that are not measurable as yet is not an adequate objection. The physicists were not able to measure mass until physics had established itself as a science. My purpose is simply to show that there is no logical reason why the labor theory of value should not be adopted and that, on the contrary, the theories that have been preferred do not stand up to scrutiny. Second, I present a rebuttal of the Marxist version of that theory. Contrary to the almost unanimously held view, even among "bourgeois" economists, Marx did not carry through to completion the labor theory of value that the classicists were supposed to have been incapable of explaining. He misinterpreted it and, above all, he strayed from the paths of science by making labor the "substance" of value, whereas the relation between value and quantity of labor is of a completely different kind. Exchange value is "proportional" to the quantity of labor, but in no way is it the labor "embodied" or, as Marx says, "crystallized" in a commodity.

But in explaining where Marx went wrong, one does much more than refute Marx. A misunderstanding is brought to light which has been a constant brake on economic thinking and the exposure of which at the same time serves to demonstrate the fallacy of the overingenious solution of marginal analysis. The misunderstanding has to do with the status of labor in economics. Although labor is what exchange value is based upon, it does not follow that labor is itself an object of exchange. It really makes no difference to switch concepts from "labor" to "labor power" as Marx did; the substitution still leaves a fundamental heterogeneity of commodities since both labor power and the products of that power are treated as commodities. I have tried to make the distinction clear and to present a solution conceptually apt to restore the homogeneity of the market. In his thinking, David Ricardo seems to have been aware of the necessity to avoid the confusion. Unfortunately his vocabulary was not on a par with his thinking, except in two or three passages that have escaped attention. The fact is that his successors—all of them to date, including Marx—have not been able to break away from the approach taken by Adam Smith, whose labor theory of value was still tainted with scholasticism since he regarded labor as an object of exchange. M. Blaug wrote in 1968, "Great chunks of the history of economic thought are about mistakes in logic and gaps in analysis, having no connection with contemporary events."[2] This is why an epistemological enquiry is so vital.

In economic thought the "epistemological break," as our structuralists would say, occurred not between Marx and the classical economists, nor between the classical economists and the moderns, but within what is rather summarily termed the classical British school, between Smith/Malthus and Ricardo. With his admirable gift for logical elucidation, Ricardo made political economy into a virtual science. To the extent that all Ricardo's successors, leapfrogging him, so to speak, consciously or unconsciously drew on Adam Smith (and on the most arguable parts of his thinking), they took economics a step backwards. Today's economic circumstances, along with the scientific progress that has been made in other areas, provide a good basis for a new start.

## Notes

1. James B. Conant, *On Understanding Science* (New Haven, CT: Yale University Press, 1947). Quoted by A. Hansen, *A Guide to Keynes* (New York: McGraw-Hill, 1953).

2. M. Blaug, *Economic Theory in Retrospect* (Cambridge, U.K.: Cambridge University Press, 1968).

*Part One*

# From Subjective Economics to Objective Economics

*1*

# The Foundations of Political Economy Overturned

## Economics Are Now Back in the "Preclassical" Age

It was around 1870 that economists like Karl Menger and Eugen von Böhm-Bawerk of Austria, Léon Walras of France (though he taught in Lausanne), and Stanley Jevons of Britain set about scrapping the Ricardian analysis of value. They thought they could prove that the exchange value (and therefore the price) of goods and services was proportional not to the quantity of labor expended in producing them but to their scarcity, it being understood (by them) that a thing is *scarce* from the moment it is both useful and limited in quantity. These economists have often been called "neoliberal" or "neoclassical" as though they were Ricardo's successors, whereas they were his contradictors.[1] It is more just and more revealing to call them by their other name, "hedonists," given them precisely because of the central importance they attached to the idea of optimum gratification of wants,[2] which they thought they could express in mathematical terms.

That, then, wrote *finis* to the classical labor theory of value, which was incapable, as the neoliberals gravely pointed out, of explaining why in a desert a glass of water which, according to them, had cost nothing to get there was of infinitely higher value than a huge diamond dug up at enormous expense from the depths of the earth. This "Robinsonade"—the word Marx would have used—is easily disproved

3

by showing that the hedonists simply forgot that exchange does not exist in a case like this. Without a blush, they confused two inseparable but distinct concepts: want and value. Setting little store by the subtle and indispensable analysis of Smith and Ricardo, they defined exchange value by use value, thus taking economics back to the preclassical age. As a consequence, the exchange value and, therefore, the price of things thenceforward depended on their "utility."[3] To remove all ambiguity, it should be pointed out that utility is obviously a necessary *condition* for a commodity, whatever it is, to possess exchange value. In simpler language, we could say that, if it is to find a buyer, a commodity supplied to the market has to be wanted because it is indispensable, pleasurable, or for any other reason (fashion, etc.).[4] It is perfectly clear that a thing manufactured at great expense will be worth nothing if no one wants it. On the other hand, once there is a demand for it, its exchange value will, in a competitive system, *tend* to be a function not of the intensity with which it is wanted, but of the quantity of labor that has had to be put into producing it.

The hedonists completely reversed the direction of economics. The vital change they made was to put the indeterminate at the center of economic thought: As a basis for value and, therefore, price, they put want—the appraisal of which is subjective—in the place of a magnitude (quantity of labor) that is *objective,* in other words perceived by the intellect, not the senses. The objection that this magnitude is, in practice, difficult to measure, which would rob its objective nature of much of its interest, is invalid because the quantity and intensity of labor are theoretically measurable categories.

Inability to measure the quantity of labor matters little; economics is interested not in the absolute value of things, but in their value relative to one another, and the scale of prices given by a market functioning in satisfactory conditions is an adequate approximation to the scale of values. The same is not true of an economy that takes the satisfaction of wants, a notion that is impossible to quantify in theory or practice, as its yardstick for exchange value. And yet economists since the end of the nineteenth century have based their reasoning on the idea that want, in whatever form (wanting a meal or wanting to own a diamond), is directly (Walras) or indirectly (Pareto and Hicks) quantifiable and they were not always above introducing *this or that quantity of want* in their workings. This artifice rests on a play on words: It is supposed that the quantity of want or the intensity of *preference* is measured by the price one is prepared to pay for the wanted object. In other words, price—which is precisely what has to be explained by value—is what enables value to be determined!

Having reached this point, we have to stop a moment to consider the distinction that the classical school made between market price and *necessary* or *natural* price. The market price is that which is established at time *t*. It is the *current price,* the resultant of all the forces effectively acting on the market. It may therefore be expected to rise, the greater the extent to which the commodity on sale is wanted. Whence it ensues that, at every moment of the period of time considered, the effects of the hedonism principle are felt. However, economic life goes on in time and were one to try to construct the "model" of a free market, in other words of a market in which productive forces are able to move from one activity to another without restriction, the logical conclusion from that freedom would be that, if profits are higher in a particular sector or activity, then capital will be attracted to it. Production would increase and eventually meet the demand. Through competition among producers, price would *tend* toward the *natural price* or cost of production (which, as we shall see, includes profit) of the least efficient producers (marginal producers) whose production is necessary to meet the demand.

The hedonist conception of value has been adopted by all non-Marxist economists—the Keynesians, naturally, but equally their opponents. Milton Friedman, for instance, refers to it specifically.[5]

I am quite prepared for the objection that for all their endorsement of the hedonist conception of value, Friedman and the other neoliberals still use the Ricardian analysis of the market price, which they call the short-term price, and the natural price, which they call the long-term price. But this only appears so, and for two reasons. First, the modern liberals* base their analysis on the cost of production to the enterprise. For Ricardo the cost of production is a social cost; it is proportional, as a first approximation (we shall see later the significance of that qualification), to the quantity of labor which, at each given stage of technical progress, the human community has to expend on average in order to produce a particular commodity or service. *The social cost of production* cannot, therefore, be measured directly—perhaps it could be today by computer, once the unit of labor were defined. This is why Ricardian analysis, the standpoint of which is the economy as a whole

---

*Translator's note: The words *liberal* and *liberalism* are used throughout this book in the European sense. In the United States the equivalent would be "free-marketer" and "free-market economics."

(i.e., one of objectivity), has been passed over in favor of an analysis from the standpoint of the enterprise. And yet Ricardo's analysis contained in embryo a radical criticism of the misuses of the market economy. Each time an enterprise's cost of production is chronically higher than the social cost of production there is undoubtedly wrongful use of the productive forces. Today, many firms make a profit only because they are free to use and pollute natural but limited resources (air, water, etc.) which belong to the whole of society. The concept of social cost, pushed into the background for a century and a half, is now reemerging in a new light. What is more important to note here is that the "social cost of production" theory (that of Ricardo, not that of Marx) provides us with a solid base on which to reconstruct a conjoint macro- and microeconomic theory. Conversely, the reason why macro- and microeconomic theories in their present form are irreconcilable is that Ricardo's analysis, from the standpoint of the overall economy (objectivity), has been rejected in favor of another type of analysis that is subjective.

Secondly and even more ominously, the neoliberal economists' substitute for the Ricardian analysis of the price mechanism is fallacious. Their intention was laudable. Ricardo's dry and precise theory was virtually unusable by practitioners because it was too general and too abstract. When they created the celebrated marginalist theory the neoliberals gave theirs a mathematical formulation. But that theory turns its back squarely on reality, since it rests on assumptions that are too particular (one being the concept of scarcity): It is simply an overgeneralization of the Ricardian theory of rent (which itself is right). Far be it from me to maintain that mathematics are not essential to economics just as they are to the other sciences; but before mathematics can be employed there has to be a close analysis of the concepts used. If these are inconsistent, then no matter how many equations are worked out, the results will be inconsistent too. It happens all too often in the human sciences that a façade of scientific language is considered enough.

Let us dwell for a moment on this question of prices which was our starting point. Value, per se, is simply a mental construct that only becomes reality through the price that expresses it, but it does not follow that price should be treated as indistinguishable from value. For price to reflect value, even shakily, in other words for the "appearance" to be significant, to correspond to the reality of "what is"—in this case for it to correspond to the social cost of production, which certainly represents something real (the work of the engineer, the effort of the laborer)—economic activity has to be rationally organized (a market is a form of rational organization) in order to be as proof as possible against the arbitrary. Otherwise, price is simply the reflection of contingent bargaining power or contingent policy decisions.

## Down with Revolution

More is at stake than at first appears. Relations between human beings, what priority is given to building the future—a need that is almost inevitably sacrificed in an interventionist system[6]—the direction in which economic activity is steered, all these differ as night from day according to whether the system is one where the social cost of production, corresponding to something as real as labor, is *present* behind the price at which goods and services are bought, or one where prices, set by reference to a subjective scale of wants, are "nonpresences" to use the word of Parmenides. Looked at from this angle, today's societies are only distinguishable by the degree of arbitrariness they admit. Capitalist societies are more "objective" than socialist societies, notably because market mechanisms play a bigger role there (this greater objectivity is the reason why socialist planners find they are compelled to refer to the price system of the world market). But this advantage will not be decisive as long as the capitalist societies' price system is two-dimensional, lacking the third—time—so that the prices of the commodities to be produced in the future are irremediably distorted for want of an adequate monetary instrument. The dispute over the gold standard hinges, in fact, on this fundamental question.

Revolution pursues the impossible dream of Marx, bent on proving there were no rational (real) bases of political economy. Revolution, in its pure form, like *Das Kapital,* is a grandiose and monstrous endeavor to deny what is, to subject the universe to man's will and pleasure. Liberal society (in the European sense) stems from the awareness that nothing is fixed or constant but that this instability does not mean that the value of things is no more than an appearance.

The only liberating way open to us is to bring the economic and political systems back to objectivity. Then they would stop pressuring us constantly with psychological stimuli to new enslaving wants. Then at last, delivered from the continual enticements of government propaganda and the machinery of marketing and advertising, imagination would find full expression in its rightful sphere—art, love, recreation. Only by bringing society back to rationality—in other words, the real—

will it be possible to open wide the field of possibilities where such a field really exists.

## A Postulate That Sums Up the Whole of Contemporary Economics

In 1874, Léon Walras, having based value on "want," was committed therefore to pronounce this judgment which sums up the whole of contemporary economics, both practical and theoretical: "In the phenomenon of exchange . . . demand has to be regarded as the principal fact, and *supply as a subordinate fact.*"[7] Léon Walras, and with him all the economists (Keynes first and foremost) who base themselves on this concept, are doubtless unaware of the dialectic of master and slave: They have refused to see that to make demand supreme is ultimately to make supply omnipotent.

However, as I have already remarked, the modern doctrine, even if it has founded a society that in many respects is entirely new, takes us back a very long way. In the seventeenth and eighteenth centuries the infant economists by and large based the concept of value on a subjective notion of the conscience. A hundred years before Menger, Jevons, and Walras, Condillac for example formulated a theory of value based on utility and scarcity, in terms which those three representatives of the hedonist school would not have disowned. But more percipient than his successors, Condillac saw very well that since "the value of things (was) based on their utility or, which amounts to the same thing, on how much we want them or, which still amounts to the same thing, on the use we can make of them," we were inclined to attach greater value to things that would satisfy a present and therefore more "highly-felt" want than to those that would gratify a remote want.[8]

A society actuated by psychology is inevitably a society that will seek maximum immediate gratification, even at the expense of future wants which, because they are farther off, seem less pressing. It is just as if the heedless extravagance and self-centeredness of the eighteenth-century nobility had been sown into broader and broader segments of the population. That is one of the characteristics of our modern society. Far from being "democratic" in the full sense of the word, which would imply a certain virtue of simplicity, since an adult people does not "look up" for its model, our society apes with a greater or lesser degree of vulgarity the ostentation, passing crazes, and other bad habits of the wealthy classes.[9]

Only when the future is brought into the picture does one become aware of the full significance of the thinking of Adam Smith and David Ricardo, who placed nascent political economy on less shifting ground than the subjective assessment of wants by introducing the idea that although, in order to have a market value, a commodity must be useful, it does not derive its value from utility. Basing value on a relation with labor (and the effect of accumulation upon exchange) was to have this very important corollary: The relative value of things did not depend on the fact that those things could be used today or tomorrow.

The future was placed by political economy on the same footing as the present, and even on a more favorable one. The twentieth century, in returning to the earlier concepts of value, let out the secret of why the nineteenth century was, other things being equal, the greatest period of capital accumulation in history. Today still, in many countries (including, above all, the poorest), public transport, housing, and even schools, to say nothing of the ocean-linking canals, are to a large extent legacies of the last century. With its Plans and its "long-term projections," the twentieth century dreams aloud of the future but is too deeply engrossed in the "fair and fleeting present."

Living in the now is, in a way, the highest form of individual existence. But—and this is the whole point—for individuals to be able to live in the present, from generation to generation, their society has to be one that collectively develops in time. Those readers who like to draw parallels may note that at the time the "hedonist" economists were winning the day, Gide was writing *Les Nourritures Terrestres*. The tragedy is that, after three-quarters of a century of bourgeois hedonism, Nathanael, Gide's hero, is no longer able to plunge into streams of pure water. The fruit he eats is tasteless, the air he breathes is polluted, and the song of the nightingale is silenced.

## Is the Liberal Economy Individualist?

This cavalier disregard for the future is reflected in the doctrines of the day. Classical economics drew a distinction in economic phenomena between the short and the long term, the latter extending over several generations, since a major place is given in Ricardian reasoning to the adjustment of population trends to the demand for labor, the increase in wealth, and so on. Keynes's horizon is far more limited. In an oft-quoted quip, that master of contemporary thought exclaimed: "In the long run we are all dead." Up to Keynes, economists—and men in general—would have said: In the long run our grandchildren will take our place. The noneuclidean economics he claims to have invented tragically lacks one dimension. It is the equivalent in time to what plane geometry is in space. It perceives phenomena only in the short term.

Obsession with the now runs through all the economic language used in our time. For instance, it is common to speak of the "burdens" which the support of old people and education of the younger generations place on the labor force, when in fact, for old people, society can never do more than give them back part of the income from their labor that they have not consumed and that has served for the accumulation of capital. After all, the labor force's consumption is also a "burden" on society if, as is the case at present, it eats into society's substance by failing to renew and develop community facilities, by polluting rivers, and so on. In the classical economic school, the present, which is only transitory and in which subjectivity operates, was in no way favored over the future. It is that school of thought's way of treating time that reveals, most fundamentally, its quality as a social science, its almost biological impartiality.

If political economy is to be conceded any rights to serve as a guiding thread for thinking afresh about the problems of our time, we need to demonstrate that its claims to objectivity are not vain, that they constitute a preliminary and therefore incomplete victory of the scientific mind in a particularly important area of social life. Marx—at any rate, to believe one of his most famous commentators, Althusser[10]—did not classify "scientific knowledge" as such under the concept of superstructure. Even had he done so, this would in no way have resolved the question. The economic laws that resulted from the classical liberal theory have, as we shall see, an objectivity which Marxian production relations do not. Changing production relations will not overturn the scientific law, but refraining from placing obstacles in the way of that law will change production relations sooner or later according to the circumstances.

The act of exchange is fundamental to all economic activity and it is on that act that economists, of whatever school of thought, have built their theories. What distinguishes the classical school is that *it posits the act of exchange as a relation of equality seen from the outside.* That is the fundamental difference from the hedonist school, which, by nature, is bound to consider exchange from the point of view of each of the two parties in turn. The classical economists are to the "neoliberal economists" what the modern novelist is to the traditional

novelist. The modern novelist faults the traditional novelist for identifying too much with his characters, for thinking and feeling too much
for them, vicariously, when in fact it is never possible to inhabit
someone else's brain, but only to relate to what he says, to what he
does, and so on. In classical political economy, when exchange takes
place on a competitive market, it tends to be analyzed as the reciprocal
transfer of two commodities requiring the same quantity of labor
(allowing, as we shall see, for the rate of profit) to produce, whoever
the two parties to the exchange happen to be. The exchange is that of
two commodities (or two services, or one commodity for one service)
the value of which is measurable by anyone, including, therefore, any
third parties who observe the exchange without participating.

To see the act of exchange as a relationship of equality implies a
conception of social life that very much limits the area of self-interested action regarded as "legitimate" (i.e., in conformity with the laws
of economics). The concept of profit maximization (deriving from the
concept of optimum satisfaction), so typical of neoliberal economics,
sorts ill with the classical pattern of thinking, which is content with
"the market rate of profit."

## Notes

1. Nothing can be more misleading than the way Keynes used the word
*classical* "to cover everyone from Ricardo to Pigou" (Joan Robinson, *The
Generalization of the General Theory and other Essays* [New York: St. Martin,
1979]). In this book, whenever I use the word *classical*, I refer to Ricardian
economics.

2. Vilfredo Pareto gave to the principle of pleasure the name *ophelimity,*
taken from a Greek word meaning "what is advantageous or profitable." The
modern concept of the "quality of life" and its social and philosophical
implications is the latest form taken by this principle.

3. *Utility* used in the widest sense. Useful is that which, "good" or "bad,"
is wanted. Tobacco is useful on the same score as bread.

4. This self-evident fact is noted on the first page of David Ricardo, *On the
Principles of Political Economy and Taxation,* vol. 1 of *Complete Works,* ed.
Piero Sraffa (Cambridge, U.K.: Cambridge University Press, 1966).

5. Milton Friedman, *Price Theory* (Chicago: Aldine, 1976), pp. 38–39.

6. A genuinely free market system, in contrast to an interventionist system,
is almost biological in nature.

7. My italics. This quotation is taken from Walras' *Elements of Pure
Economics (Abrégé des éléments d'economie politique pure ou théorie de la
richesse sociale* [Paris: R. Pichon et Durand-Auzias, 1952]), lesson 5.

8. However, Condillac felt intuitively that there was a "cost of production"
value. In two passages in his remarkable treatise entitled *Le Commerce et le
Gouvernement considérés relativement l'un à l'autre,* he almost got there: All

that was missing was the tool of analysis constituted by the fundamental distinction that Adam Smith made between use value and exchange value. *Le Commerce et le Gouvernement* appeared in 1776, the year in which Smith's great work *The Wealth of Nations* was published.

9. In his biography of Goya, Ortega y Gasset says that the explanation for the style of gesture and elegance of carriage among the poorest people of Spain is a particular circumstance in the history of that nation: The aristocracy had sunk so low by the end of the seventeenth century that, unlike what happened in the other countries of Europe, it ceased to be a model for the remainder of the population to look up to. So the common people invented their own system of communication.

10. *Lire le Capital,* vol. 1, p. 169, published by Maspéro, 1970. I would add that if Marx had put scientific knowledge as such into the superstructure, then Marxist thinking would be referring neverendingly back to itself, which is perhaps the case.

## 2

# What Is Capital?

### Enter the Marxist Concept of Surplus Value

Marx credits the classical school with two achievements: seeing a relation of equivalence in exchange and basing that equivalence on an objective conception of value. His critique consisted not in questioning these basic principles, as the hedonists of the late nineteenth century did, but in showing that having formulated them, the classical economists were unfaithful to them. Did that relation of equivalence which they brought to light and explained so brilliantly still apply in the case of the most important of all exchanges—that between the worker who sells his services for a wage and the employer who buys those services? Friedrich Engels wrote that the school of Ricardo came to grief on "the impossibility of bringing the mutual exchange of capital and labour into accordance with the Ricardian law of the determination of value by labour"[1] and that Marx had to be given the credit for being the first to solve the difficulty. Since value is created by labor, that part of value which the capitalist appropriates and which constitutes his profit must necessarily have been created by labor. But in that case, what happens to the celebrated law whereby each of the two parties to an exchange gives the other a product or a service of equal value if, in the labor contract, the price the capitalist pays for labor is lower than its value?

We know how Marx thought he had resolved the contradiction.

**For Marx, the capitalist does not buy labor but "labor power." The relation of equivalence is straightway restored and the origin of profit revealed.**

What does the worker sell on the so-called labor market? The only thing he really owns: his labor power. This labor power is bought by the capitalist who, once he has bought it, naturally has full use of it. Marx then says that the use value of labor power is labor.[2]

This restores the relation of equivalence; but, far from founding a regime of justice, the relation is the very basis of social injustice. Let us assume that a man works eight hours a day and produces, during the first four hours' work, a quantity of goods (cotton yarn, for example) the value of which is equal to the average value of his daily subsistence—in other words, what he needs to sustain his labor power (and to raise children who will provide that power in his place when it is exhausted). It would follow that the capitalist is buying labor power at its true price because the value of that labor power, *like that of any other commodity,* is determined by the quantity of work necessary to produce it! The wage paid to the workman will be equivalent to the *working time necessary* to keep the worker alive. He will receive no more and no less than the value of the commodity he is selling, so what has he to complain about? Are not the principles of classical economics respected? The other four hours that the worker spends working are what Marx calls surplus labor. The value produced during this *surplus labor time* is the surplus value pocketed by the capitalist (in the example given, the "rate of exploitation" is 100 percent because the surplus value is of the same magnitude as the wage).

Marx's criticism of Ricardo, therefore, was that he stopped halfway, so to speak, and did not take his reasoning far enough.

If it had been any other economist, Marx would have written something like this about him: If he has not taken to its conclusion an analysis so well begun, it is because of "an apologetic dread of a scientific analysis of value and surplus-value which might produce a result unpalatable to the powers that be."[3] But since it is Ricardo, Marx makes no such ill-natured remark. Throughout *Capital* he is careful to spare his great adversary, his intellectual equal, the kind of sarcasm he poured on "the vulgar economists." To believe Marx, if Ricardo had come to terms with his own thinking, he could not have failed to come to the conclusion that the law of value does not apply in the labor contract unless it is considered that the capitalist does not buy a worker's labor but his labor power.

Up to this point, Marx seems satisfied just to explain Ricardo's theory, but the analysis of capital that he derives from the surplus value concept is where he makes a complete break with Ricardian thinking.

All the rest stems from this parting of the ways and so we need to stop here a moment.

## Capital Is a Set in Which Money Has No Part

What, for classical economics, is capital? The most significant definition is again to be found in Ricardo: "Capital is that part of the wealth of a country which is employed in production, and consists of food, clothing, tools, raw materials, machinery, etc. necessary to give effect to labour."[4]

The most important part of this definition is that capital is seen as "wealth." The word is not chosen by chance. In the Ricardian vocabulary (and more generally in classical economic language), wealth has a precise meaning: goods regarded from the standpoint of their use value.

Note that Ricardo's sentence contains a definition by intention and a definition by extension because (a) he tells us what the set (capital) consists of (wealth employed in production) and (b) he gives us a nonexhaustive list of examples (clothing, tools, etc.).

This definition implies that the two expressions, in Ricardo's sentence, "employed in production" and "give effect to labour," are not synonymous. Capital is a part of the set comprising the various elements of wealth employed in production, that part being characterized by the fact that it gives effect to labor. We will need to have elucidated the reciprocal relationships between capital and profit to understand the words "give effect to labour."

The definition is remarkable both for what it contains and for what it excludes.

A first exclusion is everything that is not a product of labor. Many forms of wealth[5] supplied free by nature—river water, air (without which no chemical reaction could take place), and so on—are "employed in production," but they do not "give effect to labour" in the sense meant by Ricardo in that expression (see Chapter 5). Thus the Ricardian definition of capital is homogeneous: The products of labor, and they alone, give effect to labor.

Two other exclusions merit attention. Neither money nor man himself constitutes capital as far as political economy is concerned. And the reason why the term "capital" has given rise to so many fuzzy doctrines and so many misleading interpretations for the last century and a half is essentially because capital often continues to be mistaken either for its user, namely man (the so-called "human capital," an expression as hazy as it is empty of substance), or for the means used to acquire it or mobilize it, namely money.

By excluding man from its definition of capital, political economy proclaims its *liberal* origins (in the European sense). It excludes the state of slavery in all its forms and at all its degrees. It refuses to reason on any other basis than that of a society in which man is free and consequently cannot be considered as a thing that might be the object of an exchange. Perhaps this is an absolute requirement which disregards the facts. Possibly: but that is the theory and as far as it is concerned, alienation, in the literal sense of the word, begins every time this basic hypothesis ceases to apply.

It will not have escaped the reader's notice that, in his definition, Ricardo deliberately puts clothing and the food consumed by the worker on the same plane as materials used in manufacture. What else can this mean but that he wishes, at this point, to reason in a theoretical universe without money? In such a universe, the entrepreneur will need to have a stock of clothing, food, and so on, from which he can pay wages *in kind* to the workers he has taken on. In the world as it is, the exchange process is less direct. Money is used as a medium. In addition to his buildings, machinery, and so on, the entrepreneur will have to have the use of a certain circulating capital in the form of money from which he can draw the sums necessary to pay his workmen. In classical terminology, circulating capital is that which is rapidly renewed. The expression applies not to money but to the real goods (food, clothing, etc.) that money paid in the form of wages can be used to acquire. Without any doubt, therefore, the criteria used by Ricardo to characterize the members of the set "capital" absolutely preclude completing his nondefinitive list by the addition of money. Money is not "wealth employed in production," but an instrument for appropriating wealth. (Strictly speaking, money is not wealth; it is a means for acquiring a certain *quantum* of wealth.) Neither is it money that "gives effect to labour."

In reality, the exclusion of money from the definition of capital can be construed as a logical consequence of Ricardo's opting to reason in macroeconomic terms.[6] At the level of the enterprise, it is legitimate to include monetary holdings in *capital,* because they represent the enterprise's entitlement to a certain quantity of real goods, existing on the market, which will make up its fixed capital and its circulating capital. At the level of the nation, the inclusion is no longer warranted because monetary assets cancel each other out, those held by economic agents being liabilities of the banking system. The only monetary capital rightly so called would be the net worth of the bank of issue, assuming the latter would operate as a privately owned for profit central bank, but a discussion of this proposition would be outside the bounds of our present subject.

The striking thing in Ricardo's definition of capital, therefore, is its both permanent and ahistorical nature. Whatever the degree of development of the nation concerned, capital will always consist of food, clothing, tools, machinery, and so on, save that in a primitive society the only tools will be rudimentary instruments, whereas in a more highly developed society the machines will be both infinitely more numerous and infinitely more sophisticated. It is therefore definitely true that in all cases capital is defined by its use value—the opposite, as we shall see in a moment, of the Marxist conception.

Similarly, the classical definition is not concerned with the political, legal, or social system, as though it considered that, before asking to whom capital belongs, it is first necessary to know what the right of ownership relates to.

## Marx's Monetarist Conception of Capital

Against this conception stands that of Marx, for whom capital is an historical notion.

"The production of commodities[7] and their circulation in its developed form, namely trade, form the historic suppositions under which capital arises," he wrote[8] at the beginning of the chapter where he begins his analysis of capital. And in what form does it appear? Money is "the first form of appearance of capital," he replied a few lines later.

This analysis brings Marx to postulate the "general formula for capital": M–C–M'. With money (M), I buy a commodity (C) (cotton, for example), which I transform into yarn and sell for a higher amount (M') which includes, on top of the cost to me (price of C and cost of maintaining the work force), an increment, the *surplus value* produced by the "surplus labor" of the workers I have taken on to spin the cotton. The immediate purpose of the production process is not to create use value. To me, whether the cotton yarn is useful or not is of little concern; my only object is to sell it at its price and, in order that this price should give me a profit (derived from surplus value), it is necessary and sufficient that that price represent the value of the whole of the labor "incorporated" in the yarn.[9] The only thing that matters to me, therefore, is the exchange value of the commodities I manufacture; and that value which has become, so to speak, independent and takes by turns the form of money and the form of the commodity is what Marx calls capital. With money capital, I buy my raw material and "labor power." Labor power converts the raw material into "commodities," including in their value the value of the "surplus labor" for which the worker is not paid. And that is how the trick is done: All I have to do now is to sell the commodity at its *full value* and there I am, comfortably installed as a newborn capitalist, an English mill owner with a well-to-do look and a well-rounded paunch.

For Marx, exchange value becomes capital through money.

> In the circulation M–C–M', value suddenly presents itself as a self-moving substance which passes through a process of its own, and for which commodities and money are both mere forms. But there is more to come: instead of simply representing the relations of commodities, it now enters into a private relationship with itself, as it were. It differentiates itself as original value from itself as surplus-value, just as God the Father differentiates himself from himself as God the Son, although both are of the same age and form, in fact one single person; for only by the surplus-value of £10 does the £100 originally advanced become capital, and as soon as this has happened, as soon as the son has become created and, through the son, the father, their difference vanishes again, and both become one: £110.
>
> Value therefore now becomes value in process, money in process, and as such capital.[10]

In Marx's view, the classical definition of capital is foreign, so to speak, to political economy. It is technical in nature and therefore, according to him, does not help to explain what the production of commodities consists of. He writes: "If we consider the process of production from the point of view of the simple labour-process, the labourer stands in relation to the means of production, not in their quality as capital, but as the mere means and material of his own intelligent productive activity. In tanning, e.g., he deals with the skins as his simple object of labour. It is not the capitalist whose skin he tans."[11] In other words, Marx holds the classical definition to be unilateral: It considers capital only from the standpoint of its use value and neglects the most important aspect once capital enters into circulation: its exchange value.

In fact, classical political economy does not take this simplistic view of things at all. Its definition of capital by the use made of it (which is to be "employed in production") and by the effect capital produces (which is to "give effect to labour") does not mean that it forgets that, like any other product of labor, capital has a determinable exchange value—in other words, it can be bought and sold for *a certain amount* of other commodities or a certain amount of money. There is no question whatsoever of denying that, in the course of economic life, capital takes the form of both goods and money. But classical political economy does not on that account espouse the arguments of an all-in-all somewhat vulgar empiricism that would put money and commodities on the same footing. Capital cannot be said to be capital and, at the same time, power over capital. Yet that is the confusion that the Marxist conception fails to avoid.

To say that value has become money in process and, as such, capital would also appear to suggest that exchange value has a life of its own, whereas it must always have a use value as its substratum. To try to rescue their laborious construct, the Marxists invented the "dialectical nature" of capital, sometimes depending on the use value of the commodity and sometimes on that of money, the use value of money being none other than the function it performs as an instrument for acquiring raw materials, machinery, and also the labor power of other persons. This mere play on words cannot hide the inversion of the order of factors committed by Marx, who perceives exchange value in capital before he sees its use value. Marx does not take the monetarist conception to its conclusion. He never says that to generate capital it is sufficient to create money; but by failing to give capital a "real" content and by giving pride of place to its "money" form, Marx, under cover of a reasoning that starts out from an analysis of surplus value, follows the paths of empiricism.

### The Imaginary Reenters the Picture

Because of the method he uses, Marx can no longer reason in a "homogeneous field," to borrow an expression from Louis Althusser, one of his modern disciples. All along, his argument unfolds at two wholly distinct levels which nothing can ever bring into coincidence—that of concepts and that of history.

In the preceding section, I referred to the undoubtedly insoluble problems that Marx raised by assimilating capital with exchange value. In developing my argument, I seemed not to attach any special importance to the fact that, in Marx's reasoning, it is via money that capital becomes value. However, exchange value is a concept whereas money is an instrument created by man. To make the one equivalent to the other is typical of empirical thinking. Marx observes that, in capitalist society in the form in which it has existed since, say, the sixteenth century, capital is found in the shape of money. Therefrom he concludes that capital corresponds to exchange value expressed by money, which reverses the sequence required by scientific argument where the concept, far from being the reflection of observed phenomena, serves, on the contrary, to determine their order.

Whereas the advent of money could, in a pinch, be given a date in history, it is clear that exchange value, by its very nature, cannot be dated. Replacing the status of use value, which political economy assigned to capital by that of exchange value and saying that the latter has the "money form" as its equivalent, although money is only a *token,* a medium invented at some point in history to represent exchangeable value, is to be condemned to an endless to-and-fro between concept and symbol without ever touching ground, and therefore without ever being able to grasp the tangible subject matter of economic science. By introducing money at the center of his system of thought, Marx also introduces the imaginary. If I had no scruple about making unjust generalizations, I would be tempted to say: Look what happens to British political economy at the hands of a German philosopher!

**The Marxist analysis of capital is philosophical in nature; it is not scientific, since it is not based on a concept as such.**

Asked in an interview published in *Le Monde* of 14 May 1971, "Do you regard your last book *L'Idiot de la famille* as a scientific work?" Sartre replied: "No and that is why I am having it published in the *Bibliothèque de philosophie.* Scientific would imply rigour in *concepts.* Philosophical means that I try to be rigourous in *notions* and the distinction I make between the two is this. A concept is a definition in exteriority and, also, atemporal; a notion, as I see it, is a definition in interiority which embraces not only the time implied by the subject of the notion but also the time of one's own knowing. In other words it is a thought in which time is inherent."

From a careful study of the work of Marx it is clear that capital there is defined "in interiority" and that this definition embraces not only the time implied by the subject but also Marx's own time of knowing—in this case, the nineteenth century. The Marxist analysis of capital is philosophical because the idea it forms of its subject is a *notion*. The classical analysis, on the other hand, is straightway more abstract because it reaches for the concept, although the mere fact that a discipline uses atemporal concepts is not, of course, sufficient to substantiate its claim to be a science. My purpose in this book is to show that, though Ricardian political economy may not have been a science in the real sense, it did create the possibility of constructing a science of economics.

The plunge into concepts, inevitable at the beginnings of a science when the subject of the research is being defined, forced the first economists to reason "in real terms" and therefore to conceive of a theoretical world without money. But this term *real,* explicit though it may be, was a further source of confusion. What is real, in the current sense, is the economic world, complete with money as we know it. So an effort of mental adjustment is necessary in order to conceive of what a moneyless economy would be like.

It is this difficulty that also prompted even the greatest of the first economists to use, or rather overuse, "Robinsonades" and to refer to a "pseudo-prehistory"[12] where the deer hunter and salmon fisher exchanged their products without the aid of cash. Marx, who substitutes sarcasm for argument in many important instances, was quick to seize upon the naiveté of the approach but failed to understand the reason for it, with the result that he fell into the same trap as his opponents but, unlike them, was unable to get out of it. Their starting point was a simplified society in which value was bartered for like value. Then they introduced money in order to draw closer to the world as it is. Also they realized full well that barter cannot be supposed an ideal process of exchange except for purposes of hypothetical argument because, in the concrete world, it is a primitive medium incomparably cruder than money as a way of comparing the value of things. Marx argues in the reverse order. Instead of following the usual scientific method, which is to formulate a theory and then compare it with the facts of experience, he uses as the starting point for his explanation of how capitalism works the form that capitalism normally assumes in a developed society. The apparently innocuous finding that capital is present in the form of money leads him to assert that capital *is* that money, which represents exchangeable value. To explain capitalism, he describes capitalism.

## The Archangel of Socialism

In making capital equivalent to exchange value, Marx blandly transfers the latter from its rightful level—that of concepts—to the level of a subject to be studied in terms of how it is accumulated and the transformations it undergoes in the development of capitalist society. Impelled by Marx's power of thought, the concept of exchange value becomes a strange thing that has no name in any language and is a kind of amalgam of the mortal being and the mythical dragon, capital, which carries off men in its infernal course, feeding on their labor and transforming it into increasing amounts of exchange value—in other words, more capital. Marx himself has no hesitation in calling it an ogre. Therefore it needed the archangel of socialism to come and banish this vermin from the face of the earth and give back to the exhausted worker the fruits of his labor that the huge leech glued to his skin was sucking from every pore just as soon as he produced it. But what does it look like, this world that Marx has rid of protean Capital which at one moment takes the form of commodities and at another that of money? It is stripped of everything that made it a society operating with the fine action of a watch movement. The society he leaves is nothing more than a gigantic Robinsonade with no more wage earners, probably no more money (he does not say), and where everyone—why not?—receives according to his needs, though we are not told what those needs are nor why they should not be endless—which would immediately rule out any possibility of satisfying them.

## The Consequence of Marx's Empiricism: His Inability to Tell the Future

Empirical thinking can never see into the future because it cannot detach itself from what is right before its eyes. It is because he did not go back to the true nature of capital that Marx found himself immured in the historical experience of the nineteenth century. Between his monetary conception of capital and the fact that events disproved what he said would happen there is a direct causal relationship. Marx's theory leads him to assert, for example, that as capital increases, the situation of the workers will become more endangered. According to him, the growth of capitalism *inevitably* reduces their purchasing power and creates unemployment. From time to time, for circumstantial reasons, there may be some improvement in the lot of the workers, but that can only be temporary. The reason is that if real wages increase, entrepreneurs necessarily have to buy machinery and improve their plant in order to improve the productivity of the labor power that has suddenly become more costly. Up to this point, the reasoning is neither original nor, for that matter, particularly enlightening. It is a plain commonsense observation and all economists, whether Marxist or not, would readily agree.

They begin to go their separate ways when Marx systematizes his observation by referring to his "initial discovery" concerning the surplus value mechanism. Because his critique of political economy rests wholly on the idea that the capitalist buys the product of labor at the price of labor power, he introduces a distinction (which Engels and all Marxists after him held to be "fundamental") between variable capital, which is that part of monetary capital used to buy labor power, and constant capital, the purpose of which is to buy all the other commodities necessary for production (raw materials, machinery, etc.).

### Variable capital and constant capital in Marx; circulating capital and fixed capital in Ricardo

The response of the entrepreneurs to the increase in wages, according to Marx, brings about a change in the composition of capital. Because the entrepreneurs buy more modern plant and spend more on improving their production equipment, they increase their proportion of constant capital but commensurately reduce the other variable component of their capital. This reduction in available variable capital—in other words, in the *monetary resources* available to entrepreneurs to pay out in wages—will obviously have one or both of the following consequences for workers: further layoffs and/or wage cuts. A third consequence, this time to the disadvantage of the capitalists, will be a reduction in the rate of surplus value, because, according to Marxist theory, surplus value can only come from variable capital (that which "exploits" labor).

As I said a little earlier, Marx, at his starting point, is very close to the reasoning of the classicists. They too maintain—self-evidently—

that "the effective demand for labour must depend upon the increase of that part of capital in which the wages of labour are paid."[13] Which is why they draw a distinction between the two kinds of capital according to the length of time for which they are used. "Circulating" capital is reconstituted (or, if preferred, amortized) in a very short space of time and "fixed" capital is consumed slowly and therefore takes several years to be amortized. It is immediately clear that this classification is rather arbitrary even though it can be very useful. It depends on the subjective idea one has of the duration of a "long" or "short" space of time. Ricardo therefore specifically points out that this division is "not essential" and that, in it, "the line of demarcation cannot be accurately drawn."[14]

So here we are again at one of those crossroads in economic thinking where we see the two adversaries going off in opposite directions though starting from the same finding. Both Ricardo and Marx agree that the level of employment will be a function of the quantity of "that part of capital in which the wages of labour are paid." But Ricardo refuses to consider the distinction between circulating and fixed capital as "essential," whereas Marx bases the whole of his analysis on the distinction derived from the foregoing (but different from it) that he makes between variable and constant capital. Is it because Ricardo is not concerned with "full employment," whereas Marx, on the contrary, is obsessed with the danger of unemployment? This explanation will not hold water and Marx himself rejected it outright as we shall shortly see. There are two reasons for the divergence.

The first stems from the mathematical form of Ricardian thought. To distinguish between circulating and fixed capital in the aggregate formed by capital, it has to be possible to answer yes or no to the question "Is this capital of long duration or not?" Since this notion of duration is highly subjective, Ricardo decides not to regard the distinction as important. At first sight, Marxist concepts lend themselves better to the test. Since, for Marx, capital takes the form of "money," it is easy to identify variable capital as that part of capital used to pay wages. At enterprise level, this part of capital is indeed easy to identify, but at the macroeconomic level this is no longer the case. The reason is that, at that level, the distinction between variable monetary capital and constant monetary capital no longer has any meaning because it is clear that money, at the macroeconomic level, can be related only to income. There is no longer monetary capital for buying labour power on the one hand and monetary capital for buying machinery on the other. All the money is distributed in the form of income, either as wages or profits (the wages and profits of the manufacturers of the machinery as well as the wages and profits of its users). Maintaining at all costs the distinction between variable and constant capital is tantamount to making the mistake, familiar to economists, of mixing up the notions of income flow and capital stock. It is an established fact that, as and when a society uses more machinery—and therefore increases, to use the Marxist term, its constant capital—the proportion of wage earners in the total working population also increases. The necessary conclusion, in complete opposition to the Marxist doctrine, is that the effect of increasing mechanization is to enlarge the relative share of variable capital for entrepreneurs *taken as a whole*. The truth is that the concept of variable capital does not allow any quantifiable magnitude to be identified and therefore has no scientific value. Could it be that the Marxist concepts merely serve to expose Marx's doctrine, rather like the concepts of scholasticism that did no more than rehash the same old dogmas?

The second of the two reasons compels us to anticipate the result of this enquiry. Marx attaches crucial importance to the change in the "organic composition" of capital because, in his mind, only variable capital is capable of generating surplus value or future capital. We shall see the real process of profit formation via exchange in Chapter 4. That will lead us to conclude that, although profit, as Marx thought, is indeed always the product of fresh labor, there is no distinction to be made as regards its genesis, between the two categories of capital: variable or constant, circulating or fixed.

For the moment it must suffice to see how classical political economy, in its *system of thought,* overcomes the apparent contradiction with which we are faced. On the one hand, it too recognizes that the introduction of machinery (fixed capital) must necessarily put an end to certain jobs. On the other, the general definition it gives of capital—all commodities employed in production and necessary *to give effect to labor*—induces it to assert that the more capital grows, the more the demand for labor will increase.

Eventually Ricardo realized this contradiction, and economists know that this was how he came to write one of the most famous and controversial studies in political economy: the well-known chapter 31 of the *Principles* entitled "On Machinery." Ricardo added this chapter afterwards (which is why it appears almost at the end of the book—there are 32 chapters in all) to correct the mistake he made, he tells us, by maintaining at first that, *in all circumstances,* the introduction of machinery, by reducing the cost of making commodities, would be beneficial to all classes of society, including the workers.

To understand Ricardo's reasoning fully—and it is just as valid today as it was in his time—we have to remember that it was not really a retraction ("Although I am not aware," he wrote, "that I have ever published anything respecting machinery which it is necessary for me to retract, yet I have in other ways given my support to doctrines which I now think erroneous");[15] his conclusion, again, is that the increase in capital—a general phenomenon of which the growth of machinery is just one particular case—will, eventually, be favorable to all classes of society.

But he admits—and this is the new fact—that, temporarily, the substitution of machinery for human labor may be "very injurious" to the working class. For that to be so, two conditions have to apply: (1) the new machinery has to be "suddenly discovered and extensively used"; and (2) its use does not have to bring any increase in gross revenue.

The argument goes like this. It is assumed that entrepreneurs employing fewer workers after introducing new machinery will consider themselves satisfied if they obtain the same net product as before. Net product being what is left after covering production costs (including labor costs), it is clear that it will be possible, from now on, to derive the same net product from a smaller gross product, since gross product (production costs plus net product) will have been relieved of part of the wage bill. "Reducing wage costs" is an expression of monetary economics. Put into real terms, it means a contraction of circulating capital. The increase in fixed capital will have been possible only by transferring workers producing circulating capital and having them make machinery, or fixed capital. Now circulating capital is made up of food, clothing, and so on—in short, all those goods that serve to sustain the life of the working population.

However, Ricardo warns us that he makes this supposition purely for the convenience of his argument. It would be wrong, according to him, to leave things there:[16] "The statements which I have made will not, I hope, lead to the inference that machinery should not be encouraged."[17] Why does Ricardo remain so optimistic? First of all because, as he says, it is rare for new machines to be introduced "suddenly" and "extensively." In most cases they are brought in gradually. Another reason is because the installation of more sophisticated plant will *always* have the effect of increasing the net product, and at least part of that increased net product will be saved—in other words, converted into fresh capital, a part of which at least will take the form of circulating capital (food, clothing, etc.), the effect of which will be to ensure an increased demand for labor. Through accumulation, therefore, a larger mass of capital will ultimately be created than that which was initially withdrawn from circulation because of the contraction of the gross product due to the replacement of human labor by machinery.

Ricardo therefore concludes, prudently but firmly, "It is not easy, I think, to conceive that under any circumstances, an increase of capital should not be followed by an increased demand for labor; the most that can be said is that the demand will be in a diminishing ratio."[18] Events have confirmed, and more than confirmed, this judgment, particularly since Ricardo had the suspicion that the labor previously employed by industry would find work in the "services."[19] Even the recent advances made by automation in the twentieth century thanks to electronics—the principle of automation itself was already known in the nineteenth century[20]—have not been followed by any fall in employment although, early in the 1960s, they did resurrect the terrible fear of the Lyons silk weavers who smashed the looms that were believed to carry the curse of unemployment.

There has been an extraordinary increase in the working population of all those countries that have accumulated capital and therefore qualify to be called "capitalist" from the standpoint of political economy—the Soviet Union during some periods just as much as the United States, Germany, the United Kingdom, France, Japan, and so on. On the contrary, events have given the lie to Marx's forecast that under the "production of commodities" system, which he regarded as a mode of production governed by special laws, the technological progress that brought more machines into use, far from opening up new employment opportunities, would reduce them considerably. If it were a question of crystal gazing it would matter little, except for the record, who was right and who was wrong. But the question at issue is not who was the best prophet but which of the two, Ricardo or Marx, was the founder of a scientific method.

This inability of Marxist theory to account for the functioning of a concrete economy, even if it were socialist, ought not to come as a surprise. Reading and rereading *Capital,* one perceives that Marxist economics does not exist as such. It exists in the form of a critique of classical political economy. Marxism comes on the scene as a dissertation on political economy, history, or even all the other sciences, but never as a specific segment of any science in particular. On the supposition that Marxism is, as its supporters claim, the "science" of capitalism, this would bring us back to the previous proposition in the following terms: Marxism is the *justified* critique of capitalism. But a sound criticism of political economy could either prove the latter's futility as a particular discipline or point the way to a different political economy. Marx never tells us which of these two sides he takes but it is the former, or so it seems to me, that emerges from his long submission.

If Marx had really pointed the way to a *different* political economy, he would have to show the existence, under the ruins of classical political economy, of other laws governing economic phenomena. Perhaps Marx did not have the time to formulate, himself, the political economy that his critique of the classical school implied, but for his work to have been taken further in that direction by his followers, it would have had to contain, at least potentially, the principles of a different political economy. A strong presumption that this potentiality is not there is provided by the fact that, to save their plans from being mere declarations of intent, the socialist countries were forced to use the old categories of the political economy that Marx dethroned (profit on capital, wages paid to workers, etc.). Only then can these plans become "operational."

### "Après moi, le déluge!"

As a further illustration of the empirical—and sometimes even crudely empirical—character of the Marxist method, called an "immense theoretical revolution" by devotees like Althusser, here is another example (and there are hundreds more) taken from *Capital*. In the chapter dealing with the "working day" Marx writes: *"Après moi, le déluge!* is the watchword of every capitalist and of every capitalist nation."[21] This opinion contradicts the very idea of capital, which is that part of the product intended to be *reproduced* instead of being consumed immediately and irreplaceably. Given that a capitalist society is one that accumulates capital, is not its behavior, by definition, dictated by concern for the future? But let us stay with Marx, who goes on to say: "Capital *therefore* [my italics] takes no account of the health and the length of life of the worker, unless society forces it to do so." From the observation of a fact that was unhappily true (the excessive lengthening of the working day in British factories in the mid-nineteenth century), Marx induces a principle of general application: *"Après moi . . . ."* From this principle, what does he then deduce? The fact that he has observed! To assert that capitalism, by its nature, is not concerned about the future is to handle logic no better than someone saying: "In every age, workers have resisted the introduction of more modern machinery—*therefore* the working class is against progress."

Marxist philosophers will try to find a methodological "excuse" for Marx. Perhaps they will point out that the sentence quoted is taken from a purely descriptive chapter in which Marx is more copywriter than economist. They may say that capital is concerned about its own future, not that of the workers. The fact remains that Marx's statement is faulty. Capital is not a conscious subject that can "take account" of anything. Marx is constantly personifying capital.[22] It has a "voracious appetite," it "sucks" the labor of others, it is "celebrating its orgies." We should not quibble about these expressions; they are figures of speech. Nevertheless, such analogies are out of place in scientific thinking. No one now would accept a chemist's attributing human (or inhuman) feelings to arsenic. Ricardo, the object of whose highly modern method is the specific critique of the "language" used by economists, whether his predecessors or contemporaries, would never have suffered such a lapse of language.[23] The completely objective definition of capital he proposes preserved him from the temptation. How can any feeling be attributed, even metaphorically, to that "which is employed in production and gives effect to labour"? Conversely, Marx's definition, half-conceptual, half-historical, and therefore really neither, lends itself to unending *literary* expatiation.

As we have seen, Marx proceeds in the opposite direction to classical political economy. From the principle he induces from the data of experience he deduces these same data. The system he constructs with this method is doomed to subjectivity. As the data specific to his time slowly pass away, he loses the apparent contact he had with the real. This is why he has to present the *feelings* and *desires* of the capitalist as inherent attributes of capital. Consequently, he is led to the finding that the capitalist is really seeking one thing only and that is to increase his capital by every possible means, even if the health of his workmen should suffer. It is easy to acquiesce. The whole of economic history shows that whoever has command of capital, whether it be an individual (cf. the experience of capitalism in the nineteenth century) or the state (cf. the experience of Stalinism in the twentieth century), shows little spontaneous concern for the well-being of the workers "unless society forces it to do so.'' But that has nothing to do with the nature or the function of capital.

## Notes

1. Preface by Friedrich Engels to vol. 2 of Marx, *Capital* (Harmondsworth, U.K.: Penguin Books, 1978).

2. Marx, *Capital,* vol. 1, chap. 7.

3. Marx's comment on a critic by the name of Johann Christoph Gottsched in *Capital,* vol. 1, pp. 325–26.

4. Ricardo, *Principles,* chap. 5.

5. Ricardo does not always use the word *wealth* (or riches) to mean the products of labor, but if the quoted definition is related to its context and to *all* the other passages where the word *capital* is used, it may be unhesitatingly concluded that, for him, capital is always a product of labor and not a gift of nature. A *raw material,* for example, is capital when it has been extracted from the ground by human labor. As long as it remains buried in the earth it is neither capital nor even an economic good.

6. The exclusion of money from the set ''capital'' and the corollary of that exclusion (namely that interest on money—earned by securities, bonds, and so on—has its origin in the profit on *real capital*) run against the economic models in currency today, derived from the famous IS-LM model of the economist John Hicks.

7. By production of commodities, Marx means the capitalist mode of production, characterized in his eyes by the fact that the products of human labor are transformed into commodities intended for sale on the market.

8. Marx, *Capital,* vol. 1, p. 247.

9. The argument here is confined to the basis of Marxist theory as set out in volume 1 of *Capital,* disregarding the distribution of the surplus value, the effect of which is to equalize the rate of profit among all the capitalists, including those whose capital generates no surplus value.

10. Ibid., vol. 1, chap. 4, p. 256.

11. Ibid., chap. 11.

12. Bringing metaphors into scientific reasoning is, of itself, fraught with many dangers on which there is no need to dwell. The risks are even greater when the images appear to relate to an earlier phase of human history, because the reader may wrongly assume that the author has deeper motives than simply to illustrate his argument with a fictitious example chosen as an aid to understanding.

13. David Ricardo, *Notes on Malthus,* vol. 2 of *Complete Works*, ed. Piero Sraffa (Cambridge, U.K.: Cambridge University Press, 1966), p. 234.

14. Ricardo, *Principles,* chap. 1, sect. 4.

15. Ibid., chap. 31.

16. One may wonder whether Marx did not, precisely, leave things there. It is, indeed, highly likely that it was from this chapter "On Machinery," bristling with logical restrictions because Ricardo sets out a series of particular cases in it, that Marx derived his theory of variable and constant capital which he believes to be of general application. An argument in favor of this interpretation is that Marx regards "On Machinery" as a veritable retraction on Ricardo's part—for which he praises him to the skies, as we shall see, whereas it was simply a clarification. In *Capital,* vol. 1, chap. 15, sect. 6, Marx says that with "a whole series of bourgeois political economists, including James Mill, MacCullogh, Torrens, Senior and John Stuart Mill," Ricardo for a time held that machinery was favorable to employment. But, Marx then adds, "Ricardo originally shared this view, but afterwards expressly disclaimed it, with *the scientific impartiality and love of truth characteristic of him"* (my italics).

17. Ricardo, *Principles,* chap. 31.

18. Ibid.

19. It is true that the service he was thinking of was primarily domestic but it might be held that most "services" in the modern sense of the word are activities that were performed in the past by those "in service" in the houses of well-to-do people, for example, catering, laundering, lighting, heating, health care, and so on.

20. Marx, not perhaps the most penetrating theoretician of his century but at least a great historian, gives a striking description of the phenomenon: "A system of machinery, whether it reposes on the mere cooperation of similar machines, as in weaving, or on a combination of different machines, as in spinning, constitutes in itself a huge automaton" (*Capital,* vol. 1, chap. 15).

21. Ibid., chap. 10.

22. There are perhaps better quotes I might have picked—for example, this sentence taken from volume 1, chapter 10 on the working day: "As a capitalist, he is only capital personified; his soul is the soul of capital."

23. Thus, after quoting from Adam Smith, Ricardo writes (*Principles,* chap. 1, "On Value"): "Now it is against this language that I protest." The expression "it is against this language that I protest" recurs throughout the *Principles.* Ricardo subjects the economic language of his day to continuous logical criticism.

*3*

# There Is No Such Thing as the "Labor Market"

## Concerning the Most Significant Play on Words
## in Modern History

No matter how many times political economy may have routed its critics, the fact remains that Marx was the first to object to the idea that in our society human labor should be treated as a commodity like any other, to be bought and sold on the market. He may have been unable to overturn the logic of the earlier system but that logic is nonetheless diabolical. At best, one can only put up with capitalism until such time as "another way" can be found, another system that exposes the intolerable scandal of labor as commodity.

It would not take much prompting for most of our contemporaries, including the self-styled "liberals" (in the European sense), to start using this sort of language.

Is it right to say that in a market economy labor is "a commodity like any other"? I propose now to try to answer that question and in doing so I shall be obliged again, with apologies to the reader, to quote from texts that in some cases require no small effort to interpret. But over and above the texts and the historical origins of the thought, there is the argument itself, as it stands complete, and I shall begin by summarizing it.

In a market, supply and demand meet. If supply in a market exceeds

33

demand, then the sellers—in this case the workers, those who "supply"[1] their labor—will in the ordinary way bring down their price and supply at a discount in order to obtain employment. If, on the other hand, demand exceeds supply, then the buyers—in this case the employers, those who represent the "demand" for labor—will bid up the price and offer higher and higher wages to get the labor which is in short supply.

Something else that is true of any market and therefore applies to the case we are considering here is that the sellers set a limit to their margin of reduction: In other words, there is a price below which they prefer not to sell. This lower limit is usually the price that will just cover the cost of production. Similarly, the buyers will not bid up indefinitely: There is a price above which they prefer not to buy. If the buyer is buying in order to resell, this upper limit will be somewhere below the price at which the product bought will be resold. The transaction will take place if the price bid and the price asked coincide—in other words, only if the lowest the seller is prepared to go does not exceed the highest the buyer is prepared to go.

But what is the significance, on the market we are considering here, of the wage rate below which the worker will refuse a job? The very terms of the question demonstrate its ambiguity, at any rate if we take the case of one specific worker. If we assume that he has a family to keep and no other means of support than his job (no parents to give him a home, no welfare state to pay him benefits), the likelihood is that he will always prefer to work for however low a wage rather than starve. The question becomes meaningful only when posed for the working population as a whole. Then we see that the wage rate determines the structure of employment, and the concept of the minimum wage below which job seekers refuse paid employment has real meaning. It helps us to understand, for example, why the poorest countries have the smallest proportion of wage earners. In those countries labor productivity is so low that as a rule the level of wages is likewise very low. Even supposing that they were offered jobs, many people, rather than receive a pittance at the end of a hard day's work, would still prefer to do nothing and beg a living or content themselves with the scant and chancy earnings from some business, however modest, of their own (selling postcards, rickshaw driving, etc.). It is a fact that in the least developed regions of the world one finds an army of one-man businesses and middlemen of all kinds.

In southern Algeria I have seen the same kilo of dates go through a dozen pairs of hands before reaching the packaging firm. Once a country's wealth starts to grow and "economic takeoff" occurs, more and more of the self-employed will prefer to shed the business risk and sell their services to a small local entrepreneur, *the reason being that the wage rate has risen.* As that rate rises, the size of businesses grows. The same trend is to be found at all stages of development. I have taken the case of a poor country, but the same thing is occurring in France: The rise in the level of wages, due to economic growth, is causing increasing numbers of small tradesmen, small farmers, and small businessmen to look for jobs.

As to how the minimum wage is determined, economists always come back to the old classical idea, borrowed by Marx, that the minimum wage is determined by the habits and customs of each country and each era. What an IBM worker regards as a minimum acceptable wage today would have seemed an undreamed of luxury to his great-grandfather; it would still seem unattainable riches now to an Algerian fellah or an Indochinese coolie. In other words, the lowest wage at which the "supplier of labor" is prepared to work for someone else cannot be determined mathematically; it is largely a matter of general opinion.

Conversely, nearly all modern economists maintain that the "maximum wage," above which the employer prefers not to take on another worker, can in theory be determined precisely. In no case, they say, can the wage be higher than the value of the product which the last worker hired will make it possible to manufacture (or the value of the *service* which the last worker hired will make it possible to produce), otherwise the entrepreneur will lose on the deal. This postulate is the keystone of the marginalist doctrine. That doctrine is delivered ex cathedra, with an abundance of highly elegant geometrical demonstrations, in all the unversities on both sides of the Atlantic. And this—let it be said right away—despite its inconsistent logic and therefore its pseudomathematical character, and despite the contempt in which experience-schooled businessmen generally hold it (when they do not, the reason is not that they have found marginalist theory borne out by facts but that they keep at a respectful distance from all theorists). The whole of today's economic doctrine rests on the conclusion to which marginal analysis arrives, namely that in a competitive market the payment for labor will ultimately become just equal to the net marginal product of that labor. It seems logical enough, since until that equality is reached, it will be in the employer's interests to hire an additional worker.

This relationship of equality is the implicit reply that the so-called "neoclassical" school has made, since the end of the nineteenth century, to the Marxist theory of wages. Whereas the Marxist theory rests on an erroneous explanation of the origin of profit—due to a misinterpretation of the labor theory of value—the marginalist theory has been constructed *in contradiction to* the labor theory of value and, in the extreme case, excludes profit. Since the wage is equal to the marginal product of labor, then by definition the last worker hired (or, to put it another way, the last hour's work performed by a worker) brings no profit.

In another interpretation of the theory, the value of the marginal product does include profit, or at any rate the marginal value (or marginal cost) of the product includes the interest on the value of the capital (plant and inventory) employed in the production process. But then no convincing theory is put forward to explain interest. The very fact that profit can be alternatively included or excluded shows how vague the theory is on a point that is, after all, fundamental.

The rebuttal presented in this book will attempt to show that, whatever the hypothesis used (constant, increasing, or diminishing return), the wage is not equal to the marginal product of labor, but that since the wage is, from the employer's standpoint, that part of his capital which he invests in labor (an ambiguous expression I will replace by another later on), the wage must be placed in relation to the profit expected. This means that the critique of both marginalism and the Marxist wage theory cannot be fully developed until the question of what profit is and how it arises have been elucidated, which will be the subject of the next chapter.

In this chapter, I enquire more particularly into what is covered by the supply price proposed by the sellers, that is, the workers, and the nature of the commodity they are selling in the so-called labor market. This question is of paramount importance, since until it is answered the investigation cannot be taken any further nor, in particular, can the profit generation process be examined.

The almost impossible difficulties that have been posed by analysis of the wage, considered as the minimum compensation acceptable to workers, stem from the attempts made by the classical economists to reason in terms of the "cost of production of labor." It was concern for symmetry that led them to create this rather dubious concept. Since, in the last resort, value—or, to put it more simply, the price of anything—is determined by its cost of production, then "labour, like all other things which are purchased and sold . . . has its natural . . . price," as Ricardo wrote in the opening paragraph of his chapter on wages (*Principles*). So, despite our efforts, we are back where we began. Both sides have been heard: Labor is a commodity like any other, the proof being that it costs a certain price to produce. That price corresponds to the wage. Thus, Marx had only to take over Ricardo's notion of the "natural price of labor" to construct his concept of the "cost of reproduction of labor power."

The amazing thing about this notion is that although it seems quite impossible to accept, it cannot be rejected either. The idea of a wage level below which the worker will refuse to work has been corroborated by experience. The refusal takes different forms, depending on the era and the country. Nowadays young Portuguese people leave their country because they cannot find any employment there or because, if they do, the pay they will get seems to them too low by comparison with, say, wages in France or Germany. This emigration is causing some shortage of manpower in the country, so Portuguese wage levels are beginning to rise again. This brings us back to the Ricardian theory that the wage rate cannot remain lastingly below the "natural price of labor," because, if the effective wage is lower than that price, the working population will shrink to the point where the "price of labor" begins to rise again. This is why the idea still has a place in modern economic textbooks. Raymond Barre, in his book, quotes this passage from a modern French author (F. de Menthon):

> The labouring class thinks that, however difficult the conditions of production, however great the numbers out of work, there is a certain level below which the wage cannot fall. Public opinion thinks likewise and so does the entrepreneur. This minimum is based on the estimation of a certain standard of living and a certain price of labour, both of them governed by acquired habits and by evaluations of "what is fair" based on comparisons.[2]

From the "cost of production of labor," determined in each era and in each country by the prevailing habits and customs, it is a perfectly natural step to the "minimum wage claimed" which the interested party calculates by reference to what it feels entitled to demand. This transition from the passive to the active, so characteristic of the history of modern societies, was foreseen; in fact it was expressly recommended by Ricardo (but not by neoliberals or neomarginalists.)

But it would be too easy to leave it at that. It is not because the "cost of production of labor" could, in a capitalist society, serve as the foundation for a just claim on the part of labor that this notion would be cleansed of its original sin, so to speak. If, in fact, economics really does allow that human labor *per se* has a "price" and that its cost of production is calculable, then it is hard to see what distinction it makes between wage labor and the labor performed by a beast of burden. Admittedly a plough horse is not paid a wage, but its upkeep costs something, and if the animal were, as Aesop would have it, endowed with the gift of speech and could exercise its free will, there could be an advantage, rather than provide it from day to day with stabling and provender, in paying it a wage commensurate with its daily wants. With those who might object that my analogy is pointless because the status of a horse is not that of a worker but that of a slave, I would agree that the horse is *capital,* like the slave, since it can be bought and sold, whereas the wage laborer can dispose of himself as he will. Even so, if the human wage laborer "sells" his labor, his legal emancipation does not fundamentally change his economic status, since on the market he will still be forced to "supply" the power generated by his brain and his brawn.

Political economy is not intrinsically a "moral discipline," but if there were a definitive admission that its theorems were valid only because human labor was regarded at the outset as a commodity, then no one could rest until another system were proposed based on different axiomatics in which human labor would not be deemed to be "like all other things."

My purpose is to show that the issue is not yet resolved and that the expression "like all other things" ought to have opened the way to a solution of the riddle. The one I propose leads to a theory of profit that answers many questions raised by classical economics but remains within the framework of its reasoning. No attempt here at "noneuclidean" economics (as Keynes would have put it)!

The most extreme of the interpretations to which classical political economy gave rise is that of Marx, since it carries fallacy to a point where the disequilibrium is such that the mind is all but compelled by the force of circumstances to reestablish the truth. According to the modern Marxologists, and Althusser in particular, Marx brilliantly filled the "lacunae" that existed in Ricardo's analysis despite the apparent closeness of the reasoning. They maintain it was because Ricardo had left "blanks" in his reasoning that he had been unable to bring the labor contract within the general law of exchange (see Chapter 2, p. 13, Engels' quotation). The world had to wait for Marx and his revelations to make light where there had been darkness, since, the argument runs, when the classical economists assimilated the wage with the "price of labor," they became prisoners of an insoluble contradiction. So everything becomes crystal clear once Marx has revealed that each time the classicists write "price of labor" one should read "price of labor power."

What an extraordinary slip. But the fact remains that Marx's substitute expression, which was to be so influential in the history of economic thought—and in history generally—is not, if one may say so, the last word. Marx was right in stating that the expression "price of labor" has no concrete significance, but his substitute is just as unsuitable and equally a betrayal of the scientific spirit he claims to have. I propose here to substitute for the classicists' expression "price of labor" another one, which is not that of Marx.

What makes me inclined to think that this substitute expression is more than just an interpretation is that after reasoning had led me to it, I looked more deeply and carefully into Ricardo's work—particularly his *Notes on Malthus*—and I found that he had used it himself. This new change of term would at best be of no more than historical interest if it did not contain a number of inferences that could well serve to alter the view most people have of economics. The most commonly held is that any production process is analyzed as the combination of heterogeneous factors of production: capital, labor, and natural resources. But it could well be that this classification is the result of a confusion of concepts.

To believe that the employer buys "labor," or "labor power," is the wrong way of looking at it. What interests him is the product of labor, which he can then resell. The illusion derives from the fact that, at the time the bargain is struck, the worker "sells" a product or service (the "produce" of his labor) which only its buyer, the employer, knows. The seller (worker) knows only his own wants and he sets his price according to his estimate of those wants. This situation is the reverse of the one generally presented, where it is the seller who knows the product he is selling and the buyer who is thinking of the want he wishes to satisfy. This reversal, due to the specific circumstances of the "labor contract," has given rise to more than one misunderstanding. (This could be likened to a forward purchase: The purchaser buys a product to be delivered at a set date, at a price that is determined when the contract is concluded but that will not be paid until the due date.)

## Ricardian Wage Theory

### The so-called "iron law"

The misunderstanding most fraught with consequences arose in connection with the passage where Ricardo defined the "natural price" of labor as "that price which is necessary to enable the labourers, one with another, to subsist and to perpetuate their race, without either increase or diminution."[3] Second-rate German economists in the mid-nineteenth century claimed that Ricardo had in that passage formulated what they called "the iron law of wages": By some irresistible force or other, the amount of wages will always be brought down to the subsistence level. The expression really caught on, despite the paucity of the thought, and still today even good authors commonly accept that Ricardo, either to simplify his argument or because this is what he really believed, took for granted that the wage could never stay very long above the vital minimum. This particular interpretation (denounced on several occasions, notably by Alfred Marshall) cannot survive any reasonably careful scrutiny of Ricardo's writings. It hinges on two ambiguities: One of them, the meaning of "necessary," is comparatively easy to resolve. The other, the meaning of "natural," is not.

Let us begin, therefore, with the word "necessary." Ricardo took pains to explain what he meant by it. Yet the passage in which he did so has often been misunderstood—with the notable exception of Marx, who to all intents and purposes made it his own. Ricardo wrote:

> It is not to be understood that the natural price of labour, estimated even in food and necessaries, is absolutely fixed and constant. It varies at different times in the same country, and very materially differs in different countries. It essentially depends on the habits and customs of the people. An English labourer would consider his wages under their natural rate, and too scanty to support a family, if they enabled him to purchase no other food than potatoes, and to live in no better habitation than a mud cabin; yet these moderate demands of nature are often deemed sufficient in countries where *man's life is cheap* and his wants easily satisfied. Many of the conveniences now enjoyed in an English cottage would have been thought luxuries at an earlier period of our history.[4]

In these few sentences Ricardo says two important things, both of which contradict the Germans' interpretation of his thought. First, he says that the list of goods considered necessaries of life for the lowest-paid workers can be extended almost indefinitely according to the progress of "habits and customs." With this specific reference to the progress of habits, Ricardo makes room in his logical construct for what today would be called "the consumer society," the positive aspect of which is that it enables new classes of society to consume a luxury (for them) which the wealthy classes have always considered "necessary" to their material comfort (travel, vacations in the country, and so on). There is nothing very remarkable in this particular glimpse of the future, since the idea of a society of plenty is as old as creation. Ricardo's merit is to have perceived the relative nature of that idea through time and space. The authors of our time do not always have as clear a vision of things, and the best of them have succumbed to the illusion that we are at last living in an "affluent society," whereas, to our grandchildren, this "affluent society" will probably appear poor, crude, and absurdly sophisticated.

Ricardo goes further. He does not simply say that today's luxuries are tomorrow's necessities. He adds that it is a purely academic hypothesis to regard the wage as what is just enough to procure the "necessaries" of life, however largely defined. Let us go back to the passage I have just quoted. "It is not to be understood that the natural price of labour, *estimated even in food and necessaries, is* absolutely fixed and constant," he wrote. If the phrase I have italicized has a significance (and Ricardo was no casual writer), then what can be the meaning of the qualification "even"? It can mean only one thing: that the natural price of labor, or wage, may become high enough to leave something over after all the necessary wants—and "necessary wants," as we have just seen, mean much more than mere subsistence—have been met. In other words, the wage earner will earn enough to be able to save part of his income. This is of great significance, since to save is to contribute to the formation of society's net capital. This interpretation is confirmed by another passage in *Principles* where Ricardo deals with the distribution of income among the different classes and says this: "Perhaps this is expressed too strongly, as more is generally allotted to the labourer under the name of wages than the absolutely *necessary* expenses of production. In that case a part of the *net produce* of the country is received by the labourer, and may be saved or expended by him" (my italics).[5]

Here is a further textual argument proving that nothing could be more alien to Ricardian thought than the idea that the worker is condemned to a subsistence wage.

Marx, who sticks very close to Ricardo in this area—even on the question of net product—shares the same relative conception of the "necessary." He says that "The number and extent of [the laborer's] so-called necessary requirements, as also the manner in which they are satisfied, are themselves products of history and depend therefore to a great extent on the level of civilization attained by a country." To which he feels able to add this: "*In contrast . . . with the case of other commodities* the determination of the value of labour-power contains an historical and moral element" (my italics). This last clause shows that Marx, although he borrowed heavily from classical political economy, did not go so far as to emulate the closeness of its reasoning. In strict logic, he was wrong in maintaining that the existence of this "historical and moral element" distinguishes labor from all other commodities. Let us assume, for example, that tastes and habits require motor cars to be equipped with extras that have a solely decorative purpose: The cost of these embellishments will nonetheless enter into the car's total production cost and correspondingly raise its value, in the Ricardian or Marxian sense of the term. Ricardo, a better logician than Marx, does not say that the "natural price" of labor is determined differently from that of *all* other commodities, as the German philosopher rashly affirmed.

This brings us to the second, and more serious, cause of the misunderstanding, the ambiguity of the word *natural*. We have already seen that Ricardo used the expression "natural price" to designate the theoretical price, the price that never materializes in the market or rather does exist in the market but as a trend (the "long-term price," as modern economists would say). There is nothing really surprising, especially if one remembers the age in which he was writing, in Ricardo's choice of the word *natural* to express something the distinguishing feature of which is that it is not to be found in nature! The word matches a thought of platonic inspiration in which natural equals belonging to the world of logic. One could for example say that Pythagoras' theorem belongs to the "nature" of our universe and that knowledge of the theorem helps us to reveal that nature, even though the perfect triangle is something we shall never see in this life. Ricardo uses the concept of "natural price" or "necessary price"—two expressions which for him are interchangeable[6]—each time he tries to resolve the almost insoluble methodological problem presented to the economist by the fact that (a) a host of different factors are at work simultaneously and (b) these factors change as economic phenomena develop over time. So what the economist first has to do if he considers he is justified in trying to establish a causal relationship between two facts—the price, for example, of any kind of product consumed by the worker, and the amount of the wage—is to leave temporarily out of account all other factors (in this case, the wage) that might influence the magnitude whose main cause of variation he seeks to identify.

Hence the importance, as pointed out so many times,[7] of the proviso *ceteris paribus*, it being understood that the causal relationship that has been identified can be used in applied science only if one is capable of specifying, *first*, which elements are assumed constant and, *second*, what relationships can be established between them when, in order to construct a model more consistent with reality, one ceases to consider them arbitrarily as constant.[8]

Let us return to the key passage quoted at the beginning of this section, where Ricardo defines the "natural price of labour" as "that price which is necessary to enable the labourers, one with another, to subsist and to perpetuate *their race, without either increase or diminution.*" I particularly stress the last phrase since, of itself, that phrase shows that by *natural price* Ricardo means a hypothetical price that would materialize in a simplified world. And here is the proof: Throughout the rest of the chapter he dwells on the tendency which the population would have, in his view, to adjust, slowly but surely, to the level of wages.[9] He also reintroduces as active causes a number of other variables initially assumed constant, such as the volume of capital and the state of techniques. What, ultimately, in the mind of Ricardo, is a "natural and constant" causal relationship like that which makes the wage determinable by the prices of the necessaries of life for the worker? He answers this question himself when he writes that the "natural price" of any commodity is "that power (of exchange) which it would possess if not disturbed by any temporary or accidental cause." Ricardo's method is to leave out of account these temporary or accidental causes, whose intervention would most probably claim the entire attention of "empirical" minds and make them overlook the essential.

After having so painstakingly fashioned his concept of the "natural price of labour," which is valid only for an economy assumed to be static with a constant population level, Ricardo moves on in the same chapter to a dynamic economy and concludes, categorically, that "Notwithstanding the tendency of wages to conform to the natural rate, their market rate may, in an improving society, for an indefinite period, be constantly above it; for no sooner may the impulse which an increased capital gives to a new demand for labour be obeyed, than another increase of capital may produce the same effect; and thus, if the increase of capital be gradual and constant, the demand for labour may give a continued stimulus to an increase of people."[10]

It is clear that, in Ricardo's mind, the conditions prevailing in a real (and dynamic) economic life are very far removed from his initial and purely theoretical assumption of a "price of labour" just sufficient to "perpetuate" the working population "without either increase or diminution."

### From the custom-dictated wage to the claimed wage

The most interesting thing in this long disquisition is the way Ricardo, starting out from the idea that in each era and each country there is a sort of "minimum wage" corresponding to what today would be called the standard budget of a working-class family, arrived at this other infinitely more provocative idea that if workers are not to be condemned to a life of poverty they must cease to take habits and customs as an unchangeable datum and demand a more "comfortable" and "enjoyable" life—in other words, draw up their typical budget themselves, adding in the current value of a number of articles or services of which they, too, want to avail themselves. One might almost have thought that classical political economy conceived of society as being moved by *objective* forces that held the subjectivity of economic agents in check, a society in which no collective or, still less, individual will is able to predominate in a market that is perfectly competitive and where the law of large numbers neutralizes the desire of the sellers by the opposite desire of the buyers.

However, economic theory bears no more than a rather remote resemblance to mechanics. It cannot be equated with a mechanical science, because its subject matter is living.[11] If it is not to lose contact with reality and become no more than an intellectual pastime, it must make room for improvisation somewhere in the "system" it conceives and in the model it constructs, even if this means accepting that equilibrium may be upset and that there are circumstances in which everything must be started again from scratch. It cannot be content to describe phenomena and discover the more or less hypothetical laws that govern their sequential development. If it is not to put its reputation for objectivity at risk, it must occasionally become *praxis:* It must come out into the street and spell out a course of action. In many ways it was a dangerous misjudgment to fabricate the scholastic-sounding concept of the "natural price" and so be forced ultimately to the commonplace conclusion that for each country and each era a definition emerges of what constitutes the necessary minimum for the worker. Yet the effect of this confession of semi-impotence—the acknowledgement that, all things considered, the level of wages depends on habits and customs—is to implant the unforeseeable and, up to a point, the arbitrary, at the heart of the system, since no philosopher has ever claimed that habits and customs are inviolable—not even Marx, who cites many cases where society "forced" employers to reduce the working day and even to pay "reasonable wages."

Let us go back once again to that (virtually inexhaustible) fountainhead, Ricardo's chapter "On Wages" in his *Principles*. In it he develops a three-stage theory, working with two variables.

*First stage:* "The friends of humanity," he writes in Chapter 5 of the *Principles,* "cannot but wish that in all countries the labouring classes should have a taste for comforts and enjoyments, and that they should be stimulated *by all legal means* in their exertions to procure them" (my italics). This passage, incidentally, probably escaped the notice of the free trade–advocating politicians of the nineteenth century who made any workers' association illegal.

*Second stage:* Why did Ricardo want workers to enjoy a well-being hitherto reserved for landowners and capitalists? Because, he says, "there cannot be a better security against a superabundant population." And he goes on (again, *Principles,* Chapter 5): "In those countries where the labouring classes have the fewest wants, and are contented with the cheapest food, the people are exposed to the greatest vicissitudes and miseries. They have no place of refuge from calamity; they cannot seek safety in a lower station; they are already so low that they can fall no lower. On any deficiency of the chief article of their subsistence there are few substitutes of which they can avail themselves and dearth to them is attended with almost all the evils of famine." One could argue that this description could be applied, more or less as it stands, to some countries of the Third World today.[12] It is quite remarkable that in the early nineteenth century the greatest of the "liberal" economists should have recommended an increase in the wants of the working classes as a remedy for overpopulation.[13]

*Third stage:* We have just seen (Chapter 2, pp. 25–26) how Ricardo considers it likely that with the introduction of more and more sophisticated machinery the demand for labor generated by the growth of capital will increase less than that capital. We see now that with growth and diversification of the wants felt by workers, it is population growth that will be held back. If the volume of capital grows rapidly, what will happen? Demand for labor, even if it does not increase as fast as the volume of capital, will still grow faster than the population. *Consequently, the demand for labor will always exceed the supply.* The result will be that wages will always tend to be higher than the natural price that serves as a gauge of the minimum acceptable to the worker on the lowest rung of the ladder.[14] This, according to Ricardo, is the situation that can prevail indefinitely "in an improving society." Ricardo's conclusion, it should be emphasized, is the very opposite of Malthus' conception, which even today has currency.

In short, the classical school reminds us that workers' best guarantee of seeing their purchasing power grow is their freedom to bargain over "the price of their labour."

The proof that this is no illusory advantage is that even those who consider themselves to be the worst enemies of liberalism, like the left-wing trade unions, refuse—and how right they are—to commit themselves lastingly to any income policy which would restrict that freedom.

It is just as though they (the trade unions) admitted that the existence, in one form or another, of a free "labor market" enabled workers to place their subjective needs on the same plane as the constraints of production. What better vindication could there be of Ricardo's theory?

### The two (apparent) "gaps" in classical theory

However relevant to modern life, our theory appears to have two big gaps in it.

First, it seems precisely to make no allowance for production constraints. What kind of wage theory would it be if it were concerned only with the supply price of labor on the market (in other words, the workers' price) but never the demand price (the price that employers are prepared to pay)? Such a theory would really be no more than a pseudo-theory. It would imply that the wage level was entirely arbitrary and depended solely on what the workers saw as their wants. No law of a "scientific" character could therefore be based on it, since economic phenomena would apparently not be bound by any necessary physical constraints, as though floating weightlessly in some dimension ruled by the imaginary and the indeterminate.

Marxist theory, let it be noted, invites the same criticism, with the aggravating circumstance that Marx, like a stage magician, makes the one element serve twice: The worker's minimum supply price—set, as we have seen, by reference to his minimum wants as determined by historical evolution—becomes the price imposed by the employer. This is a strange conceit, since it would imply that the employer calculates the wage by reference to something he is not supposed to know: the wants of the workers. The only thing that he knows and that in this case interests him is the product he has the worker produce in order to sell it on the market. So it may be concluded, on the face of it, that he will base the wage rate he is prepared to pay on his production schedule (possibly allowing for competition from other firms for labor, if this is in short supply). If truth be told, Marx's idea of the "labor market" is understandable only if it is assumed that, in his mind, employers always have the upper hand and can therefore always lower the wage rate to the minimum level still acceptable to the worker. It is hardly necessary to point out that this notion has been belied by facts and that, here again, Marx reveals himself to be very inferior to his mentor, Ricardo.

The second lacuna brings us back to the central question posed by Marxism: Even if the wage is high, where is the equivalence of exchange between worker and employer, given that the employer's profit has to come from somewhere?

## Marginalism Seemingly Provides an Overall Answer

Marginal analysis, devised by the late nineteenth century economists mentioned earlier—the Austrians and Jevons, Walras, and Marshall—was an attempt at bridging these two gaps.

### Marginalism and the "demand price of labor"

The marginalists are careful not to get mired in interminable discussions about the rock-bottom minimum wage. They begin, often the best way of bypassing a difficulty, by assuming that the problem is resolved—by taking the wage as *given;* it is of little concern to them whether the wage is determined by the transactors' psychological assessment of an acceptable standard of living, by the balance of power between trade unions and employers at any given time, or by the greater or lesser degree of direct intervention by the government to enforce a minimum wage. Economics, the marginalists say, must confine itself to observing facts, and the market wage is a fact like any other. Yet economics, they add, is able to reveal a fundamental relationship; it is possible, even certain, that in the very first instance the amount of the wage is set arbitrarily, but once that amount exists then science reasserts itself and explains how enterprises will adjust to it. The arbitrary ceases forthwith and gives place to a logical sequence of facts.

What marginal analysis claimed to demonstrate irrefutably was the link that, according to the theory, has to exist at all times and in all countries between the level of the wage and the level of employment. Each enterprise, considered individually, will find it advantageous to hire extra workers as long as the wage remains lower than the net marginal product of labor. Recruitment will cease, in the words familiar to anyone who has ever read an economics textbook, when the marginal product (that is, the receipt from the sale of the additional product produced by an extra worker) equals the price (in this case, the wage) of the factor of production (in this case, labor).

The particular feature of this theory is therefore that profit is something left after subtraction. The "last" worker hired brings his employer no profit, since by definition he receives a wage equal to the product of his labor.[15] It has to be assumed, therefore, *that the return diminishes with every further worker hired.*

What is attractive at first sight about this new construct, as compared with the old, is that when set out in full it introduces simultaneously the demand price and the supply price, thus giving each of the two protagonists on the market—the employer and the worker—his role to play. For their demonstration the marginalists devised, as we know, a demand curve and a supply curve (Figure 3.1). For each curve the quantity of labor (level of employment) is plotted against the amount of the wage. The demand curve slopes downward from left to right, reflecting the fact that the ability of employers to hire workers increases as the wage decreases (the lower the wage, the lower the value of the marginal product). The supply curve slopes upward from left to right, reflecting the fact that the number of suppliers of labor increases as the wage level rises. According to this system, work contract is concluded only if the demand and supply curves intersect. The point of intersection shows at what wage level the demand for labor is equal to the supply of labor.

Note that marginal analysis—and this is another point that might seem to be in its favor—turns its back on the pseudoscientific method that goes by the name of "dialectic." And yet if there is one area in which we would be tempted to see a dialectic, it is this one. Is not the market wage a kind of "synthesis" which for the time being resolves

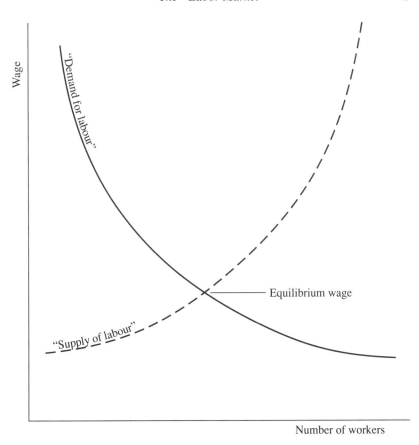

**Figure 3.1** Supply and demand curves. For the marginalist, labor is a commodity, and the wage its price.

the "contradiction" between the price proposed (the lowest possible) by the employer and the price asked (the highest possible) by the supplier of labor? However, for there to be "synthesis" in the sense in which Marxian or Hegelian dialectic takes that word, it has to represent something new in relation to "thesis" and "antithesis." But there is nothing of the kind here, since the wage rate at which labor supply equals labor demand *was already built into* each of the two curves.

In the event, everything seemed to become clear thanks to the new explanation. If Marx (and Ricardo) had been right, then the wage, in a given location and at a given moment of time, would be the same in all enterprises. But it is higher in those enterprises which are the most productive. Does this not prove that there are really as many labor markets (with their own supply and demand curves) as there are enterprises and that in each enterprise the level of wages is determined by the productivity of labor? This is why the new theory seemed to present the twofold advantage of refuting Marx and "supplementing" Ricardo.

But though giving the impression of supplementing or improving on classical political economy, marginal analysis actually made a complete break with it, in at least three fundamental ways.

1. Its reasoning is valid only if, as extra workers are hired, their productivity decreases. In other words, it postulates that the enterprise operates with diminishing returns. But this is seldom true in real life. Businessmen know by experience that they could produce more without their unit costs of production rising. What usually deters them from taking on more workers—or buying new machinery—is the limitation of their financial resources or their inability to expand their clientele, or both, but not a fall in productivity. This is one important reason why marginal analysis is proving to be of no use in guiding the action of businessmen.

There is another equally decisive reason. Even supposing that the diminishing returns hypothesis were borne out, in this or that particular case, is it true that the last worker hired will inevitably bring no profit? No sooner is the question asked than it can be answered: *Never,* in normal circumstances, does an entrepreneur commit the least part of his capital if he does not expect a profit from it. If instead of posing the question in relation to the wage earner, one were to pose it relative to capital equipment—the marginalist reasoning is supposed to be applicable to all the "factors of production"—the answer is even more obvious. Does an entrepreneur manage his business in such a way that his least productive machine (the "marginal" machine) brings him no profit? If the machine in question has ceased to be profitable, the good businessman will replace it.

Today's marginalists, of course, are not unaware of the criticism that their school holds a theory that is valid only on the assumption of increasing costs. For their reply, one of the most significant books to consult is the one in which Milton Friedman expounds to his students the theory of prices.[16] Friedman does not shirk the issue; he goes all out for marginalism as the absolute economic rationality and makes it the touchstone of general liberalism (whereas it is essentially its negation, as we shall see).

For Friedman the diminishing returns hypothesis which is the basis of the theory is always borne out, provided it is correctly interpreted, of course: It is sufficient to assume an increase in the use of one factor of production (in this case, labor) while all the others remain constant, since if an increasing number of workers are assigned to a constant quantity of capital equipment, there will inevitably come a time when the productivity of the labor assigned to that fixed capital will diminish.[17] This finding emboldens Freidman to present the argument on the highest level:

> This then is the law of variable proportions relevant for economics: insofar as possible, production will take place by the use of such a combination of factors that the average returns to each separately will diminish (or at most remain constant) with an increase in the amount of that factor used relative to the amounts of other factors. And this "law" is not a fact of nature, in the sense that nothing else is possible, or that it is demonstrated by repeated physical experiments; it is a maxim of rational conduct.

What still needs to be determined is if, understood in this way, the hypothesis remains generally valid. A firm may make its plant operate at a faster or slower rate, as the case may be, but when a manufacturer buys a new piece of machinery he usually knows how many engineers and operatives are needed to work it, with very little room for variation. In this particular case, as in many others, making the quantity of one production factor vary while the others remain constant leads to artificiality of reasoning.

Friedman's argument is therefore unlikely to reconcile us with the diminishing returns hypothesis. What is more, it must be remembered that this explanation is intended to answer the first objection to the hypothesis (namely that firms stop recruiting or expanding their production capacity for other reasons, apart from a fall in returns). But it does not answer—and for a good reason—the second, even more important objection (namely that *all* the capital employed must bring a profit).

It is here that one begins to suspect that marginalism is nothing other than a wrong interpretation of the (right) Ricardian theory of rent.

Ricardo's first conclusion is that the price of the quintal of wheat will be determined by reference to the cost of production of that same quantity produced under the worst conditions. But in the perfectly competitive economy conceived for the purpose of Ricardo's reasoning, a capitalist will only agree to put his capital into a venture if he can expect to get the average market rate of profit. How can this be reconciled with the fact that successive additions of capital (and labor) are less and less productive? Ricardo's theory of rent provides the answer: The landowner will demand for himself the difference between the return from the least productive capital and the return from the most productive capital. Thus, all the successive additions of capital will bring the same rate of profit. It is easier to state the theory by reasoning in terms of lands of varying fertility.[18] Land A yields 45 quintals per hectare, land B 40 quintals per hectare, and the marginal land C 35 quintals. Let us assume that on land C the sale of 32 quintals covers the operating costs (labor, fertilizer, depreciation, etc.). This leaves a profit equivalent to the value of 3 quintals. Land B yields a profit of $40 - 32 = 8$ q, and land A, $45 - 32$ q $= 13$ q. However, if the farmer cultivating land B pays a rent equal to the difference in yield between B and C—that is, 5 quintals—his profit will be reduced to 3 quintals; and if the farmer cultivating land A pays a rent equal to the difference between A and C—that is, 10 quintals—his profit will likewise be reduced to 3 quintals. The foundation of the reasoning is that the farmer capitalist cannot refuse the landowner the rent, because use of the land is a sine qua non for the farmer's trade (and what is more, the rate of profit is the same in industry and commerce as in agriculture).

In Ricardian reasoning, therefore, marginal farming (or the "marginal input" of capital and labor in total agricultural production) most certainly does yield a profit; in fact it is the rate of profit from the less productive farm that ultimately determines the rate of profit for the whole sector and even for the whole economy. Rent is the result of a difference, but profit is not. The origin of profit is, as I shall endeavor to show, attributable to another mechanism (see Chapter 4).

One last point: Ricardo specifies that rent can only arise in a context of diminishing returns, and he confines this to agriculture (*Principles,* chap. 2) and mining (*Principles,* chap. 3), whence it can be deduced, conversely, that for the other activities Ricardo normally assumes constant if not increasing returns. I shall return to that conclusion and its far-reaching implications and show that it admits of no doubt whatsoever, even if an entire tradition maintains the contrary.

2. Whereas Ricardo spoke only of the supplier's price, the marginalists concentrate on the price offered by "demanders" of labor, that is, employers. This is a complete change of perspective with which we are already familiar. The modern doctrine—and this is its fundamental

characteristic from which all the others derive—makes demand central to economic life, whereas the classical school assigned that place to supply.

It is really not surprising that Ricardo should take this view if one just remembers his central argument regarding price formation. Why is Ricardo interested only in the supply price of labor—governed by the "production cost"—and unconcerned with the demand price? Once again, it is because he is reasoning over the long term, as evident from his use of the expression "the *natural* price of labor," *and because over the long term that price, according to him, is in no way governed by the relationship between supply and demand:* It is governed purely by the competition between sellers. It is so customary to explain the functioning of an economy primarily in terms of the interplay of supply and demand that the reader will probably still be surprised to hear once again that for Ricardo this is secondary. In his approach to the problem, demand is a sine qua non for, but not a cause of, value. For our purpose here this means, for example, that if the wage asked by suppliers of labor were equal to or greater than the value of the product of labor, the employer would cease to be a demander of labor since he could expect no profit. We shall see (in Chapter 4, pp. 121–24) why this eventuality is precluded in normal circumstances.

3. This brings us to the third point at which marginal analysis breaks with classical theory and also, it must be repeated, with observed facts.

In establishing a necessary relationship between the level of the wage and the level of employment, the marginalists made their system so rigid as almost to exclude the intervention of free will. If the trade unions wrest further wage increases from employers, or if the government—whether at the unions' insistence or not—decides to raise the minimum wage, what will *inevitably* happen if the increased wage exceeds the "marginal product of labor" for many firms? The result, according to the theory, will be unemployment for the workers who have been pushed outside the margin, since no employer can afford to go on employing them at a loss. The only way to avoid this terrible result would be to increase the marginal productivity of labor, by introducing new machinery, by better management, and so on.

In this connection Friedman writes in *Price Theory:*

> The marginal productivity analysis is a mean of analyzing the ways in which the wage rate in, say, a particular occupation can be changed by

human action. It can be raised by any action that will raise the marginal productivity of the number of employees hired; this can be accomplished by reducing the number hired, by raising the efficiency of the workers, by increasing the efficiency of the management, by increasing the amount of capital with which they work, etc.

But, in *equating* an increase in the marginal productivity of labor obtained by reducing the number of employees with an increase in that productivity obtained by any other means (improved labor efficiency or management, increase in the volume of capital, etc.), Friedman disregards the ceteris paribus proviso. If other things are indeed equal, the only way employers can raise the wage, according to the marginalist theory, is by increasing the marginal productivity of labor through a reduction in the number of employees. All other means presuppose the intervention of new factors—technological progress of all kinds, additions to existing capital equipment—none of which are given at the outset. It goes without saying, I need hardly add, that in real life these factors often play a decisive role, and the entrepreneur could hardly care less whether the variables on which he operates are exogenous or endogenous. What is at issue here is a question of methodology.

But in fact the "labor market," even if other things remain equal, cannot be contained within the confines of the theoreticians' model, as experience has shown time and again. That is why in the last 45 years or so a number of economists, foremost among them John Hicks (Nobel Prize for economics in 1972), have rejected the idea that there could be a functional relationship between wage level and employment level. However, their demonstration remains very sketchy because they have not gone the limit with their "discovery," preferring ultimately to remain faithful to marginalism.

It is not possible, in my opinion, to provide a rational explanation of the phenomenon unless, utterly repudiating the increasingly dubious legacy bequeathed by Walras, one reconstructs a model on the basis of Ricardian thinking. Then one would be capable of justifying *theoretically* the great flexibility shown by the system *in practice*. If, other things being equal, a rise in wages does not necessarily have a negative effect on employment, it is because, contrary to what the marginalists maintain, even the least productive worker brings his employer a profit. It follows that the wage increase, provided it is not too steep, will result not in a loss but in a decrease in the relative share of income which the capitalist claims. The system's flexibility is based on the changes in the rate of capital return that it admits over time.

This brings us back to our point of departure: the old story of the lack of equality between employee and employer.

### Marginal analysis and equivalence of exchange between employee and employer

Marginal analysis seemed finally to provide an answer to the question posed by Marx and Engels: Since the employee receives in the form of a wage the equivalent of the marginal product of his labor, the relationship of equality is reestablished with the last employee hired.[19] However, even supposing that one accepts the theory's premise (the unacceptable assumption of diminishing returns in all circumstances), serious objections suggest themselves.

Marginalism sidesteps the question of profit. It does not answer Marx and Engels, or rather it does but with a pseudo-answer: It reestablishes the relationship of equality in the exchange between employer and employee "at the margin," but at the margin it makes profit disappear.

However, the evasion (of the subject) does not end there. The marginalists have ultimately taken economic thought back more than a century, as I shall try to show in the rest of this chapter. On the basis of their analysis, modern economics is convinced that it has once and for all laid to rest the old labor theory of value, which it considers useless for the purpose of explaining the origin of profit. In fact it has, without ever realizing this (as far as I know), reverted to the first and false version of that theory, the version which Adam Smith professed and which Ricardo refuted. But Ricardo's refutation, which would have opened the way to a theory of profit—it is the purpose of this book to offer—gave such a shock to received ideas and implicit reasonings that it has never really been heard—whether by the marginalists or, before them, Marx. This failure to understand has been a severe constraint on economic thinking ever since. Part of the fault lies with Ricardo himself, who, after making his breakthrough, was unable to match his writing to his thought.

The misunderstanding still persists, since economists continue to speak, as Ricardo did, of the *price of labor,* a highly ambiguous expression indeed.

## A Quick Look at Accounts

Neither for the employer nor for the employee does the wage, strictly speaking, represent the "value of labor" or its price. In the employer's accounts, wages are one of a number of operating costs. To determine the cost price of each item that he produces he will break down his expenditure among the different accounts for the different items. Let us consider a hypothetical set of such accounts. To produce *x* pairs of stockings with an estimated inventory value of 100 francs, he will have had to buy forty francs' worth of cotton, pay thirty francs for ten man-hours of labor, write off three francs as depreciation of the loom, and so on. *It could be said that the firm had bought with the wage a portion of the finished product,* just as with another sum it has bought the raw material incorporated in that product and with yet another sum the fraction of the machine's value, reflecting depreciation, in the cost price of the *x* pairs of stockings. No business is interested in buying labor or labor power as such. The businessman will judge his worker's labor by its result—in other words, by the product it yields and nothing else.[20]

Let us now look at the accounts of the man whom, by deference to convention, I have been content to call the "seller" or "supplier" of labor, but who in fact has provided the firm not with his labor as such but with the product of his labor. He will set against the wage he has received the different uses he has made of the relevant sum of money: purchase of food and clothing, rent, his transport, expenditure on "cultural items" (books, visits to the movie theater), vacations, and so on. If he knows something about economic thought and if he has been told, in the party cell of which he is a member, what the wage is in Marxist theory, he will call this set of expenditures the "costs of sustaining his labor power." If by chance, instead of having read Marx, he has read Ricardo, he may consider this expenditure a fair representation of the "natural price" of his labor. But let us assume—and this is important to the rest of our enquiry—that without detracting from what he considers his "normal" life-style, our man sees that his wage leaves him with a little something over. In that case, to conform to the Ricardian teaching he prefers, he will say that his wage is higher than the "natural price" of his labor insofar as, after his daily wants have been satisfied, he is still left with a certain portion of income which he can either save (for example, by buying shares on the stock market) or spend for his enjoyment. Our man can tell himself all this, but even so he will have a suspicion that whether his wage is seen according to the Marxian conception—as the sum that will just cover the cost of sustaining his labor power—or according to the Ricardian conception—as the sum that will probably more than cover the expenses he regards as "normally" necessary to meet his wants—this is simply a matter of interpretation. What he will learn from his accounts will be simpler and more to the point, namely that the sum of money he has received as a wage has been used for this or that category of expenditure, including the portion saved, since saving is also a use of resources which has to correspond to an expenditure—for example, purchase of shares.[21]

As to whether the value of this set of expenditures is less than, equal to, or more than the "price of labor," or less than, equal to, or more than the cost of sustaining "labor power," these questions are wrongly formulated. And here is the reason: Although labor is the basis of value, it does not have—since it is not itself a product of labor—any market value. Labor as such is not a category for the purpose of economics, which is concerned solely with the relationships between the products of labor.

Let me make myself quite clear: This is no manipulation of words to suit the purposes of my argument. It is not a question of substituting the expression "price of the product of labor" (or price of the service provided by labor) for the expression "price of labor" in order to dispose conveniently of the idea of "exploitation" of the worker. That workers have many times and in many countries, including the most developed, been exploited—in other words, deprived of the benefits of the economic progress made by the community as a whole and, by definition, by themselves—is certain. Far from denying this fact, political economy serves to reveal what it consists in—namely, too high a rate of profit—and what its effects are.

For the time being, however, we are discussing the concepts used in economic reasoning. What seems to me very important is to show that there is no congenital fault in that reasoning, as there would be if it put, say, the cement market on the same footing as the labor market for bricklayers, as the vocabulary used seems to imply. Not only is labor not a commodity like any other, but, for the purposes of economic analysis, it is not a commodity at all. A clear understanding of the meaning of the concept of value, a rigorous assessment of the function performed by labor in an exchange economy, and—without any trickery or semantic contrivance—this fundamental point will stand revealed.

## The Expenditure of Labor Is Measurable in Calories, Not in Money

If there is one idea that seems to go without saying, it is that a rise in wages must be matched by an increase in productivity. If only, it is thought, workers would agree to limit their wage demands in accordance with that rule, inflation would cease and "stable growth" would be ensured. I shall try to show that the theory that the wage should, in every case, vary commensurately with productivity, is directly linked to the conception of labor as a "commodity." It is simply the translation into terms of economic policy of the marginalists' equation: wage = marginal product of labor.

Having said this, we must not draw over-hasty conclusions from the exposition that follows. If, for example, it disproves the view that there is a functional relationship between wage growth and productivity growth (and the contrariness of facts here might already be taken as an indication that this view is not sound), it does not necessarily follow that there is no case for a wage–productivity link. There may be lasting circumstances in which it is possible and desirable for pay roughly to keep pace with productivity, but what is important is to be aware that this proportionality is not dictated by some economic law.

The labor theory of value consists in stating that quantity of labor assigned to the production of any commodity determines its exchange value, which means that this commodity will be exchanged for another which, to be produced, requires approximately the same quantity of labor. But this principle, as Ricardo rightly pointed out, can be "considerably modified" by accumulation of capital, as we shall see in Chapters 4 and 5. Let us leave for the moment this important complicating factor to make the point that one can say very rightly that one deer is worth three salmon or one-half gram of gold, or conversely that three salmon are worth one deer, or again that one-half gram of gold is worth one deer or three salmon, in the event that the quantity of labor required to hunt one deer, catch three salmon, or mine one-half gram of gold is approximately the same, say ten hours. *The logical fallacy would be to conclude that ten hours' labor is worth one deer, or three salmon, or one-half gram of gold.*

Ten hours' labor represents an expenditure measurable neither in deer, nor in salmon, nor in gold, nor in francs or dollars, nor in any other medium of exchange. Why? Because labor is not an expenditure in the economic sense of the term, but an expenditure of energy measurable in calories. Measurement of this quantity of energy is a matter for the biologists; economics is incapable of shedding any light at all on this phenomenon. Similarly, mechanics, which studies the laws of equilibrium and motion, is incapable of explaining the force that imparts movement. The fact remains, however, that mechanics would have continued to progress, and its laws would have continued to be verifiable, even if physics had ceased to be concerned with the question of what energy is and how it is measured.

Labor, per se, is not an economic category. That is the fundamental point. Only the products of labor are exchanged on a market, never labor itself. By way of example, let us assume that in the workshop where, all-unobserved, he plies his trade, a worker has invented a process that will enable him to save three-quarters of his labors. Whereas his fellow workers, in other workshops, work eight hours a day, he only needs two hours in which to accomplish the same task. The remainder of the time he rests, smokes cigarettes, and so on. Yet he will be paid the same as the others, for the simple reason that the employer is not concerned with his expenditure of muscular and nervous energy, but with the product of that expenditure. The day our worker's secret process is discovered, a higher output will be asked of *all* the workers, but that problem does not concern us at this stage. We might note, however, that the new hourly wage is most unlikely to be four times as much as the old!

## Ricardo Excludes Value as Such from Political Economy

As to that expenditure of muscular and nervous effort—which is what, let it be said, all human activity consists of, not only paid work but sport, dancing, combat, and walking—its equivalent, I repeat, is not an expenditure of money or any other commodity with an exchange value, but an expenditure of energy. I shall be told that to provide for this expenditure of energy the worker (and the sportsman, dancer, soldier, and Sunday afternoon stroller, too) needs to feed and clothe himself and rent somewhere to live and sleep, and so on. But that is another problem altogether because there is no presumptive relationship of *equivalence* between the expenditure of energy and expenditure on food, clothing, housing, and so on (I shall be just as warmly clothed in a simple pullover as in an expensive suit cut by one of the top tailors), save in one possible case: Whenever an employer is in a position to squeeze the last drop of blood and energy out of his workers, then *everything seems to suggest that the "labor market" is governed by this alleged relationship of equivalence,* theoretically untenable though it is seen to be. In these unfortunate circumstances, wages are reduced to the bare minimum and the pittance paid to the worker allows him to buy no more than the calories necessary to keep him and his family alive. But this conception of the "natural price" of labor equivalent to the biological minimum for subsistence was never that of Ricardo nor, incidentally, that of Marx (see above, "Ricardian Wage Theory," p. 40 ff).

To say that ten hours of labor are worth three salmon or a half gram of gold (or $x, representing 0.5 g of gold) is to say that the value of the product of labor is a measure of the value of the labor itself; but that is impossible. There is no device whereby a common denominator can ever be found for labor and for the product of labor, because the two are heterogeneous. To say that labor or labor power has an exchange value is to commit as gross an error as to use a unit of weight to express distance. Saying that labor is the source of value is simply stating that, on a market, the products of labor will be exchanged for one another *in proportion* to the quantity of labor that has had to go into making them, due account being taken of the average status of technology, production organization, management, and so on. It does not in any way mean that exchange value is that quantity of labor. Ricardo made himself clear at least three times, to my knowledge, on this point that was obvious to him but not to either Adam Smith or Malthus. Both admitted, the former quite explicitly and the latter at least implicitly, that "ten hours of labor *are worth* three salmon." Their error would be of interest only to an historian of economic doctrine, were it not for the fact that it is still a central tenet of economics.[22]

What is important is to realize that by showing that the exchange value of commodities is "in proportion to the quantity of labour . . . *but is essentially different from the labour itself,*" Ricardo removed all scholastic overtones from the labor theory of value. He was right to see the expenditure of labor as the fundamental origin of the value of economic goods because it gave his sytem a far sounder basis than want—ophelimity.[23] But we can safely go a step further in stating that it was sufficient, once and for all, to relate the effect to its cause, after which no further mention need be made of it.[24] The only thing one can know is the value of commodities or services in relation to one another. It varies in proportion to the quantity of labor: Three salmon are worth one-half gram of gold because, roughly speaking, the same amount of labor is needed to catch three fish as to mine and refine one-half gram of the precious metal.

To sum up, value is not a quality inherent in the products or services that are exchanged. It is *the rate* at which a product of labor can be exchanged for another product of labor. Making value an attribute of commodities would amount to reducing economy to a "literary" and sterile disquisition on value, as though value existed per se independently of the act of exchange and the resulting relation between two commodities (three salmon = one-half gram of gold).

## How Adam Smith's Pseudo-equation Was Taken Over by the Marginalists

The corollary to Adam Smith's false theorem, which states that ten hours of labor are worth three salmon or half a gram of gold, is that if the productivity of the fisherman (or the miner) falls, say by half, the remuneration he receives for his labor will then be reduced by half. If, on the contrary, his productivity is doubled (six salmon caught or one gram of gold mined in ten hours), the effect—by application of the same corollary—will be a doubling of the remuneration of the fisherman's (or miner's) labor. Ricardo takes a categoric stand against this pseudo-reasoning in a rather long passage which I nevertheless quote in full because of its exceptional significance for economic theory.

This text, probably because of the inadequacies of vocabulary already addressed, seems not to have been properly understood, and is at the heart of the controversy that has persisted over the years between Ricardian thought—poor in its expression but faultless in its logic—and the thinking on the one hand of Adam Smith, Malthus, and their latter-day successors (both the neoliberals like Milton Friedman and the Keynesians and neo-Keynesians) and on the other of Marx, sometimes seemingly clearer but in fact irrational.

Ricardo writes:

Adam Smith, who so accurately defined the original source of exchangeable value, and who was bound in consistency to maintain that all things became more or less valuable in proportion as more or less labour was bestowed on their production, has himself erected another standard measure of value, and speaks of things being more or less valuable in proportion as they will exchange for more or less of this standard measure. Sometimes he speaks of corn, at other times of labour, as a standard measure; not the quantity of labour bestowed on the production of any object, but the quantity which it can command in the market: as if these were two equivalent expressions, and as if, because a man's labour had become doubly efficient, and he could therefore produce twice the quantity of a commodity, he would necessarily[25] receive twice the former quantity in exchange for it.

If this indeed were true, if the reward of the labourer were always[26] in proportion to what he produced, the quantity of labour bestowed on a commodity, and the quantity of labour which that commodity would purchase, would be equal, and either might accurately measure the variations of other things; but they are not equal; the first is under many circumstances[27] an invariable standard, indicating correctly the variations of other things; the latter is subject to as many variations as the commodities compared with it. (*Principles,* chap. 1, sec. 1)

To show that his conception of the wage is valid in all cases, Ricardo maintains on the next page that if, on the contrary, productivity should happen to fall steeply, say by half, in the production of goods and services consumed by the wage earners, there is no reason for wages to fall in the same proportion; in his view the most probable result will be for wages hardly to fall at all.

In the same country double the quantity of labour may be required to produce a given quantity of food and necessaries at one time that may be necessary at another and a distant time; yet the labourer's reward may possibly be very little diminished. If the labourer's wages at the former period were a certain quantity of food and necessaries, he probably could not have subsisted if that quantity had been reduced. Food and necessaries in this case will have risen 100 percent if estimated by the *quantity* of labour necessary to their production, while they will scarcely have increased in value if measured by the quantity of labour for which they will *exchange*.

The ambiguity of this passage is similarly dispelled if it is borne in mind that the value of commodities varies depending on whether a greater or lesser quantity of labor has gone into their production, but that this quantity of labor is not itself the object of the exchange, even though one may have that impression ("by paying X a wage of so much I buy ten hours of his labor").

In these long quoted passages, Ricardo is seen to explain that Adam Smith, under the same expression "quantity of labour," lumps together two unconnected things. Adam Smith argued that, with the value produced by ten hours of labor, the worker could buy ten hours of labor from another worker; in other words, the value produced by a worker and the value of his labor were one and the same thing. This is exactly *what the marginalist school asserts in a seemingly more sophisticated form.*[28]

This relationship of equality is imaginary because the two sides of the equation relate to different objects. On the one side we have the ten hours of labor that the worker has spent making this or that product and on the other we have the wage paid to a worker corresponding to the latter's needs if he is employed at full time. Those needs do not change immediately as labor becomes more "or less" productive.

We are now in a position to reestablish the meaning of the, at first sight equivocal, Ricardian expression "natural price of labour." What I have earlier referred to as a possible weakness in his reasoning now helps us to clear away any ambiguity as to what he understood by wages. I said that Ricardo nowhere referred to the demand price for labor, as though labor as such was not bought, and that, on the contrary, he dwelt on the supply price. The reason is that, in his eyes, the remuneration for labor is largely unrelated to the output of that labor,[29] whereas it would be directly related to it if labor, as such, had a market value. In the long term, wages are governed by the worker's needs as estimated at any given time in any given country. The practical consequence of this argument is that there is no theoretical justification for output-related wages and the trade unions are therefore right to demand their abolition. The Taylor system is related to the psychological phase of political economy.

This analysis also holds the key to other difficulties of interpretation to which classical political economy has given rise. For instance, Ricardo states that the "natural price," or "value," or again "production cost" of labor (three expressions he uses synonymously) increases and decreases with that of wheat and other products that workers consume. If ever a proposition caused ink to flow it was that one. But in fact it can be seen from what I have just said that this is a tautological proposition in which Ricardo's fault was to have become entangled in his vocabulary. The value of labor increases or decreases with the value of wheat and other products consumed by the worker because the so-called value of labor is—and is nothing other than—the value of wheat and the other products consumed by the worker.

In view of the importance of what is at stake—nothing more nor less than the status awarded to human labor by the best theory of capitalism that has yet been formulated—I shall again risk trying the reader's patience by quoting the two passages where, to my knowledge, Ricardo seems to be confusedly aware of the gap between his theory and its very inadequate formulation, and corrects himself. If labor were a "commodity," then its "production cost" (or "natural price") would have to mean the quantity of labor necessary to "produce" it, which would be absurd. That this is not the right interpretation is made clear by Ricardo in the letter (a famous letter, incidentally) which he sent to Malthus in August 1823 a few weeks before he died. Malthus had written to him that "in the progress of society" more labor must be required to produce labor (a reference to the increasing difficulty of producing food). Ricardo took him up on his language in these terms: "You must mean 'to produce the remuneration paid for it.' "[30]

In the other passage (*Principles*, chap. 7 "On Foreign Trade"), Ricardo ponders the effects of what we would call progress of productivity. "The rate of profit is never increased by a better distribution of labour, by the invention of machinery, by the establishment of roads and canals, or by any means of abridging labour either in the manufacture or in the conveyance of goods."

"These are causes," he says, "which operate on price, and never fail to be highly beneficial to consumers: since they enable them, *with the same labour*, or *with the value of the produce of the same labour* [my italics], to obtain in exchange a greater quantity of the commodity to which the improvement is applied."

Today, the expressions "price of labor" and "labor market" are still in constant use by politicians, journalists, and, less pardonably, economists. Ricardo too—save in the rare instances I have referred to— used the same erroneous terms, but his theory was sounder than his language. Basing ourselves on that theory, we may perhaps be able to set human labor free from all the circumstances that combine, in our liberal societies (in the European sense), to make of it—de facto if not de jure—a commodity.

It is because modern economics has no clear conception of labor, capital, and value that at the close of the twentieth century we are still in thrall to the fantasies of Adam Smith and the mythical aspects of his thinking—and perhaps to an even greater degree than the reader suspects.

### The Contrast Between the Homogeneous Realm of Ricardian Theory and the Absurdity of the Labor Standard

Once labor is given a "market value," there is no limit to conceptual anarchy. If labor had a "value" and could itself be exchanged, surely it was the ideal standard measure for value. That is what Smith believed (see the passage from Ricardo quoted on pp. 61–62) and, after him, Malthus. We know how the idea of the labor standard flourished again in the twentieth century; it was the official doctrine of Naziism and it is found again, in another form, in Keynes. Since the exchange value of commodities depends on the greater or lesser quantity of labor bestowed on their production, Smith and Malthus deduced that labor was the invariable standard for measuring the value of commodities! The part of the letter from Malthus to Ricardo that I quoted on page 64 shows the confusion to which this view of things could lead. Malthus, who mixed up many things, is unable to produce one clear idea from the jumble he has created. He believes that (a) labor has a value, (b) that value is invariable, and (c) the value of labor, like any other value, depends on the labor necessary to produce it (*labor is produced by labor*). But he also believes that as society progresses and the population grows, food will cost more to produce. Should not this rise in cost affect what he claims to be the invariable value of labor?

Contrasting with this hotchpotch is the homogeneous realm in which Ricardian theory is developed. Only "products of labour"[31] obey the laws of exchange and only they have "value" in the sense in which political economy uses the word. The value standard can only, therefore, be a product of labor (gold, for example, or any other commodity) by virtue of the elementary principle that "Length can only be measured by length, capacity by capacity and value by value" (*Notes on Malthus*).

We can see here, incidentally, the kind of "liberation" the "gold demonetization" program represents. Its proponents would have us believe that man suffers an intolerable loss by taking the precious metal as the center of his price system. "We will not crucify the United States on a cross of gold," exclaimed a candidate for the White House in 1894, a famous saying that is still remembered in the United States and echoed today in the American leaders' avowed intention to demonetize gold.[32]

As for Hitler, he wanted to set the German people free, once for all, from subservience to gold and make the labor of German workers the supreme standard of value. It is not for the purposes of my argument that I compare these fulminations and these programs that answer one another down the course of history. Unfortunately they have a common source and the reason why they reappear so easily and find as many ready listeners each time is that they are now embedded deep in the West's economic and social ideology. Let a more or less unscrupulous politician get his hands on them and they will surface again. This doctrine, in spite of the many detours it has made, stems from the sophism of Smith, whose dubious legacy has bypassed Ricardo and come down to us. This sophism makes "labor" the measure of value, whence the sacrosanctness of the idea that wages should increase in proportion with productivity. My conclusion is this. To make labor, expressly or implicitly, the measure of value is, in fact, to reduce it to the level of a commodity. The real way to remove labor as such from the clutches of the market—or the discretionary power of the state—is to have as a standard of value a product of labor the value of which relates to other products of labor.

## The Epistemological Break

By comparison with the confused thinking and the dubious program of action to which neoliberal doctrine or "marginalism" has given rise, do we have to expect more rigor from Marxism? To see things clearly, we shall have to forget the widely admitted interpretation on both sides of the Atlantic. According to this interpretation, Marx, having inherited the labor theory of value from the great British classical economists, Smith, Malthus, and Ricardo, carried it through to completion, after which "serious" economists finally jettisoned the old theory. What a cavalier treatment of the real descent of ideas! As we have seen, what separates Smith and Malthus from Ricardo is more than just niceties of thought. It is a basic opposition about the status of labor in political economy, a conflict that was a constant source of correspondence between Malthus and Ricardo until the latter died. For the former, labor so definitely has value that it is promoted to the rank of standard of value. For Ricardo at his best, exchange is confined to the products of labor. Thus, Ricardo's interpretation of the labor theory of value makes—to use the language of the structuralists—an "epistemological break" with the old theory of Adam Smith as taken over by Malthus,[33] from whom it passed on to the "serious" economists of the end of the nineteenth century, the founders of present-day economics.

## The Immense "Theoretical Revolution" of Marxism Is Ultimately No More Than a Misinterpretation

Is Marx the descendant of Ricardo or of Smith–Malthus? At first glance, there seems no room for doubt. Does not the whole of Marxism hinge on the realization that labor as such has no value?

In his celebrated preface to volume 2 of *Capital,* Friedrich Engels describes the difficulty which had "caused the Ricardian school to founder" about the year 1830 (see also Chapter 2, page 13 above):

Labour is the measure of value. Now living labour, in exchange with capital, has a lesser value than the objectified labour for which it is exchanged. Wages, the value of a definite quantity of living labour, are always smaller than the value of the product that is produced by this quantity of living labour, or in which this is expressed. The question is in fact insoluble, in this form. Marx posed it correctly, and thereby answered it. *It is not the labour that has a value. Labour, as value-creating activity, can just as little have a particular value as heaviness can have a particular weight, heat a particular temperature, or electricity a particular intensity of current.* It is not labour which is bought and sold as a commodity, but labour-power. (my italics)

Let us leave the last sentence to one side for the moment in order to concentrate on the other part of the text and, in particular, on the part in italics. Friedrich Engels seems to credit Marx with having understood that "as value-creating activity" labor can have no "particular value." Ricardo had said the same thing (but not in the same cumbersome philosophical language) and it is not his fault if his successors (his "school") failed to understand him. After all, this question of who said it first would be unimportant if Marx's thinking on this subject had been as clear as Engels' précis seems to suggest. Let us hear Marx himself.

In *Capital,* volume 1, chapter 1, he writes: "Human labour-power in its fluid state, or human labour, creates value, but is not itself value." The case therefore seems to be closed: Marx is categorical. But there is something disturbing about this "in its fluid state" that has slipped into the sentence which puts us on our guard, however much at home— and one never manages to be completely at home with it—we may be with the metaphorical style of the author. He confirms our misgivings when he says, in the next sentence: "It [labor] becomes value only in its coagulated state, in objective form."

So, when I buy a bicycle, I would really be paying for the fifteen hours of labor it took to make, the bicycle being "the form" taken by labor in becoming value. In the fluid state, labor has no more value than heaviness in the abstract has a particular weight, but as soon as labor is trapped within a material object it acquires value. We know this way of talking (and thinking?). It is the way the schoolmen talked when they used words like the substance or essence of things.

These are in fact the words used by Marx in his analysis. Readers will remember the distinction—in his eyes, vital—that he makes between useful or concrete labor (for instance, that of the tailor making up a suit) and "abstract labour" defined as the expenditure of human energy, the common denominator of all useful labor. In his view, it is the system of "capitalist production," the effect of which is to reduce all the qualitatively different types of useful labor to abstract labor— that is, reckoned only in quantitative terms. And the way this miracle comes about is through exchange. Exchange transforms the products of useful labor into commodities that are worth more or less in accordance with the greater or smaller quantity of human labor "crystallised" or "congealed" or "embodied" within them (all these expressions are found in Marx).[34] Marx then concludes: "Now we know the substance of value. It is labour. We know the measure of its magnitude. It is labour-time" (*Capital,* chap. 1). The word *substance* was not written just by chance. In the same chapter, a little further on, he also refers to *the essence* of value. How different from the strict formulations of Ricardo for whom value is "*essentially* different from the labour itself" (see above p. 60).

This is how, in the very opening pages of *Capital,* Marx takes the first step toward endowing a concept, exchange value, with an existence of its own in the form of capital. Marx can tell us as much as he likes that the value of commodities has only "a social reality" (whoever said otherwise? For Ricardo this value was nothing other than the *ratio* of exchange). Carried away by his conception of labor as the "substance" of value, Marx inevitably ends by giving value a kind of immanence. From writing in metaphors he eventually goes on to thinking in metaphors. "The value of a commodity is expressed in its price before it enters into circulation, and it is therefore a pre-condition of circulation, not its result" (*Capital,* vol. 1, chap. 5). The truth is that value has no separate existence from the price expressing it. In volume 3 of *Capital,* Marx's parting with this simple proposition is even more irreversible. There he strives to show how surplus value, generated solely by variable capital, is divided up among the various capitalists. This is possible only if certain commodities (those that embody a large proportion of surplus value) are sold for less than their value, whereas others (embodying little or no surplus value) are sold above it. As Marx says (so that the premises set down in volume 1 will be compatible with the formation of an average rate of profit), "The prices of commodities have to be distinct from the value of commodities." Marx, understandably, offers no experimental proof of this strange conception in which what was left of classical political economy is finally submerged (value ceasing to be an exchange ratio).

Applied to Marx's thinking, the adjective "scholastic" will seem sacrilegious. And yet that is the term applicable to *Capital,* perhaps even more than the reader might suspect. Is not scholasticism that method of reasoning that the philosophers of the Middle Ages believed derived from Aristotle? It was in order to explain "the great investigator who was the first to analyse the value-form" that Marx constructed his own labor theory of value. Unfortunately for Aristotle, he hardly fared any better at the hands of Marx than he had with the doctors of the twelfth century. Thinking to say what the Greek philosopher had left unsaid, Marx slips into the same rut as his predecessors. He quotes the following passage from Aristotle: "There can be no exchange without equality, and no equality without commensurability." "Here, however, he falters," adds Marx, "and abandons the further analysis of the form of value." We shall never know whether Aristotle faltered or gave up or, if so, why he did. It was unfortunate for future economic thought that Marx—who introduces his concept of the "substance" of value at this point—did not give up also. If two commodities are exchanged, the reason in Marx's eyes is that the same quantity of human labor is *crystallized* in them. And so that no one should fail to grasp this essential identity, he uses another metaphor borrowed from chemistry: "Butyric acid is a different substance from propyl formate. Yet both are made up of the same chemical substances, carbon (C), hydrogen (H), and oxygen (O). Moreover, these substances are combined together in the same porportions in each case, namely $C_4H_8O_2$" (*Capital,* vol. 1, chap. 5).

How is it that a Greek thinker of the fourth century BC is wiser than a German philosopher of the nineteenth century? The history of civilization has yet to be written.

Now we come to Marx's real discovery, for which Friedrich Engels and, after him, the Marxists of today praise him so highly. To believe one of them, Althusser, Marx truly "inaugurated science" by causing an "epistemological break" with earlier political economy, which had been no more than a mere "ideological" dissertation. How did he sweep away obscurantism and bring light in its place? By uncovering the true meaning of the relationship of equality established by Ricardo. Wage is equal not to the price of labor but to the price of labor power. In Ricardo's text, Althusser goes on, there was a "blank." Marx's genius consisted in revealing the existence of that blank. By filling the void, Marx converted the imprecise Ricardian proposition into a scientific one. Replace the word "labour" by the words "labour-power" and the meaning is made whole. Althusser writes as though Marx had made visible the unseen and audible the silences of classical political economy. These "silences," these "absences" now take form, thanks to "the immense theoretical revolution" brought about by Marx's power of analysis, as so many "symptoms" of a meandering train of thought which, knowingly or not, hide that part of the truth that it is to the advantage of the bourgeoisie not to reveal. Thus it was that Marx's "symptomal reading" of Ricardo opened the way (*dixit* Althusser) to science.

Marx's "immense theoretical revolution" consisted in falling into the trap laid by Smith's prelogical thinking that Ricardo had been at such pains to uncover in the passage I quoted on pages 61–62. According to Engels (see above, p. 67), the school of Ricardo had come to grief because of its inability to explain why, in a system based on the equivalence of exchange, "wages, the value of a definite quantity of living labour, are always smaller than the value of the product that is produced by this quantity of living labour. . . . The question is in fact insoluble, in this form."

I have no idea of the form in which the Ricardian school put the problem (and it matters little), but quite certainly *Ricardo, for his part, refused in the most categorical fashion to put it in these indeed insoluble terms*. Engels fails to realize that he is describing to us the analysis made by Adam Smith as Ricardo presents it, only to reject it outright in the opening pages of the *Principles*. One has only to refer again to the passage I quote on page 61–62. In it, Ricardo states that there is no possible relation of equality between "the quantity of labour bestowed on a commodity"—what Engels calls in this context the quantity of "living labour" that has generated the value of the product—and "the quantity of labour which that commodity would purchase"—corresponding to the quantity of foods and other goods and services consumed by a wage earner, that the exchange value of that commodity would allow to acquire. Althusser prophesies in *Lire le Capital* (vol. 1, p. 33) that "one day Engels's extraordinary preface to Vol. III [of *Capital*] will be studied in the classroom." It may be that his political friends, if one day they come to undivided power, will make this pseudoscientific work compulsory reading for schoolchildren [written in 1973]. Worse things have been done to them over the years and mankind has survived worse mistakes.

So the suspicion first aroused by the variations on the theme of the "substance" of value is wholly confirmed by Friedrich Engels' indeed highly informative preface. Marx's critique really applies not to Ricardo's political economy, but to that of the "Ricardian school." Unfortunately, Ricardo's disciples, having failed to assimilate the Ricardian theory, got into Adam Smith's shoes which, far from being seven-league boots, could only enable them to mark time. Adam Smith's proposition blocked the whole system and made it unintelligible because, if a man working ten hours receives a wage equal in value to the value produced by ten hours' labor, profit disappears. More perceptive here than economists like Léon Walras or Milton Friedman and his like, who think the problem can be solved "at the margin," Karl Marx recognizes the unresolvable contradiction implied if it is put "in this form." But it is not the form of the problem that he changes, only one of the sides of the false equation proposed by Smith. Marx thinks he can overcome the contradiction by replacing "labour" by "labour-power." In so doing, he continues to reason—he, the inventor of the method known as historical materialism—in the same mental universe as the eighteenth-century ex-clergyman who, although writing a work of genius (*The Wealth of Nations*), believed that the object of exchange was labor. Marx puts this crude mistake right but only to assert that the capitalist purchases the power that generates labor as though it were labor per se in which the capitalist was interested. Marx takes the mistake to its ultimate conclusion.

The syllogistic reasoning the conclusion of which seems to him to reveal the truth is set out in Engels' preface.

As what may labor, ultimately, be analyzed? As an expenditure of human energy. This expenditure of energy, "as value-creating activity," cannot "have a particular value." So what is bought and sold on the labor market is not labor.

But, though labor itself has no value, sustaining labor power costs a certain price in food, clothing, housing, and other commodities necessary for the laborer to live. Thus, labor power *may* have a value.

It does indeed have that value "once this [labor power] becomes a commodity."

The conclusion is then self-evident: "*Thus* [my italics[35]] the sale and purchase of labour-power on the basis of its value in no way contradicts the economic law of value."[36]

In the same passage, Friedrich Engels tells us (see p. 67) that "the question is in fact insoluble, in this form" and that "Marx posed it correctly, and thereby answered it." This is an admission that Marx put the *same* question in *another form*.

In actual fact, it is the question that needed changing. Having failed to do this, Marx gives a reply that is predetermined by the approach of the "Ricardian school," which—in spite of its name—simply took over the Smithian theory. According to this approach to the problem, there is a market on which capitalists buy "something other" than the products of labor. Smith had defined that "something" as labor itself, without further explanation. Marx fills in its outline and reveals that what is really meant is labor power. Sometimes, nothing is more dangerous than a new explanation in reply to a question not so far resolved. Believing at last to have the solution, we forget to question whether the problem, *in whatever form it is put,* does in fact have one.

The only explanation for the theory formulated by Marx is that he took literally the disastrous *figure of speech* describing labor as that which is produced by labor. If, after the first step in their reasoning ("labour, as value-creating activity, has no particular value"), Marx and Engels had continued along this same path instead of wanting, a priori, to identify a "commodity" in order to be able to use it in place of this labor which was impossible to classify as a "commodity" per se, they would no doubt have come up with the real questions.

The "critique of political economy" set out by Marx in *Capital* is therefore not conclusive because, in reality, it is the critique of the "vulgar" political economy that held sway in the mid-nineteenth century. Marx had little difficulty in besting his puny adversaries who, even when they claimed allegiance to Ricardo, were the successors of Adam Smith. But, in his substantial book, Smith had, so to speak, exhausted all his possibilities. To continue his work, what was needed, after taking over from his thinking everything that deserved to be kept (and in particular the notion—and how fertile it was—that all value proceeds from labor), was to subject it to radical criticism. This was the self-appointed task of Ricardo whose *Principles,* literally from the first page to the last, are in the form of a critique of Smith's theory and language (as I have already pointed out), either for the purpose of approving it or to expose its inadequacies and contradictions.[37]

The revival of free market economics in our age is often placed under the auspices of Smith—so far so good—but the key to going further has to be found in Ricardo's analysis.

In the first appendix to this chapter (page 80) the reader will find a systematic statement of the opposed theses of Ricardo and Marx on the "labor market."

## Marxism and Marginalism Both Have Common Ground in Pre-Ricardian Thought

The marginalists were duped by the Smithian mirage even more irretrievably than Marx. They have more credibility, however, because they discarded prescientific language—words like the "substance" or "essence" of value—and no longer quote Aristotle (in which they are sometimes wrong). Instead they use mathematics, which gives a stamp of profundity. Even the old alchemists used instruments—stills, for example—which could be found in a *real* chemical laboratory. To resume, the marginalists made their theory an equation; but what did they (re)discover? The relation of equality postulated by the eighteenth-century Scottish professor. The fact that this relation has thereafter been regarded as applying *at the margin* changes nothing at the root of the matter. The pseudo-demonstrations we have inherited from Walras, Jevons, and the economists of the Austrian school increasingly fail to hide the nonscientific and therefore nonmathematical character of their doctrine: Economics has to be remodeled from top to bottom.

The current notion of the origins of modern political economy is that Adam Smith, author of a venerable opus that appeared in 1776, was its long-distant founder. This interpretation is even truer than is generally believed in the sense that the author of *The Wealth of Nations* is the common source of the two official economic doctrines between which the world is split today [written before 1973]. It would be an excellent thing if neoliberal and Marxist economics both stemmed from the scientific part of Smith's work (for example, the parable of the invisible hand denoted the modesty in the face of facts that characterizes the attitude of the man of science). Unfortunately this is not the case. Both Marxist and marginalist doctrines derive from the least defensible part of the work that Smith handed down.

For once, we might be tempted to approve Michel Foucault when he writes (*Les Mots et les Choses,* chap. 7, the section devoted to Ricardo): "At the deepest level of Western knowledge, Marxism did not introduce any fundamental break." But he seems to me a little too precipitate when he dismisses both "bourgeois economics and the revolutionary economics of the 19th century" by saying that "their arguments may have made a few waves and brought some ripples to the surface but these are just storms in a teacup."

The storm was sometimes so violent—pace Monsieur Foucault—that one would like to know what started it off. But the main point is that our author commits the traditional mistake of lumping together, under the heading of "bourgeois economics," theories and doctrines that are highly different. In particular he does not see that the "real break" was between Smith and Ricardo and that, in many respects, the lessons have yet to be drawn. To do so would lead to constructing very different models from those that exist today. In a flash of insight, Maurice Allais (Nobel Prize 1988), a well-known French economist, recently said that the work accomplished by economists over the past twenty years has undoubtedly advanced mathematics but not economics.[38] It is high time that economics should again be able to profit from the use of mathematics.

## Subjectivity in the Parties to an Exchange Regains Certain Rights

The reason why the complete absence of any significance in the terms "price of labor" generally goes unnoticed is the highly subjective nature of the expression. It describes wages as seen by the worker. Whether I am a laborer, an engineer, a foreman, or a hairdresser I shall automatically tend to compare the amount of my earnings to the effort I have put into the product of my labor. Economics, however, has to aim at objectivity because otherwise it would have no hope of establishing itself as a science. Objectivity requires that the act of exchange should be considered from the outside; it must not be identified with the particular view of it that each of the two parties to the exchange inevitably takes. Economics is not bourgeois, nor has it any reason to be proletarian either, even if the lot of the proletariat merits more attention than that of the employer.

A further source of confusion stems from the fact that the market is not completely insensitive to subjectivity in the exchange process. There have always been arduous trades commanding higher wages than others because, if not, no one would be found to do the work. This is the normal result of the supply and demand mechanism. There is no general law to be derived from this fact of life. Moreover, the ranking of wages according to the difficulty or prestige of the job would seem unlikely to change as time goes by. Adam Smith already remarked that miners and butchers were paid more. In our time, Peter Wiles, a British author, writes with humor: "Since the Middle Ages, there has been great technical progress in the production of wheat, a little in the building of houses and none in the saving of souls. Yet the relative incomes of farmers, bricklayers and priests have not, after making all qualifications, greatly changed. . . ." I do not know whether Peter Wiles realized or not that he was paraphrasing Ricardo, who expresses exactly the same idea (taking *his* inspiration from a passage in Smith):

In speaking, however, of labour, as being the foundation of all value, and the relative quantity of labour as almost exclusively determining the relative value of commodities, I must not be supposed to be inattentive to the different qualities of labour, and the difficulty of comparing an hour's or a day's labour, in one employment, with the same duration of labour in another. The estimation in which different qualities of labour are held, comes soon to be adjusted in the market with sufficient precision for all practical purposes, and depends much on the comparative skill of the labourer, and intensity of the labour performed. If a day's labour of a working jeweller be more valuable than a day's labour of a common labourer, it has long ago been adjusted and placed in its proper position in the scale of value. (*Principles*, chap. 1)

The point to remember from these paragraphs is that the hierarchy of wages develops empirically on the market as a function, among other things, of the degree of arduousness of the work and the degree of skill it requires.

To conclude, I would add that although Ricardo, victim of colloquial language, used faulty terminology in calling "natural price" or "value of labour"—both expressions void of meaning—what is actually the "natural price" or value of the products and services judged necessary for the worker to live his life, the concept that he formulated in this way, but worded badly, has since proved to be more fecund than might have been expected. The idea that there is a "minimum wage," corresponding to what is regarded in each country and at each period of time as the lowest acceptable standard of living, has become established. The statisticians have finally quantified the enigmatic "natural price of labour" under the name of "minimum wage." That does not mean that there is no danger in giving a legal basis to such "minimum wage," because in doing so, a government sets a general rule that does not allow for the diversity of individual cases. Man is gradually ceasing to be the plaything of the uses and customs he has himself developed and is making conscious choices and assessing his needs in full knowledge of the facts. To do so he has to apply to the reality of his experience the logical abstractions of economics.

In addition to the appendix (on page 80) setting out the opposed theses of Ricardo and Marx on the subject of the labor market, the reader will find a second appendix on page 85, which discusses the contention that Ricardo predicted the tendency for wages to fall.

## Notes

1. The terminology I use here is the reverse of current usage, which ranges employers on the supply side (they supply jobs) of the labor market and

workers on the demand side. It is here logical to say that employees "supply" their labor—or rather, as we shall see, the products or services that their labor produces—and that the "demand" for those products or services comes from the employers.

2. Raymond Barre, *Economie politique*, vol. 2 (Paris: Presses Universitaires de France, 1955), p. 113. Raymond Barre, who has been prime minister (1976–81), was a professor of economics and the author of a famous textbook.

3. Ricardo, *Principles*, chap. 5.

4. Ibid.

5. These sentences are taken from ibid., chap. 26, bk. 1. The similarity of expression—the use of the word "necessary"—is remarkable.

6. In Ricardo's writings, "natural" can also convey the more usual meaning of "in conformity with experience." In this case, natural "is distinguished from any merely necessary connection" as N. B. de Marchi points out in the British review *Economica* of August 1970 in an article entitled "The Empirical Content and Longevity of Ricardian Economics."

7. In later writings, notably in de Marchi, "The Empirical Content and Longevity."

8. Not forgetting that, in order to be able to build a model, all the elements in question must be quantifiable.

9. In modern economic parlance one would say that the population figure, included at a first stage by Ricardo in ceteris paribus, is reintroduced at a second stage as an endogenous factor, in that its own variations depend on— and in turn influence—the variable (wages) included in the causal relationship singled out. In many other cases Ricardo does not say whether the factors he has assumed constant are endogenous or whether they are exogenous (i.e., linked to a cause independent of the causal relationship in question). This is a further source of ambiguity. On this point, see the article in *Economica* mentioned in note 6.

10. See Appendix 2 following this chapter.

11. Claude Lévi-Strauss, in an interview with the magazine *L'Express* (15–21 March 1971), said this: "Science studies objects, and it is particularly difficult for man to agree to regard himself as an object and disregard his existence as a subject, since he is one and the other at the same time. One can foresee that, as they progress, the human sciences, even more than the other sciences, *will always come up against this irreducible antinomy*" (my italics). Political economy resolves, at least temporarily, this irreducible antinomy by showing, for example, that the wage claims of economic *subjects* cannot be met unless output is sufficient to permit an increase in wages.

12. It would only need the rice crop to fail in a number of Asian countries for them to be in a state of near famine.

13. For Ricardo, overpopulation is always a relative notion. There are some countries, he says, in which "the evil proceeds from bad government, from the insecurity of property, and from a want of education in all ranks of the

people." What should be done in such cases? "To be made happier, they [the countries] require only to be better governed and instructed, as the augmentation of capital, beyond the augmentation of people, would be the inevitable result. No increase in the population can be too great, as the powers of production are still greater" (*Principles,* chap. 5).

14. In modern economic parlance one would say that workers as a whole would be prepared to work even if the wage were a little lower.

15. In the most sophisticated exposition of the theory, the "last" worker need not be chronologically the last to have been hired. But the refinement does not change the reasoning.

16. Milton Friedman, *Price Theory* (Chicago: Aldine, 1976).

17. In *Price Theory,* Friedman writes: "At bottom, the issue in question has little or no relation to this distinction between fixed and variable factors; it is rather concerned with the effect of varying the proportions in which different factors are employed and all factors enter in completely symmetrical fashions. Accordingly it will perhaps avoid misunderstanding to call it 'law of variable proportions.' "

18. See Chapter 12, note 11.

19. It is also reestablished with each employee hired if it is considered— another way of expounding the theory—that his hourly wage is determined by the marginal hourly product of his labor—in other words, by the product of the last hour worked (the hour during which he is supposed to be least productive, according to the artificial hypothesis used).

20. In most cases this product takes the form of a service.

21. Even so-called liquid saving can be likened to a purchase: By depositing money in a commercial or savings bank, I acquire a claim on that bank that is repayable on demand.

22. This is what Ricardo writes (in a half-erased note, says Piero Sraffa) in his *Notes on Malthus:* "I do not say a commodity will be worth its cost in labour, but in proportion to its cost in labour." Further on, p. 79, in a text all of which has been preserved, he says: "But what is meant by a quantity of labour, being the cost of a commodity?—By cost, is always meant the expense of production estimated in some commodity which has value, and it always includes profits of stock. The cost of production of two commodities, as I before observed, may be in proportion to the quantity of labour employed on them, but *it is essentially different from the labour itself*" (my italics). In the *Principles,* and particularly in chapter 1, Ricardo writes that exchangeable value "is in proportion to the quantity of labour" (see below in the text).

23. Vilfredo Pareto gave to the principle of pleasure the name *ophelimity,* taken from a Greek word meaning "what is advantageous or profitable."

24. But, as will be seen in Chapter 4, economic science cannot, any more than the other sciences, do without "non-operational" concepts (to use Althusser's expression).

25. By inserting the word "necessarily" here, Ricardo shows clearly that it

*could* indeed be that the remuneration is doubled in the circumstance in mind but that this is not a *necessary* consequence of the doubling of labor productivity.

26. The use of "always" here further supports note 25.

27. For convenience, I have kept to the simplified version of the labor theory of value. Ricardo does not take the same precaution in this passage even though it comes at the very beginning of his book. Then he adds the extra difficulty of implying—the implication is in the words "under many circumstances"—that the same quantum of labor may be reflected by differing exchange values. He explains the circumstances in which invariability ceases to obtain a few pages later when he shows how two products requiring the same quantity of labor have different exchange values because the proportions of fixed and circulating capital used in their manufacture are not the same or because, if these proportions are the same, the fixed capitals (machinery, etc.) employed in the two cases are of unequal duration. Further on, when he deals with the theory of foreign trade, in the admirable chapter of that title, and the functioning of the gold standard, he presents other exceptions to the invariability of this "standard measure."

28. Milton Friedman writes (*Price Theory*, p. 187), "The price of the factor of production (labor is one of these factors) is equal to the marginal value product of the factor." Similarly, further on (p. 194), he writes: "Each laborer gets the value of his marginal product."

29. This lack of dependence is argued at the macroeconomic level, which is Ricardo's standpoint, as is clear from the passage quoted on page 62, which, highly significantly, refers to the economy of a country as a whole ("*In the same country* . . .").

30. It is in the same letter that Ricardo admits to being discouraged, the question of value being, he says, "the most difficult question in political economy," adding, with regard to the solution he had put forward, "though not without fault it is the best." I shall show, subsequently (Chapter 5), that the objections he put to himself fall away if the expression "product of labour" is substituted for "labour."

31. And not just any kind of labor. The laws of exchange apply only to the products of standardized labor (see Chapter 9).

32. Written before 1974.

33. Malthus also occasionally "corrects" the work of Smith and in those cases he is generally in accord with Ricardo. The most celebrated example is that of the explanation of rent.

34. I quote these expressions because a careful scrutiny of Marx's work shows the extent to which he is ensnared in his own words. For him, exchange value is human labor "crystallised" or "congealed" or "embodied" in a commodity, as if these expressions had more than metaphorical meaning. What a contrast to this picturesque but inappropriate style is the sober language of Ricardo who simply says that a commodity is worth more or less

according as more or less labor has been employed or bestowed on its manufacture. Even from the literary standpoint, the style of the great British economist is superior to that of the German philosopher. There is more poetry in precise language than in an abundance of approximate images.

35. By a kind of "symptomal" inevitability, the use of the word "thus" is often a sign that the author's reasoning is at fault—as if the insertion of the word is intended to bridge a gap in the logic.

36. After noting that "it is not labour which is bought and sold as a commodity, but labour-power" (see quotation on p. 67), Engels writes: "Once this [labor power] becomes a commodity, its value is governed by the labour embodied in it as a social product; it is equal to the labour necessary for its production and reproduction. Hence the sale and purchase of labour-power on the basis of its value in no way contradicts the economic law of value." The reader would have noted the phrase "Once this becomes a commodity. . . ." This is to beg the question.

37. The first sentence in the book is a quotation from Adam Smith and the last also refers to a passage from Smith quoted by Malthus. Both relate to the question of value.

38. I refer to the paper given by Maurice Allais at the Congress of French-language economists held in Lausanne in May 1971 to celebrate the centenary of Walras. (M. Allais's address is reproduced in *Revue d'économie politique*, published by Sirey, June 1971.) See also on this subject, Chapter 10, "Outlines of a Critique of General Equilibrium."

*Appendix 1*

## RICARDO VERSUS MARX ON THE "LABOR MARKET"—
## A SYSTEMATIC COMPARISON

### In the "Labor Theory of Value," What Relationship Is There Between Labor and Value?

For Marx, labor is the "substance" or "essence" of value.

This contrasts with Ricardo's critique encapsulated in this one sentence (quoted in note 22, page 77): "The cost of production [*synonym for value in the Ricardian vocabulary*] . . . may be in proportion to the quantity of labour . . . but it is essentially different from the labour itself."

In using the word *essentially*, Ricardo would seem to have wanted to refute in advance the errors to which his theory was to give rise. Why is labor "essentially different"? Ricardo does not say, but the reason is clear: It is because only the products of labor have a production cost and therefore a value.

Labor proper creates value but is not value. When analyzed it proves, as I pointed out in Chapter 3, to be an expenditure not of money (which is a matter of economics), but of energy (which is a matter of biology).

### What Does a Worker Supply on the Labor Market?

Value being essentially different from labor, it follows in the Ricardian theory that labor as such is not something that can be exchanged. Unfortunately, Ricardo did not match his vocabulary to his "prodigous discovery" (to use the pompous language of Marxist intellectuals). In a rare lapse from his usual consistency of terminology, he failed to guard against the inaccuracy of everyday language and continued to speak of the "price of labour" as though the expression meant something. This slip had incalculable consequences. In his defense let it be said that, 150 years after his death, all economists without exception are still using the term without questioning its validity in any way; and at least Ricardo can be credited with having put matters straight on a number of rare occasions (of considerable value because they enable us to establish what he really meant). On this point I quoted, on page 64, a passage in *Principles* where, after apparently attributing exchange value to labor, he corrects himself and explains that this exchange value is that of the "produce of . . . labour."[1]

In short, for him what the worker supplies is the "product of his labor." But there is more to it than that. Economically, the contract of hiring out one's services is an exchange between (a) the wage paid to the employee, which is part of the capitalist's capital, and (b) the profit that the latter expects from his investment. Up to the moment that the employee has reconstituted the value of his wage he has contributed nothing to his side of the bargain. Marx's mistake was to see that reconstitution as an exchange (whence his "labour-power" concept).

There is no point in trying to reconcile Marx with Ricardo's labor theory of value by equating "labour-power" with product of labor. Marx precludes any such interpretation by telling us that the capitalist, when he buys labor power, is securing the "use value" of that power, that is, the labor of the worker.

### Whose reasoning does experience bear out, that of Ricardo or that of Marx?

The strongest evidence in support of Ricardo's thesis is supplied by double-entry bookkeeping, the study of which, let it be said in passing, is a far better introduction to economics than Hegel's philosophy. What the employer enters in his trading account is the product of the labor of his employees—he could not care less about their labor as such or their labor power. In Chapter 3 I showed why a worker often has the *impression* that he is selling his toil; this provided me with a further opportunity to point to the deeply psychological nature of Marxist theory—probably the reason for its success.

### What determines the "price of labor"?

Put this way, the question has no meaning for either Ricardo or Marx. We saw (see page 64) how Ricardo picks Malthus up when he wrote that, with the passing of time, labor "must require more labour to produce it." Ricardo offers him the right expression: "You must mean 'to produce the remuneration paid for it.' " Labor can only produce products of labor—not labor itself.

Marx, too, "corrects" Malthus (who in this field as in many others is the direct heir of Smith): "It is labour-power, not labour, that is

produced by labour.'' This change of term is no doubt an improvement
on the Smith–Malthus conception. But there is no point in trying to
improve a conception that is absurd; it has to be rejected completely,
otherwise one is still its captive.

Having made this substitution, Marx answers the question in Malthus' very terms: "This peculiar commodity, labour-power, must now
be examined more closely. Like all other commodities it has a value.
How is that value determined? The value of labour-power is determined, as in the case of every other commodity, by the labour-time
necessary for the production and consequently also the reproduction,
of the specific article."[2] For Malthus, labor produces labor; for Marx,
labor produces labor power. Nowhere does the vacillation of Marx's
thinking appear more clearly than in the reasoning leading him to this
conclusion. First he says that labor "in the fluid state" has no value
but that in the "congealed state" it forms the substance of that same
value.

*Proposition One:* "In so far as it [labor power] has value, it represents no more than a definite quantity of the average social labour
objectified in it."[3] Here Marx is right in the Smithian realm of the
imaginary. Even if it did have a value, labor power could in no case
"represent" a quantity of social labor since—as Marx and Engels both
say—the quantity of social labor has no value. It would have been
more reasonable for Marx to write that, insofar as it has value, labor
power represents the value of the products necessary for the worker to
subsist.

*Proposition Two:* "Labour-power exists only as a capacity of the
living individual. Its production consequently presupposes his existence. Given the existence of the individual, the production of labour-
power consists in his reproduction of himself or his maintenance."
This is a clumsy truism which would have made a classical British
economist blush in writing it, but which is no doubt intended to tell us
that the worker, in selling his labor power, is parting with its "use
value."

*Proposition Three:* "For his maintenance he requires a certain
quantity of the means of subsistence. Therefore the labour-time necessary for the production of labour-power is the same as that necessary
for the production of those means of subsistence."

Here, Marx blandly changes key. First he tells us that, insofar as it
has value, labor power represents a certain quantity of social labor.

But he does not stay with this Smithian proposition. To take his theory to completion he turns to Ricardo, and thus the value of labor power is finally related to the value of the "means of subsistence," that is, the products of social labor. But to arrive at this result, Marx had to link up three propositions of which the first is imaginary, the second tautological, and the third a combination of the two: (1) Value of labor power equals quantity of social labor objectified in it; (2) labor time necessary for the production of labor power equals labor time necessary for the production of the means of subsistence; (3) value of labor power equals value of means of subsistence.

It will be noted that Proposition Two, the essential link between the first and the third, is simply a rewording of Ricardo's unduly famous definition of the "price of labour,"[4] which is not, as we have seen, the brightest jewel of English political economy. The concept of the value of labor power, insofar as it relates to the value of the goods necessary for the possessor of that labor power to live, is a needless and dangerous detour because it perpetuates and aggravates, in another form, the verbal ambiguity of the Ricardian reasoning. When Marx breaks away from Smith's ideas it is to draw close to Ricardo's thinking, without ever penetrating it.

Ricardian analysis made it possible to found an economic science. It quite simply consisted in revealing that the "labour cost of production" of the means of subsistence (or, to use the Marxist vocabulary, "quantity of social labour objectified in it") refers purely and simply to the value of those *products* consumed by the worker. It is quite simply a delusion to believe that this cost refers to the value of labor (Smithian–Malthusian version of the labor theory of value) or the value of "labour-power" (Marx's revised version of that theory), the reason being, let it be said again, that the concept of exchange value can apply only to the products of labor and never to labor or labor power.

## The Marxist Nonsolution to the Nonproblem Put by Smith

Thus Marx's argument is as open as that of Smith to Ricardo's criticism quoted on pages 61–62. Marx believed he had solved the riddle by showing that the wage corresponds to the "necessary labour-time" during which the worker reproduces the value of his labor power. This would confirm Smith's equation: "The quantity of labour bestowed on the production of any object"—here the means of subsistence—is equal to "the quantity [of labor] which it can command on the market." The value produced during the "necessary labour-time" (six hours, say, out of a ten-hour day) is equal to the value of the labor power on the market. This is how Marx found a solution to the *insoluble problem* set by Smith and, after him, by the Ricardian school. Since the problem is a nonproblem, the solution is likewise a nonsolution. Marx's central proposition says in effect that the value of the products necessary to a worker's life is equal to the wage, which is just another way of saying what has been said already. The fact that the worker should produce more than that value during the course of his day is also self-evident because his employer gets a "profit." As the reader will see, my Chapter 4 with its appendix on the origin of profit is one way of reconciling the labor theory of value, correctly interpreted, with the equivalence intrinsic to exchange. On the basis of what we know already, we can say that when Ricardo spoke of the "value of labour" (although, in his theory, labor can have no value), he used the wrong words—whereas Marx, explicitly attributing value to labor power (as Smith had to labor), was guilty of confused thinking. Marx's error was all the more serious in that he had Ricardo's analysis to guide him.

## Notes

1. Sometimes Ricardo avoids the ambiguity by using the word *work* (i.e., produce of labor).

2. Marx, *Capital,* vol. 1, chap. 6, p. 274.

3. Ibid. The three propositions quoted here in turn from *Capital* follow one another directly in the text.

4. "The natural price of labour is that price which is necessary to enable the labourers, one with another, to subsist and to perpetuate their race"; see above p. 40.

*Appendix 2*

# RICARDO AND THE SO-CALLED "IRON LAW OF WAGES"

The incorrect interpretation of the word *natural* as used by Ricardo has been the source of serious misunderstandings that have done much to misshape contemporary economic thought. Ricardo is accused of having predicted that wages would diminish.[1] Because this "prediction" has not proved true and was—or so Ricardo's critics have claimed—"consubstantial with his doctrine," that doctrine is held to be flawed from beginning to end. And yet a reading of the famous chapter "On Wages" gives the lie to this interpretation. No less than seven times in that chapter Ricardo submits that, as society progresses, wages will tend to be above their natural level and that, therefore, "the condition of the labourer is flourishing and happy." Ricardo's argument is even far more categorical than has been noticed by those economists who have taken his words purely at face value. This is what he says: "Thus, then, with every improvement of society, with every increase in its capital, the market wages of labour will rise; but the permanence of their rise will depend on the question whether the natural price of labour has also risen; and this again will depend on the rise in the natural price of those necessaries on which the wages of labour are expended." This last sentence refers, as we know, to a very remote and indefinite time in the future when an increasing share of the gross product is devoted to the production of "necessaries" because of the diminishing returns in agriculture. Further on, however, Ricardo shows that in a gold standard system it is impossible for the rise in wages (generally, he says, because the increase of wealth and capital will have occasioned a new demand for labor) to be lastingly reflected in higher prices for basic consumer products. On the contrary, those prices will necessarily fall, otherwise it would be impossible to import the extra gold needed for an extra volume of production to circulate.[2] If this last statement is compared with the previous passage, one has to conclude that in an improving society where there is no inflation the rise in real wages is a permanent phenomenon.

Now I come to the essential point which, to my knowledge, has been overlooked. Against this impressive array of arguments designed to show that the "price of labor" must, in the circumstances that may normally be expected, rise, what arguments are produced to prove the opposite? The key passage here is the one where Ricardo says: "In the *natural*[3] advance of society, the wages of labour will have a tendency to fall, as far as they are regulated by supply and demand" (*Principles,* chap. 5).

In this passage, Ricardo returns to his argument that the rate of accumulation must diminish with the rising cost of production. The supply of labor must therefore be expected to exceed the demand for it.

"If, for instance," he writes, "wages were regulated by a yearly increase of capital at the rate of 2%, they would fall when it accumulated only at the rate of 1.5%."

But this hypothesis is valid only in the case of "the natural advance of society." I repeat, the word "natural" in the writings of Ricardo, as he himself says in explicit terms, applies to any process that is not frustrated, deviated, or amplified by the advent of new factors. A "natural" process is, as we have already seen, an academic supposition framed for the convenience of the reasoning because so many causes are simultaneously at work in economic life that the first task of economics must be to try to isolate them from one another. The natural advance of society implies, for example, that technological progress has ceased, whereas Ricardo considers that, in the case of industry, technical improvements are continuous (in agriculture, however, he admits that progress takes place sporadically). It also implies that the population will continue to increase as long as capital increases, whereas population growth will be less rapid than capital growth in a country where the normal effect of the desire for well-being is to inhibit the birthrate. Now, on this last point, Ricardo allowed no doubt to subsist. Whenever capital grows faster than population, the result will be that wages will rise. This is probably the weightiest argument against the so-called "law of iron."

There is another and, to my mind, just as conclusive argument. In the Ricardian analysis there can be no increase in wages without a fall in the rate of profit, and vice versa. But in the following chapter on profit, he writes that "the natural tendency of profits then is to fall."[4] The reason is that, with the passing of time, the production of food will absorb practically the whole of the gross product, leaving nothing for profit. But in this admittedly academic hypothesis, the real winners in the long run will be the landowners (who collect rent). The wage earners, even though they may receive more money, will in reality receive a smaller proportion of the total product. In that case, profits and wages, if regarded as a percentage of total product, may indeed both diminish.

The truth is that the use of the word "natural" relates each time to hypothetical situations so narrowly defined that it is dangerous to draw conclusions from them to be applied to the ordinary circumstances for which Ricardian economic theory was conceived. For those ordinary circumstances, Ricardo considered a continuous rise in wages in terms of product (Chapter 3) and maintenance of their real value—that is, in his words, as a percentage of gross product—to be both possible and desirable (this point is clarified in Chapters 5 and 6 where it is shown that if the rate of profit in general remains fairly stable, a similar stability will apply to wage rates).

## Notes

1. See, for example, Mark Blaug, "The Empirical Contents of Ricardian Economics," *Journal of Political Economy* 64 (1956).

2. If paper money wholly replaced gold in internal circulation (which was true of England during the Napoleonic wars, when Ricardo was writing), the process would be exactly the same, says Ricardo.

3. My italics (see also Chapter 7). The word *natural* implies the singling out of a particular factor as applying to a particular concept. If it is a matter, for example, of defining the "natural wage," it is assumed that the labor force remains unchanged. If it is a matter of defining the "natural advance" of a society, the archetypal variable "population" is reintroduced. This is a striking illustration of the transition from static to dynamic economics.

4. See Chapter 7, page 200.

*4*

# Profit in the General Scheme of Exchange

We now come to the very heart of the exchange mechanism. Let us first of all take a look at the "labor contract," because of the very special importance that that contract has in industrial relations and also because of the errors of interpretation to which the theory of capitalism has almost invariably given rise concerning it.

In the previous chapter we saw that in his contract with the employer the worker does not deliver his labor nor his labor power, but the product of his labor. As to the employer, he takes possession of that product (in most cases this takes the form of a service) by paying the worker a "wage," the amount of which, as we have seen, is largely determined by the "stage of historical development" of society. If the analysis is taken no further than that, it seems that the classical theory of capitalism cannot make the labor contract amenable to the general law of exchange because it is evident that *in every case* the wage with which the worker will obtain the products of labor regarded as necessary to his existence represents a value lower than the product of his own labor which he delivers to his employer under the contract. And the reason is that if the first of these values were not lower than the second, the proportion of the employer's capital invested in labor would bring no profit. Let us say that the employer has spent 1000 francs of his capital on hiring the services of Pierre—in other words, he pays Pierre a wage of F.1000, a sum which represents the equivalent of the different products that Pierre will consume in order to subsist and support his family (food, rent, cigarettes, transport, etc.). If Pierre's labor yields a "product" which is likewise worth F.1000, there seems no reason why the employer should hire him.

Other than in exceptional and very short-lived circumstances, Pierre's services will be asked for only if he is able to deliver a product worth, say, F.1100 or F.1200, in other words, a product from which the employer can expect a profit—equal in the first case to 10 percent of the capital invested and in the second to 20 percent.

To what does this profit correspond? In other words, how is it generated? How is its existence reconcilable with the Aristotelian—and Ricardian—principle of equivalence of exchange? Is *any* capital or only the capital invested in *labor* able to bring a profit? And in the event that it is any capital, is it still possible to maintain that labor is the sole source of value?

These are the questions I shall try to answer in this chapter. My answers will be built around the following idea: Profit—or, properly speaking, the value of the product representing profit—is what is actually exchanged.

One first point—to which I have already referred in Chapter 3—has to be made. The explanation of profit, if it is not to be invalidated, has to be all-embracing: In other words, it has to be valid whatever the assumption, be it increasing, constant or diminishing costs. It is pointless—worse, dishonest—to maintain that profit makes its appearance only by subtraction; that the wage being equal to the marginal product of labor, there is profit only when the marginal product is less than the average product (increasing cost hypothesis). A theory that is valid only on that condition is radically insufficient to explain this most important phenomenon of an exchange economy (or capitalism). What reveals the inconsequence of the marginalist school is its cavalier treatment of the phenomenon: One minute it suggests that the value of the "marginal product" includes profit,[1] the next that it does not. Either way, it has to jump through hoops before finally introducing profit into a system of which it is not a built-in part. The work of Milton Friedman, regarded as the purest representative of neoliberalism (new new economics), provides the most extreme illustration of these ingenious but ineffectual contrivances. The fact that marginalist theory, as taught in all the universities of the West, offers no explanation of profit and is reduced to seeing it as a "residual" attributable to a factor as vague and subjective as "entrepreneurial capacity" is eloquent testimony of its inability to account for economic phenomena and therefore to serve as a tool of thought that can be a guide to action.

This is not to say—let us be quite clear on this point—that entrepreneurial capacity plays a minor role. It is a decisive factor in economic progress. Reversing the viewpoint, it develops most effectively in a system based on the exchange mechanism.

## The Two Elements of Growth

In this chapter I shall tackle the phenomenon of exchange from the standpoint of the reproduction of value. This process is the thread that runs throughout the entire economic system, since the reproduction of value is nothing other than exchange phased over time. It is at the root of all management, whether of a business or of the economy as a whole, and it is the basis of the rules of accounting. Since value does not exist on its own, it has to be transmitted through the production of new commodities or new services, which, in deference to convention, we shall call "products" or "wealth" according to context.

In modern societies, progress in technology and labor organization is constant. As a result, more commodities are produced with the same quantity of labor. This means that to transmit the same value, more wealth is needed. Accepted economic doctrine as taught in all the universities of the Western world deprives itself, from the very outset, of an essential tool of analysis when it feigns ignorance of the distinction between value and wealth. This obliteration of fundamental notions is not fortuitous; it is the result of a theory that bases value on want. It is just as if the glorification of the commodity had finally got the better of the most elementary logical distinctions. In a system where the customer is being wooed on all sides there is no place for an idea which for classical political economy would be self-evident—namely that the sum total of consumer goods diminishes in value as it becomes possible to produce those goods *more easily*. This is simply the logical follow-on from what we have established previously. The exchange value of a commodity depends on the quantity of labor that went into making it (in the case of a service, the amount of labor expended to perform it). It follows that if, as the result of a technical advance, better organization of labor, more efficient management, and so on, a firm manufactures, say, 2000 pairs of shoes in ten hours instead of 1000 pairs (assuming a capital of equal value and durability), in a *fully competitive market* the 2000 pairs will have the same exchange value as the 1000 which the firm was producing before: They will likewise be exchanged for another batch of commodities produced with ten hours' labor, say for five TV sets or $x$ grams of gold.

If during that same period of time no technological advance has been made by the manufacturers of TV sets or by the producers of gold, it will be said that the value of the shoes relative to gold (and relative to TV sets) has fallen by half. Exchange ratios never tell us and *cannot* tell us the absolute value of things. For this to be otherwise, it would have to be assumed that mankind has at all times had a commodity serving as a standard, the cost of production of which has never varied (and even that condition would not be enough, as we shall see). This is not so and never will be: A perfect standard of value like this might well be disastrous since it alone would retain an immutable value, while the relative value of virtually all other commodities would fall as techniques improved. The result would be that the price of anything, expressed in this invariable unit of measurement, would fall almost continuously, and this would probably be prejudicial (at any rate according to the arguably prejudiced view that currently prevails) to the development of economic activity. This deflation is something that the world, save during brief periods, has eluded if only because the commodity chosen as a standard has also declined in value. And this is because technical progress spreads through all areas of activity, with the result that as society develops, it produces more cheaply nearly all the items it thinks it needs. This is true, too, of the commodity chosen as the monetary standard. Let us take the case of gold, which has long served as a standard. No one doubts that the quantity of labor needed to produce it has decreased as mining processes have improved and ever richer deposits have been discovered: Today more gold is mined each year than arrived in Europe during the entire century that fol-lowed the discovery of America by Christopher Columbus! Is it not infinitely probable that the quantum of human energy expended in getting the 750 tonnes or so of gold to Europe between the years of 1500 and 1600 was very considerably more than the quantum of energy now expended over twelve months in the South African gold mines, which alone can produce 1000 tonnes in certain years?

It is because the value of gold has fallen that gold prices, over the long run, have remained stable. Stability of gold prices (never yet a complete reality, I need hardly add) is possible only if the value of gold diminishes in the same proportion as the value of commodities ex-pressed in terms of gold.

I do not want to give the impression that I am trying to explain monetary phenomena and price movements solely by changes in the value of gold. In fact, and especially in today's world, the value of money[2] is no longer linked to that of gold other than nominally or symbolically (we shall see that this is not necessarily a step forward!); consequently, the continuous fall in the value of money is attributable to causes that have nothing to do with the fall in the value of gold, which—until further notice—is now a standard in name only.[3] What I have tried to show here is quite simply that the famous price stability attributed to the gold standard is a more complex phenomenon than would appear at first sight, since it implies a continuous fall in the value of gold because of the decrease in the labor time necessary to produce it. One of the great discoveries of classical economics—and one that will ensure its revival—is that in the economic system there is no *fixed point,* nor can there ever be.

It can be maintained without any hesitation that economic history, especially since the industrial revolution, has seen a continuous fall in the *value* of commodities (capital and consumer goods) as well as an extraordinary growth in their quantity. This becomes obvious once it is recognized that the value of a commodity decreases as the labor time needed to produce it diminishes.

The proposition will hold good in any number of hypotheses. For example:

*First hypothesis.* Let it be assumed that the total quantum of labor remains constant over time, either because the size of the work force (likewise the number of hours worked) does not change, or because the work force is increased while the number of hours worked per employee is reduced. In this case the total value of output remains stationary, but the output itself increases each year owing to technical progress, better organization of labor, and so on, with the result that the unit value of each item produced decreases commensurately.

*Second hypothesis.* The population grows rapidly and so the quantum of labor increases even though the working day becomes shorter. The total value of output increases proportionately, but unit product values decrease, because while the quantum of labor has grown by, say, 5 percent during the year, the actual volume of output has grown by 15 percent.

*Third hypothesis.* The trade unions decide to press for a drastic reduction of working hours, and the outcome is that the annual quantum of labor decreases. So, too, does the total value of output; but there is a big advance in productivity, and output grows more than ever, with the result that unit values fall more rapidly than the total value of output.

Whatever hypothesis is chosen, the conclusion reached is always the same: As the absolute unit value of each product diminishes, so man becomes wealthier, since, strictly speaking, becoming wealthier does not mean possessing more *value* but being able to obtain a greater number of goods and services of all kinds. The trend of market prices is fundamentally incapable of telling us anything about the divergent movements of wealth and value, since money prices can only show the value of one commodity relative to another (and then only if the monetary system is functioning perfectly, since any operational defect may distort relative values). Now, clearly, relative value may rise even though absolute value falls. If the absolute value of money falls faster than the absolute value of other commodities, money prices will rise. The same thing will happen if, meanwhile, the monetary unit is changed (e.g., through devaluation). If the reverse is assumed, the same conclusion is reached: The growth of a society's wealth, including the wealth of the gold producers, is not basically affected by upward or downward fluctuations in the absolute value of the money standard over a given period. Let us assume that over ten years the gold producers make no progress; every year they mine exactly the same quantity with the same number of workers (and the same capital equipment). Gold will not decrease—nor, for that matter, increase—in absolute value. Let us also assume that, at the same time, the manufacturers of shoes and TV sets, the wheat producers, and so on, have succeeded, still with the same work force, in doubling their respective outputs. The total value of their outputs expressed in terms of gold will not have changed at all. But they will be twice as wealthy because they will have twice as many shoes to provide protection for the feet, twice as many clothes to keep them warm, twice as much wheat to provide food, twice as many TV sets to provide entertainment, and so on. And the gold producers, too, will be twice as wealthy, since they will have exchanged a quantity of gold unchanged in value for twice the quantity of *useful* products. Of all the goods that exist, money is the only one that does not constitute *wealth* in the economic sense of the term. It does not matter, at least theoretically, whether money is produced in greater or lesser quantity: Since its utility, or use value, is to measure exchange value, the latter is all that counts. Mankind may find it more *convenient* to have more gold if it uses that metal as a medium of exchange, but this, far from increasing its wealth[4] in the slightest degree, tends to reduce it since mankind has to allocate more resources to the production of a good with no direct utility.[5] If monetary gold does not constitute wealth in the strict sense, the same is true of the other forms that money may take, like specie or bank-notes.The proposition is elementary, yet the so-called "modern" theory leaves it vague, since because the concepts of use value and exchange value are no longer clearly differentiated, money in whatever form is classed as an economic good.

Having established these preliminaries, we must be careful not to conclude in our turn that the increase of wealth eliminates the problem of value. Until that problem has been posed—and resolved—the economic system will remain largely unintelligible. The growth phenomenon has to be broken down into two distinct elements that have to be carefully separated. First there is accumulation itself, a process which is at the root of all economic development, whether or not there is accompanying technical progress, whether or not there is private appropriation of the factors of production. Accumulation appears, as we shall find out in a moment, once the value produced is retained. In order to understand better how value is transmitted—and the purpose of accounting is to describe that particular process—we shall, in this chapter and also in its Appendix 1,[6] imagine a world in which machines have the same productivity as human labor and in which, *as a result, the introduction of machines would not have the effect of reducing the unit values of the items produced.* Second there is the complication of the accumulation process by the fact that machinery considerably increases the productivity of human labor, which I shall deal with in the next chapter. This return to reality will enable us to ascertain that classical political economy is much better equipped conceptually than Marxist and neoliberal doctrines to explain and guide the progress of modern societies.

## Capital Is Exchanged for Profit Over Time

It is by concentrating on the time of utilization of capital that one discovers why Marx fell victim to a false impression and tried to solve a problem which does not arise in the terms he defined.

Let us imagine, for argument's sake, that Pierre lives solely on wild fruit. In ten hours of intensive search (there is nothing to prevent us from already applying the term "labor" to this expenditure of human energy) he gathers on average, say, 2.4 kg of apples, pears, and so on, while 1.2 kg would suffice for his food. If Pierre behaves like the gentle savage he is, he will "work" only one day in two or, what amounts to the same thing, five hours a day. As long as he limits his fruit gathering to his "wants," spending the rest of the time sunning himself or making love (if, by so doing, he begets children, the problem will become somewhat more complicated, but let us leave this interesting possibility aside just now), his life will lie outside the compass of "economics," which will exist only as a potentiality. But this will no longer be the case if one fine day—or one evil day, the point could be argued forever—Pierre ceases to be content with what he has and decides to accumulate *wealth*. That day he will work ten full hours and, if he is averagely lucky, gather 2.4 kg of fruit. Of this he will eat half and the other half he will "save." So the rate of saving will be 50 percent.

$$\frac{1200 \text{ g (quantity saved or net product)}[7]}{2400 \text{ g (gross product)}}$$

The initial rate of saving might have been different, of course—either higher or lower. Let us assume that Pierre, instead of consuming 1200 g of fruit, has consumed 1600 g. I should say, incidentally, that in that quantity of fruit I include all the products that Pierre consumes in order to satisfy his wants, whatever they may be. It is possible, for example, that he continues to eat only 1200 g of fruit and that the other 400 g represents the value of the other products he uses in order to clothe, adorn, and amuse himself, move from one place to another, and so on. In that case the rate of saving would have been 33⅓ percent, since he would only have been able to save

$$2400 \text{ g} - 1600 \text{ g} = 800 \text{ g per day}; \therefore \frac{800 \text{ g}}{2400 \text{ g}} = 33.333\%$$

In these new circumstances, Pierre would have had to work two full ten-hour days before being able to build up a saving of 800 g + 800 g = 1600 g equal to his daily ration.[8]

If Pierre wants to hold on to what he has saved, he will have to forgo rest on the next day and work again. For how long? That will depend on the quantity of produce he consumes. In the first hypothesis, he will need to work only five hours, the time approximately required in order to gather another 1200 g. He will then again hold 2400 g, of which he will consume the first half and "carry forward" the second to his next day's holding, and so on and so forth. In the second hypothesis, he will have to work six hours and forty minutes, the average time he would need to gather 1600 g. He will then have 3200 g of fruit, of which he will consume half and carry forward the other half. Pierre will then have had to work only *one* stretch of five hours (or 6 hours 40 minutes) without consuming the product of his labor *always* to have a saving of 1200 g (or 1600 g for 6 hours 40 minutes work). This simple proposition already encapsulates both the economic efficiency of capitalism and the social difficulties to which its development almost invariably gives rise.

To stay ahead, Pierre will therefore have to work every day in order to meet his daily wants, which implies that if one day he fails to gather his 1200 g (or 1600 g) of fruit, he must be prepared to reduce his daily ration proportionately so as not to eat into his savings.

Marx explains this self-evident finding (in *Capital*, vol. 1, chap. 11) as follows: "If this worker were in possession of his own means of production, and were satisfied to live as a worker, he could make do with the amount of labour-time necessary to reproduce his means of subsistence, say 8 hours a day." From a simple proposition on which capitalism is founded he derives an argument against it. Marx's sentence is worth quoting because his special way of reasoning becomes glaringly apparent. If the possessor of labor power were provided with the means of production, he would no longer be one of the proletariat but—surely—a capitalist (quod erat demonstrandum). "No," says Marx, because the means of production in question would simply renew itself and there would be no further accumulation. But the renewal is already the first stage of the process that leads logically to accumulation, as we shall now see.

Let us come back to Pierre and establish that (a) if he did not work enough to satisfy his wants each day, he would quickly return to the status of *homo praeeconomicus,* which, incidentally, he has not yet completely shed, and (b) by working no more than five hours a day (or 6 hours 40 minutes), he has reduced his rate of saving from 50 percent (or 33⅓%) to 0 percent.

To become a real *homo economicus* Pierre will have to do two more things. First, he will have to find a rational use for his extra quantity of produce instead of contenting himself with the hitherto unknown feeling of security it gave him. Second, he will have to bring his rate of saving back up to 50 percent (for a daily ration of 1200 g) or to 33⅓ percent (for a ration of 1600 g), or to $x$ percent (in any other hypothesis). Only by finding this rational use, understandably, will he be able to maintain a certain rate of saving, i.e., continue to accumulate wealth.

As long as there are no machines to do the work that man has so far been doing, Pierre has only one course open to him if he is to achieve his first aim, and that is to propose to Jacques, who also lives by gathering fruit, the following deal: "I'll hand over to you now, as a wage, the 1200 g of fruit you need, and in exchange you bring me this evening the fruit you have gathered." What quantity of fruit does Jacques, now Pierre's "employee," have to bring back in order to keep his side of the bargain proposed by Pierre? If he brings back only 1200 g, Pierre will have "got back" in the evening what he handed over in the morning. But what point would there have been to making the arrangement with Jacques? It is clear that the outcome would have been exactly the same for Pierre if he had not handed over his provision. Whereas Jacques has appropriated the wage by consuming it, Pierre has received nothing in exchange by receiving back a saving he has not consumed. *For the deal to be worthwhile, Jacques, after giving back to Pierre what he had received from him (1200 g of fruit), has to provide him, over the same length of time as that taken to accumulate the amount saved, with an income the value of which will tend toward equivalence with the value of that saving.* Only then will the amount that Pierre has saved (and paid over to Jacques as a wage) become for him a *capital* from which the income forms a *profit.* In this particular case Pierre will agree to commit his capital for one day if he can reasonably expect Jacques to bring him 2400 g, of which 1200 g is repayment and the other 1200 g the equivalent value (or profit) of the produce received by Jacques and consumed by him. The reader will almost certainly protest indignantly at the idea of such a contract, and rightly. I would just ask him to hear me out until the end of this chapter.

It is probable that Pierre will agree to commit his capital for a longer period—two days—if the wage considered necessary (and here we come back to a familiar idea that was discussed at length in Chapter 3) rises from 1200 g to 1600 g. This is because it will have taken Pierre, our budding capitalist, two days to save 1600 g, and also because Jacques will have had to work two ten-hour days in order to produce a profit the value of which, as related to the amount of time worked, will be equal to the initial capital advanced. In this new hypothesis, the capital saved will have had to circulate twice before bringing a profit equal to it.[9]

For convenience sake I shall from now on use expressions of an already semimonetary nature, and therefore more familiar, to designate the different values involved here, for example, by postulating that it takes ten hours' labor to mine and refine a gram of gold, so that any product requiring ten hours' labor *is worth* 1 g of gold.

Pierre has solved only his first problem, and perhaps not even that, since his own consumption has to be taken into account. In hypothesis 1 (wage of 1200 g) Pierre retains the savings he has advanced but that is all: Of the 2.4 kg of fruit that Jacques brings him back at the end of the day, he eats half and keeps the other half as capital available for him to use to recommence the same operation the next day. In hypothesis 2 (wage of 1600 g) he does not do so well. If he wants to conserve the capital he has advanced, he will have to eat only on every other day (or be content with a half-ration a day). In that hypothesis, Pierre could get by only if he had saved twice as much at the outset so that he could have hired two workers, Jacques and Henri. Only if he has a capital of 1600 g × 2 = 3200 g to begin with, can he manage to remain *stationary*, in other words with a rate of saving down to zero (because the capitalist is consuming his profit). Otherwise he will have either to reduce his consumption or—a solution which would not last long—to eat into his capital, that is, dissave (negative rate of saving).

Pierre will increase his holding over time only if his rate of saving remains positive. In other words, to one saving he must add another saving, and so on and so forth. Now he can make this accumulation all on his own, but if he does so he will soon find that an increasing share of his capital is lying idle. On the first day he works ten hours and consumes half the fruit he has gathered, that is, 1200 g (the same process of accumulation would occur if he consumed two-thirds of his output, or 1600 g, except that it would take longer). The next day he works another ten hours and consumes the 1200 g saved from the day before. At the end of the second day he has a saving of 2400 g. On the third day he again works ten hours, continuing to pay himself a wage of 1200 g. At the end of the third day he has savings of 2400 g (new produce) plus 1200 g (half of the produce brought back the previous day and not consumed) = 3600 g. If with this capital of 3600 g Pierre hires three workers, in the circumstances described earlier, he will turn his capital to full account, which means that he will considerably speed up the rate of accumulation. In today's language we would say that "he is putting his capital to work," an execrable saying which is utterly at odds with the spirit of political economy, since it is always man who works with the aid of capital.

At this point in our story we can now see just where Marx began to go wrong in his reasoning (almost at the very beginning of the causal chain), and we can also understand why his theory, although entirely fallacious, had the impact it did. Just as Ptolemy's astronomy seemed to provide the perfect explanation of why night follows day, so Marxist doctrine seems to make the phenomenon of profit intelligible. In our example, Pierre's accumulation of capital (over and above what he has accumulated himself) appears to derive from the fact that Jacques, Henri, and all the other employees have each worked ten hours but have received as a wage only the product of five hours' work. Surely the one-sidedness of the bargain constitutes irrefutable evidence that the capitalist exploits the labor he employs "in his service."

But the conclusion we reached in the previous chapter must make us automatically wary of the terms in which Marx puts the problem. I showed that labor time was the common denominator of two commodities that are exchanged, *but that, since labor time itself is not a commodity, it is not an object of exchange,* even if it may seem so because the worker is paid by the hour, the week, or the month. So what we have to concentrate on is not labor time but the products that are exchanged. And what do we find? Jacques brings Pierre the product of ten hours' labor whereas he has received the product of five hours as a wage. This wage has to be deducted from what he brings in. Let us ask why that deduction can be assumed to be legitimate. Jacques has appropriated the 1200 g of fruit, and during the first five hours of his workday he replaces the value (saved by Pierre) of that fruit; up to that point he has contributed nothing to his side of the bargain with Pierre. Jacques begins to make a contribution, and thereby in turn to play his part in the social process of production only when he embarks on the second half of his workday, the phase devoted to the production of the "net product." It is ultimately that net product (or the entrepreneur's profit) which will determine *retroactively* the wage he has been paid *in exchange,* which in our ultrasimplified example is equal to 1200 g of fruit worth 0.5 g of gold. *What is exchanged over time is capital saved in return for future profit.*

## Replacement of Capital Is Not an Act of Exchange

To make the terms of exchange quite clear, let us look again (cf. pp. 98–99) at the complete breakdown of the transaction from Pierre's standpoint in terms of labor time. His saving (1200 g of fruit) is the product of five hours' labor, but to amass it he has had to work ten hours. Assuming that the rate of saving is not 50 percent but 33⅓ percent (rate of profit of 50%), the labor time needed in order to build up the relevant saving (1600 g) would be twenty hours. If one measures the labor time of his employee Jacques, one sees that in the first hypothesis it is ten hours and in the second twenty hours (see note 9). If Pierre invests his capital, he will want to receive in return a product having needed as much labor time as his investment.

The value of the initial capital has been replaced at the end of the first five hours of the workday, but it is quite clear that the exchange does not consist in replacing a value that has not been spent by the owner of that capital. For there to be exchange, either the two products exchanged must both exist at the time the transaction takes place or, if one of them has been destroyed by use meanwhile, its value must have been replaced. In our example, when Pierre recovers his capital he is not receiving a new product in exchange for what he has handed over: He has resumed ownership of the latter. For there to be exchange of value for like value, at the time the exchange is completed the sum of the values of the two items exchanged must be twice the value of each one.

It is this capital which, at the time it is paid over in the form of a wage, is being exchanged for future profit. That holds good, the Marxists would probably say, only if the wage is regarded as an advance. But Marx, they would add, anticipated the argument by observing that in real life the opposite occurs. Is it not the working man who gives his employer an advance equivalent to the wage, since the employer will pay the working man his wage only when the job has been done? Once again, Marx draws a general conclusion from just a few observations (the journeyman baker who receives his wage only when the bread he has baked has been sold, and so on). If truth be told, Marx himself, throughout *Capital,* considers "variable capital" to be accumulated capital, at least implicitly. And when, in an isolated passage, he comes to maintain that the working man makes an advance of his wage, he is contradicting himself since, if that were so, what would happen to the famous relationship of equivalence he thought he had reestablished in stating that "labour-power" was in fact purchased at its true price? It is a fact that the wage is generally paid when the wage earners have delivered the product of their labor (at the end of the week or month). Against this it can be maintained that, in most cases, the wage is paid in advance in the sense that it is paid *before* the products of labor have been sold; but a more cogent argument would be this: The journeyman baker is able to bake bread only because the means of production needed to give effect to this kind of labor have been accumulated by his employer. It is the accumulation of productive capital and the product it enables the worker to deliver that determines the general level of wages.

To sum up, this is the basic pattern that emerges from our reasoning so far:

*First proposition.* There is no exchange between the wage paid by Pierre and the labor supplied by Jacques.

*Second proposition.* The exchange is effected over time between, on the one hand, Pierre's capital—namely, the labor product which has been accumulated by Pierre and which can therefore be destroyed only through consumption by Pierre—and, on the other hand, the profit deriving from the *new labor* provided by Jacques.

This is so because Jacques has meanwhile consumed (destroyed) the product accumulated by Pierre and paid to Jacques as a wage. He therefore has to replace its value, and only as of that moment does the process of exchange over time begin.

## The Rate of Profit

The ultrasimplification of the hypothesis on which I have reasoned lies chiefly in the fact that the rate of profit is assumed to be 100 percent (see note 7) and that the wage paid is assumed to be the only capital expenditure incurred by "Pierre Inc." The outcome of these twin circumstances is that the wage paid is equal to the profit. Obviously things are very different in a real business: Capital expenditure represents not only wage payments, but also equipment, raw materials, and so on. As for the rate of profit, it will almost certainly be a lot less than 100 percent. In other words, the business will have to wait much longer than one day (or one year if the year is the unit of time), for the deferred exchange to be completed.

In Marx's interpretation of the labor theory of value, the rate of surplus value, which we can equate here with the rate of profit,[10] is equal to the degree of exploitation. Jacques has worked ten hours in all, of which five were "necessary" to produce the value of his wage. The five additional hours' work are "extra time" during which "surplus labor'' is performed, the product of which is, without further ado, pocketed by the capitalist:

$$\frac{5 \text{ hours' surplus labor}}{5 \text{ hours' necessary labor}} = 100\%$$

In the interpretation of labor value I give here, the rate of profit is the same, but it is calculated by reference to the rate of saving of which I spoke earlier. The gross product is 2400 g of fruit and the net product 1200 g, hence a rate of saving of 50 percent. A rate of saving of 50 percent corresponds to a rate of profit of

$$\frac{1200 \text{ g (net product)}}{1200 \text{ g (invested saving or capital)}} = 100\%$$

Note that, in our example here, ''invested saving or capital'' is equal to the ''share consumed'' by the worker in the production process. The same is true of any capital, once it is invested. This becomes particularly apparent when capital is invested as a wage. The corresponding amount of money—or goods of any kind (fruit in our simplified example)—is accumulated capital as long as it remains in the employer's hands; once it passes into the employee's hands, it becomes the share that is consumed (unless the employee sets aside part of his income, in which case he builds a new capital for himself which has nothing to do with the old). The ''consumed share'' will reappear as the replaced capital of the employer only at the end of the process of production and sale of output.

Let us sum up by saying that a *daily* rate of profit of 100 percent means that in one day the invested saving recoups its value and brings in an equal amount of profit. If the *annual* rate of profit is 100 percent, a full cycle of replacement of capital as thus defined will be completed in twelve months.

In our second hypothesis we have assumed that the daily ration is increased to 1600 g of fruit, with the result that the rate of saving falls from 50 to 33⅓ percent. A rate of saving of 33⅓ percent corresponds, of course, to a rate of profit of

$$\frac{800 \text{ g (net product)}}{1600 \text{ g (invested saving)}} = 50\%$$

it being understood that the daily gross product is still 2400 g. Since the period of reference is one day, the new rate means that it now takes two days for the capital (or, more accurately, the invested saving, that is, the saving which has been used to produce or to acquire that capital) to go through its full reproduction cycle. If the reference period were one year, a 50 percent rate of profit would mean that the full cycle of reproduction of the saving's value would be two years; a 10 percent rate would mean a ten-year cycle, a 5 percent rate a twenty-year cycle, and so on.

Thus, the length of the cycle of capital replacement through phased exchange is expressed by the rate of capitalization, which is the reciprocal of the rate of profit.

An annual rate of profit of 100 percent corresponds to a rate of capitalization of 100/100 = 1 year; a rate of 50 percent corresponds to a capitalization ratio of 100/50 = 2 years, a rate of 5 percent corresponds to a capitalization ratio of 100/5 = 20 years, and so on and so forth. The rate of capitalization determines the length of time at the end of which the invested saving is replaced and produces an amount of income equal to itself.

## Why There Is Relatively So Little Wage Labor in Primitive Economies

It is quite possible, the reader will say, that according to the theoretical scheme of exchange Pierre does not "exploit" Jacques when he contracts to pay him a wage of 1200 g of fruit. Even so, the reader will add quite rightly, the end result is the same: If Jacques, instead of working for Pierre, gathered fruit for himself, he would earn twice as much a day on average. This is absolutely true, and that is why there is little likelihood that Pierre, possessing only the very rudimentary capital I have endowed him with, will become the employer of numerous workers, or even one for that matter. The fact is that Jacques (and likewise his companions) will have understood that by working *on his own account* for ten hours a day, he will in all probability earn more than by hiring out his services to Pierre, even if the first hypothesis is discarded for the second (wage of 1600 g), or even for a hypothesis much more favorable to the employee. Jacques will only begin to think seriously of working for Pierre instead of being his own boss if fruit gathering becomes more difficult (or requires the prior accumulation of tools) and if there begins to be a real risk of not being able to gather in *one full workday* of ten hours at least 1200 g (or 1600 g). In the latter case, he may prefer to be assured of his subsistence, the employer being better placed to make out by the law of averages since the days of zero and minus profit will be offset by the bumper days.[11] However, historical experience confirms that even this risk is not enough to make Jacques and all his companions become employees. In the least developed countries, *those where the greater share of capital is "circulating"* (in the form of food, clothing, etc.), only a relatively small proportion of the total population is wage earning, whereas there are multitudes of small craftsmen or traders— in short, all those who themselves make their little capital "circulate" pitifully. Pitifully but, let it be noted, with a very high rate of profit (sometimes as much as 50%, if not more), which just enables them to get by.[12]

Wage labor begins to develop on a big scale when the capital needed to produce consists not only of food and clothing but also, and most importantly, of tools and machines: in other words, equipment of greater or lesser durability which, directly or indirectly, multiplies the productive effects of labor. In such circumstances, Jacques will earn more by becoming an employee, *since he will be unable himself to get together enough capital to make his labor sufficiently productive.*

## The Marxist Explanation of Profit Is Not Consistent with the Labor Theory of Value

Here I embark on the second part of my refutation of the Marxist explanation of profit, a refutation which differs from those already put forward in that it rests on the labor theory of value which Marx drew upon and which he misinterpreted.

Marx held that only variable capital—in his language, the capital invested in wages—is capable of generating surplus value (and hence profit). To arrive at this erroneous conclusion he starts out from a correct principle, namely that only fresh labor (living labor, to keep to his vocabulary) can create fresh value. If from a correct principle he draws a false conclusion, it is because of his scholastic conception of value. He, the materialist philosopher, has committed the error characteristic of idealism, which is to substantify mental constructs (see above, Chapter 3). According to Marx, if the sale of product A is to bring a profit, it is because, during the production process, fresh value has been "embodied" in the value already possessed by the ingredients of A. This fresh value can come only from the "surplus labor" provided by the workers in making A. So it is just as if Marx regarded value as a property of the product; if a product is the result of ten hours' labor, then it *possesses* such and such a value; if it is the result of five hours' labor, it possesses half the value of the previous product, and so on.

One can see how fallacious this reasoning is. Value is not an intrinsic quality of a product, it is not labor "crystallized" in the product, it is not a quantum of labor contained in the product—all of these being expressions used by Marx in his exposition, as we have seen. Value is the rate at which any product of labor[13] is exchanged for another product of labor; value is not a substance but a ratio. So there are absolutely no grounds for presuming that the fresh labor that generates the value materialized in the profit *has been applied directly to the manufacture of product A*. On the contrary, everything would suggest that the introduction of this fresh labor takes place at another stage.

For product A to be exchanged, fresh labor has of course to be performed in order to make product B (or to provide service B, as the case may be). Otherwise, not only is no profit conceivable but no exchange is possible. Pierre has invested a capital of 1200 g of fruit (wage paid to Jacques) so as in the evening to find himself in possession of the product of ten hours' work by Jacques—that is, 2400 g of fruit. He exchanges that 2400 g of fruit for another product which likewise has required ten hours of work, let us say 1 g of gold. Marx maintains that the profit realized by Pierre in selling his fruit for 1 g of gold— profit equal to 0.5 g of gold—was created by Jacques' *surplus labor*. Marx thus mistakenly merges two successive exchange transactions into one.

### Marx Wrongly Merged Two Exchange Transactions into One

To begin with, there is a first exchange between Pierre and Jacques. When Pierre had 1200 g of fruit in hand, he possessed, strictly speaking—and the propriety of terms is just as vital to economics as it is to mathematics or physics—no value. He possessed fruit. The notion of value appears only when Pierre exchanges his provision not for Jacques' labor, still less for Jacques' labor power, but for the product of Jacques' labor. But this is where the mere observation of facts can easily lead us to some fanciful conclusion, like the one Marx reached.

Pierre hands over a provision of 1200 g of fruit to Jacques as a wage; and Jacques brings back 2400 g of fruit. So why not conclude that the provision handed over to Jacques *is worth* 2400 g of fruit? Is this not a correct mode of expression (or reasoning) since, value being an exchange ratio, the value of a product can be expressed only in terms of another product: This motor car is worth 1.5 kg of gold or five TV sets or $10,000, say, and so on. Here the value of a stock of fruit is expressed in terms of other fruit gathered later. However, from what has gone before, we can immediately see why we fortunately do not have to endorse so patent an absurdity as the idea that a capital of 1200 g of fruit *is worth* 2400 g of fruit. We know that deferred exchange has taken place between the 1200 g advanced to Jacques and the profit (1200 g of fruit). Meanwhile Jacques has consumed that provision and replaced its value: This replacement has remained outside the exchange transaction, since in no circumstances can *replacement* be regarded as an exchange (see p. 100). These are two logically separate concepts which only dialectic could manage to transpose! So when Marx, emboldened by his "prodigious discovery," deduces that labor power, like any other commodity, is exchanged in the market at its true value, his conclusion is absurd for two reasons: first, because (cf. the previous chapter) labor power is not a commodity, and second, because replacement by the worker (during "the necessary labour-time") of the value he has received as a wage is not an exchange. The Ricardian theory, on the contrary, is confirmed. In Chapter 3, I showed how, according to that theory, the "price of labour" is simply the value, materialized in the wage, of the goods and services consumed by the worker, for the very good reasons that the wage is not exchanged for labor time (because labor time is not an exchangeable commodity). The analysis of exchange leads us, by a different itinerary, to the same conclusion by showing up the conceptual difference between the replacement of a temporarily destroyed value and exchange.

As to the second exchange transaction, it takes place when Pierre, now in possession of 2400 g of fruit—of which 1200 g represents his initial capital—enters the market to exchange it. It will not be enough for him to announce "here is the product of ten hours' labor, say 1 gram of fine gold." For the exchange to take place, it will be necessary—a condition that seems so self-evident, it tends to be forgotten—for *fresh labor* to have been provided by Pierre's exchange partner, say to mine that gram of gold. Otherwise there is no chance of an exchange of value for like value, and Pierre will receive none or only part of the value of his product.

Let us return to the first exchange transaction. Here it is as though Pierre, with a capital of 1200 g, indefinitely spares himself the effort of five hours' labor per day.[14] It is Jacques who supplies the effort instead. But suppose that a machine does the work and not Jacques. Would this mean that there would be no profit? Quite the reverse.

*Now we come to the heart of the argument I am developing in this book.* (For easier reading I have set one passage apart from the main body of the text [see Appendix 1 to Chapter 4, page 131].)

*I shall show that a machine—which for the purposes of the argument I shall assume to be entirely automated and the productivity of which is equal to that of human labor—takes on the status of capital only if it yields a product the value of which is sufficient (a) to replace the value of the machine when it has to be scrapped and (b) to provide the machine's owner with a profit.*

How can this condition be reconciled with the labor theory of value according to which value is proportional to the quantity of labor? At first sight this theory would suggest that the total value of the machine's output can in no case exceed the machine's value, given the assumption that human labor alone is capable of creating value. This is what Marx maintained so peremptorily when he said that a machine "transfers" to the products it serves to manufacture its own value and nothing more. If, for example, a loom has cost F.150,000, a total value of F.150,000 will have been "embodied" in the value of the fabrics it has woven during the time it has been in use. It would follow that the capital invested in the loom cannot itself have yielded any profit. This is the contention of Marx, who claimed that surplus value, the source of profit, can only derive directly or indirectly from the exploitation of human labor power.

Marx's mistake was that he reasoned that *fresh labor,* which alone is capable of generating the value that constitutes profit, has to derive from the weaving process. This is what causes fresh value to be "added to" or "embodied in" the fabrics. But this conception betrays the scholasticism in Marx's thinking. In no circumstances is value a substance which can be "embodied" in a product or "added" to the value it possesses already. Value *does not exist as such;* it is only an exchange *ratio.* The real question is at what rate the fabrics will be exchanged for other products (or for money to the value of those other products). Formulated in these terms, the problem has a solution that bears no relation to that proposed by Marx but that, I think, provides the key to the puzzle set by the Ricardian labor theory of value.

The first condition for the exchange of the loom-woven fabrics to bring a profit is for *fresh labor* to have gone into the making of the products *for which* the fabrics are exchanged.[15] This obvious condition is necessary but not in itself sufficient. A second condition is that the loom's total output should be such that it can be exchanged for a value equal to the real cost of the investment represented by the loom.

As regards the evaluation of that cost, the sad truth is that Marx has made another blunder. If the loom costs F.150,000, which on the market represents the equivalent of, say, the product of one hundred hours' labor, in no way does it follow that the investment cost is no more than that sum. If the businessman—or the Soviet or Chinese planner (the arithmetic does not suddenly become different in a socialist economy!)—estimates the investment cost at F.150,000, then he would do better to quit business, or planning. But suppose he does estimate it as such. What will happen the day the machine comes to the end of its useful life? Its value will now appear in the form of fabrics. But what will have become of the value of the savings *in exchange for which* the machine was acquired? It will be lost for good. Yet the fact that this value must continue to be taken into account is implicit in the principle of exchange set out earlier (p. 101) and is explained at length in the first part of Appendix 1 to this chapter.

To be "capital," the machine has to be capable of reproducing the *total* value of the investment cost—and we already know that value is nothing other than a "cost"—which it has occasioned. The total cost (or capitalized cost) comprises, in addition to the machine's price, what mathematicians call the "present value" of a perpetuity that would cover infinitely many replacements. So here may be glimpsed the implications of a theory defining *the conditions* that a given tool of production must fulfil, at each stage of economic development, in order to perform the function of capital (it explains, for instance, why use of the technically most sophisticated machines is not advantageous, *in present circumstances,* in China or the Ivory Coast).

Let me add two clarifications.

The first is that instead of using a loom as my example, I have preferred to take the more unusual case of an "automated fruit gatherer" in order to show, using my previous example, that the conditions that have to be fulfilled for capital to bring a profit are exactly the same whether the capital is invested in a wage (see above) or invested in machinery that can function without human aid.

The second is that the analysis set out below and in the relevant appendix is in every way consistent with the methods currently used in all the industrialized countries to calculate the cost of investment (this will be made quite apparent in Chapter 5). This will clinch my case that the old labor theory of value (not Marx's but Ricardo's) tallies perfectly with the most modern techniques of capital valuation. But let us not look too far ahead.

### What Makes an Accumulated Product of Labor Become Capital?

Not every accumulated product of labor automatically becomes capital. What is needed for this to happen? Let us return to Pierre. He is still intent on increasing his well-being, and so it occurs to him to build a machine that will do his fruit gathering for him. He has thought his idea out carefully and, notwithstanding the rudimentary state of his knowledge, he is capable—at least we shall presume so—of building in ten hours an entirely automated fruit-gathering machine (for simplicity's sake, let it be assumed that the value of the energy needed to make the machine run is negligible). Let us assume, too, that the machine will work for no more than ten hours and that it does so only during the day (in other words, there is no question of its operating during the hours of sleep); during those ten hours it will gather 2400 g of fruit.

In designing and building this contraption Pierre has graduated with flying colors to the rank of *homo artifex,* but at the same time he has slipped back from the rank of *homo economicus* which he has just attained. And this is because the machine, as it stands, is not capital. *This is the paradox of the machine that has the same output as a man.*

The very basic reasoning that now follows holds good even for an economy as complex as today's. Take the Concorde: It may be a brilliant feat of engineering, but it is not capital for the same reasons that Pierre's fruit-gathering machine is not. The proof is that it brings no gain to its owner. So this means that in fact its use is a loss-making operation.

This is not immediately apparent from the business balance sheet and we can readily forgive Pierre for not having seen it straightaway, since far more erudite minds than his—Marx to begin with—have made the same mistake.

On the face of it, the advent of the machine has made Pierre neither better off nor worse off. On Monday morning, before starting work, he had to have 1200 g of fruit in hand if he were not to succumb to the pangs of hunger on the day of his memorable technological exploit. At the end of the day he possesses the automated fruit gatherer. The next day he sets the machine running, and in the evening—having gathered 2400 g of fruit—it dies on him. But what would Pierre have to complain about? He is exactly as he would have been if he had not built the machine. The only change, if any, is the nature of his occupation; its tangible outcome is still the same. If, instead of spending ten hours of his time on Monday making the automated fruit gatherer, he had spent five hours on Monday and five hours on Tuesday gathering fruit in his usual way, he would still have ended up with 2400 g of fruit—in other words, his food for those two days—and, assuming that on Monday he consumed a prior stock of 1200 g of fruit, he would still have had 1200 g in hand on Wednesday morning. Whether Pierre spends his time building the machine or continuing to gather fruit himself, the result is apparently the same. There appears to be no economic motive for his choosing one solution over the other. If he preferred the machine, it would be because he had developed a liking for engineering and so found it more enjoyable to build a machine than to look for fruit in the forest.

But Pierre is not content to let matters rest there and realizes that in fact there are two very different situations.

*Situation A. He invests in one day's gathering a capital produced with five hours' labor and with the tangible form of a provision of 1200 g of fruit.* This brings him a net "profit" of 1200 g of fruit. That is the position if on Monday he consumes the provision of 1200 g and spends ten full hours gathering fruit by hand.

*Situation B. He invests a capital of twice the value and taking the material form of a machine (built with ten hours' labor); however, this bigger investment, far from bringing him more profit, leaves him none at all, since he has completely lost the product accumulated on Monday.* Let us consider for a moment what this double investment consists of. To make his machine on Monday, Pierre has had to consume 1200 g of fruit, the provision (capital) which he had laid in earlier by working five hours without consuming the product of his labor. Then Pierre replaces the value of that expenditure of 1200 g by working the first five hours of the Monday on making the machine. After which he continues his efforts for another five hours in order to finish the machine. We can say that Pierre has reinvested in the machine the profit derived from employing his initial capital of 1200 g.

On Monday morning he began his day with a saving of 1200 g of fruit valued at 0.5 g of fine gold; since in ten hours of labor he has not only replaced that value after having consumed it (this replacement is what the classical economists very aptly called *reproductive consumption*) but has also saved the product of five more hours' labor, he may legitimately be considered to have doubled the capital he originally advanced. At the outset Pierre had a saving (or capital, or permanent advance—see p. 165) equivalent to 0.5 g of gold, so it seems justifiable to maintain that the saving is now equivalent to 1 g of gold.

In principle, Pierre will preserve this advance of capital for as long as he does not consume it unproductively. However, the machine he has made, with the performance of which we know it to be capable, will not do well enough for Pierre to be able to do so. During its lifetime (10 hours) it gathers 2400 g of fruit; afterwards, Pierre will certainly recoup in another form—fruit again—the assumed value of his now useless machine, but in the meantime what he advanced will have vanished. This is why the making of the machine has, economically, been a loss-making operation. One may argue that Pierre does not mind. He has no wish to accumulate. All he wants is to feed himself and indulge in his penchant for engineering. *This objection holds good only if Pierre renounces once and for all the advantages of exchange.*

The truth of what has just been said can be cross-checked by answering the question that follows. If Pierre, instead of operating his machine himself, wanted to sell it, would he find a buyer at his *asking price,* that is, 1 g of gold or any other product having cost ten hours' labor? The odds are he would not find a buyer and here is the reason. Suppose that Jean is a possible taker: He possesses 1 g of gold, which has taken him ten hours to mine and refine. But if he wanted to acquire 2.4 kg of fruit, he could do so *immediately* by paying over his gram of gold. Now suppose Jean, instead of mining and refining gold, has gone fruit gathering like everyone else, and therefore has 2.4 kg of fruit. In that case the purchase of the machine for 2.4 kg of fruit would appear to be even more absurd. Why burden himself with the machine for a day by handing over 2.4 kg of fruit, since he will find himself at the end of the day with 2.4 kg of fruit and only that amount, the machine having come to the end of its useful life? It is not just that Jean will have no motive for acquiring such a machine; he will have a definite motive for not buying it at the *asking price,* since to buy it would postpone by ten hours the time of his entry into possession of 2.4 kg of fruit, without his deriving the least advantage from the postpone-ment. The argument would be even more compelling if the machine's life, instead of being one day, were a week, a month, a year, and so on.

What condition must the machine fulfil for Pierre to be able either to sell it at its "full price" (i.e., in exchange for a product which has likewise cost ten hours' labor) or to operate it himself and derive some advantage? That condition has to do with the actual circumstances of the machine's manufacture. Pierre will not really recover the full value of his investment unless he obtains in the output of his machine (a) the value of the now useless machine (in my example it is written off in one go, since the machine's useful life is the same as the unit of time reckoned with—in this case, one day), and (b) an income—his profit—equal, in the context of our example, to his permanent advance or capital. If the machine gathers only 2400 g of fruit in its ten-hour lifetime, the first condition will be met, but not the second.

The two conditions would be fulfilled if, *other things being equal and in particular the rate of profit,* the machine gathered in its ten-hour lifetime not 2400 g, but 4800 g.

## Marx's Faulty Accounting

This conclusion is completely at variance with Marxist theory, which would have maintained in our example that doubling the machine's output halves the unit value of the fruit.

Why? Because, the theory goes, the machine, which is accumulated "dead labor," can transmit no more than its own exchange value (1 g of gold or any other commodity likewise having required 10 hours' labor). If, therefore, a machine made in ten hours of labor gathers 4800 g of fruit, the exchange value of the 4800 g can never exceed that of a product likewise having required ten hours' labor, except where the machine's owner has used workers to make it operate—which is not the case here. Admittedly Marxist theory does not deny that the owner of an entirely automated machine, like the one here, can make a profit. But according to the theory, that profit has to come from the transfer of surplus value from enterprises exploiting a large work force to enterprises that have very few (and possibly no) workers and a large amount of fixed capital.[16]

And yet, can it be held that, *in the circumstances here,* the unit value of the fruit will be halved if the machine gathers 4800 g of fruit, with the result that the quantity can now only be exchanged for 1 g of gold? Absolutely not, *since the machine has to be capable of this output if its yield is to be equal to that of human labor.*

This is what emerges from the reckoning in labor time of the machine's construction, a reckoning that corresponds to what we shall call in the next chapter the *capitalized investment cost.* To build the machine Pierre will have had to begin by working a first day during which he will have "set aside" the 1200 g of fruit he will need for a second ten-hour day spent in making the machine. In all, twenty hours' labor. Let us suppose that the rate of saving has fallen to 33⅓ percent (corresponding to a 50% rate of profit). It will have taken Pierre two days (20 hours' labor) to save a ration of 1600 g of fruit. To which must be added a ten-hour day to build the machine, making a total of thirty hours' labor. In this last hypothesis, the machine would pay for itself, which in our example means that it will have the same yield as a man, if during its lifetime (10 hours) it is capable of gathering 3.6 kg of fruit, that is, 2.4 kg as the equivalent (renewal) value of the machine and 1.2 kg profit (at a rate of 50%). Two successive machines will be necessary in order to complete the full cycle of savings reconstitution (and likewise the exchange between the initial saving and the profit) since the rate of capitalization is equal to two days. The two machines will then together have produced $3.6 \times 2 = 7.2$ kg of fruit (quantity gathered in 30 hours' labor by hand).

In a developed economy, Pierre the entrepreneur will seldom make his own equipment, although this is fairly common in specialized firms. More often than not he will buy his equipment from another entrepreneur. This does not in any way change the nature of the operation just described. If Pierre has made the machine himself, he will still in effect have purchased it through an exchange of his own assets. And even if he buys it from Paul, the same internal exchange will take place, because Paul will only deliver the machine in exchange for a product that has needed ten hours' labor, let us say 1 g of gold. Pierre will therefore have had to accumulate that gram of gold before he can acquire the machine.

Note that a similar exchange has taken place between Paul's own assets: To get the gram of gold he has had to deliver a machine that is the product of ten hours' labor.

We shall see (in greater detail) in Appendix 1 how the exchange might figure in the accounts.

## The Influence of the Rate of Profit on the Return from Machines in a Primitive Economy

It was pointed out a little earlier that, to bring a sufficient return, the machine had to produce a minimum of 4.8 kg of fruit in ten hours. If it produced less, *other things being equal and in particular the rate of profit,* it would be to Pierre's advantage to use his capital in employing Jacques and Henri. If it produces more, the unit value of the fruit will inevitably fall.[17] The reader may be tempted to think that, having been sent out through the door, the exploitation of man by capital has sneaked back in through the window. What authorizes me to say that the fruit gatherer will be economically viable—and thus have the status of capital—only if it produces 4.8 kg a day? Simply the comparison with the profit derived by Pierre from the "contract" he has made with Jacques and Henri. If capitalism's concern were to ease the labors of men, the machine would be advantageously used as of the moment it produced a little more than 2.4 kg per day. Why? Because if it produces a shade more than that amount it becomes more productive to spend ten hours making a machine, an indirect way of gathering fruit, than to spend the same time and effort gathering directly by hand. This is undeniable, and for that reason it is necessary to introduce into our model another variable, the rate of profit.

It is purely for convenience that thus far I have assumed the rate of profit to be unchangeable. Actually the rate of profit depends in the last analysis on the ratio of net income to gross income (a ratio equal to the rate of saving if the whole of the net product is saved). That ratio depends in turn on a multitude of factors, some affecting the amount of gross income—like the amount of time worked, for example—the others affecting its distribution: The greater the share consumed, the smaller the disposable share and vice versa. In our example the machine will not be *profitable* if it produces less than 4.8 kg of fruit because I have assumed, among other things, that the labor time is kept at ten hours. But there is nothing inevitable about this. If the length of the working day were suddenly to shorten, the result, other things being equal, would be an automatic decrease in net income; in other words the rate of profit would have fallen. In that case it would be advantageous to gather fruit by means of a machine less productive than the one used for the purposes of our argument so far.

We reach exactly the same conclusion if we assume that the workday remains set at ten hours but that the share of the gross product consumed in the production process increases, with a corresponding fall in net income. This is the assumption already used for the case where the wage rises from 1200 to 1600 g of fruit.

The assumptions can be varied ad infinitum. The rate of profit, for example, can be lowered by the combination of a shortening of the workday and an increase in the share consumed. In a developed society, the factors depressing or pushing up the rate of profit are constantly making their influence felt and offsetting one another to varying extents. Our first assumption was that the gross income from a ten-hour workday was equal to 2.4 kg of fruit and then that a man's daily ration was 1.2 kg, whence the "saving" (accumulated product) of 1.2 kg if the length of the workday remains ten hours:

$$\text{rate of profit: } \frac{\text{daily profit}}{\text{invested saving (capital)}} = \frac{1.2}{1.2} = 100\%$$

The simple question we have to answer is this. Suppose that the rate of profit falls to 50 percent because daily consumption rises from 1200 g to 1600 g. What will the machine's performance have to be for there to be "no difference" between using an automated fruit gatherer and using human labor? The machine will have to gather 3.6 kg of fruit during its ten-hour lifespan (see also pp. 113–14).

Pierre built the fruit gatherer on Monday and allowed himself a food ration of 1600 g, which he accumulated by not consuming during the previous week the product of six hours forty minutes' labor. During the first six hours forty minutes of the workday on Monday he reinvested the value of 1600 g of fruit in the construction of his machine; then he completed his engineering feat by working an additional three hours twenty minutes during which he produced a value equivalent to 800 g of fruit. Those 800 g are profit (from a capital of 1600 g) reinvested in the machine's construction. If the machine, by operating on Tuesday, brings him 3600 g of fruit, it reproduces the value he produced on Monday (equal to 2.4 kg of fruit) and in addition brings him a profit of 50 percent—in other words, 1200 g. This is the profit he would have made if, with a capital of 2.4 kg (the value of which is the same as that of the machine), he had hired, on Tuesday, two employees: Jacques full-time (a wage of 1600 g) and Henri half-time (a wage of 800 g).[18] To Pierre, having a machine or a provision of 2.4 kg of fruit to advance as circulating capital is the same thing.

The chronological order in which I have introduced the different types of machine is the reverse of historical experience. I have assumed that Pierre began by designing a machine capable of gathering 4.8 kg of fruit in ten hours, then, the rate of profit having fallen, a machine capable of gathering only 3.6 kg in ten hours. Clearly, in real life the sequence would be reversed. It is very likely that Pierre will first design the machine with the lower yield. But, as we have seen, with a yield of 3.6 kg the machine's operation does not bring a satisfactory return if the rate of profit is 100 percent; in other words, at that rate the machine is not capital. More likely than not, Pierre's employees will want more enjoyment in their lives and therefore will try to get an increased daily ration of fruit, which, other things being equal, will have the result of lowering the rate of profit. At that moment a machine that hitherto did not bring a sufficient return begins to do so. The reason is that the relationship between the two phenomena— rate of profit, and invention of new production techniques—is not simply one-way. The mere fact that an operable machine has been designed—provided that the rate of profit falls, say, from 100 to 50 percent, or from 50 to 30 percent, or from 30 to 25 percent, and so on—will cause consumption and saving habits to be readjusted to that rate.

This is not to say that technological progress invariably makes the rate of profit fall. This happens only in the strictly defined conditions of the hypothetical cases discussed here. The examination of these hypothetical cases makes it easier to understand why the economic takeoff of an underdeveloped country almost always presupposes a rise in wages. Mechanization becomes possible only when a larger share of gross income is absorbed in higher living standards. As long as the rate of profit remains high, competition to the work force will have to come from machines that have a very high yield and are probably too costly for most businesses. Those businesses, on the other hand, can content themselves with acquiring machines with a lower yield once the wage level rises—assuming constant labor productivity.

In my example Pierre would have to be clever enough to make a machine that gathers 4800 g of fruit in ten hours when a man's ration is 1200 g a day. In all likelihood that machine—assuming Pierre is technically capable of making it—would require more than ten hours of his labor. So he would have to do without it. But when the daily ration rises to 1600 g, he will simply need a machine producing 3600 g of fruit. Perhaps he will be capable of building that less sophisticated fruit gatherer in the time required for the operation to be profitable—in other words, ten hours.

It should not be concluded that the higher the level of wages in a country, the less advanced the technology needs to be. That would be another instance of fallacious reasoning due once more to neglect of the famous ceteris paribus clause. It would be to forget that in the advanced countries, those where wage levels are highest, labor productivity is also several times higher (largely through the use of machines) than in the poorest countries. And the reasoning in my example required that labor productivity be constant.

## The Capital Renewal Cycle

In all the preceding examples I have assumed that intervals of time are equal which, in real economic life, hardly ever are. In the hypothesis of a 100 percent rate of profit (1200 g of fruit saved each day) I assumed that the cycle of renewal of the value of the invested saving, the time taken to manufacture the machine (physical capital), and the latter's useful life were all equal to one day.

With hypothesis 2 (wage at 1600 g, hence a lowering of the rate of profit to 50%) we were already closer to reality. It took two days for the savings renewal cycle—that is, the exchange between saving and future profit—to be completed, while the machine lasted only one day. Remember that to acquire the machine it was necessary to invest the product of ten hours' labor. In ten hours of operation the machine replaced its own value (2.4 kg) and in addition brought a profit in the form of 1200 g of fruit. For the phased value-for-like-value exchange of invested saving for future profit to take place, Pierre had to use two machines in succession. On Tuesday evening, when the first machine has come to the end of its useful life, he immediately acquires another, which he can do by handing over 2.4 kg of fruit (from the total output of 3.6 kg). The second machine will operate on Wednesday and, on the evening of that day, Pierre will again find himself with the replaced value of the machine (2.4 kg of fruit), while the successive use of the two machines will additionally have left him with a profit of 1.2 kg × 2 = 2.4 kg, equal to the saving he invested at the outset. The rate of capitalization determines the length of the period over which the deferred value-for-like-value exchange of saving for profit takes place. In everyday language we would say that the machine is written off in ten hours, while the investment yields a profit of 100 percent in the first example and 50 percent in the second. For the purpose of describing the exchange mechanism, it is necessary to distinguish carefully between *replacement* of the machine's value and *reconstitution* of the invested savings by profit.

In our two examples, the time taken to build the machine was the same as the machine's useful life, but again this is not true in practice. One can imagine, for example, that the machine will last two, three, four, five, six days, and so on (whereas it always takes 10 hours' labor to make the machine). Suppose the machine operated for six days: What would its daily output have to be for the yield to continue to be equal to that of human labor? At a 50 percent rate of profit, replacement of the machine's value at the rate of ⅙ per day would be:

$$\frac{2400 \text{ g}}{6}$$
$$+ 50\% \text{ profit on the invested capital}$$

| | |
|---|---|
| 400 g | |
| 1200 g | |
| 1600 g | |

In that case the machine would have to gather 1.6 kg of fruit per day for six days. Before going any further, we should note that Pierre will probably realize that it is hardly consistent with the rationality of the *homo economicus* he has become to put aside for six days 400 g of fruit in order to replace the value of the machine. That rationality tells him to employ the output productively until such time as he needs to be able to use it to replace the machine. Logically, therefore, on the basis of a slightly more complicated calculation (which introduces compound interest), to equal human labor output the machine need produce not 1600 g, but only about 1315 g:

| | |
|---|---|
| daily amount of the annuity which, at a daily rate of 50%, will replace in 6 days the product of 10 hours' labor (2.4 kg of fruit or one machine) | 115 g |
| + daily profit of 50% on the capital invested | 1200 g |
| | 1315 g |

Note that use of the machine would have brought a total profit of 1200 g × 6 = 7200 g of fruit and, at the end of the machine's useful life, a replacement value in the form of 2400 g of fruit. Since the invested saving constitutes a permanent reserve, it makes no difference to the capitalist, in theory, whether he invests his capital daily for six successive days or ties it up once over a six-day period. In practice, there are other considerations that will determine whether the one solution is more advantageous (or less risky) than the other.

The reverse situation also occurs very often in reality. The effective life of a machine is shorter (e.g., 3 years) than the average cycle of reconstitution of the invested saving (10 years if the average rate of profit is 10%). In that eventuality it will be necessary to use several machines in succession before the phased exchange of capital for profit can be completed.

Physical capital is the material medium of investment (or invested saving, still also referred to here as "capital employed" or "committed"). Its lifespan determines the number of times the savings renewal cycle will take place before the savings are invested in another physical capital asset. The number of times may also be a fraction if, for example, a machine's lifespan is two years while the rate of capitalization is equal to twenty years (corresponding to a 5% rate of profit).

## Special Case of an Exchange Between the Products of Two Automated Machines

Now we shall see whether the labor theory of value can hold good in a circumstance which in modern economic life occurs millions of times a day. It can be summed up very simply: Suppose that Pierre is not alone in having developed a special talent for engineering. While he has been making the automatic fruit gatherer, François has built a mill with, mutatis mutandis, the same characteristics in that it was constructed in ten hours of labor and its milling capacity is 4 kg of flour, it being assumed that in ten hours one man can mill *by hand* 2 kg of flour (and that with 1 kg he can feed himself, leaving a rate of profit of 100%). I assume, too, that the mill functions entirely automatically without entailing for its owner any expenditure—in the economic sense of the term—in respect of energy (no fuel, electric power, etc.), an assumption which, in this particular example, brings us closer to known reality instead of further away from it, since it can be assumed that the mill made by François is a good old-fashioned windmill.

It is obvious that, in the circumstances defined here, 4 kg of flour *has the same value* as 4.8 kg of fruit, and that if Pierre and François exchange the outputs of their respective machines they will each obtain a *profit* that will enable them to get back the full value of their respective investments.

In this case there has thus been profit and, apparently, no fresh labor. But this particular hypothesis includes nothing that has not been said earlier and I introduce it only to dispel the false impression that it conveys on superficial examination. The profit obtained by Pierre (in exchanging his fruit for flour) and by François (in exchanging his flour for fruit) simply resuscitates, as it were, the latent value of the capital which each has committed at a 100 percent rate of profit, Pierre to construct the gatherer and François to build the mill. When the exchange is completed, they find themselves with values proportionate to the amount of time they worked earlier. Pierre had made an investment the full reckoning of which in labor time is twenty hours (100% rate of profit); François had likewise made an investment that necessitated twenty hours' labor. They end up respectively with 4 kg of flour (product of 20 hours' labor) and 4.8 kg of fruit (product of 20 hours' labor). If Pierre and François, instead of consuming the flour and fruit unproductively, now use them as capital, we shall continue to see, through a succession of exchanges, the phenomenon (already mentioned at the beginning of Chapter 4) of preservation of the value of the saving, which, once the first cycle has been completed, can give rise to accumulation. The conclusion would be the same if we were to imagine that *the automated machines reproduced themselves,* each of them capable of generating a whole succession of identical machines.[19] In that case the exchange, from the standpoint that concerns us here, would have only one effect—namely to bring out, with each generation of machine, the permanent nature of the initial saving (or capital) as a reserve. For the exchange to embrace new values, the output of the machines would at some time have to be exchanged for the product of fresh labor (a new type of machine, for example).

One final point concerning Pierre and François: The fresh labor necessary to produce Pierre's profit is the labor performed by François in building the mill, while the fresh labor needed for François to obtain a profit is that performed by Pierre in making the gatherer.

## On What Does the Rate of Profit Depend?

What in the last analysis determines the average rate of profit in a given society at a given moment? The reader will point out that I have already answered this question by implication. Like many other interpreters of Ricardo's work, I have made the rate of profit depend on the distribution of gross income. This interpretation is a first step in our

search, but even so it leaves us in want of an explanation. Its acceptance as such means that the rate of profit is determined at the whim
of highly subjective forces: On the one hand those which impel the
trade unions to keep raising their assessment of the goods regarded as
"necessary" to the employee, and on the other those which almost
always incline employers to resist the most legitimate of claims with
such arguments as "It would be spending money before we get it" or
"The country is already living beyond its means," and so on. Might
there not be, beyond this trade-off between the satisfaction of wants
and the formation of capital—which, in the free market economies,
seems to resolve itself into a perpetual confrontation between empoy-
ers and the working class or classes—might there not be, at the heart
of the exchange mechanism, a spring the action of which predeter-
mines, as the case may be, either the result of the apparent struggle
over "the share-out of the cake," or the seemingly arbitrary decision
of the central planning body?

If the wage rate—and hence the rate of profit—is in fact finally
determined by the consumption habits of the working population (an
expression to be taken in its broadest sense to include, besides workers, all those who contribute to production), is there any reason why
gross income should not be entirely eaten up by production costs?
What is there to stop the unions, provided that the political circumstances are right, from pushing their demands *to the limit*? Conversely,
what is there to stop the employers or the omnipotent planner from
putting maximum pressure on the people to squeeze the maximum
amount of capital out of them?

Determination of the rate of profit is necessarily another component
of the theory of value. Once there is accumulation (which is the case
with all goods and services offered on the market), exchange value is,
as we know, not only proportionate to the quantity of labor, it also
depends on the rate of profit. But does not profit—unlike the quantity
of labor, which is an independent variable that relates to nothing other
than itself—result from a comparison between the cost of production
and the selling price (exchange value) on the market? The objective
value theory, as we have outlined it, is valid only to the extent that the
rate of profit can be determined without any reference to the price
system. One approach to the problem is to suppose that Ricardo
argued (although he did not) from the simplified example of an economy whose sole input was wheat plus some other products and whose
sole output was wheat, plus the same products, too. Profit then would
be determined by technical factors; it would be that share of output

(surplus) which exceeded the sum total of production costs.[20] But does really this line of reasoning result in an explanation? Does not one beg the question in assuming a certain model of consumption which implies a surplus above the costs of production?

It would be necessary to imagine a wide range of possible variation for the rate of profit. This could be very high when the wage is very low, and quite low when the sum of goods allocated to the wage earner becomes relatively large. The upper limit has almost been reached in the economically underdeveloped countries, where the wage is close to the minimum subsistence level and where consequently, in spite of the still rudimentary state of production techniques, the labor time spent in producing the goods consumed by the wage earner is small. As for the lower limit, this is harder to determine. It brings us back to the question asked earlier: What principle has it that wage earners in the developed countries fail to obtain almost the whole of the product? The reason probably lies first and foremost in the functioning of the market. On the one side, any reduction in the rate of profit below a certain limit would mean a withdrawal of capital or, put another way, a refusal by capitalists to invest. The inevitable consequence of a decrease, absolute or relative, in the volume of invested capital is a fall in demand for the services performed by labor,[21] hence lower wages or higher unemployment, or both. On the other side of the market, competition between job seekers has the effect of making the wage level decline low enough for the capitalist to be prepared to put his capital into hiring them. These two rules apply even to the centrally planned economies, since there too it is virtually never true that the market mechanisms fail to make themselves felt (the only situation in which these mechanisms are totally eliminated is in the economy of a country at war where all the forces of production are mobilized not in the service of the population but in the service of defense).

We still have to form some idea of how the rate of profit is determined in normal conditions. Intuitively I would reply that this rate is in inverse proportion to the *average* length of time taken to accumulate the saving the community needs to acquire the volume of capital (food, clothing, machinery, buildings, etc.) necessary to give effect to the (available) labor—that is to say, to ensure full employment. If it took ten years to accumulate this saving (for which, in our example, the capital goods produced are exchanged), the rate of profit would be something like 10 percent; if it took twenty years, the rate would be about 5 percent, and so on. This hypothesis seems to me the most plausible and I would add that this question of profit, so important for

the advancement of economic science, calls for research both theoretical and empirical, which will probably be undertaken on the scale
desirable the day that economists finally cease to regard profit as a
"residual."

The accumulation process stems from the exchange mechanism and
the latter, once the stage of the subsistence economy is passed,
governs all economic activity, even where all the instruments of
production belong to a single legal entity such as the state (see
Appendix 1).

The law of equivalence of exchange, which implies the earning of a
certain profit, ultimately restores the conditions necessary to ensure
this profit by eliminating, in one way or another, the claims that would
immediately absorb the net product if they were to be satisfied. In
certain circumstances (when monetary authorities are accommodating)
the short-term adjustment can be made through inflation. Suppose that
the trade unions obtain wage increases so large that businesses will be
unable, at current market price, to obtain a profit from their operations.
If that happens, then prices will almost invariably rise, so that the rate
of profit will ultimately stay much the same. (This is true for the first
phases of inflation, which, as it develops, inevitably becomes a factor
in its own right in the reduction of firms' profit-making capacity.)

Determination of the distribution of gross income by the exchange
mechanism explains the often-noted disquieting fact that the overall
wage level (measured in terms of real purchasing power) depends very
little if at all, in sectors where there is keen competition, on trade
union action. During the late 1960s and early 1970s in the United
States, wages rose faster in those occupations which were not union-
ized, or only very little. This was a strong indication of the validity of
the theory that the "share-out of the cake" depends on objective
conditions and is virtually uninfluenced by the subjective desires
expressed with greater or lesser force by employers and employees.

But this only really holds good if other things are equal: In the long
run the struggles to improve the lot of the workers, to introduce more
acceptable working conditions, make their effects felt. More often than
not the process is basically as follows: Businessmen, obliged as they
are to pay higher wages, to forgo forms of labor organization that are
particularly convenient—for them (as in the case of today's assembly
line)—have no choice but to increase output through technical progress
and new division-of-labor methods. The increased wants of wage
earners can then be satisfied and at the same time an adequate rate of
profit maintained.

## Profit Rate, Wage Rate, and Population

We are now at last in a position to understand better the wage theory expounded by Ricardo (see Chapter 3). We have seen how Ricardo is concerned only with the "supply price of labor" (the minimum considered necessary) and does not even mention the "demand price" (the maximum that employers are prepared to pay). In spite of our efforts we had not quite managed, I think, to explain this seemingly astonishing one-sidedness. The reason was that it is impossible to account for wage rate determination without reference to the rate of profit, since it is the latter that plays the central role in *any accumulative economy* (whether free market or socialist). The logical chain of events would be roughly as follows:

1. The volume of expressed wants gradually determines the volume of capital necessary, "to give effect to labor," taking into account the current state of production techniques. Hence the importance of the "natural price of labor" (an expression I can now use without compunction since we know where we stand with it).

2. The rate of profit adjusts itself to this volume of saving. In an exchange economy this rate of profit will gradually be established by the market. Since the production process breaks down into a sequence of exchanges over time, the rate of profit is the most important price of all. In the general model of exchange the wage rate appears as a resultant of the rate of profit, and that is why the theory does not have to mention the demand price of labor, since employers set it in accordance with the profit they expect.

The reader will doubtless have realized that, thus presented, the general model of exchange is still incomplete. We started out from the idea that the volume of capital is that which is necessary to give effect to the labor of the working population, taking into account the technological state of the art. How do wants adjust to the society's productive capacity? Ricardian economics answers that question by introducing a third variable (the most important of all for the destiny of mankind) to which I have already referred in the previous chapter (see in particular pp. 45–46). This is the population variable. Provided a sufficiently long period of time is envisaged, the adjustment between wants and the material means to meet them will take place through the changes in population numbers. There is no area in which Ricardo's theory is more radically opposed to that of Malthus. For Ricardo, the population figure *depends,* in the last analysis, on the material means ("capital stock") with which to feed people and, more generally, to meet the wants they consider "necessary." But for the causal relationship to be in that direction, *men have to have become aware of their wants* (see above, p. 45). Otherwise, population runs wild; it develops independently of the "capital stock" variable, and the gloomy predictions of Malthus threaten to materialize (see Chapter 7, p. 204), as tends to be the case in the poorest countries—not in genuinely developing countries, because in such countries the reference to the capital stock available in the coming future somehow makes its influence felt. In the countries that have had their industrial revolution, on the other hand, Ricardo's theory seems to be confirmed beyond any possible doubt. With the advances of birth control, population growth will probably become increasingly regulated by economic factors, in accordance with the theoretical pattern of society proposed by Ricardo 150 years ago.

The average rate of profit is therefore difficult to ascertain in practice, although studies on the subject are undertaken from time to time by American statisticians. The long-term rate of interest probably approximates it.

To come back to my hypothesis, I would point out that the time needed to accumulate the savings with which the existing volume of capital has been acquired may be short for two different reasons. The first is that the country concerned may be economically underdeveloped, which is another way of saying that it possesses very little capital. In such a country the rate of profit will tend to be high.[22] The second possible reason is quite different: It is that the share of national income which is saved may be considerable. A country where the rate of saving is very high is in a position to accumulate much more rapidly. The rate of profit is higher than in a country where saving is smaller in relative value.

One argument in favor of the hypothesis is that it would satisfactorily explain why, in the least developed countries, the rate of profit is always very high, sometimes as much as 50 percent.

I would point out here that a Ricardian model has actually served as the foundation for the "construction of socialism." In China, new capital wants expressed by production units were supposed to be calculated according to the time taken to recoup the capital employed. This is the so-called "pay-back" formula, the primitive nature of which is due to the fact that it presupposes a different rate of profit for each sector of activity (the more advanced socialist countries prefer the more conventional and more modern "discounted present value" technique).

The question of the rate of profit is so important that we shall have occasion to return to it several times in the course of this book, notably to show that the so-called "law" of declining rate of profit—expounded in different ways, on the one hand by "bourgeois" economists beginning with Adam Smith, followed by Malthus and then Keynes, and on the other hand by Marx—is without foundation.

## Abolition of Wage Labor = Universalization of Profit

While the share of gross product taken by profit is, for the reasons I have just outlined, destined to be maintained in our societies despite the pressures exerted by the other parties with claims on the gross income, it is an interesting theoretical exercise to envisage other models of society in which profit would either ultimately disappear or be all consuming. By the mathematical nature of his thinking, Ricardo was led to examine these two extreme hypotheses (especially the first). We shall look at this in more detail in Chapters 5 and 6. But in pursuit of our present line of enquiry it is useful to consider at this point what those hypotheses represent.

The absorption of total gross income by profit can come about only on one condition: namely that output in its entirety comes from completely automated machines which also have the property of being everlasting—or of reproducing themselves without the aid of new human labor. In that eventuality, the entirety of the machines' product would be distributed as profit. One could even imagine that the machines would be so designed as to be able, over the course of time, to increase their output and improve themselves! But there would be no creation of new value, as the increase in output would result in a fall in unit product values. The proposition still holds good that there can be no new value without new labor.

Conceptually it is impossible to visualize abolition of wage labor other than in the purely theoretical and probably forever unrealistic circumstances I have just imagined. This is a logical consequence of the fact that the entirety of any society's income is shared between wages and profit (rent being, by definition, taken out of profit). If labor disappears there is no more wage, and if there is no more wage, then income consists solely of profit. By reasoning in terms of this extreme case we see, yet again, the logical inconsistency of Marxism. Marx wants to abolish wage labor by establishing socialism. But abolition of wage labor logically implies the absorption of total income by profit.

In the reverse hypothesis, profit is abolished because income in its entirety is absorbed and consumed[23] by the workers: The rate of *profit* falls to zero, which implies that capital accumulation ceases. With a zero rate of profit it may be wondered how long the status quo could be preserved, since without any prospect of profit there would be a great temptation to consume the capital already accumulated. Reduction of the rate of profit to zero would probably, sooner or later, set off a process of dissaving which would take the society back to a more primitive state.

In terms of modern political parties, it might be said that abolition of wage labor through general distribution of profit corresponds, if not to Marxist theory, at least to the Marxist vision of society, to the extent that Marxist politicians and ideologists want, through accelerated technical progress—made possible, according to them, by the establishment of socialism—to free man from uniform and dictated labor so that he may reach the state where there is no longer any direct link between labor and the satisfaction of wants. This link will indeed be broken the moment that *all* men become *rentiers* of the savings accumulated by their predecessors to construct automated and self-reproducing machines. Ironically, the greatest book ever written in the cause of freeing the worker from the status of wage laborer is entitled *Capital*. In choosing his title, Marx, in a way, showed himself to be more percipient than in formulating his critique of political economy.

As for zero growth and, *more importantly,* the regressive state caused by the disappearance of the rate of profit, this would reflect in its own way the leftist vision of society.

The reader will find that the two appendixes to this chapter deal respectively with profit in the general mode of exchange and the various meanings of the word *capital*. Also useful is the essay, following Chapter 12, entitled "Notes on Piero Sraffa's 'Prelude.' "

## Notes

1. But it seems that for the marginalist school, the remuneration of the production factor "capital" has not to be considered as profit proper.

2. In his *Treatise on Money* (London: Macmillan for the Royal Economic Society, n.d.), Keynes categorically rejects the idea that changes in the general

price level are determined by "changes on the side of money." Any revival of monetary theory must, to my way of thinking, begin by reinstating the idea of "value of money" (which Keynes called both a "mirage" and a "will-o'-the-wisp"). I would add that this particular idea holds good whatever monetary system is in operation.

3. Written before 1973, when the value of currencies was still legally expressed in terms of gold.

4. Here I am considering gold purely from the standpoint of its monetary function. Clearly, if gold is used as an industrial raw material, an increase in its quantity will constitute an increase in wealth.

5. *Theoretically,* all production of monetary gold diminishes the output of directly useful goods. However, while the monetary system may *function* better because of an increase in the quantity of gold, this will not strictly speaking create any additional wealth but will *facilitate* increased generation of wealth. Here we have stumbled on a discovery: the "empirical" nature of any monetary system, however rational.

6. See Appendix 1 to Chapter 4, p. 131.

7. A rate of saving of 50 percent would represent a rate of profit of 100 percent.

$$\left[ \frac{1200 \text{ g (net product)}}{1200 \text{ g (quantity consumed)}} \right]$$

8. A 33⅓ percent rate of saving would represent a 50 percent rate of profit.

$$\left[ \frac{800 \text{ g (net product)}}{1600 \text{ g (quantity consumed)}} \right]$$

9. Day 1: Pierre pays a wage of 1600 g to Jacques, who brings him back 2400 g; so Pierre gets back the 1600 g (capital) plus 800 g profit. Day 2: the operation is repeated; at the end of the day Pierre gets back the 1600 g capital he has employed a second time, plus another 800 g profit. At the end of the second day, therefore, he possesses 1600 g (initial capital) + 1600 g profit, that is, a total of 3200 g.

10. It is pointless, at this stage of the reasoning, to take into account the second part of Marxist theory (set out in volume 3 of *Capital*), namely the distribution of surplus value among the different categories of capitalists. This distribution has the effect of reducing the average rate of profit to less than the rate of surplus value.

11. This would suggest that the real "raison d'être" of wage labor is the elimination of the aforementioned risk. In the poorest countries the employer tends to hold on to his employees even when business is bad; instead of dismissing them, he will reduce their (already very low) wage. This is true even in Japan, a country which has retained many of the characteristics of a primitive society despite the enormous economic progress it has made.

12. We already reached this conclusion, though by another route, in the preceding chapter (see page 34).

13. It may be a material object or a service. In our example the product of labor is in fact a service, since the fruit has not been made but *gathered* by Pierre or by Jacques.

14. The five hours' labor performed in order to produce the profit.

15. If, as is likely, the fabrics are sold for a sum of money, the problem is simply displaced one remove but it arises in the same terms, since the seller will use the money he has received to buy other products.

16. The distribution of surplus value among capitalists is explained by Marx in volume 3 of *Capital*.

17. This phenomenon, which is central to economic development through mechanization, is examined in Chapter 5.

18. By working ten hours Jacques would have gathered 2.4 kg of fruit, of which 1.6 kg would have replaced the value of his wage and 800 g would have constituted Pierre's profit. In five hours Henri would have produced 1.2 kg of fruit (800 g plus a profit of 400 g).

19. It is possible that this hypothesis is included in the famous work by Piero Sraffa, *Production of Commodities by Means of Commodities: Prelude to a Critique of Economic Theory* (Cambridge, U.K.: Cambridge University Press, 1977). But Sraffa, despite being the leading authority on Ricardo this century, seems to have been unable to formulate clearly the exchange mechanism and the meaning of the labor theory of value as understood by Ricardo. Even so, the intuition that "labor" as such does not enter into the exchange circuit is implicit in the title (see "Notes on Piero Sraffa's 'Prelude' " at the end of the present volume, page 335).

20. Compare Sraffa, *Production of Commodities by Means of Commodities*.

21. This expression is preferable, as we know, to that of "demand for labor on the market."

22. We have seen that in a country of this kind the labor time spent in producing the goods consumed by the worker is short. Need it be added that those goods consumed by the worker form an integral part of the country's capital, and often the bulk of it?

23. If the workers do not consume the entirety of their wage, the share saved is intended to bring a profit, and our hypothesis cannot apply.

*Appendix 1*

## PROFIT IN THE EXCHANGE PROCESS

### The Full Account of the Exchange Between Pierre and Paul

1. First there is Paul's balance sheet. He has made the machine and sold it for one gram of gold. His balance sheet looks like this:

| *Assets* | *Liabilities* |
|---|---|
| Cash: 1 g gold[1] | Capital: value of accumulated product of 10 hours of labor |

Here I am using the word "capital" in its ordinary legal or accounting sense (see Appendix 2, Chapter 4). In this acceptation, capital expresses the extent of the rights that the owner has over the assets. Here, Paul possesses the whole of the value of the assets because he has not borrowed anything from anyone to acquire them. He gained the money by selling a machine, the product of ten hours of his labor. The value of the capital is therefore equal to that of a product of ten hours of labor.

2. Next is Pierre's balance sheet. He has given Paul the gram of gold in exchange for the machine:

| *Assets* | *Liabilities* |
|---|---|
| Fixed asset: 1 machine = value of 1 g gold | Capital: value of accumulated product of 10 hours of labor |

These two balance sheets do not cancel each other out, they complement each other. At the moment that they are drawn up, the two assets do indeed exist. The gram of gold is in Paul's till and the machine is in Pierre's workshop. Each of these balance sheets is simply a "still photograph" of the property (or estate) of each of the two parties to the exchange taken at moment $t + 1$, immediately after the exchange has taken place. At that moment, Paul possesses one gram of gold and Pierre one machine and that is what appears on each one's balance sheets.

At moment $t - 1$, just before the exchange, Pierre's balance sheet looked like this:

131

|           *Assets*          |           *Liabilities*          |
| Cash: value of 1 g gold | Capital: value of accumulated |
|                         | product of 10 hours of labor |

At moment $t + 1$, following the exchange, this balance sheet became the balance sheet shown earlier.

If Pierre wishes to draw up the complete account of the transaction he has just been involved in, he cannot confine himself to the balance sheet as such. In the complete account of the instantaneous exchange between Pierre and Paul, two assets are related which appear simultaneously in two different "estates." In the complete account of the deferred exchange between Pierre and Pierre at two different moments in time we have two assets that appear successively in one property.

### Value Has No Reality Beyond That of a Figure in an Account

In spending his gram of gold to buy the machine, Pierre has accumulated; in other words, instead of causing the value of this gram of gold to cease to be part of his property, which would have happened if he had spent it on his own personal consumption, he has *exchanged* it for a machine as a productive investment. It is at this point that we need to be on our guard against metaphorical pseudo-reasoning. Old habits of language—the trap that Marx failed to perceive and he promoted to the status of "dialectical movement"—almost inevitably lead us to conclude that the value of the gram of gold has passed into that of the machine and that, therefore, it only needs counting once. But value is not a thing; it cannot be "transmitted" from one commodity to another. *Value has no reality other than that of a figure appearing in an account.* The only mischance that can befall it is to be entered arbitrarily or, on the contrary, to be forgotten and not entered at all. In either case there is nothing that value can do about it; the accountant is the one who is to blame! In our example, if Pierre wants to enter the total account of his investment in his ledger from the outset, not only is it not arbitrary but it is necessary that he enter under assets, alongside the value of the machine, that of the gram of gold with which he purchased the machine. The value of this gram of gold, which he no longer has, represents the latent value of the savings initially accumulated to acquire the machine. The speed with which he will recover the value of these savings will depend on the rate of profit. And since there is nothing for the moment to offset this value on the other side (liabilities) of the balance sheet, we will accept that it be entered in italics for now. Equilibrium will not be reached until later when a new exchange transaction—the sale of the fruit gathered by the machine—has brought in the *profit.*

**The full account of the exchange within Pierre's property**

This explains why a description of the exchange that has taken place within Pierre's property requires that a statement of assets and liabilities be drawn up that is fuller than the normal balance sheet as at moment $t + 1$. The extended balance sheet will look like this:

| *Assets* | | *Liabilities* |
|---|---|---|
| Fixed asset: | value | Capital: claim on asset consist- |
| 1 machine: | 1 g gold | ing of 1 machine |
| *Accumulated product* | | *Profit to come: equivalent of* |
| *of 10 hours of labor:* | 1 g gold | *savings representing the prod-* |
| Total: | 2 g gold | *uct of 10 hours of labor* |
| | | Total: value of accumulated |
| | | product of 20 hours of labor |

That is Pierre's extended balance sheet. Paul's will be like this:

| *Assets* | | *Liabilities* |
|---|---|---|
| | value | Capital: claim on assets consist- |
| Cash: | 1 g gold | ing of 1 g of gold |
| *Accumulated product* | | *Profit to come: equivalent of* |
| *of 10 hours of labor* | 1 g gold | *savings representing the accu-* |
| Total: | 2 g gold | *mulated product of 10 hours of* |
| | | *labor* |
| | | Total: value of accumulated |
| | | product of 20 hours of labor |

That Paul should expect a profit from the gram of gold received in exchange for the machine may come as a surprise, but one only needs to assume that this gram of gold is employed productively—for example, to buy a loom (of similar productivity to that of the gathering machine) or to employ labor. If, instead, Paul spends the gram of gold on his own personal consumption, its value will be lost for good. He will have dissaved.

In practice, it would be dangerous and arbitrary for Pierre (or Paul) to keep his books this way. Pierre has only just taken delivery of the machine. He has not yet made it work. It would be very rash on his part to enter in advance the profit he hopes to make from an activity necessarily fraught with risk. But for us, there is no reason for the same caution. We are not Pierre the entrepreneur but observers studying the exchange from outside without being involved in it. So there is nothing to prevent us describing it in its entirety before it has reached completion. And that is why, on the assets side of Pierre's extended balance sheet, I have entered—in addition to the value of the machine—the value of the product that Pierre has accumulated in order to acquire the machine and, on the liabilities side, as *future capital or profit,* the equivalent of that accumulated product that has been exchanged over time.

Before we go any further, the following point needs noting because it is important for a clear understanding of the exchange phenomenon. The general case is not the exchange between Pierre and Paul at the same moment in the period concerned, but the exchange between Pierre and Pierre at two successive moments. This is because there are two possibilities. Either Pierre is both manufacturer and user of the machine, in which case the exchange is between the accumulated product of labor on the one hand and the machine on the other. Or else Paul is the maker of the machine and Pierre the buyer/user, in which case the instantaneous exchange between Paul and Pierre may be analyzed as two symmetrical exchange transactions phased over time, one within Pierre's property and the other within Paul's property.

### Exchange Does Not Generate Profit but There Is No Profit Without Exchange

Let us return to Pierre who is now trying to sell the fruit gathered by the machine. His earnings from doing so (exchange) will produce a profit (equal here to the value of the capital committed because the rate of profit is 100%), plus the value of the machine destroyed by use, only on one condition—so self-evident, as I have already pointed out, that it could easily be overlooked—namely that someone comes forward who has in the meantime expended *new labor* to produce a commodity that can be exchanged for the product of the machine used by Pierre.[2] This is sufficient of itself to resolve the apparent paradox that baffled Marx: Exchange per se is incapable of generating profit, and yet it is only via exchange—or, if you prefer, sale—that a profit can be made. What follows, therefore, is simply the transposal to the case of the machine of what I said on page 107 about the sale (exchange) by Pierre of the fruit that Jacques, his employee, has brought back to him.

Here let us go back to our extended balance sheet and assume that once the accumulated product of labor (saving) has been substituted for the machine within Pierre's property, either directly (case no. 1, in which Pierre himself makes the machine he is going to use) or indirectly (case no. 2, in which Pierre purchases the machine from Paul), *neither Paul nor Pierre—nor anyone else—does any more work*. What will happen when the machine comes to the end of its life, after gathering, as foreseen, 4.8 kg of fruit?

Pierre could be content to eat the fruit he has. It will last him four days. I mention this possibility only for the sake of exhaustiveness, since quite clearly it lies outside our field of study. If Pierre eats the machine's output, the problem of value no longer arises. No one has ever eaten value: Value is not an intrinsic quality of the product (as Marx stated in his leaden language and without drawing all the inferences, value is simply a social relation).

Another possibility is for Pierre to try to make a fresh exchange with the 4.8 kg of fruit:

*Hypothesis 1: exchange within his own property.* This exchange takes place within Pierre's property. On his balance sheet he had booked the machine at one gram of gold (the value of the product of ten hours' labor). The machine has, physically, disappeared. The only thing that Pierre can do, if he continues to keep accounts, is to replace the item "machine" on his balance sheet by the item "fruit." But since the machine was evaluated at one gram of gold it is this same amount that he enters against the item "fruit."

*Hypothesis 2: exchange with Paul.* Pierre approaches Paul who, having added nothing to his property, owns the value of one gram of gold and that is all. He cannot offer more to Pierre. The latter "sells" 4.8 kg of fruit for one gram of gold.

In both cases, no real value can be found to meet the claim in italics on Pierre's balance sheet (p. 133), representing the accumulated product of his labor invested in the manufacture (or purchase) of the machine.

Business practice is to calculate the price at which the product of an instrument of production—a machine, for example—needs to be sold for that instrument to give a "return." In what I have just said, my purpose was to run this process in reverse and show *on what conditions the product in question can be exchanged at that price*. To determine those conditions is to show how profit is generated by new labor.

## Ex Ante Balance Sheet and Ex Post Balance Sheet

The rules of standard accountancy seem, at first sight (as already noted on page 133), to be in contradiction with the pattern I have just outlined. Here, the discrepancy stems from the fact that one of the most constant, and least debatable, principles of corporate accountancy is that costs are based on original value. An industrial firm will base its estimate of the value of its products on the cost price of the various components that went into their manufacture (raw materials, manpower, depreciation of plant, etc.). That is the principle and one can only go along with it. Would it not be giving free rein to the arbitrary to allow a firm to enter its various assets in the balance sheet at the value that they would probably realize? If such a practice were for some reason to be allowed, one of the primary aims of any accounting system—namely, as objective as possible an evaluation of trading results—would be placed utterly out of reach. Arriving at such an evaluation raises problems of all kinds as yet imperfectly resolved, so what possible chance could there be of overcoming so many difficulties if it is decided to dispense with the only solid basis that is available and that itself is so difficult to establish: calculating costs on the basis of the original value of the components of manufacture, making no allowance at all for expected profit?

However, the point is that economics does not have to view things from the same standpoint as the entrepreneur or the accountant. The role of the entrepreneur requires him to stand upstream of the act of exchange. Whether he be a distributor or a manufacturer, it is with that act in view that he organizes the life of his firm or draws up its accounts. From his accounts he requires as precise as possible analytical knowledge of all the activities carried on in the different offices, workshops, warehouses, and so on (the different management and operating accounts) and overall knowledge (the balance sheet proper). Economics is not uninterested in the problems of companies (if it were, it could become no more than an otiose discourse or a mathematical exposition with no direct bearing on reality) but its first aim is to embrace all the phenomena of economic life; and to do so objectively, it has to consider them from a vantage point. The economist does not have to prepare for the act of exchange like the entrepreneur does. He has to analyze it, explain it, and for that he has to understand it at the moment that it takes place. It is surely evident that at the instant that the act of exchange takes place, the profit—if profit there be—is included in the price. Just as it would be dangerous and arbitrary for the entrepreneur to include—and therefore anticipate—his profit in the value of the goods that make up his assets, so it would be absurd and arbitrary on the part of the economist to exclude that component of the selling price since, at the moment the economist is exercising his power of investigation, that profit is most certainly included.

Let us see how Pierre would have described, in his balance sheet, what happened during the ten hours that the gathering machine was working. He would have had to cancel, on the assets side, the value of the machine (1 g gold) because after ten hours of operation the machine has to be scrapped. This value he would have transferred to a new item in his balance sheet: "fruit gathered by the machine." The 4.8 kg of fruit would therefore have been entered, temporarily, on the assets side as worth only one gram of gold (counterpart value of the machine that cost 10 hours of labor).

But, lo and behold, the proceeds of the sale of the fruit amount to two grams of gold! Instead of appearing as an integral part of the full value of the commodity, the one gram profit generated by the exchange seems to have fallen like manna from heaven. Accountancy is always brought up short by this problem of the transition from value of origin (at cost prices) to realized value. Between the two poles, accountancy experts hesitate. As to the economists and philosophers, they have, for over a century, been trying to come up with every kind of intellectual device to explain a phenomenon that is apparently fortuitous, but which, as we have just seen, is inherent in exchange.

To show that future profit is potentially included in the value of the fruit as soon as it has been gathered, we have to look at the ex post balance sheet as we have done here. This point is obscured when we reason ex ante, as is quite properly done in standard accountancy. Then we have the impression—but it is only an impression—that profit is a certain rate (10, 50, 100%, etc. as the case may be) applied *after the event* to the cost price of a product or service. But the labor theory of value—Ricardo's not Marx's—holds the key. It provides a rational basis for what seems the most arbitrary aspect of double-entry bookkeeping, so that profit no longer appears as manna from heaven but for what it is—namely, the product of new labor expended by the party to the exchange. I have described this profit as potential. It would have been better to say that its existence depends on a suspensive condition, warranting—in the eyes of the theoretician—the caution of the accountant for whom the book value of the fruit is only one gram of gold, the value of the destroyed machine.

The 4.8 kg of fruit cannot be exchanged for its full value—that is, including profit—unless new labor is also expended by the other party to the exchange. Then, Pierre can sell his 4.8 kg of fruit for the product of twenty hours of labor—say, one gram of gold and another machine. The other party to the exchange to whom I refer is not necessarily, I would repeat, someone other than Pierre. It is perfectly reasonable to suppose that the exchange takes place between Pierre and himself, if it is Pierre who expends the new labor. *The existence of profit, far from being an exception to the law of equivalence of exchange, is a sine qua non for that equivalence to exist.*


### Robinson Was a Capitalist Before Man Friday Came to the Scene

All alone on his island, Robinson was a capitalist—well before he met Man Friday. Daniel Defoe's book, published at the beginning of the eighteenth century, may well have owed its immense success primarily to the fact that, in a Britain which was still rural, it heralded the explosion of capitalism by showing how a man thrown back on his own resources can create for himself a comfortable life on a desert island by *accumulating* the products of his labor. Robinson was the antisavage in the sense that he was prepared to work ten hours whereas five would have sufficed for him to gather his daily food and meet his elementary needs.

For Robinson to be able to buy from himself, so to speak, the full value of the output of his machine, in other words for him to retain the benefit of the advance he built up by accumulating on Monday, in the form of a machine (or in any other form), the product of ten hours of labor, then on Tuesday—while his machine operates on its own—he has to work another ten hours making, say, another machine to replace the machine that will be worn out at the end of the day. *This is how, all alone on his island, Robinson has become a capitalist simply through the principle of exchange.* We have seen what would have happened if he had not worked on Tuesday. Since he would have consumed, during the first two days of the week, 2.4 kg of fruit—that is, half the output of the machine—on Tuesday evening he would have been left with 2.4 kg in "credit," whereas the business he had set up ("Robinson & Robinson") would have been "owing" him the value of a product that cost twenty hours of labor for the reasons set out above. As a result, the firm of Robinson & Robinson would have been running at a loss and its only shareholder, Robinson, would have had to accept a reduction of his claim on himself. To avoid that, there is no alternative but for Robinson to work ten hours on Tuesday. This means that he sets up a second company, Robinson II & Robinson II, whose output will be exchanged, value for like value, for the output of firm Robinson I & Robinson I. Failing which, Robinson will have wasted his time and effort. Yet capitalism is nothing other than the system enabling man to regain the full value of the product of his labor. Marx poked fun at Robinsonades—maybe it was because the real story of Robinson was the simplest and most definitive rebuttal of his explanation of capitalism.

## Notes

1. Received in exchange for the machine.
2. The argument developed in this chapter being that the general model of exchange is implicitly contained in the Ricardian labor theory of value, I now quote a passage proving that the idea that the value of a commodity includes the value produced by labor not directly applied to the manufacture of that commodity was espoused by Ricardo himself. In the chapter "On Value," section 5 (*Principles,* p. 24), he writes: "If fixed capital be not of durable nature it will require a great quantity of labour annually to keep it in its original state of efficiency; *but the labour so bestowed may be considered as really expended on the commodity manufactured* [my italics] (with the aid of the fixed capital) which must bear a value in proportion to such labour."

*Appendix 2*

## VARIOUS MEANINGS OF THE WORD "CAPITAL"

In political economy, capital is the "accumulated product of labor." In accountancy, equity capital is a claim on the company and therefore appears on the liabilities side of the balance sheet. In economic analysis, the "accumulated product of labor," also called "saving," is what generates the claim, entered under liabilities, that the capitalist holds against the company's assets. Lastly, the word "capital" is also regularly used, as it is in this book, in another sense. In practice, the "accumulated product of labor" takes many forms: buildings, tools, machinery, food, clothing, and so on—in short, all goods "employed in production" in accordance with the definition I quoted in the early pages of Chapter 4. In this case, instead of being a synonym of the abstract notion of "saving" or "accumulated product of labor," capital means all those things produced by human labor—whether tangible like plant and machinery, or intangible like patents—used to "give effect to labor."[1] These "capital goods" form so many assets owned by companies or the nation as a whole.

It would be very useful to have at least two different words for capital according to whether it appears as an asset or a liability. Up to a point the British classical economists made this distinction, by sometimes using the word *stock* (assets sense) and sometimes the word *capital* (liabilities/assets sense depending on the case). In the rest of this book I shall try to keep to the following rule:

accumulated product of labor = invested saving = capital committed
= original stake (liabilities sense)
capital good = instrument of production (assets sense)

The bookkeeper's concept of capital, which has the latter appear on the *assets* side of the balance sheet as the value of the production apparatus designed to bring in a profit and on the *liabilities* side as a claim on the *value* of the saving previously constituted in order to purchase this production apparatus, shows up the incredible deceit inherent in dialectical reasoning. The Marxists say that capital has a dialectical nature. Its value is sometimes in "commodity" form and sometimes in "money" form. In reality, the meaning of this oscillation—if, expressed in such language, it has any—is to be found in the two columns drawn up for double-entry bookkeeping. But double-entry bookkeeping, I need hardly repeat, owes nothing to philosophical reflection on the various "forms" of value. It is the result of a *logical* elucidation of the function of capital. Precisely because of its logicality, double-entry bookkeeping provides a better introduction to the study of economics than Hegelian dialectics (revised by Marx)!

## Note

1. A patent is capital from the legal standpoint, and the standpoint of any company in particular; but in terms of macroeconomics, technology cannot be regarded as capital.

# The Labor Theory of Value Fits In with the Modern Method of Calculating the Cost of Investment

## The Computer as Capital

I would like to explain how the ultrasimplified examples I have argued from in my attempt to show the workings of an entirely revised labor theory of value fit in with the modern method of calculating the cost of investment.

The reader will remember that my object was to establish the conditions in which Pierre's automated fruit gatherer could function as capital: in other words, the conditions it would have to meet to be "profitable."

Here we switch abruptly from Robinson Crusoe–land to the most modern industry of the day and transpose our argument to an example that is less naive[1] than the previous one and will ultimately enable us to outline the general scheme of deferred exchange.

I shall therefore assume that the long-term market rate of interest—which I shall equate with the average rate of profit—is 10 percent and that Peter Ltd. is a company with an initial capital (savings) of F.1,500,000, wholly invested in the purchase of a computer with a lifetime of twenty years. I shall further suppose (to prevent our case from becoming unnecessarily complicated) that the computer operates automatically, being powered by a battery with a twenty-year charge (the cost of which is included in the purchase price). What is the minimum price at which Peter Ltd. has to sell the computer's services each year for the investment to yield a satisfactory return?

To justify its cost of F.1,500,000, the computer would have to bring in each year, in the form of earnings or reduction of costs, an amount of F.176,189.43 made up as follows:

| | |
|---|---|
| 10% annual interest on "capital employed" | F.150,000 |
| The annuity which, after 20 years at a rate of 10% interest, will replace a value of F.1,500,000$^2$ | F.  26,189.43 |
| | F.176,189.43 |

Another way of arriving at this figure is to work out the annuity that F.1,500,000 would buy today for twenty years if the rate of interest were 10 percent.

Over the lifetime of the computer, Peter Ltd. will earn a total profit of F.150,000 × 20 = F.3,000,000 on the capital employed. There is nothing surprising in this. A 10 percent rate of interest corresponds to a ten-year capital reconstitution cycle (rate of capitalization = 10). After ten years, therefore, Peter Ltd. will, in accordance with the theory of deferred exchange, have made a profit equal to the company's initial investment or "capital." From time $t + 10$ on, a new capital reconstitution cycle begins, regardless of the fact that it is still the same machine that is the physical basis of this "capital" (a fact with which we are all familiar). At the end of the second ten-year period, Peter Ltd. will, in the ordinary way, have earned a second profit equal to the firm's initial investment.

It is only after two full cycles of reconstruction of the capital employed that the value of the physical capital (the computer) in which the company invested is replaced by successive transfers, at the rate of F.26,189.43 a year, to the cost of the service rendered by the computer.

A point to note, in passing, is that the computer has, in principle, already lost one-twentieth of its value by the end of its first year of operation and that, therefore, there is no longer any equivalence between the value of the "capital employed"—which continues to be reckoned at F.1,500,000 in the balance sheet (and yields 10% of that amount every year)—and the value of the computer in which this initially employed capital was invested.

For the annual product of the computer to be *effectively* exchanged for other products (services) at a value of F.176,189.43, certain conditions which we have already encountered and which concern the performance of the machine have to be met. On the assumption that a product worth F.1,500,000 requires 30,000 hours of direct and indirect labor[3] in the present average state of the art and in the given place, the computer has to be productive enough for the services it renders to enable approximately the following to be saved, *in the production of other goods:*

$$3,000 + 53 = 3,053 \text{ hours of labor}[4]$$

Let us now compare this formulation with the concept of capitalization used in investment calculus[5] on the basis of which Ricardo built his theory—but not so (however strange it may sound), the modern theories of capital.

## Periodic Investment Cost and Capitalized Cost

Business economists calculate what they call the periodic investment cost ($H$), to which the sum of F.176,189.43 corresponds in the above example. The calculation is based on the following reasoning: If the company owning the F.1,500,000 had not purchased the computer and had invested this sum, denoted by the letter $C$ ($C$ = initial cost of investment, which I have called "capital employed or saving"), at the going rate of interest $i$ (10% in my example) it would have yielded every year, for an indefinite period, a revenue of $Ci$ or F.150,000.

$Ci$ therefore represents the interest forgone because Peter Ltd. purchased an asset—the computer in my example—instead of putting the money on deposit. In addition, because the cost of replacing the machine in twenty years' time will be F.1,500,000, Peter Ltd. would be well advised to pay an annuity of F.26,189.43 (called $R$) into a sinking fund. The accumulation of this amount over twenty years will reconstitute the "principal," that is, F.1,500,000, which would otherwise have been lost. Hence the classical formula:

$$H = Ci + R$$
$$H = \text{F.150,000} + 26,189.43 = \text{F.176,189.43}$$

It is quite clear that if the use of the computer does not bring Peter Ltd. an annual income of F.176,189.43—the annual cost of the investment—the capital will have been employed at a loss.

From *the periodic investment cost* we can calculate the *capitalized cost* of the investment. Quite simply, this is the amount of capital $K$ which, put out at the current rate of interest, would yield the money necessary to meet the periodic cost.[6] In my example, the *capitalized cost* is:

$$K = \frac{F.176,189.43}{0.10} = F.1,761,894.3$$

If that amount were put out at 10 percent, it would yield F.176,189.43 every year, which would enable interest of 10 percent to be earned on the principal (initial cost of the investment) and the value of that principal to be reconstituted every twenty years.

### Reenter the Labor Theory of Value

The periodic investment cost concept throws light on the labor theory of value. According to that theory, if 30,000 hours of labor have gone, directly or indirectly, into the making of a computer, that computer will be exchanged on the market for another product of 30,000 hours of labor, here assumed to be worth F.1,500,000[7] regardless of its useful life. If the computer purchased by Peter Ltd. were designed to last ten years, say, instead of twenty, its price would be the same if it had taken 30,000 hours of labor to make.

Its price would be the same, but obviously the annual investment cost would not. That would be F.244,118 (instead of F.176,189.43), broken down as follows:

| | |
|---|---:|
| 10% annual interest on "capital employed" | F.150,000 |
| The annuity which, after 10 years at 10% interest, will replace a value of F.1,500,000 | F. 94,111 |
| | F.244,118 |

As for the *capitalized cost,* that will be

$$\frac{F.244,118}{0.10} = F.2,441,180$$

which, invested at 10 percent, would enable an annual income of 10 percent to be obtained on the principal (F.1,500,000) and the value of that principal to be replaced after ten years.

The fundamental idea of capitalized cost corresponds so closely to the nature of things that it is what—without giving it a name—the maker of the automated fruit gatherer, whose imaginary story I told at length in Chapter 4 and the ensuing Appendix 1, based himself upon. The reader will remember that Pierre had almost fallen into the crude accounting error committed by Marx when he thought that his machine had "cost" him ten hours of labor because this was the number of hours he had spent making it and that, furthermore, he could have exchanged it, had he wanted, for the product of another ten hours of labor. But he quickly realized that the full amount—the capitalized cost—of his investment in labor time was twenty hours if the rate of profit was 100 percent (see pp. 113–14). Last, the fruit gatherer in the conditions prevailing on the market (rate of profit: 100%) could pay for itself only if it could yield 4.8 kg of fruit: in other words, exactly the product of twenty hours' labor.

In this ultrasimplified example, the useful life of the capital good (the fruit gatherer) was the same length as the savings reconstitution cycle—that is, one day. The same applies to the computer intended to operate for ten years if the long-term interest rate is 10 percent. The only noteworthy difference between the calculations made by Pierre and by Peter Ltd. is that the sum deducted every year to replace the value of the computer is capitalized at compound interest, which Pierre clearly cannot do in our example because the value of the fruit gatherer is replaced in a single day. But we have seen Pierre use the compound interest calculation (see p. 119) for the machine he made when the rate of interest fell to 50 percent.

As can be seen, the fact that—if the rate at which the deferred exchange is made is 10 percent a year—just F.26,189.43 has to be paid out each year to get back a value of F.1,500,000 at the end of twenty years is not the result of some quirk of monetary economics. Cash accounts simply express to the nearest cent—in other words, with more than acceptable accuracy—the reality of things.

Here I am describing a simplified process. In real economic life, it is perfectly obvious that Peter Ltd. will not be prepared to spend F.1,500,000 on a computer with a lifetime of twenty years unless the firm expects to earn far more than F.176,189.43 annually during the first few years it is in use, the reason being that, in real life, Peter Ltd. will have to allow for a multitude of unknowns that in fact prevent it from reliably forecasting the return on any investment beyond a certain horizon. In our example, the management of the company will be well aware of, among other things, the danger of seeing computer makers launch a new model on the market in a few years' time with a far higher performance (but costing the same), thus forcing them to buy new hardware ahead of time and virtually to write off the old computer, though it be still in perfect working order.

The fact remains—and that is what I wanted to show here—that profit (or, if preferred, the interest on capital) is a vital consideration in deciding whether it pays or not, from the strictly economic standpoint, to make a particular investment. If the investment does not bring the expected return, it means at bottom that *a number of hours of human labor will have been wasted.*

## Ricardo's Futuristic Example

For the central argument of this book, it is of the utmost interest to point out that the analysis of capitalized cost and periodic investment cost, on which the practitioners of investments base themselves, is described in full in Ricardo's work. The circumstances under which Ricardo was induced to change the first exposition he made of his theory of value in relation to the accumulation of capital constitute a highly significant episode in the history of the hostility that fundamental research in this field has practically always encountered. The story is worth telling because, if Ricardo had not given in to his second-rate critics and changed the example from which he had first argued, the history of Western thought might have been different. Ricardo argued first from a "futuristic" example having nothing in common with any type of production known or even foreseeable in his time. He had thought of a hypothetical machine that would last a hundred years and produce certain goods over the whole of that time without the assistance of any human labor whatsoever.

Suppose that an engine is made, which will last for a hundred years, and that its value is £20,000. Suppose too that this machine, without any labour whatsoever, could produce a certain quantity or commodities annually, and that profits were 10%: the whole value of the goods produced would be annually £2,000 2s 11d for

    the profit of £20,000 at 10% per annum is    £2,000
    and an annuity of 2s 11d for 100 years

at 10% will, at the end of that period,
replace a capital of £20,000[8]           2s 11d
                                  ———————
                              £2,000 2s 11d

After which, Ricardo—for the purposes of his argument—varies the rate of profit and calculates what the price of the goods produced would be for each such rate.

Nowadays, there would be nothing unusual about such a supposition. It is no longer utopian, for example, to imagine the building of a nuclear power station electronically remote-controlled and programed in advance, powered by a fast breeder reactor and capable, in those conditions, of operating for one hundred years without any human intervention whatsoever. We may be sure that Ricardo had not the slightest intention of acting the futurologist in a field—technology—which was not his own. He devised his example of an entirely automated, hundred-year machine as an extreme case enabling him, by eliminating labor and payment of labor, to study what would be the value of the goods the sale of which would produce income only in the form of profit. His argument is of the utmost interest to anyone trying to elucidate the classical theory of value, profit, and capital, because he compares the extreme case of the machine without a human operator with a different extreme, that of capital (again £20,000) wholly "employed in supporting productive labour." This brings us to the very heart of the question put by British political economy and to which Marx attempted a reply: How can it be that, if value is based on labor, the product of a machine operating entirely without labor should have sufficient value to produce a profit (over and above replacement of the value of the machine)?

If Marx, who may be thought to have been inspired by the same impartial love of the truth as his illustrious predecessor, had thought about the implications of Ricardo's example, maybe he would have found the true explanation for the problem set by Ricardian theory. The reason he did not pause to think about the futuristic hypothesis of the automated hundred-year machine is probably that Ricardo, in the second edition of *Principles,* had already removed it from his book (nor is it to be found in later editions, all based on the third edition, which was published during Ricardo's lifetime). What made him do this?

The reason is that, in an article which appeared in November 1817, a critic in the *British Review* reviewing the first edition of *Principles,* had ridiculed Ricardo's example. Ricardo then deleted the example from the second edition, although he explained the excision with the following footnote: "To put the principle in a strong point of view, I have supposed a machine to do work without any assistance from human labour, which is evidently impossible. A writer in the *British Review* has absurdly argued as if the supposition was essential to the truth of the principle."[9] This unfortunate episode also shows that to discover phenomena are interlinked, economics—like physics—sometimes has to argue from wholly hypothetical cases that anticipate any possible observation of fact. Seeing in economics no more than the reflection of the conditions and modes of production specific to each era is to deny it all chance of ever acceding to the rank of science. In the first quarter of the nineteenth century, it was inconceivable that a machine could ever operate for a long period without the assistance of any human labor. But there was one great economist who formulated the (true) theory of an economy in which such machines would be in use. In the fourth quarter of the twentieth century such machines already exist (oil refineries, power stations, computers, etc.), but, too busy dressing up the pseudo-logic of Menger, Walras, and Keynes in new trappings, the economists of our day have no time to study the theory of capital, as is clear from the confusion in which the well-known Cambridge controversy on the subject ended.[10]

## Two Riddles Solved

The mechanism of deferred exchange is the only explanation one can give for the creation of value by labor and the origin of profit. This explanation has the merit of converting all the cases that Ricardo saw as exceptions to the theory of value into confirmations of the general principle. In addition, it answers the questions about the origin of value that Ricardo went on asking himself to the last day of his life without ever finding a reply that fully satisfied him.

The objections he put to himself about his own theory turned on two riddles: One, here are two commodities with the same exchange value and yet one requires a considerable amount of labor in its production and the other very little; two, here are two commodities that have required the same quantity of labor to produce and yet their exchange value is different because the time taken to make them is not the same.

It is worth spending some time on these two riddles, for I think it highly probable that future progress in economic science will depend on the rehabilitation of the labor theory of value. Since Marx is of no help to us here, we have no alternative but to take up the question where Ricardo left it.

### Different quantities of labor but same values

Ricardo imagines the following case:[11]

Five wage earners work one year making iron that is then sold at a profit of 20 percent. This profit is added to the capital and, with the increased sum he now has, our entrepreneur takes on six instead of the former five workers. The six make more iron that, at the end of the year, is again sold at a profit of 20 percent, and so on, for twenty years. At the end of that time, the iron has been sold for £100. Ricardo then imagines that the first year a different entrepreneur employs five men to plant oak trees in a field. At the end of twenty years, without any additional work being done in the meantime, he sells the unfelled timber for £100. If one goes no further than the simplistic version of the labor theory of value—that of the author of the "general formula of capital,"[12] say—one is taken aback by this identity of value produced by such disporportionate quantities of labor. Ricardo considers that the question is "completely answered" by the fact that different quantities of "fixed capital" have been employed. It would have been just as simple on his part to have said that the initial capital was *exchanged* several times before the product was sold on the market at a price allowing for this series of exchanges. The point is that it is only because he hopes to sell his timber for £100 that entrepreneur No. 2 is prepared to have lie idle for twenty years the capital that he has committed the first year to pay his five men. If he is unable to sell his final production for £100, he will have failed to capitalize his initial investment at 20 percent. The fact remains that all the oak timber will have required is the labor of five men for twelve months and that it is worth as much as the iron it took twenty years to make in all—the first year five men, the second six, and so on.

To produce the oak timber there was no possible shortcut, no other way of doing it than that followed by the entrepreneur, which was to have five men work for one year to prepare the ground, plant the saplings, and so on.[13] He therefore has to commit an amount of capital corresponding to five wages for twelve months. This capital will be tied up for twenty years. If the sale of the timber did not produce a sum for the entrepreneur equal to this capital invested at 20 percent compound interest for twenty years, he would do better to employ it differently. But since we are supposing (a) that there is a demand for oak timber and (b) that there is no more economical way of making it grow, the conclusion is self-evident: The entrepreneur will exchange the timber, value for like value, for the iron produced in the conditions described above.

One last comment before winding up our consideration of this example. In the eighteenth century, the physiocrats would have found, had they studied such a case, confirmation of their pseudo-theory according to which value was created by nature. In reality, a completely different problem is involved. In any case, whatever the activity concerned, man's productive work always consists in using the laws of nature for his own purposes. In the above example, "nature" is involved both in the growing of the trees and in the making of the iron. What, after all, does an iron maker do but put to use the natural action of heat on materials nature provides? The only difference is that in tree growing, all that is necessary to harness the forces of nature is to work once—every twenty years, say—whereas in iron making the work is continuous, year in, year out. Nature as such causes trees to grow but it never creates value, an obvious fact that, even today, the economics who describe land as "natural capital" are constantly inclined to forget.

### Same quantity of labor but different values

Whenever unequal exchange values correspond to equal quantities of labor, the cause is always the same—the commodity that has more value is the commodity that has required capital to be tied up longer.

Ricardo imagines the following example: An entrepreneur has a capital of £2,000 with the aid of which he engages forty men for one year.[14] It is assumed, for convenience, that our entrepreneur incurs no other expenditure. The raw material his workmen process is assumed to be supplied to him free of charge. If the rate of profit is 10 percent, he will sell the commodity he has produced by the end of the year for £2,200. Another entrepreneur has a capital of £1,000 and takes on twenty workers to tan leather (supplied free of charge). At the end of the year he decides not to sell the leather but to take on twenty workmen again on the same terms to complete the tanning work already begun. At what price does entrepreneur No. 2 have to sell the leather at the end of the second year to be on equal terms with entrepreneur No. 1? One might think that the output of entrepreneur No. 2 has exactly the same exchange value as the output of entrepreneur No. 1 because, in both cases, the same quantity of labor has been spent on it (the labor of 40 men for one year in one case and the labor of 20 men for 2 years in the other). And yet, entrepreneur No. 2, to get the same return on his capital, will have to sell his commodity for £2,310. Why? Because he invested, in the first year, a capital of £1,000 and, in the second year, a capital of £2,100, that is, £1,000 to pay the wages plus £1,100 representing the value of the gross product of the labor supplied by the twenty men during the first year they tanned the leather. Why £1,100? Because, if entrepreneur No. 2 had sold his leather output at the end of that first year he would have received £1,100: £1,000 to recover what he had advanced in wages to his workers and £100 in profit (or net product). Instead of consuming this product, he reinvests it in his enterprise; in other words he defers its exchange. He therefore has to recover its value when the exchange does finally take place.

The reason why this example is so significant is that it immediately makes plain that capital, in all cases, is nothing else but the *accumulated* product of labor and that profit is a result of the exchange of this accumulated product phased over time. This, therefore, brings us to the important finding that ultimately proves, as we shall see, the coherence of the theory of value as here explained: Even in an economy in which human labor were not assisted by any machine, exchange values would not be proportional to labor time if the production processes are of different durations. This seems further reason why the expression "labour theory of value," used traditionally to denote either the theory propounded by the classicists or that developed by Marx, has to be regarded as unsatisfactory. It already has the major drawback, as was made clear in Chapter 4, of seeming to attribute a value to labor, which conflicts with the idea that exchange value is proportional to labor time. But that proportionality is itself valid only for products manufactured in exactly the same conditions.

Once the accumulation of capital takes longer in one production process than in another the principle ceases to hold good, because then allowance has to be made for the incidence of the phenomenon of exchange between capital and profit in which the rate of profit is involved. Let it be noted, however, that in terms of labor time, the capitalized cost of investment No. 1 is higher than that of investment No. 2, which confirms the logic of the theory here set out. *Exchange is inherent in the production process itself.* It is not dissociated from it, as believed by Marx, for whom exchange occurs only before (in the case of labor power) or after the production process (in other words, once the products of labor are offered as commodities on the market). Instead of the labor theory of value, a better expression would be the objective value theory. I shall continue to use the former sometimes because it is the name by which it is known (with all the ambiguities that we have so fully discussed).

### Effect on Exchange Value of a Change in the Rate of Profit

The example prompts a question of considerable interest for economic and monetary theory: What will be the effect of a change in the rate of profit on the relative value of the commodities produced by the two entrepreneurs? Let us suppose that the rate of profit falls from 10 to 5 percent. Does that mean that the price of entrepreneur No. 1's commodity will fall to the same extent? The objective value theory points to the opposite conclusion. The product of the labor of forty men tanning leather for one year will continue to be exchanged for the product of other labor also furnished by forty men in the same conditions. The fall in the rate of profit changes nothing in this fundamental equivalence. Its effect will be to bring about a different share-out of the revenue from the exchange (sale) of the tanned leather. Let us supposed that the leather is exchanged for £2,200.[15] When the rate of profit was 10 percent of the capital, the capitalist kept £200 for himself. The fall in the rate of profit means nothing more than a new distribution of the proceeds to the benefit of the wage earners. A lower rate of profit therefore corresponds to higher wage rates. To pay forty men, our entrepreneur will now need an initial capital of about £2,095 on which he will make 5 percent profit—say, about £104.7. The product will continue to sell for £2,200.

Here we can see why the law of equivalence of exchange, if it is not to be frustrated by the use of money, requires a monetary system in which the money tokens represent the value of a certain product of labor—for example, a given weight of mined and refined gold. Thus, with the gold standard system, the fall in the rate of profit from 10 to 5 percent leaves the monetary value of the tanned leather unchanged: It will always be worth £2,200, or roughly that amount, but this sum will then be differently split between capitalist and wage earners.

The exchange value of the commodity produced by entrepreneur No. 2, however, will be affected by the fall in the rate of profit. Now he will need a capital of about £1,047.6 to employ twenty men the first year. In the second year the capital employed will be:

$$1,047.6 + (0.05 \times 1,047.6) + 1,047.6 = £2,147.6$$

on which value he will make a profit of 5 percent, giving him £2,255 instead of the £2,310 he made when the rate of profit was 10 percent. A more paradoxical twist is given to this conclusion if we say that, other things being equal, an increase in wages—an expression equivalent in Ricardian thinking to a fall in the rate of profit—will have the inevitable effect not of increasing the price of products made by labor-intensive industries but of reducing the prices of manufactured products in whose production the proportion of fixed capital is high, the point being that what distinguishes entrepreneur No. 2 from entrepreneur No. 1 is that his capital has a longer duration than that of entrepreneur No. 1.

The underlying reason why a change in the rate of profit has different effects on the exchange value of the products of our two enterprises is this: In enterprise No. 1, the fall in the rate of profit inevitably has the effect of raising wages, but this reciprocal relationship cannot exist when the rate of profit applies to an *accumulated* product of labor: in other words, the product of past labor.

Many readers will find this explanation beside the point, being too remote from the present conditions of economic life.[16] Even so, the argument is of considerable scientific interest because it explains why it is in practice and *in theory* impossible to have a standard capable of measuring variations in value in time and space. I have already on several occasions referred to the main reason for this impossibility, namely that we do not have and cannot hope to have a commodity the production time of which in hours of labor would be invariable. But even if that condition were met, it would still not be sufficient. The exchange value of our standard in relation to that of other commodities would still, as Ricardo pointed out, be affected by the inevitable changes in the rate of profit. The standard commodity would be an accurate instrument for measuring exchange values only for those commodities the cost price of which incorporated exactly the same proportion of circulating capital and fixed capital (of the same duration). Scientifically speaking, most exchange values are not commensurable. The logic thus confirms that any monetary system, however perfect, is by nature *empirical,* if only because of the fact that prices are always expressed by rational numbers. In no case can money be taken as the equivalent of the exchange value. Here again, it needs to be pointed out that, when Marx and Ricardo talk about measuring value, they stand on completely different ground. The former attributes an historical function to money capital and the latter refers to an abstract standard of value that he calls—for convenience—gold but that has nothing in common—and he repeats this frequently—with real gold[17] and no equivalent in any conceivable commodity. The only advantage to him of the reference to gold is that he wishes to make it clearly understood that, to measure the value of the products of labor, one cannot imagine anything other than a product of labor (gold is the monetary standard, not in the form of natural wealth but as a metal *mined* and *refined* by human labor).

## The Justification of the Full Definition of Capital

It is only after the meaning of the labor theory of value is explained that Ricardo's definition of capital which I quoted early in Chapter 2—"Capital is that part of the wealth of a country which is employed in production . . . necessary to give effect to labour"—becomes clear. Does the last part of this sentence define an essential characteristic of capital goods, in which case the latter would be a subset of goods *employed in production;* or, conversely, is it just a redundancy, a stylistic device to give the sentence a better balance? It would be ridiculous—for Ricardo or anyone else—to resurrect the infallibility argument (adduced so long in the case of Marx, Lenin, and so on) and to advance as a principle that Ricardo can never be wrong. And yet, in dealing with a logical mind of this caliber, the instinct for elementary prudence which, in the absence of modesty, should guide the scientist, requires that he should assume the onus of proof. Before concluding that the definition is rickety or needlessly overelaborate, it needs to be examined in all its aspects. In the light of what has just been said, it is certain that Ricardo did not formulate his definition lightly and that it is not complete without its second part. The reason is that one can imagine many circumstances in which there would be production but no profit. In such a case, the goods employed in production do not, in the strict sense, play the part of capital and, as we have seen, the result then is that the hours of labor spent building up the savings with which these goods have been acquired are *lost* for good. The use made of goods "employed in production" therefore has to make a profit in order "to give effect to labour."

## Notes

1. This in fact is taken directly from Ricardo's work, with a few minor changes to make it less "futuristic"! (See p. 148.)

2. I could just as well have assumed that the replacement cost was lower or higher than the initial cost.

3. Labor applied indirectly to the manufacture of a given commodity is that used in producing the machines, raw materials, and so on that go into the manufacture of that commodity.

4. Three thousand = 10 percent of 30,000 hours plus 53 hours, being roughly, in the circumstances we are considering, the labor time necessary to produce any commodity worth F.26,189.43. In actual fact the calculation is more complicated since we know that, because of capital accumulation in the production process, the exchange value is not exactly proportional to labor time. The phrase "in the production of other goods" is italicized in the text in order to stress that the labor saving concerned is not, of course, the time saving possible with a computer by comparison with manual calculation. This time saving is certainly a large multiple of the labor time spent on manufacturing the machine (with a computer, calculations can be carried out that a hundred human brains working continuously throughout their life would not have enough time for).

5. Compare the excellent *Mathematics of Finance* by Hummel & Secback, published by McGraw-Hill (3d ed., 1970), as practiced by economists when they have to solve problems for a firm.

6. Here that cost is annual but the basis could be daily (as in my simplified example of the automated fruit gatherer), or monthly or quarterly, or again every two, three, or four years, and so on.

7. The labor theory of value assumes that there be some objective base for the value of money. With the franc at its present gold equivalent, F.1,500,000 is equal to 240 kg of 22 carat gold. If gold were really performing its function as a monetary standard, that would mean, in our example, that roughly 30,000 hours of labor would be needed to mine and refine 240 kg of gold (in 1973 values).

8. Ricardo, *Principles* (1st ed.), appendix to chap. 1.

9. Ricardo, *Principles* (2d ed.).

10. That controversy, between the neo-Keynesians (Joan Robinson in particular), who seem to be feeling their way back to classicism, and the American neoliberals (Samuelson, Solow, etc.) is highly interesting, primarily because it reveals below the surface the theoretical confusion in contemporary economics due to unclarified general concepts. Much of the reason for the controversy was that the protagonists did not agree on the very subject of their debate, as Solow admitted when he wrote, in 1962, "I have long since abandoned the illusion that participants in this debate actually communicate with one another, so I omit the standard polemical introduction and get down to business at once." The fact remains that, through this controversy, we can see the basic Ricardian concepts laboriously gaining ground in the minds of the participants or, at least, supplying the answers to questions which they have put, better in some cases than in others, and left unanswered.

11. In Ricardo's *Fragments on Torrens,* vol. 4 of *Complete Works,* ed. Piero Sraffa (Cambridge, U.K.: Cambridge University Press, 1966), pp. 312–13.

12. Marx, see present volume, p. 17.

13. In reality, some work would have to be done looking after the trees, weeding, clearing, and so on, for the following nineteen years, but for the convenience of argument, it is assumed that this expenditure is negligible or else included in the capital expenditure of the first year.

14. Ricardo, *Principles,* chap. 1, sec. 4.

15. That amount being assumed to represent the value of a quantity of gold mined and refined by forty men in the same conditions. Since, however, the gold industry does not require the same proportion of fixed and circulating capital, the change in the rate of profit causes slight changes in gold prices, which are disregarded here.

16. Although it does explain why, in our present period of inflation, a steep increase in wages has far less effect on the prices of manufactured products than on the prices of services.

17. The essential difference being that the cost of producing gold varies with time.

*6*

# The Structure of Capitalism

The objective value theory of which the British classical school laid the foundations explains better than any other the workings of capitalism, for which it would be preferable to substitute the term *exchange economy*.

## Capitalism "Condemns" Human Society to Work

Because of the fact that, for enterprise X to make its profit, enterprise Y has to have expended "fresh labor," and vice versa, an economy based on freedom of exchange is, by nature, highly dynamic. Exchange (i.e., trade) is an unending summons to produce new goods and new services and, as we shall see, the exchange economy is the more dynamic in that it favors production rather than value.

In the preceding pages, we showed the identity of savings and capital, profit being nothing more, at bottom, than the phased reconstitution of savings. It is relevant to note that the most modern economic thinking bases its explanation of the phenomenon of growth on that identity.

The Swedish economist Göran Ohlin, who is professor at Uppsala University, writes:

Saving or capital formation then corresponds exactly to the income to capital. It is interesting to *recall that the classic economists generally assumed that the incomes of capitalists were saved and used for capital*

159

*formation*. Here, however, it is sufficient that saving is as large as the income to capital regardless of how saving is actually achieved. Another way of expressing these conditions for a growth path that yields maximum consumption at all times is to say that *real interest or the yield from capital must be exactly the same as the natural rate of growth,* neither higher nor lower.[1]

Profit is the "net product": in other words, what is left of the gross product after reconstituting the value of the products consumed by the production process. Several modern economists call this net product "surplus," which is almost exactly the same as the expression used by Ricardo ("overplus"). It designates the excess of production over the consumption necessary for that prod˙˙ ˙tion.[2]
Basically, there are the following alter˙. ˙ves.

Profit may be reinvested in whole or in part. The growth rate is at its maximum if all the profit is reinvested.

The profit may be wholly applied to nonproductive spending by private persons or by the state. In this case accumulation ceases (zero growth).

The third alternative is more theoretical: The rate of profit itself may fall to zero. According to Ricardo this could arise from only one cause: the growing scarcity of natural resources (primarily arable land), which would increase the price of food so much that the whole of the gross product would be used up in the form of wages (see Chapter 7). There being no profit; saving would become impossible. The difference between this and the preceding hypothesis (profit maintained but zero saving) is that society—or the capitalists—would have to forgo the enjoyment procured by the nonproductive spending.

Two stationary states are therefore conceivable, one with the net product maintained but wholly applied to nonproductive expenditure and the other with zero profit.

### As it progresses, economics comes closer to the classical model

Once we accept that profit or *net income* is nothing other than the phased reconstitution of earlier savings, it is clear, logically, that the object of this reconstituted value is to act as savings in its turn (being exchanged for the product of fresh labor) so as to perpetuate the process of accumulation. This logic, however, can operate fully only as from a certain level of economic development. For as long as most of the capital is "circulating" and entrepreneurs are also the owners of their enterprises, profit is personal income and, as such, is highly likely to be partly dissipated in nonproductive spending. As soon as the proportion of fixed capital becomes larger, things are no longer the same.

Here is a fresh illustration of the logical and, at the same time, historical nature of the gradual objectivization of economics. As long as the personal enterprise predominates, profit is, partly at least, a personal income. When the differentiated type of enterprise—in which the management function is no longer merged with ownership—takes its place, profit is employed for its destined purpose; it *appears* as what it *is*, namely that part of total income used to increase existing capital.

Modern economics, therefore, puts into effect, for the first time, the theoretical construct of the classical economists, for whom all income from capital was reinvested.

**The nonwidening gap**

The apparent paradox of the situation of the underdeveloped countries is now being finally dispelled. In these countries, the rate of profit is very high (about 30% at least) and yet growth there is still generally weak. The explanation is that profit is largely spent as income by the capitalists. This state of affairs is now changing rapidly in several countries especially those where the government systematically favors the entrepreneurial class, whose function is precisely to find "profitable" uses for the potential capital that profit represents. In most cases the transition from the state of underdevelopment to an accumulative economy appears to be the result of the deliberate intervention of *political* power.

The renewal and growth of the capital stock puts one in mind of the process whereby the human species is renewed and grows. Every ten to twelve years—every two to five years in the poor countries where fixed capital is undeveloped—there is a new generation of capital, just as every twenty-five to thirty years there is a new generation of human beings. This pattern of existence and development ought to have put the columnists—with certain economists, unfortunately, among their number—on guard against the logically inconsistent and yet widespread idea that the expansion of our economic system must *necessarily* mean that the gap between developed and less developed countries (LDCs) will widen still further as time goes by. In its simplicity, the argument seems faultless. In country A—one of the rich ones—per capita income is, say, $2,500 a year. In country B, on the bottom rung of the ladder, per capita income—taking the good years with the bad, but the bad years outnumber the good—is $400. Even on the highly optimistic assumption that growth rates in national income and population are the same in both countries, the per capita income gap will keep increasing by geometric progression. In the first year considered, the gap was $2,500 − 400 = $2,100. After four years, assuming a 3 percent annual growth rate in per capita income, the gap will be

$$2,500 (1 + 0.03)^4 - 400 (1 + 0.03)^4$$
$$= \$2,813.7 - \$450.2 = \$2,363.5$$

This, if we are to believe certain reports from international institutions, is "mathematical" reasoning.

Here I would like the reader to consider this purely empirical thought: The exponential equation being about the only thing (perhaps because it *appeals to the imagination*) that nonmathematicians remember about mathematics, the fact is that a theory based on geometric progression has a good chance of being wrong, because this formula is often applied just for the sake of it.

Here, we arrive at a very different conclusion if we allow for the rate of profit being usually much higher in LDCs. The big problem is to reinvest the profit instead of spending it nonproductively. Success (for which the spur of intelligent policymaking is necessary) will almost always produce a rate of growth far higher than growth rates in the developed countries, so that it is possible to catch up.

The object here, need I add, is purely to arrive at the internal logic of a system: Reality of course is less simple. Without any doubt, the existence of an old industrial—or cultural—tradition is an advantage of the first order; with but a few exceptions, takeoff is possible only if there is a long-established core of activity or culture.

**Profit is proportional to the capital employed, not the number of workers taken on**

The reason here lies in the deferred exchange mechanism as explained in earlier chapters. Say one entrepreneur puts all his capital (F.1,000,000) into employing workmen and another invests all his capital (same figure) in long-duration fixed plant. On a competitive market, they ought in principle to make about the same annual profit on their capital—say 10 percent—because, if that were not the case, capital would shift from one activity to another. According to the labor theory of value as interpreted by Marx, the profit of the highly mechanized firm could come only from a redistribution among the various enterprises of the surplus value generated by the labor-intensive industries percolating through the whole of the capitalist class. This is what he explains so laboriously in volume 3 of *Capital*. So this would mean that profit, which finances—we should remember—future investment, is the responsibility of technologically the least developed sectors of the economy. In France, for example, the declining textile industries of the Vosges would, indirectly, be the source of the abundant self-financing resources available to the petrochemical industry with its small work force relative to the value of its capital! It is sufficient to spell out the practical implications of Marxist theory to realize its absurdity. Apart from any other argument, Ockham's principle—according to which, of two theories explaining the same phenomenon the one to choose is that which goes more directly to the point—would be enough to prefer Ricardo's approach to labor theory of value to that of Marx.

**Inflation imposes a subjective conception of time**

Unless things are distorted for one reason or another—and the most frequent of these causes of deviation is monetary inflation—the capitalist system is favorable to long-term investment. If I have the following choice for investing a capital of F.1,500,000—to buy an automatic machine that will run for twenty years yielding an annual product of F.176,189.43 (see Chapter 5, pp. 143–44) or to take on workmen the product of whose labor I could sell for F.1,650,000 a year—there would be serious arguments in favor of the first alternative although both would produce the same annual income:

*1st alternative*—annual product F.176,189.43, of which F.150,000 is profit and F.26,189.43 is depreciation;
*2nd alternative*—annual product F.1,650,000, of which F.150,000 is profit and F.1,500,000 is recovery of the capital paid out in wages.

The second alternative is less attractive in many respects than the first. It involves the trouble caused by a far higher annual turnover (F.1,650,000 instead of F.176,189.43) and the risks are much greater because I shall be obliged to replace every year the value of my material capital since otherwise I would not be in a position to keep my enterprise going on the same scale.

The comparison of these two examples calls for one other general comment. Early on in this book I stressed the point that in classical political economy the present was given no precedence over the future. The proof that this was not simply an opinion is that, on the basis of purely economic considerations unaffected by any moral or philosophical aspect, long-term investment seems from several standpoints to be more advantageous or in any case at least as favorable.

Such a state of affairs cannot, however, exist without a sufficiently objective monetary system—that is to say, one that enables the phased exchange mechanism to operate up to the limits of the economic horizon (20–30 years?). Such a system, as I have already had occasion to point out several times, has to be founded on a standard the value of which, too, is determined by the labor time necessary to produce it. The system's stability is ensured by the fact that the quantity of labor (to which—allowing for the rate of profit—value is proportional) needed to produce the standard commodity may be expected to vary roughly to the same degree as for all goods and services supplied on the market.

Here, therefore, we have the organic link between economic system and monetary system. For its conception of time to prevail, objective economics has to have an adequate monetary system. As we know, for economics, time has, so to speak, a uniform character whatever moment is being considered. By means of the deferred exchange mechanism, any product currently available can be exchanged for the product of future labor. It is sufficient to know the rate of profit—which undergoes only slight variations over time, as we have also had occasion to note—to calculate straightaway the present value of a future product or the future value of a present product used as capital. The calculation of *capitalized cost* (discussed at length in Chapter 5) has to be based on the neutrality of objective economic science toward different moments in time, because this cost is defined as the sum of the initial expenditure (first cost) *effectively* incurred in purchasing (or producing) a given asset—such as a machine, a house, and so on—and the "present value" at which the perpetuity which would cover the cost of replacing that asset is *estimated by calculation*.

It is therefore solely in the fact that the present moment has no absolute value eclipsing all else, that economics is a *social* science.

## Capital Is a Permanent Advance

As long as a person who has built up savings in the circumstances that I have described does not decide to consume them, they are available to him for use as a permanent advance. The point is that the reproduction process to which he commits his savings (capital employed) results in his being reimbursed their value at more or less frequent intervals (depending on the rate of profit). Once the phased exchange has come to an end, the transaction must be regarded as completed. Most probably, however, the "capitalist" will recommit his initial stake (and possibly part of the profit he will have earned) in the same enterprise. For the economist, this would be a fresh investment. The "permanent advance" function of capital explains why, in countries where the legal system conforms with the law of exchange, all "nationalization" or expropriation measures give rise to "fair compensation" regardless of the number of times that the capital has already turned over.

This does not necessarily imply that a government is always in the wrong to refuse to pay all the compensation claimed by a particular foreign company. It may be justified, since the big companies of the West have often misused their power to exploit the natural wealth of economically undeveloped and politically weak countries.

It is appropriate here to stress once again that the principle of equivalence of exchange, while it provides a seemingly unshakeable basis for the economic system, could well have unacceptable consequences at the social level. The fact that capital has this nature of a "permanent advance" means that there is a constant tendency toward accumulation of wealth by the few, and experience shows that even the fiercest competition between producers (the effect of which is to challenge established positions) and the spread of saving to new strata of the population change the distribution of the national wealth among the various categories of the population only slowly and inadequately.

The aim of economics is not to justify the existing "social order." It is to explain the mechanisms of economic life which it is pointless to ignore. It is absurd, for example, to demand an improvement in the physical well-being of the population and at the same time to want to abolish profit when profit is the source of new capital and when, consequently, an economy ceasing to produce profit would cease to make any material progress. That having been said, the question of the distribution of the fruits of growth cannot be settled purely by applying the equivalence-of-exchange principle.

It would be futile to pretend that the system, left to itself, would not lead to the concentration of practically all capital in the hands of a restricted number of individuals and families. The fact is that this state of affairs is in general fairly well accepted since one finds that invariably far less policing is necessary to enforce the law in the *inegalitarian* society of the liberal countries (in the European sense) based on the *equivalence-of-exchange principle,* than in the egalitarian or egalitarian-oriented societies of the socialist countries. The underlying reason is probably that, if all men are to be equal, there have to be more prohibitions in order to reduce exchanges between them to the minimum. At least, that is the explanation that political economy suggests.

## The Compound Rate of Interest, or the Paradox of the Franc Invested in AD 1

The "permanent advance" function of capital also explains the mechanism of the rate of interest, something else to have been almost wholly obscured through the invasion of economics by psychological (or pseudo-psychological) concepts.

The rate of interest is generally termed the "cost of money." It is the ratio (expressed as a percentage) between the income from capital and the amount of that capital. It is supposed that this income is in the form of a perpetuity, which amount is divided by the value of the corresponding capital. We are familiar with the misunderstanding to which this concept has given rise in the minds of laymen. How is it that in exchange for the present payment of a *finite sum of money* (a capital of F.1, for example) one can obtain an *infinite* sequence of income (e.g., 3 centimes a year if the rate is 3%)? In layman's terms, this naive wonder could be expressed apocryphally as follows. If a man had invested in perpetuity, in the year AD 1, a coin of 160 mg of fine gold—in other words equal to the official value of one present-day franc in 1970—at 3 percent (or even at a much lower rate), the capitalized interest would then be a weight of gold equal to several times the weight of the earth. Even if the interest had been paid in paper money rather than gold, the value it would represent would be such that it would be enough to buy all the wealth that exists today several times over. The fabulous return on the franc invested in AD 1 is to economics something like what Zeno's arrow is to kinetics.

To explode the sophism, all that is necessary is to refer to one of the most evident—although one of the most regularly forgotten—propositions of the classical theory, without which economic life, taken as a whole, ceases to be intelligible, namely that money of itself is not capital because it is not money that directly gives "effect to labor."

Remember the computer (see Chapter 5). Clearly the source of the income is not the sum of F.1,500,000 but the computer. So if I want to secure a perpetual income, I shall need to scrap the old machine every twenty years and replace it by another. Similarly, if I own a house, I shall have to rebuild it every twenty (or 30, or 40 . . .) years to continue to receive the income with which it provides me.

Money, in itself, is completely inert, incapable of generating any income whatsoever. The interest it bears represents the value of the real goods and services that existing real capital produces (or yields). What is illusory in the tale of the franc invested in AD 1 is not the tale itself. It is possible, at the farthest stretch of the imagination, to conceive of an ancestor of mine investing the equivalent of one franc almost 2000 years ago and that investment being handed down to me from generation to generation (although successive generations will have consumed, i.e. destroyed, their income). The illusion is in suspending disbelief and thinking that the monetary system could operate independently of the economic system, the only producer of income.

The reader will no doubt be thinking that I have overlabored the point, but restating these obvious facts does at least have the advantage of showing that the rate of interest (on money) is purely the rate of profit (on capital) in another form. Unfortunately, modern economics turns its back on this conception without which, however, it is absolutely impossible to embark on an *objective* analysis of the causes determining the level of the rate of interest over the long term. As for the short-term level of the rate of interest, that is more directly affected by contingent decisions, depending on the monetary authorities, but the flow of the relevant income comes from real profit.

Here again, it is easy to show that the deviations to which modern theories about the rate of interest give rise have a cause with which we are familiar. It is the withdrawal from objective research in which the researcher sees exchange—including therefore exchange between the borrower (who sells a claim on himself) and the lender (who buys that claim with the money he lends)—as a fact that science has a duty to consider as such. Since the end of the nineteenth century this method has been replaced by another that consists in explaining the level of the rate of interest, like everything else, by subjective factors. The culmination of this curious "scientific" approach was the theory of Keynes, for whom the rate of interest is nothing other than the price to be paid to win "the preference" that every owner of money is supposed to have for "liquidity." Culmination but also dead end because, as soon as they are faced with reality, economists realize that the concept of "liquidity preference" is of no help to them, which is why, here too, they are in the process of rediscovering the path of objective concepts.

Keynes's theory on the rate of interest has been the source of serious errors of economics committed during the last forty-five years or so, particularly in the English-speaking countries. Keynes—who openly admits[3] that Ricardian theory is valid in the long term in the event that full employment is achieved—recommends a policy based on a reversal of the causal link established by the classical school. To increase the volume of investment, he recommends that the central bank lower the rate of interest below what he calls the "marginal efficiency of capital," his expression for the rate of profit. It was by virtue of this principle that, from 1945 up to the mid-1960s, the Bank of England attempted to reduce the cost of money by increasing the quantity of money (the Bank's purchase of public debt issues sent up their price). The most tangible result of this policy was to fuel chronic inflation, while the rate of investment in Great Britain remained at a lower level than in most comparable countries. Neither did this Keynesian-inspired policy secure full employment, because the rate of unemployment has remained consistently higher in Great Britain than in the other industrialized countries of Europe. The mistake was that a policy to reduce artificially the rate of interest must inevitably interfere with the functioning of the monetary system, while constituting a doubtful—and in any case very temporary—means of stimulating investment. The rate of interest depends on the rate of profit, not vice versa.

The psychological theory of the rate of interest also has the particular feature of favoring one of the two parties to the exchange—the lender. This bias has been systematic since the famous analysis of the rate of interest by Irving Fisher which has influenced all modern economists. Irving Fisher distinguished the real from the nominal market rate, the latter generally being higher than the former to allow for rising prices.

But this again is a psychological argument which was claimed to hold the explanation of why interest rates rise in times of inflation.[4] It is quite true that at such times lenders will seek to obtain a rate high enough to compensate for the loss they expect on the principal due to the continued inflation they think probable. But this defensive reaction is not itself the reason why the market rate goes up. The wish of the lender is matched by the hope of the borrower, who in his case counts on inflation to cheapen his debt repayments. Does this mean that the effective rate will settle at about the midway point, at a level that still satisfies the lender's expectations though appearing to be "advantageous" enough to the borrower (two requirements that are contradictory if we assume that both sides forecast the same rate of inflation)? Apart from the fundamental objection (the subject of this book) which has to be made to the psychological approach to economics, that approach presents the particular disadvantage of having ever to remain incomplete because some motive or other will always be left in the dark until it emerges, in a certain situation, as the reason why behavior in the market is what it is. What happens on the market can be better understood if, like the classicists, we concentrate on the seller (in this case the seller of claims on himself—namely, the borrower). In the economic system, he is also the producer of real goods and services and on his reckoning will depend the answers to the crucial question on which everything that follows will hinge: Is the loan worth taking or not—and if so, at what rate of interest, in light of the profit the business to be financed may be expected to yield? The long-term rate tends to be governed by the rate of profit, which is why it changes fairly slowly over time. Inflationary pressures are communicated to the financial market via the short-term rate.

Inflation begins when all borrowers issue claims (which constitute the counterpart to money in circulation) which exceed in aggregate, other things being equal, the lenders' capacity to meet those claims out of current receipts. An increase in the "supply" of claims in the money market (a better name for which would be claims or debts market) tends to lower their price, which automatically raises the rate of interest. The central bank may, for a time, be able to paper over the cracks by increasing its operations in the open market—in other words, by increasing the volume of its purchases of claims. In this way it artifically keeps the price up. It is in this sense, and in this sense only, that the increase in the money supply may, as Keynes said, bring down the rate of interest. But such a policy can be only temporary, because it stimulates fresh borrowing (through a lower interest rate than that which the market, left to itself, would establish) and merely suppresses—or damps down—for a time the effects of inflation while, below the surface, fuelling inflation itself.

From this it appears that the only way out of inflation would be to curb the discretionary power of the central bank to issue money (and thereby govern the level of interest rates) through its operations on the open market. This discretionary power is at the origin of what—although never mentioned—is probably the greatest anomaly and dysfunction of modern economies, namely the fact that at the very heart of the capitalist system—the market where money is created—prices are permanently distorted. An ideal situation would be one in which the value of debts (and therefore the level of interest rates) would be freely settled in the market, the role of the central bank (restored to its function of lender of last resort) being to regulate—not set—interest rate trends through intermittent intervention (so the intervention rate of the central bank would normally be pegged above the market rate). In such a situation, interest rates would usually be low, because commercial banks, not relying any longer on quasi-automatic refinancing through the central bank, would only admit into their assets loans that were self-liquidating (a concept that needs to be revived). The value of such claims would not need artificial support. Debt as a whole would no longer play a predominant role in financing economic activities; equity capital would be reinstated.

In this theory, only objective facts are involved. First, on the basis of an analysis of the characteristics of money and the claims markets, the mechanisms are defined that will ensure, on conditions that also have to be defined, effective regulation of the issue of money. It will then be seen that the famous psychological factors often advanced by modern economists to explain inflation (transactors' expectations, for example) are simply the reaction of transactors to the deviation (which can be determined objectively) imposed on the credit mechanisms.

The reason why inflation sends up prices is that the *value* of money is falling. What does the value of money (a concept abandoned since Keynes called it a "mirage" or "will-o'-the-wisp" in his *A Treatise on Money,* published in 1930) depend on? It depends on the value of the claims for which money is issued in counterpart. It is via the claims market that the trend in the general level of prices is brought into relation with the rate of interest.

Marx, for his part, thought he had made a startling discovery in asserting that the rate of interest is no more than transformed surplus value. This assertion is a rather pale reflection of the classical theory, which held that interest is only one of the forms taken by profit.

## Rate of Profit and the Consumer Society

With the classical definition of capital that we have adopted, the working population's consumption may be described as the destruction of capital that is constantly renewed. To see the truth of this, all we have to do is to reason, as we have often done before, in terms of real goods. It is then clear that circulating capital, instead of being distributed in wages, is in fact made up of agricultural produce, clothing, housing and transport services, vacation facilities, and so on, in short all the goods and services into which wages paid in the form of money, for greater convenience and freedom, are converted.

It is often said that consumption is the motor of growth (whence the emphasis placed on demand), but this is a superficial view of things that only proves true in the short term. By that I mean that, in economies like ours, if consumer buying were suddenly to slow down, the firms that work to supply the market would indeed also be compelled to cut back their activity. But if things are considered over a longer period, they appear in a completely different light. The more the work force consumes, the greater the share of productive effort devoted to replacing the capital employed in production. If, conversely, consumption were lower, there is no prima facie reason to suppose that total production—measured in terms of gross product—would be any less. It would be differently distributed, the share of the net product or profit being greater (at this stage in the argument I am not yet concerned with the question of who receives, or should receive, the profit—see Chapter 8). What would this mean? That a part of the new production, previously devoted to replacing capital, would be available for fresh investment at home and abroad. In other words, the growth rate would be quickened, not slowed down. This increase in the reinvested net product would also bring about a change of direction in production and a redistribution of consumption which, a point to stress, would in no way be reduced *overall*.

This last point is worth dwelling upon because no contrast is more frequently made than between "consumption" and "capital formation" (or saving). It is the old exhortation: Tighten your belts to rebuild the country, prepare the ground for the well-being of future generations, and so on. And yet, even though they contain a large element of truth, these maxims may be the cause of a misconstruction for the following reason. If one thing is certain it is that the whole of production giving rise to the distribution of gross income is *consumed*. Now in the case of a country called upon to restrain its wants in order to build up its infrastructure, a greater share of activity will be devoted to producing machines, railway lines, power stations, and so on, the consumption of which (i.e., destruction by use) will be slower. In other cases, a greater part of activity will be applied to the production of goods for export, this in many respects being the same thing as saving. The production of capital and exportable goods in the end means the payment of wages, so the following general conclusion may be formulated: The combination of lower personal consumption (in relative terms) and a high proportion of saving leads not to a fall but to a rise in employment.[5]

Our societies are able to create an enormous mass of goods and services; but since the larger part of economic activity is devoted to continuous renewal of this stock, the impression that is given of "material progress" is partly false. If net income were higher as the result of slower growth in "consumption" (the word being used here in its currently accepted meaning), the accumulation of capital would increase and by that very fact our towns and roads would become less congested because of the change in the allocation of productive resources. The (relative) decrease in consumption in the rich countries would release the resources necessary to equip the less developed countries. Today the former countries are not even investing so much as 1 percent of their national income in the Third World, in spite of the undertakings they have made. Prior to 1913, Great Britain was investing something like 10 percent of its income abroad, mainly in the poor countries (even today, the transport infrastructures of the countries of Asia and Latin America date back to the nineteenth century). If the economies of the big "capitalist" countries changed their pattern, vast additional resources could be mobilized to equip the world. The problem would be to find the legal and political arrangements to prevent the huge capital flows from being accompanied by massive transfers of ownership.

### Any Capitalist Enterprise Implies a Risk but Profit Is Only Secondarily the "Recompense of Risk"

Since a capitalist enterprise, regardless of its size and purpose and the time at which it carries on its activity, consists in committing a certain capital in an exchange phased over time, it always runs the risk of not finding another party to the exchange, which will certainly happen if, for example, the enterprise embarks on the production of an article or service the demand for which proves to be lower than expected, or if it miscalculates its costs. The fact remains that profit is not, truly speaking, the reward of that risk—which is amply shown in our analysis of profit thus far. It is one thing, however, to study the act of exchange objectively as the economist must do and another to be involved in it oneself. In the eyes of the entrepreneur, the profit he hopes for will almost inevitably seem to be his reward for the risk he has been prepared to shoulder. From his standpoint, this way of looking at things is very understandable and it would be ridiculous to chide him for it. But if the economist insists on describing profit as "compensation" for the risk, he explains nothing; he is simply making a psychological interpretation.

The marginalists go through all sorts of intellectual contortions trying to explain a phenomenon that is not a built-in feature of their model. One of the most common of their explanations is to ascribe profit to "entrepreneurial capacity." There is no question that it is vital for an enterprise to be well managed but, if it is, then the profit it makes is the result of exchange that good entrepreneurship renders possible, and not the magic of some deus ex machina. Here again, Milton Friedman's work is a typical illustration. It uses elusive concepts to mask the powerlessness of modern economics (or at least the majority current of thought in modern economics) to bring profit into its equations and curves. "Pure profit" Milton Friedman sees as "an unanticipated residual arising from uncertainty." It is true that the best managed enterprises make higher profits than the others, but how can economic analysis progress if it does no more than qualify the extra profit that is the result of this circumstance—and of certain others—as "residue"? Residue of what? The picture immediately becomes clearer if we take the classicists' viewpoint and see this extra profit as a "rent" (see Chapter 8 and 12), on top of the average rate of return on capital. Milton Friedman's "pure profit" is impure profit.

### Absence of profit is equivalent to a loss

Because profit is net income, it is customary to liken it to an *absolute gain,* the received idea which Marx enshrined in theory by introducing the surplus value concept. In reality, however, the classical labor theory of value, correctly interpreted, confirms what every entrepreneur knows from experience: Absence of profit is not a break-even operation but a loss in real terms. If an enterprise that has employed capital in its business makes no income out of its activity over and above the transfer of the value attaching to the act of production (see Appendix 1 to Chapter 4), it has nullified in the same proportion the earlier savings effort it has had to make to build up its capital. It if were possible to keep general accounts in hours of work, it would be seen that some of that time would purely and simply have been spent in vain. In the fact that absence of profit represents wasted labor can be seen the proof, to the contrary, that the generation of profit is a matter of an exchange operation.

### The method of asset evaluation

Present-day accounting seesaws constantly between two methods for evaluating balance sheet assets: one based on the cost of the asset and the other on an estimate of the "present value" of a capital asset in terms of the flow of future income expected from it. Theoretical works on this question generally state that the former method is an application of the labor theory of value whereas the latter, now increasingly frequent in practice, stems from the "psychological" or modern theory; as we saw in the two preceding chapters, the labor theory of value recognizes as capital only those assets that are capable of bringing in a certain minimum income in the future. Say I have F.1,500,000 and am a builder and that the average rate of profit is 10 percent. It would not be *worth*—in the full sense of the word—the trouble of building a house lasting twenty years unless I could reasonably expect it to produce a gross annual income of F.176,189.43, broken down as follows: net annual income F.150,000 plus depreciation F.26,189.43 (see Chapter 5, p. 144). This profitability calculation, at the level of the economy as a whole, can only be worked out by comparing the initial cost of the investment with the income *expected* of it. I stress the word "expected" because it denotes the difference in standpoint, already pointed out on several occasions, between the economist who considers the act of exchange ex post and the businessman, who will not know the overall result of the operation until later: in other words, when it is too late to redress the situation if, by chance, he has miscalculated. Suppose the builder has overestimated the qualities of the house and can only let it at an annual rent of under F.176,189. Suppose, next, that he has to sell the house. Clearly he will not find a buyer ready to pay F.1,500,000 because the buyer could not care less about how many hours of labor went into the building. The only thing he is interested in is the income that his new capital[6] will earn him. Suppose the annual rent he could get is F.155,000; he will work out the maximum price at which he is prepared to buy the house, on the basis of that income, and arrive at a figure of F.1,319,602.3.[7]

From his standpoint, this is the only rational evaluation method. But anyone can see that this standpoint is not that of the economist, who must not espouse the interests of either party to an exchange. For the purposes of economic theory, the initial investment has really cost the economy so many hours of labor. If the good created by this labor does not bring in a commensurate income it means that the house, in present market conditions, has only partly the nature of capital. Part of the labor time spent building it would have been better used elsewhere. The result is a loss that needs to be recorded in the accounts. Note here that in this example the loss is indeed sustained by the seller, who parts with the house for F.1,319,602. But to describe the exchange transaction in its entirety, the seller's figures have to be compared with those of the buyer. This comparison shows that the central fact, in drawing up the overall balance sheet, is the cost of the initial investment.

It is time for modern thinking to break, once and for all, with the doctrine of the late nineteenth and early twentieth century economists who, from the method of calculating the present value of a capital on the basis of the income it is supposed to bring in, draw the strange conclusion that the value of an asset is not determined by its production cost but by the services expected of it. This, for example, is what Irving Fisher wrote in *The Nature of Capital and Income,* chapter 11, page 88:

> The principle of present worth is of fundamental importance in the theory of value and prices. It means that the value of any article of wealth and property is dependent alone on the future, not the past. The principle has been imperfectly stated as follows: "The value of any article is not determined by its cost of production, but by its uses." But the costs of production are disservices and these, if they be *future,* enter into value on precisely the same terms as uses or services.

In saying this, Irving Fisher misunderstands the basic principle whereby depreciation is intended to enable the full value of the investment to be recovered.

It is only by reference to the labor cost of an investment and the possibility for that cost to be recouped with a profit, that we can—with some luck!—tell, from the standpoint of the community, what is and what is not capital. Economists reasoning like Irving Fisher are unable to say.[8] To go back to my example, they put themselves solely in the position of the buyer acquiring the house for F.1,319,602 without realizing that, on the basis of this price, the profit it brings in does not permit replacement of the entire amount of the savings sacrificed by the community for the building of the house. The Cambridge controversy we referred to earlier would suggest that no progress has been made in clarifying the question of capital since Irving Fisher.

Fisher's words lead us to ask another question: Does the "disservice" notion that he uses offer a real symmetry with the "service" concept? Later on, Keynes similarly used the term "disutility of labour" to describe the effort it cost the workman. The latter would stop looking for a job when the marginal disutility of labor exceeded its marginal utility measured in terms of wages. Here, the lack of symmetry seems still more conspicuous.

### The Objective Value Theory Puts Increase in Product Before Conservation of Value

From the above we shall now be able to derive what is probably the most important consequence of the objective value theory. It is the most important because, through it, classical political economy is seen to be the most powerful organizational principle available to society to increase and multiply its material wealth, including what today is called "social overhead capital," characterized in most cases by the long period of time over which its consumption extends.

That consequence is this: In an economy whose functioning is regulated by the strict rule of exchange equivalence, entrepreneurs will find they are obliged by the nature of things to sacrifice the *value* of their capital whenever this prior sacrifice has to be made to ensure an increase in production. At first sight, it seems surprising, particularly after what we have just said about reconstituting the value of the initial saving, that a theory based on the principle of objective value should lead to an increase in product being put before the conservation of value. So strange does it appear, one would almost be tempted to give this conclusion a dialectical form: Does it not consist in one assertion giving rise to its opposite? In reality, the primacy of production is imposed by the *logic* of the system. It is both rationally demonstrable and empirically verifiable. It would not be going too far to see in it the explanatory principle of economic growth. At the theoretical level, it forms the decisive issue in the conflict between the thinking of Ricardo and that of Marx, the arena where their singular combat ends in the total victory of the economist with the mathematical mind over the economist trained in the philosophy of Hegel (or what he thought to be the dialectic of Hegel).

For Marx, the raison d'être of capital, of which he says money "is the first form of appearance" (see Chapter 11), is to secrete capital—that is, in the last analysis, exchange value. For Ricardo, capital—defined as all commodities employed in production—has the "effect" of increasing the *product* of labor. Before going any further, let us dwell a moment on the vocabulary used by our two authors, any critique of economics being necessarily, at the outset, of a semantic character. Close reading of Ricardo's work will show that, to designate profit, he uses the terms "net produce" or "surplus produce." To my knowledge he only once uses the term "overplus" in the sense of extra "value" (in *Principles,* chap. 6), the expression out of which Marx fashioned his famous surplus *value* concept.

Economic science in its most modern version is now going back to Ricardian concepts in this field too, since its analyses of profit and growth are framed in terms of surplus, or net *product* available once that part of annual production intended for current consumption has been destroyed and reconstituted. But the thinking is still incomplete because of the impoverishment of the conceptual tools used by economists ever since the hedonists of the late nineteenth century once again confused value and want, as a result of which they have assimilated any increase in the number of products intended to satisfy our wants with an increase in value. This manner of presentation prevents them from putting in clear terms the permanent conflict into which the growth process resolves itself. Economic life, considered in its dynamic aspects, is driven by the tension unfailingly and continuously caused by the advent of new production processes that save labor time. The introduction of previously unknown methods to reduce the *cost of production* has the inescapable effect of knocking out of the race a large number of machines, equipment, techniques, and so on, in other words various accumulated products of past labor that have become prematurely obsolete. Put another way, progress, the sole object of which is to increase labor productivity, causes—as its first result—the loss of part of the products of labor already accumulated. In this antinomy, Marxism sees one of the many "contradictions" of capitalism. Political economy, more simply, sees in it a "problem" to be solved. One suspects that the solution is to be found in a comparison between the advantage to be expected from increased production and the disadvantage to be suffered through the loss of an item of capital that has not yet been "written off." One suspects, too, that the reasoning cannot be conducted clearly unless, from the beginning to the end of the process, a careful distinction is maintained between the product and its value: ultimately, between production and *social* cost of production. The stressing of the word "social" is more necessary here than in any other field because to tackle the problem from the specific viewpoint of the firm that is sacrificed is to become ensnared in an insoluble contradiction. The outcome then is to make absurd claims of the kind that the Marxists, in the steps of their master, have long upheld: Capitalism inhibits technological progress so as to protect the value of existing capital, and so on. Clearly, a firm in a monopoly or quasi-monopoly position will follow that policy if it suits its current interest. But capitalism forms a "system," and if the system is not hampered in its operation it is constantly driven by the dynamics of exchange toward the most productive solutions.

Put simply, the sequence of events is this. One or more firms bring into service new equipment that increases labor productivity. For example, where their competitors are making one pair of shoes in one hour of labor (that hour includes not only the time spent by the workers in the shoe factories but also that spent making the plant and the raw material used in those factories, etc.), they produce two pairs. These advanced firms will make considerable profits, part of which it may be imagined they will begin to forgo in order to broaden their markets. If reasonable conditions of competition prevail—which is not always the case in practice, but we have to start from this hypothesis in order to know what will happen, thereafter reintroducing the disruptive influence exerted by the imperfection, itself variable in degree, of competition—we shall find that after a certain time all shoemakers will be forced both to fit out their factories with the most modern equipment and to reduce their prices to the level of their new production costs (profit included).

The fact is that until the average price of shoes has been divided by two (other things being equal, including the value of money), shoemaking will be an activity bringing in a higher-than-average rate of profit. It will therefore be continually stimulated by an inflow of capital.

To describe the process, let us imagine an automatic shoemaking machine costing F.1,600,000 and lasting five years. The current rate of profit is assumed to be 10 percent. To be "profitable"—in other words, according to our definition, to qualify as capital—the value of the machine's output throughout its lifetime must be a minimum of F.422,076 × 5 = F.2,110,380, because its annual output will need to have a minimum value of

10% profit on capital employed                              F.160,000
annuity which, at the rate of 10%, will
replace a value of F.1,600,000 after 5 years    F.262,076

                                                            F.422,076

Let us suppose that this latter sum represents the value of 4200 pairs
of shoes (one pair = F.100). If we express the value of the machine in
terms of its own product, it may be said to be worth 16,000 pairs of
shoes and to be profitable only if, over five years of service, it is
capable of making approximately 4200 × 5 = 21,000 pairs of shoes.[9]
Note that if it is capable of producing more, other things being equal,
this extra production will have considerable economic significance: It
will be a sign that the machine enables existing labor productivity to
be improved and that therefore the unit *value* of one pair of shoes will
have fallen.

Let us suppose that such is the case and that, from now on, we are
technically in a position to bring into service a machine still costing
F.1,600,000[10] but capable of making twice as many shoes in five years:
42,000 pairs instead of the 21,000 with the old machine. According to
our earlier assumptions, the unit value of the shoes will fall by half, so
that F.100 will now buy two pairs (1 pair = F.50). The result of this is
that the value of the machine and its output, expressed in francs, will
not have changed but, expressed in "shoe equivalent," the machine
will now be worth 32,000 pairs and its total output will be 42,200 pairs,
corresponding to an annual output of 8440 pairs.

The old-model machines, for their part, will cease after a time to be
worth anything. The interesting question is what firms still equipped
with the obsolete plant will do during this transitional period. This is
the question put by Ricardo in his book, once again proving that
political economy did not wait for the advent of the second or third
industrial revolution to formulate the economic implications of technological progress in clear—though extremely subtle—terms. He envisages the case "of a man who has erected machinery in his manufac-
tory at a great expense, machinery which is afterwards so much
improved upon by more modern inventions that the commodities
manufactured by him very much sink in value. It would be entirely a
matter of calculation with him whether he should abandon the old
machinery, and erect the more perfect, *losing all the value of the old*[11]
or continue to avail himself of its comparatively feeble powers" (*Principles*, chap. 19). The entrepreneur's choice is relatively easy to

make—at least in theory, because in reality a large number of factors, including the rate at which prices will adjust to the new production costs, will elude him. The important thing is to note that, once the old machines cease to qualify as capital,[12] their value is destroyed. A machine worth F.1,600,000 only yesterday is today well and truly unsaleable. At best it could be sold for its *scrap value*. And yet if the old machines were operated, one could recover a certain value in the form of pairs of shoes produced. In any case, many entrepreneurs would be unable to replace their machinery and would be forced either to run their old plant at a loss or else lose all their capital and withdraw from competition.[13] The latter alternative will obviously be very much to the disadvantage of the capitalist, but society as a whole will benefit.

The choice between the loss of the out-of-date plant and the purchase of new machinery is not arbitrary as it is "a matter of calculation," but since the function of the market is to bring down the price of products now requiring less labor in their manufacture (in other words, products that have fallen in value), it is inevitable that the solution ensuring maximum production at lowest social cost, for the economy as a whole, will proceed from the sum of the individual calculations made by each of the entrepreneurs.

Here, the opposition between "society" and the interests of the individual entrepreneur is clear. Both the entrepreneur who was the first to introduce the more productive machinery and the manufacturer handicapped by the heavy investment plant now obsolete will have an advantage in maintaining the old price: in other words, inhibiting the action of the law of value, which, far from being the law of the growth of value as Marx thought, is the law that continually forces the capitalist to adjust to value's inexorable downward trend. Here again, it is clear that political economy views the economic system, in its totality, as a social phenomenon. That is how it was capable, a century and a half ago, of stating in Ricardo's words: "[Such] capital is spent with a view to augment the produce—that, it should be remembered, is the end; of what importance, then, can it be *to the society* whether half its capital be sunk in value, or even annihilated, if they obtain a greater annual quantity of production? Those who deplore the loss of capital in this case are for sacrificing the end to the means" (my italics). This passage occurs in a footnote (as do several others which have since become some of Ricardo's most famous theories). He returns to it a little later in the body of the text in the following words: "[T]he end of all commerce is to increase production, and . . . though

you may occasion partial loss, you increase the general happiness''
(*Principles,* chap. 19).

It is possible, even certain, that in real economic life some entrepreneurs will have sufficient influence to prevent the system from working,
either by setting up cartels or inducing the authorities to take protective measures. In that case, however, the task of a critique is to enquire
whether the system is *effectively* applicable, given the power of the
converging opposition it will unfailingly arouse. The mistake of Marxism is to have applied its critique to the very logic of the system when
it is powerless to catch that system in the act of contradicting itself.

## Does the Value of Obsolete Machines Still Depend on Their Production Cost?

The opposition between the interest of society and that of the
individual entrepreneur is greater than at first appears. The owner of
the obsolete machines will have a twofold interest in keeping up the
price of shoes. It will enable him both to continue to sell his output at
a profit and to preserve some value for his machines that are still
paying for themselves although technologically outdated. This latter
remark seems to bear out the modern theory inherited from Irving
Fisher, among others, according to which the price of an item of
capital equipment depends on the services expected of it. If the
exchange value of the old-model machines falls at the same time as the
expected value of the products they help to make, is that not evidence
that the exchange value of a machine depends not on its own past
production cost but, via the value of the products, on the production
cost of present-day machines? Who could fail to see that this would
introduce something into the reasoning that was not there at the start,
namely technological progress? The estimation of value is valid only if
everything else is equal. From the standpoint of society—rather than
that of each individual entrepreneur—it can be seen that the effect of
technological progress is to *take away* from the machine its quality of
capital. What is happening at enterprise level is then clear for what it
really is: Since the old machine has wholly or partly lost its capital
function,[14] it is wrong to speak—as subjectivist economists do—of the
*lowering* of its value; the right term is the total or partial *nullification*
of that value. The *exchange value* is nullified when the product has
lost its *use value*.

## A Word about the "Real Wage"

If we look beyond the image produced by the intervention of money—the effect of which is always to bring value into the foreground—and seek the real motors of economic activity, it becomes increasingly clear that maximum product comes before value as an objective. In other words, the object is not to achieve the largest possible output because that is the best way of obtaining the highest possible value; instead, the point of obtaining the highest possible value is that this is the best way of obtaining the largest possible production. Value is not what wage earners use to feed, clothe, or house themselves or to drive a car, and it is not value that "capitalists" use to build factories, develop new sites, or build supermarkets. Both, productively or nonproductively, consume products,[15] and what they share between them is the *products* of labor.

Exchange value determines the *proportion* in which the sharing of output takes place but it is not the object of that sharing. The frequent bouts of spiraling inflation we have experienced during the last few decades have at least had the advantage of making this fact clear to a large number of people. They now think not just about the amount of money reaching them in the form of wages, dividends or profits, and so on, but also about the volume and nature of the *products* (food, clothing, housing, car, factory, etc.) or services that this amount of money will enable them to purchase.

Let us imagine that, as the result of a finer division of labor (to which most advances in business management and control boil down), improvements in tooling, the introduction of new manufacturing processes, and so on, a country's industry has, in the space of a few years, become twice as productive as before, which means that for roughly the same quantity of labor[16] (expressed in number of hours) twice the volume of products are produced. Everything else, including the *quality* of the articles manufactured or services performed, being equal, the *unit* labor cost of production for each product or each service will, on average, have been reduced by half. What is going to be divided up between the parties concerned, capitalists and wage earners (there is no point here in introducing others like the central government or the landowner), is the volume of products available. If the distribution governed by the rate of profit[17] has not changed, everyone will receive a double quantity of products the *aggregate* value of which will not have changed. Economic agents will receive, *in their capacity as capitalists,* 10 percent of the value of the total product and, in their capacity as wage earners, 90 percent. The reason for my use of the words "in their capacity as" is that, in reality, one and the same person may be both wage earner and capitalist (and we shall see that this proposition goes further than at first appears, part of the country's net product probably being distributed in the form of wages).

In the meantime, as often happens in a period of rapid technological progress, the rate of profit may have risen, from 10 to 15 percent, say. In that case, the wage earners' share of total value produced will have fallen but their lot, compared with what it was before the general increase in production, will have substantially improved all the same.

Now that we are living through an era of technological revolutions, it is vital—the better to understand and control them—that we should go back to the rigor and careful precision that early political economy showed it possessed. Thus Ricardo, in the last case quoted, would have said that the *real* wage had fallen. For him, the real wage, like real profit or real rent, is a *proportion* of value produced.[18] This brings him to qualify the wage evaluated in products as *nominal, whether the product in question is a product with a use value (a cloth, for example) or the gold used as money.* This way of expressing himself, be it noted, was as disconcerting for the readers of his day as for the present-day reader because, from time immemorial, nominal wage has been the expression reserved for the wage expressed in money (even if in the form of gold sovereigns) and real wage has meant wages expressed in the goods or services (food, housing, car, hairdressing, etc.) purchased out of wages. The strict logician that Ricardo was, however, follows the method of the scientist who, to avoid the complications inherent in a measuring instrument, reasons in percentages. Because he had earlier proved that not only is there no invariable standard of value *but that it is impossible to conceive of one,* the only path left open to him, to construct his chain of propositions as rigorously as possible, was to eliminate value and refer solely to share of value.

This method seems to defy common sense to the extent that, as we saw a little earlier, it means that when the share of gross income going to the workers drops from 90 to 85 percent, the economist refers to a fall in *real* wages, even though this drop in percentage has been accompanied by a vast increase in production, the effect of which is to have increased the volume of products placed at the disposal of the worker in the form of wages. But the idea that one may be *richer* through receiving a lower *value* should not surprise us. If we are rich it is not because it costs a great deal to manufacture the products we use but because we have a large quantity of products (and services) at our disposal. Put another way, this idea means that, in an economy governed by exchange, the less effort it costs to produce riches, the less it costs to buy them. This proposition forces itself on the mind with, if I may say so, the minimum effort; all that is necessary is to differentiate between unit price and aggregate value of output.

### A Diesel Truck Is Worth More in Bombay Than in Düsseldorf

Before we go any further, we need to ask ourselves: Is the distinction between value and product purely artificial as the interpreters of neocapitalism maintain? Does it stand the test of events, which is obviously a necessary condition to lend it a certain scientific quality? Well, there is no doubt that this distinction is confirmed experimentally by economic reality—and in the most direct fashion.

In an unindustrialized country (like Africa, India, and so on), a car will have a far higher value than in a country where cars are easy to manufacture. I hope no one will argue that this higher value, expressed by a higher relative price, is explainable in the final analysis by the psychological factor of scarcity (this point will not be completely cleared up until we get to Chapter 9). It is explained by reference to the sum of the amounts that would have to be committed to make a similar object locally. Are not customs duties worked out, roughly, so that the price of the imported article is at least equal to the price of a comparable home-produced article? This is necessary if they are to
, play a protective role.[19]

Let us now take a magic carpet ride to one of these "underdeveloped" countries. Here we are in the plain of the Punjab or on the high plateau of Yunnan (the political and social regime of the country matters little). We strike up acquaintance with an Indian entrepreneur or a Chinese people's commune and we discover that either one has a few diesel trucks. Will not the exchange value of these trucks, relative to the other products available in the region, be distinctly higher than it would be in Düsseldorf or Los Angeles? Would not the entrepreneur (or the people's commune) have had to work much harder to purchase them than a German or U.S. transport operator? Of course. Yet who would imagine for an instant that because the trucks are *worth* more in the Punjab or Yunnan than in Germany or the United States, the Indian haulier and the Chinese people's commune are *richer* than the transport operator in Düsseldorf or Los Angeles? Let us complicate the hypothesis (slightly) by supposing that through unceasing self-denial and effort the people in the Punjab manage to acquire (by buying them or manufacturing them themselves) as many trucks, factories, machines, telephones, and so on, as there are in North Rhine-Westphalia or in California. We would have grounds for arguing that the Indians in the Punjab and the Chinese in Yunnan had become as "rich" as the citizens of Düsseldorf and California. And yet should we count for nothing the fact that the former acquired their wealth by sheer toil and sweat and that the latter—thanks to the lead they had built up in the form of accumulated capital, the skills of their workmen, and the technological progress applied over the years—were able to make their trucks and new machines, modernize their telephone installations, and so on, while spending their weekends in the country and clocking off at five every evening? It was to allow for this difference, a vital point in economics, that classical political economy pursued its analysis far enough to make a radical distinction between the concepts of wealth and value.

"It may be said," wrote Ricardo, "of two countries possessing precisely the same quantity of all the necessaries and comforts of life, that they are equally rich, but the value of their respective riches would depend on the comparative facility or difficulty with which they were produced" (*Principles,* chap. 20).

Value being proportional, as a first approximation, to quantity of labor, it can be seen that the classical theory of value is that of the relativity of value. The cost of production varies over time, influenced in particular by technological progress. It varies in the space dimension, too, because neither the methods nor the modernity of production are uniform in all countries.

Since the debate on value and product is the common source of the economic *doctrines* that are currently dividing the world and the universities into two different camps, it is hardly surprising to find this issue still cropping up in the argument between the philosophers and advocates of each school of thought. Raymond Aron writes the following about the passage I have just quoted from Ricardo:

> Let us suppose that facility signifies a smaller expenditure of labour. This will mean that value will be in inverse proportion to wealth. As difficulty increases, value will also increase but, at the same time, wealth will decrease—a strange consequence of a conceptual approach which, relating value to the conditions of exchange (or relative prices) and calculating those conditions in terms of quantity of labour, is unable to produce a

clear idea of aggregate national product and will not allow that the sum total of the value produced by a community is the same as the wealth of that community.[20]

If Raymond Aron has a clear idea of aggregate national product, he could give some useful practical—not just theoretical—tips to our national accountants who at the moment think that nothing is less clear and are groping their way back to the Ricardian concepts to explain to themselves what they are doing. In any case, there is no country in the world, nor are there any specialist international organizations (OECD, the UN, etc.), in which the statisticians who work out "aggregate national product" confuse product with value. If they have to work out India's national product, for example, they count the machines, trucks, and so on, manufactured in India at their cost of production in that country, even though it is almost 100 percent certain that these cost prices will be higher than those of comparable machines and trucks made in the United States or in Germany. The Indian national accountants put the wealth produced in their country at the value (price) it has there, while German national accountants give the riches produced in Germany the value they have in that country. This is not in itself a reason for disregarding the comparison between national accounts, because in the example here cited, there are also many products and services that are much cheaper in India than in Germany. The fact remains that, to ascertain the relative scale of production and respective levels of development in Germany and India, we need an itemized accounts system for goods—an inventory (so many machines, trucks, telephones, etc., made and imported each year).

## Value, Product, and Pollution

Distinguishing value from product has the further advantage of sidestepping some of the traps into which psychological economics and thereafter official national accounts nearly always fall, namely pollution problems. Let us suppose that, as a result of new "developments" in hedonist neoliberal economics, we manage to pollute all the rivers, springs, and lakes and poison the atmosphere to such an extent that, to drink and breathe, mankind has to maintain costly facilities to filter and purify the water and the air. The air and water, supplied free by nature and for thousands of years, would thereby be transferred to the category of "economic goods," whose characteristic (see Chapter

9) is that they are obtained via a detour, a certain amount of labor being necessary to make natural resources usable.[21] It would never occur to anyone that promoting elements so essential to life to the status of economic goods would represent progress for mankind. To enjoy them, a certain effort, previously not needed, would have to be made. As a community, people would be *poorer* if we accept the definition of political economy that relates wealth and poverty not to the ownership of value, but to the enjoyment of the goods (whether economic or not) at one's disposal. Only this definition can reconcile national accounting with the reality of the world today. It is indeed true that the new need to regenerate oxygen and water would be reflected in an increase in the national product in value terms for the reason that oxygen and water would now have a value where they had none before. In gross national product (GNP), this extra value would be represented by the value of the output of the new pollution control industry. Some people would like to deduct the cost of the pollution control industry from the national product on the grounds that it is a tribute paid for the growth of other activities. Let us assume that, in a national product put at F.1,000 billion, F.25 billion represents the value of the output of the chemical industry. But this industry infects watercourses and poisons the atmosphere and, to control these harmful effects, treatment stations have had to be built—the annual operating cost of which is estimated at, say, F.5 billion. Would it not be correct to deduct this F.5 billion from the F.25 billion—value produced by the chemical industry—to put a true figure on the latter's contribution to GNP? This would be as strange a way of reckoning as that consisting in deducting from the value produced by agriculture the amount it spends annually on fertilizer and ploughing to recondition the soil after the harvest. The only correct way of reckoning is to include the price of fertilizer and ploughing in the total cost (value) of agricultural produce. The same applies to our chemical industry. If it were to maintain the treatment stations at its own cost, it would sell its output not for F.25 billion but F.30 billion.

Even so, in spite of its name, gross national product is not an inventory of all the *products* made available to the population. It is an estimate *in value terms* of current production and we already know that, theoretically, value is not a measure of wealth but of the cost of production. Let us concede that, in most cases, the distinction is, in practical terms, pointless to the extent that an increase in value is almost always mirrored by an increase in wealth or products. There are, however, some cases in which this is not true and, with the dual phenomenon of pollution and the increasing difficulty of stepping up the yield from agricultural lands without exhausting them, these cases are going to become more and more frequent, thus bringing us back to the hypotheses that classical political economy, with its admirable logic, had stated at the very outset. The launching of a pollution control industry is a perfect illustration of this principle because its necessary corollary in national accounts is an at least relative increase in value coupled with an at least relative decrease in production. Factually, there are two—and only two—possibilities. Either a number of additional hours of labor are spent to perform the new tasks, or else the number of hours devoted to economic activity each year is not increased in total but part is now applied to the pollution control industry. In both cases there is a decrease in the sum of riches produced per hour of labor compared with the previous state of affairs, since part of labor time is applied to producing goods—pure air and water—which were previously available freely without the slightest effort. This is a phenomenon of impoverishment to which we shall have occasion to return (Chapter 12) in view of the importance it could have, and already has, in the contemporary world. It has no relation, I should point out, with the phenomenon of impoverishment of the masses that Marx believed to be inherent in the growth of capitalism.

Today it is fashionable to criticize national accounts. They do have serious design faults and the author of this book would not argue to the contrary. The fact remains that some of the complaints most frequently leveled at national accounting would disappear of themselves if economic thought stopped mixing up value and product as it has been doing since the late nineteenth century. It would then be realized that an increase in value is not necessarily synonymous with an increase in product and less still in well-being (a subjective notion, to do with the enjoyment of goods, not the possession of value). This confusion, implicit in the psychological theory of value according to which value is proportional to utility, is in a way consubstantial with the consumer society.

My evidence is the opposition of the most brilliant minds to any reasoning—even as clear as that in the Ricardo passage quoted in my example of Germany and the Punjab—which would challenge that theory.[22]

## Economic Laws Precede the "Relations of Production"

No matter how many errors Marx may have made, the so-called "dialectical" method would have proved rewarding if, through his critique of political economy, it were possible to arrive at a new construct, a new integrated body of thought. But this is just not the case. Marxism lands back with the very laws it claimed were contingent ("historical"), which leaves some doubt as to the reality of any dialectical reasoning.

> The field of application for machinery would be entirely different in a communist society, from what it is in a bourgeois society.[23]

Why was Marx convinced that in a communist society many more machines would be used than in a capitalist society? Because, he thought, a communist society would give the machine back its true role—not, that is, to subject labor to the law of surplus value but to make labor both easier and more productive, which would indirectly have the result of enabling man, liberated at last from the most arduous tasks, to devote his abilities to worthier occupations. In a capitalist system, Marx claimed, this cannot happen because without labor there can be no surplus value. So the machine *must*—against its nature, so to speak—bring into the work force an increasing number of operatives selling their labor power at a discount. That is why machines *cannot* be developed to the full in a capitalist system of production. However, Marx maintains, that system will not indefinitely have the better of the antagonistic forces it generates from within; it will be brought to a standstill by the effect of its inherent contradictions.

That is the doctrine. Yet everything suggests that it rests on a series of inversions: supply price treated as demand price; the objective of surplus value substituted for that of the largest possible product; conversion of money into capital presented as the hallmark of the capitalist system, when to take "conversion" in this sense is simply to play on words. The inconsistency of the metaphor stares one in the face even before one tries—and inevitably fails—to weld its incompatible terms into some kind of mathematical formula. Marx uses a figurative language devoid of scientific precision and, therefore, inaccurate since the phenomenon to which he refers is the transmission from one person to another of the value of an amount of capital by way of money, with the result that he attributes to the thing transferred a transformation that affects the assets of the successive owners.

So here we see Marx distilling his concepts with a wonder-working alchemy that had already enabled him to transmute labor power into a commodity. And all in aid of what? To build a communist society that would restore to capital the quality of use value which the theory Marx criticized said it had from the very start. So the question that has to be asked is this: Once capital has been reinstated in its role of an instrument for "giving effect to labor," do we not, then, find ourselves back with the laws that political economy had logically deduced from its definition of capital? Those laws explained how the product of the labor applied to capital would be shared out among the different actors in economic life, it being clear that these laws cease to exist, *and are not replaced by any other,* if the assumption of equivalence of exchange is discarded. Without equivalence of exchange it becomes radically impossible for the science to determine its subject matter. We are, therefore, no longer in the sphere of economics but in that of "the arbitrary," of "interventionism" in all its forms. Looked at from this angle, the mechanisms of a capitalist economy do not form a particular structure or mode of production sui generis that replacement by socialism causes to vanish.

### Marx Again Proceeds from Smith and Malthus and Precedes Keynes in Formulating the So-called Law of Declining Rate of Profit

If there is one theory that has always divided economists it is that of the fall in the rate of profit caused by capital accumulation. The idea was first put forward by Adam Smith in *The Wealth of Nations* as a sort of roughed-out pseudo-intuition: If capitalists can produce in great quantities, competition will lead them to pare their profit margins. This is roughly what Smith was saying when he wrote: "When the stocks of many rich merchants are turned into the same trade, their mutual competition naturally tends to lower its profits; and when there is a like increase of stock in all the different trades carried on in the same society, the same competition must produce the same effect in them all."

Here too, and with more serious consequences than elsewhere, many authors of textbooks have lumped together the ideas of Smith, Malthus, and Ricardo without realizing that the last, once again, is completely opposed to the other two. In no other area has the misinterpretation been so total or so constant, and in no other has it been more inexcusable, since Ricardo explained himself at great length in a chapter specifically devoted to the subject, chapter 21 of the *Principles,* entitled "Effects of Accumulation on Profits and Interest," which Ricardo opens with these words: "No accumulation of capital will permanently lower profits.'' Yet in spite of this passage, and many others, Ricardo has been made out to be the inspiration for the famous Marxist theory of the declining rate of profit. The reason for this misreading is the fact that Ricardo, in his subtle but difficult formulation, is constantly shifting from one level to another, which means that the reader has to take great care. One moment he is analyzing the workings of the economic system as it is; the next he is considering how that system will evolve over the long and even very long term. When it is a question of actual time, there can be no doubt whatsoever that he categorically rejects the theory that profits must inevitably decline. Ricardo states (Smith had already done so too, but was unable to draw the logical inferences) that men's wants are limitless. The idea that *"effectual demand"* might suddenly become insufficient to absorb the output supplied seems all the more absurd to him in that the production of any commodity is intended to procure another commodity in exchange. The only thing that can happen, if the exchange mechanism is not put out of joint by some exogenous cause, is that producers have momentarily misjudged the market and are supplying products that for one reason or another no longer correspond to the wants of the population. In that case it can be assumed that they will quickly correct their aim. In theory there can be no argument about that, since it is inconceivable that manufacturers will go on making articles for which there are no buyers. In practice, the adjustment of supply to demand may be delayed by many obstacles, especially when investments have to be decided a long time in advance.

What is important to bear in mind here is that in the classical model the infinite multiplication of exchanges does not imply any radical change in the workings of the system. The end of that system cannot come about through saturation of demand and this, I repeat, for two reasons. First, for a logical reason: since products are purchased with other products, it is inconceivable that an abundance of them would lead *in the aggregate* to an all-round fall in prices (by that I mean a fall in the prices of products to a level below their value, i.e. the cost of production, which would make exchange of value for like value impossible). Second, for a reason that in a sense is sociological or psychological: Man is made in such a way that his wants are infinite. If abundance of products is not per se a cause of decline in the rate of profit, the same of course applies to the capital accumulated in order to produce them. "While there can be no limit to the desire of 'conveniences' . . . there can be no limit to the capital that may be employed in procuring them," Ricardo wrote in the aforementioned chapter. Elsewhere, in his *Notes on Malthus,* he says: "It is here [in the passage from Malthus which he is commenting upon] inferred that a fall of profits is a necessary consequence of an accumulation of capital. No mistake can be greater."

Well before Keynes, economists were asking themselves whether the crises were not due to insufficiency of demand and whether, more generally, what they ought to do to maintain a high level of activity was not to stimulate consumption directly and bypass the supply side. That is what Malthus maintained, and his long discussion on the subject with Ricardo is one that makes the ten-year controversy between the two men so topical today.[24] For Malthus the economic system was threatened with "general stagnation,"[25] by the insufficiency of "effectual" or "effective" demand, an expression already in current use at that time.

In order to create work for the labor force, Malthus believed it necessary to encourage "effective demand," that of the wealthy classes incidentally—to which, by the way, Ricardo answered[26] that if the wealthy classes shunned conveniences and luxuries, the workers would be only too happy to have them. Contradicting Ricardo, who thought that a better result would be obtained by increasing "reproductive consumption," that is, by increasing saving (invested in capital), Malthus replied (even at that time) that capital accumulation would have the effect of depressing profit a little further and, therefore, of slowing down the economy even more. A hundred and fifteen years later Keynes, who expressly acknowledged spiritual descent from Malthus,[27] in turn emphasized the preeminent role of "effective demand," which inevitably caused him to take up the ever-renascent theory in which Ricardo discerned the supreme error: "I feel sure that the demand for capital," wrote Keynes,[28] "is strictly limited in the sense that it would not be difficult to increase the stock of capital up to a point where its marginal efficiency [marginal profit] had fallen to a very low figure." It has been seen earlier that the "marginal efficiency of capital" tends, on the contrary, to rise as technical progress accelerates and encourages rapid renewal of capital, which might explain why the rate of profit is much higher today than when Keynes brought out his *General Theory,* despite the fact that by comparison with that time the mass of accumulated capital is much larger. Yet the fact remains that theories like those of Keynes have almost always won their authors excessive esteem, even though history to date has shown that the countertheories are correct. That is why, of all the "laws" allegedly revealed by Marxist theory, that of the declining rate of profit as a necessary consequence of capital accumulation has long enjoyed especial prestige. This is another example of how Marxist analysis, with its own arguments, of course, rolls along the path traced by Smith and after him by Malthus, but regarded by Ricardo as leading nowhere.

Marx incorporates the old Smithian idea in his system because the concept he has developed of capital leads him to discover a "contradiction" in the spread of mechanization under the capitalist system of production: "Of the two factors of the surplus-value created by a given amount of capital, one, the rate of surplus-value, cannot be increased except by diminishing the other, the number of workers."[29] Nowhere better, perhaps, than in this proposition does one see the nature of Marx's reasoning. The famous contradictions he thinks he has discovered in the capitalist system he has put there himself by plastering his concepts over reality. In other words, the contradictions in question are not implicit in the subject of the research set by the researcher but have sprung (to use the language of Althusser) fully armed from the head of the thinker. They vanish if, instead of stating that "the sole aim in using machines is to increase surplus-value," one concludes with Ricardo, from the analysis of product and value, that machines, like any capital, are used for the purpose of increasing the *product,* and if one also realizes that putting value before production, far from being the hallmark of capitalism, is the surest sign of divergence from its logic.[30] That is why the "law of declining rate of profit," whether as formulated naively by Smith, ambiguously by Malthus, or sophisticatedly by Marx and Keynes, has no real justification in theory. It is hardly astonishing, then, that it should have been regularly disproved by facts and will be again in the future, even if the present period of economic euphoria [written in 1970–71] is followed by a phase of depression lasting a greater or lesser length of time.

## The Circularity of Exchange Does Not Warrant the Pitiful Analogy of the Chicken and the Egg

The complexity of economic phenomena being what it is, the temptation is great to resort to the facile analogy of the chicken and the egg. Which is cause and which effect? The circularity of exchange seems to provide the observer with a further and apparently unanswerable argument for refusing to answer. Would it not be intolerably arbitrary to assign once and for all, on any market, the preponderant role to the buyer or alternatively to the seller? It is only too obvious that one would not exist without the other and that, depending on the circumstances, the one was going to impose his will on the other or vice versa. The argument seems irrefutable and yet it does not correspond to the truth of things, or, if the reader prefers, its development reveals two relationships of different kinds where there originally seemed to be only one. In no case is it possible to relate the circularity of exchange to the existence of a supply and a demand, even supposing that they are complementary (which is not always so). The mere fact that it is possible to state that in a market you cannot demand if you cannot supply shows that supply and demand in that market are not equivalent: Logically, supply comes first and demand second.[31] Since supply and demand are linked together in a certain order, it is clear that equivalence of exchange cannot result purely from their coming together. *Only the law of markets, whereby commodities are purchased with other commodities, gives the exchange relationship the symmetry without which there can be no equivalence.*

Even a summary analysis of the workings of a market economy reveals the following two relationships: (1) a relationship of equality (and therefore symmetry) which makes it possible to speak of an exchange *circuit,* and (2) a functional relationship which establishes itself between supply and demand (production will increase as demand increases). To omit this distinction will have notable consequences on the theoretical level and also for the organization of those societies which have the advantage of having been able to remain "capitalist." The main consequence, which sums up all the others, is that by reversing the order of the factors it becomes impossible to influence events by bringing into play the causal relationships between economic phenomena. What characterizes modern economics is its abandonment, overt or covert as the case may be, of the principle of causality.

It might be useful here to consider for a moment the epistemological status of the relationship of cause and effect, since in economics, even more than in other areas, observation of facts often seems to justify reversing the order of factors, the same factor appearing at one time a cause and at another an effect. How, in the turmoil of events, can one be distinguished from the other? Let us take an example. Even if one is convinced, as I am, that inflation is, *in the last analysis,* a phenomenon caused by the malfunctioning of the money-issuing mechanism and that, consequently, it is not the rise in wages that causes prices to rise, but the other way around, it is impossible not to see that, from the moment the inflation process gets under way, wage increases will in turn accelerate that process. But the relationship of causality to which science refers is the one that appears, as I have just said, "in the last analysis"—in other words, it applies to an abstract model. The model, if it is well constructed, should make it possible to foresee what will actually happen in reality, but although it may *match* that reality, it belongs forever to another order, since it is nothing other than a mental construct. In a perspicacious little book written when he was a student at the École Polytechnique in Paris, Jacques Rueff showed that the scientist does not discover in nature, as a superficial view of scientific activity might lead us to believe, the causes of the phenomenon he is studying: He *invents* them.[32] The fundamental heterogeneity that makes the *explanation* provided by science distinct from reality is now admitted by all scientists whatever their discipline, be it physics, biology, sociology, or economics. It is in this perspective, of course, that I have attempted in this book to identify the relationship between, for example, labor and value.

I would add that the nature of the causal link thus defined makes it possible to understand why, in economics, it is often not possible to redress a situation other than by a plan of radical reform that utterly changes the circumstances of the problem. If one is content with partial measures, the chance factors that have caused confusion and foiled policy action are still allowed to operate.

If Marxism has so long exerted so much influence, the latent reason may be that many minds have believed, as a reaction against the lack of rigor of the neoliberal economists in determining cause and effect, that they have seen the light in what seems to be a structured system of thought. But Marxism has in its own way thoroughly confused things by proudly putting cause in the place of effect, and vice versa. Not the least of the contradictions in Marxist thinking is that it too rejected the law of markets while recognizing, from no less a source than Aristotle himself, the law of equivalence of exchange.

## Notes

1. Göran Ohlin, in an article published in the quarterly *Skandinavska Banker,* entitled "The Golden Rule in Modern Economic Theory." My italics.

2. In a letter to Malthus dated June 1814, Ricardo wrote: "The rate of profits and of interest must depend on the proportion of production to the consumption necessary to such production," a proposition that has been

extensively commented upon in the literature. See, for instance, in *Economica* (August 1973), "Ricardo's Analysis of the Profit Rate" by Samuel Hollander.

3. John Keynes, *The General Theory* (London: Macmillan for the Royal Economic Society, 1973), appendix to chap. 14.

4. Inflation being a dynamic phenomenon, its relationship with interest rates is not the same at all moments in time. The rate of interest will be found to rise when inflation reaches breaking point (bursting like an overinflated balloon). At that point the quickening rate at which claims depreciate automatically sends up the cost of money.

5. This combination has long been and still is to some extent a feature of Japan's growth, one of the fastest in the world.

6. Here I am ruling out the possibility of speculative buying.

7.                        $155,000.\overline{a_{20}|}\ 10\% = F.1,319.602.3$

The F.155,000 gross income breaks down as:

| | |
|---|---|
| 10% profit on capital | = F.131,960.2 |
| annuity which, in 20 years at 10%, will replace a capital of F.1,319,602 | = F. 23,040 |
| | F.155,000.2 |

8. Fisher writes: "But the failure to agree on any dividing line between wealth which is and wealth which is not capital, after a century and a half of discussion, certainly suggests the suspicion that no such line exists." That is not a reason to deprive ourselves of one of the few solid principles apt to shed some light into such an intricate subject.

9. Worth F.2,110,380 rounded off to F.2,110,000.

10. In practice, things will be more complicated. The new machine, for example, will cost 1½ times as much but will enable production to be quadrupled.

11. Ricardo's italics.

12. This can be expressed in the following way: In shoe-equivalent, the cost of production of the old machine has now become 32,000 shoes. But the machine, as we have seen, will be capable of making only 21,100 shoes over its lifetime. Who would be foolish enough to give away 32,000 pairs of shoes now so as to receive 21,100 over five years?

13. I assume that the firms have no other source of capital than that originally invested in the purchase of the obsolete machines.

14. If the performance of the new machine is incomparably better than that of the old, the latter ceases to be capable of performing the function of capital almost immediately. The day it became possible to mass-produce internal combustion engines, the owners of horse-drawn carriages, at least in sectors of activity where there was keen competition, saw the value of their capital reduced to nothing in a short space of time.

15. I do not mean that reproductive consumption is confined to capitalists

or that the latter do not consume nonproductively. The distribution of the saving function in society is one of the key points of economic life and merits separate treatment on its own (see Chapter 8).

16. Roughly, because, with things as they are, the quantity of labor cannot be calculated mathematically, the first reason being the different intensities of labor in the various tasks involved and the second being that many of the tasks performed do not directly contribute to the production of goods or even of services.

17. Here I express the rate of profit as a proportion of the gross product accruing to the capitalists and not, in the more normal way, as a percentage of invested capital.

18. Ricardo's concern for exact language to identify economic phenomena reminds one of the work of Lavoisier, who felt it was essential to have an improved language to introduce the spirit of analysis into chemistry, as pointed out by François Jacob in his book *La Logique du vivant*. François Jacob adds that science in the classical age was based on comparisons. It was the knowledge of the *relations* between things. Similarly, for Ricardo, exchange value can be known only as a ratio. The first purpose he assigns to political economy is to discover the proportions in which the value of the product is distributed between the capitalist and the worker (and the landowner).

19. It may happen that customs duties bear no relation to local production costs, but in that case they have no protective purpose. In many countries customs duties are levied as deterrents. The purpose is simply to discourage by high prices the consumption of products regarded as unnecessary or dangerous (alcohol, for example).

20. Raymond Aron, *D'une Sainte Famille à l'autre* (Paris: Gallimard, 1969), p. 196. In these lines, the assimilation of value with product, characteristic of the neocapitalist doctrine born of the psychological school of the late nineteenth century, is reaffirmed. Even so, Raymond Aron has too keen a sense of real economics not to put the cost consideration first in the analyses he makes of concrete cases. This is what he does when he points out that the so-called consumer societies are first and foremost producer societies.

21. A point to note here is that, unlike air, water has always been an economic good because cost is involved in carrying it from the spring to the kitchen sink. In ordinary circumstances, the cost is negligible and this is why, in my example, I treat water on the same basis as air.

22. In his *Sainte Famille,* Raymond Aron's criticism of Ricardo's argument is, it is true, only secondary. The purpose of his book is the critique of Marxist and Althusserian conceptions. Marxists would clearly be incapable of presenting any objective theory of value that would be other than a highly suspect imitation of Ricardian theory.

23. Marx, *Capital,* vol. 1, chap. 15, "Machinery and Large-scale Industry," p. 515, footnote 33.

24. This controversy is recorded in a great exchange of letters between the two men, which came to an end only when Ricardo died, and also in the latter's *Notes* on the *Principles of Political Economy* of Malthus. Furthermore, Ricardo's *Principles* contain two chapters in which he discusses the principles of Malthus, not to mention many other passages in which he expresses his disagreement with these.

25. The expression "general stagnation" was in fact used by Ricardo in a passage in his *Notes on Malthus* where he comments on the latter's fears.

26. Ibid., pp. 311 and 318.

27. Pointing out that mankind's great misfortune was to have believed Ricardo rather than Malthus for more than a century (see chap. 15, p. 383).

28. Keynes, *General Theory,* chap. 24 ("Concluding Notes on the Social Philosophy Towards Which the General Theory Might Lead").

29. Because the use of machines, by lowering the cost of production of the goods needed by the workers, makes it possible to reduce their wages.

30. Thus the arbitrary definition that Marx gives of capital leads him to put the stamp of theory, as it were, on the most common preconceived ideas of his time and ours. What more popular topic is there than the machine's enslavement of man? Everything was so much clearer with the classical view to the effect that capital accumulation is not accumulation of value, it is accumulation of various *products* which will, in their turn, be "employed in production . . . to give effect to labour."

31. There can be no equivalence without symmetry. The reverse relationship, "There can be no supply without demand," is not symmetrical to "There can be no demand without supply."

32. Jacques Rueff, *Des sciences physiques aux sciences morales,* first published in 1922 and republished in 1972 by Payot.

*7*

# The Zero Growth Hypothesis Brings Out Some Basic Features of Capitalism

The stationary state hypothesis, which figures prominently in the reasoning of Ricardo and other early nineteenth century economists, had been abandoned until recently and often regarded as either pointless or even false, some of its critics pretending that it was a "forecast" which facts obviously disproved. *The advent of the stationary state is not a "forecast."*

There has been an intuitive return to this line of reasoning. In the early 1970s, the idea that natural resources might run out came back into vogue—often for the wrong reasons. The reason why Ricardo (accompanied here by the other classicists) took it as a principle that the economic system was drifting toward the stationary state with accumulation coming to a halt, is that he discovered a natural limit to the infinite expansion of wealth, namely the absolute impossibility of indefinitely increasing the area and yield of arable land. This limit, he says, is ceaselessly pushed back into a hypothetical future (something which the authors of the all-too-famous report of the Club of Rome hardly seem to have thought of), because of the steady progress made in agricultural methods which increase the yield from the land. Even so, it cannot be conceived that this yield will increase indefinitely because, as everyone knows, the use of manure and other fertilizers can only *stimulate* fertility and the soil must be—or should be—constantly renewed. Modern agriculture sometimes seems to forget this obligation because of our society's abandonment of the principles of economic science, which is the science of the optimum development (from the material and demographic standpoint) of mankind in its natural environment.

The first methodological reason that requires us to consider the hypothesis of a stationary state for the economic system, therefore, is that there is at least one variable—the quantity of natural resources available—which, theoretically at least, must eventually reach a maximum.

The second reason also has affinities with mathematical reasoning. For Ricardo, the supreme problem in economics is the distribution of income among the capitalist who receives the profit, the landowner who receives the rent (a form of profit), and the workman remunerated by a wage which he assumes in most cases (although he may envisage the opposite, as we have seen) to be wholly *consumed,* leaving nothing for savings. Faced with a problem of this kind, a mathematician would wonder what would happen if one of the two variables—wage and profit—were equal to zero.[1] This is the question that Ricardo tackles with his incomparable logic, his first question being what cause would reduce the rate of profit to zero, the question being the more inevitable in that his theory of exchange had led him to conclude, contrary to Smith and Malthus, his principal references for argument, that capital could go on being accumulated without ever causing profit to diminish (see pp. 190 ff.). Once he had found that cause he could write without compunction, in spite of everything he had previously said about the permanence of profit: "The *natural* tendency of profits then is to fall."[2]

But he also writes a few pages further on: "In the natural advance of society, the wages of labour will have a tendency to fall."

It is puzzling, at first sight, to compare these two statements because Ricardo never misses a chance—as I have already said—to point out that wage and profit cannot diminish at one and the same time, because he conceives of both as parts of total gross product. In his final chapter he even goes as far as to say that it was his "endeavour to show in this work that a fall of wages would have no other effect than to raise profits." How do we reconcile this central position (and its reciprocal: An increase in wages would have no other effect than to lower profits) with the two sentences I have just quoted and which scholarly interpreters have used in some cases to argue that Ricardo had "predicted" that wages would fall to subsistence level (the "iron law") and in others to maintain that he had "forecast"—just as "wrongly"—that the rate of profit would diminish? The contradiction disappears if it is realized that when Ricardo talks of a *natural* tendency he is not making a *forecast* in the factual sense of the word because the tendency concerned is a product of the reasoning of deductive science, the necessary culmination of a causal chain, not the end point—unknowable by its very nature—of a historical process (see Chapter 3, pp. 42 ff.).

Whenever Ricardo refers to a "natural" tendency it is in connection with a cause-and-effect relationship between phenomena that he isolates, artificially, from their context. In the two cases considered here, the isolated phenomena are not the same and the chain of logic is different in the two cases. In the case of wages, he says they will tend to fall "in the natural advance of society," but we have only to read the passage in *Principles* to see that the hypothesis of this "natural advance of society" has no historical context either, as the reader will have realized from Appendix 2 to Chapter 3.[3]

As to profits, their "natural" tendency to fall is explained by the finite quantity of agricultural resources, the effects of which, *theoretically*, must be felt in the form of rising production costs of the necessaries required by the worker and therefore an increasing share of the gross product going to the wage earner. For the purpose of his argument, Ricardo applies the ceteris paribus clause, to identify the "permanent cause" of a tendency for the rate of profit to fall. This brings him to assume constant a large number of factors which in reality are not, such as the status of agricultural technology (and then, as we see in the passage quoted in note 2 on page 206, he reintroduces the variable of improvements in farming methods).

From the above it can be seen that Ricardo's critics, concluding that his theory was false because its predictions were wrong, misunderstood its meaning. Ricardo did not "predict" the stationary state characterized by the rate of profit falling to zero and, therefore, by the cessation of capitalist accumulation. It is in history that predictions materialize or fail to materialize. This does not mean that the stationary state has no "reality," but that the reality it refers to is on another level—the logical level. The stationary state would mean the cessation of growth (productive capital no longer increasing).

Intuitively (no longer logically, alas), our age has rediscovered the idea—and for the same basic reasons as Ricardo. He saw its cause in the fact that agricultural resources are finite. The announcers of zero growth apply this generally and justify their program by the fear of all life's most necessary natural resources being exhausted. But the cessation of growth described by Ricardo does not, of course, mean the halting of economic activity. That goes on. What has changed is the destination of gross product. As long as accumulation continued, gross product was split two ways, between profit—part of which was reinvested (net capital formation)—and wages. Now it is only just enough to remunerate the workers and enable the reconstitution of the capital previously accumulated. How clearly this shows the gulf separating capitalism's great theorist from the "bourgeois" economists! In the eyes of the latter, profit is the mainspring of economic activity; for Ricardo it is only the mainspring and provider of growth, which is not the same thing.

It would be wrong to view the study of this hypothesis, which will probably never materialize, as an idle exercise. Actually, the stationary state is particularly interesting to analyze because, being one extreme of the economic system, it reveals the system's essential characteristics, those which would survive once the "extra-ordinary" phenomenon of growth had disappeared of itself. We shall now attempt that analysis.

Thus *stationary state* does not mean "static state." An interesting point here is that the definition given by Ricardo (and the other classicists) for this state, and the place he allots to it in his theory, correspond with the definition that modern physics ascribes to *stationary state* (or steady state) toward which an "open system" tends, in contrast to *state of equilibrium,* toward which a closed system tends.

## Economic (Pseudo)equilibrium

Far from being of itself a factor of anarchy, competition is above all a *principle of organization.* When, conversely, objects form an inert mass, like grains of sand in the desert or stones in a garden, they are never in competition because they do not react to one another.

In the stationary state, as we have just seen, the economic *system* continues to be capable of performing its task, that of producing all that mankind needs and restoring the capital accumulated in the past as it is consumed in the production process. We could say that it continues to receive energy and raw materials from its environment and gives them back in the form of labor. It is precisely this that characterizes the stationary state of an open system (of which the living organism is the prototype) and differentiates it from the state of equilibrium reached in a closed system, the classic example of which is a chemical compound (butane, for example) shut up in a tank. A system in equilibrium like this requires no energy from outside, nor does it supply any (although, *potentially,* it contains a great quantity of energy). It is not the same as a state of rest because chemical reactions are going on inside the tank, the number of molecules destroyed being exactly equal to the number newly formed. Even so, in spite of its perpetual agitation, a closed system in a state of equilibrium is incapable of performing any work at all and no external work is necessary, either, to activate the reactions within it.

*Whichever case is considered—positive or zero growth—economic equilibrium can only be conceived as a dynamic state.* If an economic system is said to be in equilibrium, what is really meant is that it is in good working order and functioning without any serious disruption: "Demand" matches supply, external transactions are in overall balance, and so on. The endless debates of the "neoliberal" school on the transition from static to dynamic equilibrium might therefore be pointless because the notion of static equilibrium can never apply to an economic system.

## The Economic System Is "Open" to Its Environment

The characteristic of the economic system is a two-tier relation of exchange. Within the system, the production units exchange their products reciprocally. But the system as a whole is in continual exchange with its environment from which it borrows raw materials and energy in all its forms (steam, waterfalls, the combustion of oil and gas, the sun which makes the wheat sown by the farmer grow, etc.), and then restores these raw materials and energy in the form of the products of labor.

In the earlier chapters I showed that, within the economic system, exchange related only to the products of labor and never labor per se or labor power. What, then, is the position, from the political economy standpoint, of labor or the energy generated by the human brain and body? Economic science should regard human labor power as a source of energy borrowed by the economic system from the natural environment by which it is surrounded.

## A Halt to Economic Growth Halts Population Growth

To return, now, to the stationary state, two other important comments are called for.

The first is that, in its Ricardian version, the theory of the stationary state is in complete contrast to the famous proposition of Malthus that food resources would increase by arithmetic progression and the population by geometric progression. With Ricardo, the population stops growing as soon as capital accumulation ceases for the reason that, from then on, wages absorb the entirety of the gross product. With capital no longer increasing, "no additional labour can be demanded,[4] and consequently population will have reached its highest point."[5] For the master of the classical school, it is the system of capital accumulation that determines, at least in the advanced countries (refer to Chapter 2 regarding the less developed countries), the rate of population growth. Population growth in Europe, including Russia, and in North America and Japan since the advent of the industrial revolution in these different continents or countries (the most striking effect of which was to cause a tremendous acceleration in capital accumulation) certainly seems to confirm the direction of the cause-and-effect relationship formulated by Ricardo. In those countries the rapid increase in wealth-produced caused a very steep increase in population with a few exceptions, the most noteworthy being France. But in this field, even more so than in many others, a large number of factors all act simultaneously and, in any case, Ricardo does not treat the effect of capital accumulation on population growth as an infallible "law." He himself remarks that nothing obliges the worker receiving more wages to burden himself with a larger family.[6] To quote his very words, "in all probability," he will use at least a part of his increased income to improve his condition. It is clear that, in reality, the increase in income as a result of the industrial revolution was not followed, in any of the countries I have named, by a proportional increase in population. Some part of the income increase, varying with country, was applied to increasing per capita consumption.[7]

The most striking thing about Ricardian reasoning is its *modern* character, which confirms what I have several times had occasion to point out: The approach of "objective" political economy formulated for the first time in Great Britain over a century and a half ago operates fully only if a number of conditions, to be met in the future with the progress of human society, all finally materialize. The human race multiplies, therefore, only if the means of production designed to feed it—and as far as possible to feed it better—are already available. However, this relationship, established in logic, will come true in history only if men have evolved sufficiently to take economic factors into account in organizing their lives. This already applies in the industrialized countries and probably in an increasing number of the so-called Third World countries.

*Subject to what has just been said,* there is no reason for the gloomy predictions of Malthus—based on the pseudoscientific law of the arithmetic progression of resources and geometric progression of population—to come true.

Last, Ricardo's reasoning about the stationary state brings out a further feature of political economy, highlighting its ability not to "predict" events (the job of a fortune-teller, not a scientist) but at least to indicate the course they will take. Here I refer to the Marxist belief (a belief of which the "new right" seems to partake) in the gradual withering away of the state which seems to be so inconsistent with the evolution of modern societies—particularly, strangely enough, those already close to communism (written before 1973). It is interesting to consider what place, in the mind of Ricardo the liberal economist (in the European sense), the public sector occupies in the stationary state because, at first sight, it might be thought that an economic system based on interaction (competition) of the elements that make it up (independent producers)[8] and on self-regulation *would tend,* ultimately, to eradicate all traces of the state. But this is not the case. The closer the economy draws to the stationary state, the broader the field—says Ricardo—of the public sector. To prove this is so, he has no need to move out of his field of investigation. The main problem of political economy—as he says in his preface—is to determine the laws which regulate the distribution of produce to the three classes of society: landowners, the owners of capital, and workers. It is by virtue of these laws that he concludes that, long before we are brought to the stationary state, "the very low rate of profits will have arrested all accumulation, and almost the whole produce of the country after paying the labourers will be the property of the owners of land *and the receivers of titles and taxes.*"[9]

## Notes

1. Note that the "wage" variable cannot be assumed to be reduced to zero, because the workers cannot be assumed to cease consuming. Toward the end

of Chapter 4, I assumed, purely hypothetically, that the entire income was absorbed by profit, but it will be remembered that I also supposed that all the work was done by automatic machines and that everyone lived off the profit produced by the capital (the automatic machines) inherited from earlier generations.

2. (My italics.) *Principles,* chap. 6. The sentence is immediately followed by this explanation: "For, in the progress of society and wealth, the additional quantity of food required is obtained by the sacrifice of more and more labour. This tendency, this gravitation as it were of profit, is happily checked at repeated intervals by the improvements in machinery, connected with the production of necessaries, as well as by discoveries in the science of agriculture which enable us to relinquish a portion of labour before required, and therefore to lower the price of the prime necessary of the labourer."

3. If the reader cares to consult *Principles* he will see that Ricardo begins by reasoning on a hypothesis (according to which wages are regulated by labor supply and demand) which he describes, immediately afterwards, as incomplete and incapable by itself to account for reality (see p. 86).

4. Perhaps I may point out that, if the approximate language of Ricardo is replaced by the correct expressions, the logic of the proposition comes out much more clearly. For example "no additional labour can be demanded" should read "no product arising from additional labor can be demanded." And since it is the accumulated product of labor that buys the new products of labor, if there is no additional capital there can be no additional demand for the product of labor.

5. *Principles,* chap. 6, "On Profits."

6. Ibid., chap. 32.

7. Noneconomic factors have affected the trend in each country. In France, for example, the *code civil* had a downward influence on the birth rate (already declining since the middle of the eighteenth century). In Japan, a traditional frugality, coupled with the government's nationalist propaganda, long had the effect (up to 1945) of keeping population growth roughly in proportion to accumulation. That having been said, population growth, by increasing productive forces, may itself become a factor helping to raise the standard of living.

8. In its pure form, the economic system consists solely of producers who produce so as to be able to "demand" another product in exchange. Each producer is therefore the consumer of the products supplied by the other producers.

9. *Principles,* Preface (my italics).

*8*

# Enter the Political Dimension of Political Economy

## There Is No Such Thing as Perfect Competition, Even in Theory

Even assuming that the macroeconomic model founded on the classical theory has the advantage over all the others of resting on causal relationships of a "scientific" nature, this is still not enough to win it acceptance. Of what use is a model that just cannot be applied to real circumstances as we know them, the circumstances in which life goes on? And the model thus succinctly described does seem totally alien to real economic life, in which the production and distribution functions are performed by enterprises. What becomes of the enterprise in a market where perfect competition is supposed to prevail, which, among other things equally impossible in practice, implies a single rate of profit for all producers?[1] The discrepancy between the perfect market hypothesis and reality has been sufficiently illustrated for its further discussion to be unnecessary. The one alteration that could be made to the familiar picture would be to tone down the contrast, since experience provides, much more often than is admitted, examples of near-perfect markets whose efficiency should fill anyone unforewarned with admiration. One need only think of the amazing degree of spontaneous organization which ensures that the millions in a modern city can find all the food they need.

This much said, the discrepancy in question is not between theory and reality. The original theory recognizes the discrepancy and not only seeks to explain it but makes it an essential component of the model. Here I refer the reader to the distinction between "market price" and "natural price."[2] The difference between the natural (or necessary) price and the market price is that the determination of the latter introduces an indefinite number of variables that had been eliminated from the determination of the former in order to show the all-important relationship of cause and effect. The number of these variables is infinite but they all have one feature in common: They end, at any rate temporarily, the state of perfect competition.

By nature this "temporariness" must inevitably last indefinitely. The only assertion that political economy makes here is that, unless the situation is one of monopoly (or oligopoly), market forces will constantly tend to bring the effective price down to the level of the production cost (necessary price). What is required here is to define the conditions necessary for an "objective" economy, given that man's economic activity is constantly under the pull of subjectivity. The most probable outcome, in the absence of an organizational principle such as free competition among producers, is that the prices of commodities will never be "true" and will simply reflect the relative strength of the producers or consumers at any given time, with one side or the other, depending on the circumstances, being in a position to "dictate terms."

For the prices of commodities to be determined instead by their value, it is necessary to assume perfect market conditions, a hypothesis that is completely theoretical and consequently scientific. This hypothetical market ensures that the prices of goods and services will not be arbitrary, but tend—at every instant of time—to conform to their value. But it is inconceivable for market price (an empirical datum) ever to be identical with "necessary price" (a concept), since this, logically, would imply a world in which economic life had ceased to evolve in time. In a real market, forces are constantly emerging which pull effective price and natural price apart, but those forces are never powerful enough, if the competition is not distorted, to prevent the effective price from tending back toward its theoretical level. It is only if they are never materialized that concepts can be called timeless or "eternal," just as the geometric triangle consisting of three lines, themselves formed by a succession of immaterial points, is "eternal." In layman's terms one would say that Ricardo's "natural" price is the least natural imaginable, since its materialization is subject to conditions so stringent that, at best, they can only ever be very partly met.

Marx, let it be said again, does not seem quite to have realized that the classicists' natural price carries the maximum degree of improbability. The uncertainties in his thinking are due to the fact that he sees the market described by classical political economy not primarily as a set of conditions ensuring that the price of commodities bears some relation to their real value, but as a mechanism peculiar to the "bourgeois" economy, in which "prices of production" differ from exchange values because of the filtering of the rate of surplus value into the general rate of profit. Consequently he sometimes gives the impression that for him the value of commodities is a datum, as witnessed in this sentence in chapter 5 of *Capital* (volume 1): "The value of a commodity is expressed in its price before it enters into circulation, and it is therefore a pre-condition of circulation, not its result."

The looseness, to put it mildly, of Marx's thinking on this point is reflected in the conflict that divided Soviet economists during the early 1970s. One school of thought agreed with the Polish economist, Oscar Lange, that the labor value principle held good in a planned socialist economy. Yet if there were any countries in which prices had all but ceased to express objective relative values, they were the ones where competition between producers had been abolished and where the regulating mechanisms consequently no longer operated. Either, therefore, the supporters of Oscar Lange's theory had to make it their duty to reestablish those mechanisms, or else they were obliged to feel capable of devising a plan that was superior to the market as an organizational principle. A mind-boggling task, since the absence of a market implied that there were no prices to begin with. So the only answer would have been to arrive at them progressively on the basis of production cost accounting by direct reference to quanta of labor (a calculation, moreover, which would have to be done ex ante because they were required for a plan). Even then it would still have been necessary to determine whether the impact of the rate of profit would be allowed for in the case of those goods and services the production of which required a capital input (in practice, all goods and services).

The other school of Marxist economists maintained that the labor value principle fails to survive outside the capitalist system. Could this mean that Marxism comes, at the end of the road, to want-value, as the catchphrase "each according to his needs" would seem to imply? Whatever conception one has of needs, to define value by need or want is to deprive economic science of any objective foundation. These doubts of Marxism about the validity of the labor value principle are all reasons for believing that this doctrine ultimately leads to the negation of economics as a science (which in practical terms implies that mankind must stop trying to organize the most important part of its activity by scientific methods).

## The Enterprise in the Economic System

Political economy's explanation of progress and change is based solely on the imperfection of competition at each moment of time. "It is through the inequality of profits that capital is moved from one employment to another," wrote Ricardo.[3] The chain of events is well-known. When the demand for a product (or service) increases, so does the latter's price. Attracted by the high profits, producers will increase the supply until the competition among them has the effect of bringing the rate of profit down to its average level. In this model the sole regulating element is competition among the producers. It can be inhibited only by a *monopoly*, the characteristic of which is that production cannot be increased at will, either because there is an arrangement or cartel between producers to limit supply artificially (in a complete monopoly a single producer controls all production), or because of the specific nature of the products demanded. We shall see in Chapter 9 that the market for all nonreproducible goods is "monopolistic."

Far from pretending that perfect competition can become reality in economic life, the classical theory of prices sees the incessant fluctuations of the market price around the necessary price as the main source of the dynamism and adaptability of the entire system. It regards perfect competition as the extreme that would bring the economy to a standstill. It is because competition is imperfect that profits are unequal, and it is this inequality that enables the theory to bring out the salient feature of the exchange economy, the one that makes it technically superior, in our civilization, to all other systems: the great mobility (which it makes possible) of all the factors of production. Because the enterprise is constantly being "encouraged" (see note 3) by the hope of higher profit, it can contribute to progress.

One could say that what enables the enterprise to make the most of itself is its ability, by means of the advantages it gains over its competitors through modernization of its production or management methods, to be constantly challenging the state of perfect competition, which, if it existed, would preclude movement. As long as the enterprise continues to outpace its competitors, it will create to its advantage a situation of partial and temporary monopoly which will come to an end when the competitors have caught up (but then it may forge ahead again, and so on and so forth). However, if it founds its prosperity on the imperfection of competition due to the slower response of other producers, it can continue to generate progress only if it operates within an economic and legal system that is constantly striving to establish the inaccessible state of perfect competition. Otherwise, the action of the enterprise, ensconced in its monopoly situation, will start to have counterproductive effects, the first of which will be to restrict the mobility of capital. Thus the laws laid down by the "liberal state" (in the European sense) concerning competition do not aim to establish a perfect market, whose real existence is ruled out by the theory itself. They aim to ensure sufficient competition among producers for the effective market price, resulting from competition which is necessarily imperfect, to be brought closer and closer to the cost of production (profit included). Competition would be said to be perfect if there were nothing placing any limit on profitable supply.

In practice this is impossible, if only because of the production lead times[4] necessary to adjust supply to ever-changing demand. But this impracticability in no way detracts from the absoluteness of the principle which can be stated thus: An economy is governed by the principle of competition if supply increases—or decreases—to the point where output can be sold at its production cost (profit included).[5] This definition has the advantage of being valid as it stands whatever the number of competitors. If there were only one producer, prohibited by law from limiting his output, he could be regarded as competing with himself. Meanwhile the modern "game theory" has come along to confirm what the classical economists knew already: namely that if the number of competitors is very small, this considerably increases the *instability* of the system, if only because each competitor thinks he has the *power* to eliminate his rivals, and because the time is bound to come when each will try to corner the market. Hence the aggressive strategies of firms bent on eliminating all competition. Almost always this situation of conflict resolves itself in the victory of the one who has made the fewest mistakes and turned those of his competitors to maximum account. The "winner's" outright victory means there is a *monopoly*. When, on the other hand, there are very many players of roughly equal strength, none of them has the *power* to exert any influence over the outcome of the game (see Chapter 9, p. 234), and that is why plurality of producers is usually seen as the key condition for competition to thrive. But, as can be seen, this condition is not strictly *necessary*.

## For Competition the World Has to Be at Peace

The perfect competition hypothesis is an ultimate not only at the level of economic theory but also where mores are concerned. It postulates a behavior on the part of economic agents that is the exact opposite of the belligerent tendencies still prevalent in mankind. Perfect competition implies that the necessary rivalry among the cells of the economic system is channeled into purely peaceful activity. It presupposes that none of the competitors is able to influence price or demand. None of them is allowed to wield the weapons with which opponents can be eliminated violently (e.g., dumping) or surreptitiously (e.g., wooing customers with misleading advertising). Each competitor has only his own resources to keep him in the race. It is through the insecurity of each member that the maximum security of the whole is ensured, just as the health of a living organism demands that no one cell proliferate at the expense of the others.

It is inevitable that each enterprise should seek constantly to turn the rules of the game to its advantage and to equip itself with all the means of attack it can. Modern marketing idiom—words like "aggressive" and "hard sell"—clearly expresses the trend. In their own way the precepts of the kind of marketing engendered by the consumer society reflect the overdeveloped subjectivism of modern economics, which, by basing value on scarcity, introduces into the heart of its system the frenzied desire of each producer to establish a monopoly for himself.

Two types of reaction to this deviation are conceivable. One of them is maximalist and would be to establish a society in which the teeth of all economic agents are drawn to the point where competition between them is so peaceful as ultimately to cease to be competition. In a sense this would be the surest way of making perfect competition prevail, since the virtual paralysis of the system would lead to equality of profits. The second reaction would be more pragmatic and consist in outlawing much more rigorously than at present the really flagrant breaches of the principles of peaceful competition that characterize genuinely liberal economics (in the European sense). This would imply a tighter clampdown on monopolies, on misleading advertising in all its forms, and so on.

## The Two Questions Posed by the Distribution of Gross Product

The inevitable emergence of superprofits for the most dynamic businesses, or the best placed in the market, further complicates the problem of the distribution of gross income, which is already difficult to resolve even in the simplified model. The problem can be summed up in the following proposition: Exchange is based on equality, but this objective relationship of equality between the values of the products exchanged generates, and then perpetuates and exacerbates, inequality in the distribution of wealth among men. The reason is the accumulation mechanism.

I now propose to question the classical theory to find out how it views the two eminently political issues raised by the distribution of gross product between profit (net product) and wages.

1. Is it legitimate to allocate, in the form of profits, the entirety of the net product to the holders of capital, which means that the workers receive, in the form of wages, only what is judged to be "the necessaries of life" (even if the "necessaries" in question are, as we have seen in Chapter 3, understood in the broadest possible sense to include such items as expenditure on vacations, recreation, cars, and so on)?
2. Supposing that, in any progressive society, net product is divided into "profit" and "superprofit," should the latter be allocated, partly or wholly, to the "capitalists"?

I shall take the second question first since classical political economy, basing its argument on the particular case of land rent, has supplied an explicit and detailed answer.

### Generalization of the theory of rent

Rent formation occurs whenever the rate of profit differs from one enterprise to another—or more precisely, from one holding of capital to another (see Chapter 3, p. 52). The payment of rent reestablishes equality of profits. This reasoning was applied by the classicists to agriculture and mines but has to be extended to all the other activities, whether industrial or commercial. Let us first imagine business A, located close to its market and managed with exceptional skill and, second, business B, located less favorably and managed tolerably well.

In a competitive economy (and this assumption is vital, otherwise the argument falls to the ground), capitalists will invest in business B only if it can produce, taking the good years with the bad, an average return on capital. But, being better located and better managed, business A will earn more and its extra profit can be regarded as a rent attributable to these two causes.

Theory shows that rent is never a part of exchange value of any commodity, since that value is determined by the production cost for the marginal enterprise, which, by definition, pays out no rent. From the standpoint of each individual enterprise the situation is obviously quite different, since if business A pays out a rent, the amount of that rent must be included in its cost price.

If it is assumed that to equalize the rates of profit in agriculture the best-placed farmer pays a rent to the landowner, it must likewise be assumed that in industry or commerce there is no particular reason why the "surplus profit" should go to the capitalist. The principal recipients should probably be the entrepreneur and all those who help him to make his business a success—in other words the entire work force, since it is to them that the business owes its particular efficiency. That much said, surplus profit in other cases indicates the existence of a monopoly, even if only temporary, in which case the consumer is the sufferer. Taxation might be one indirect way of reestablishing equality of exchange. Things are also complicated in periods of inflation when firms take over the saving function. In any case some measure of caution is required, particularly in view of the difficulty of calculating the average rate of profit and its variations over time. The long-term rate of interest—roughly 9 percent in Western Europe in the early 1970s—is a good approximation, however. How far the practical conclusions suggested by the theory are taken will depend on whether the viewpoint is conservative or progressive. Only one thing is certain: The classical theory gives no justification for the system now in force in the capitalist countries.

The reader may object that to challenge the capitalists' exclusive title to "surplus profit" is to rob the system of the mobility of which so much was made a little earlier on. This is not necessarily so. Though the capitalist (or saver) is free to choose where he places his capital—and this freedom of choice is fundamental—he will not as a rule exercise that option at random. He may be expected, according to his natural inclination, to pick either the businesses that are most dynamic or those which to him seem the most sound. In either case his choice will be influenced by the way in which the businesses are managed. In the last analysis capital comes to the entrepreneur, rather than the entrepreneur to capital. The saving function is therefore pretty well disconnected from the use-of-savings function. I would add one more thing: Since profits and surplus profits are normally reinvested, any scheme for profit distribution must in principle aim at capital formation. Capital must as far as possible be marketable. One solution (though it is difficult to specify how it would work in practice) would be to increase the number of share issues and earmark part of the new shares for employees and possibly also for associations representing the public. Here too, the degree of priority which, in many respects, it is desirable to give the initial shareholders will depend on whether the viewpoint is conservative or progressive.

### "Net product" does not go in its entirety to capitalists

It is the rate of profit which determines the division of gross product between (1) the share used to reconstitute the capital spent in the production process and (2) net product. This rate is itself, as we have seen, largely determined by objective factors about which employers and employees can do little or nothing. Does this mean that the distribution of gross income between the different social classes is in a sense "objectively" governed by the logic of the system?[6] However that may be, there is very little or no scope for government to correct the consequences of capital accumulation, short of outright confiscation, which is what very high inheritance taxes, for example, amount to. It would be both pointless and absurd to try to conceal the fact that, in practice, this is the way things are. The statistics on distribution of wealth in the most advanced industrial societies are proof enough. Economic progress spreads the ownership of wealth only very slowly and very imperfectly. The concentration of capital in a few hands is still—and will probably continue to be—one of the features of an economic society governed by exchange. Anyone carried away by the elation of egalitarianism can only reject the whole capitalist system outright. But what about those who more moderately find unacceptable an *excessive* inequality in the distribution of wealth, which almost inevitably generates inequalities in all the other areas; what must their view of capitalism be?

Clasiscal political economy admits of no determinism in the distribution of gross product. The reason is that, true though it is that gross product is necessarily shared between wage and profit, that does not mean between wage earner and capitalist.

According to the classical reasoning, there is nothing to prevent a portion of the net product from being allocated to the workers, whose wage would thus include a share of profit. But this does not mean that net product is no longer net product. Ricardo speaks about this in a passage of *Principles* already quoted in part on page 41:

> More is generally allotted to the labourer under the name of wages than the absolutely necessary expenses of production. In that case a part of the net produce of the country is received by the labourer, and may be saved or expended by him; or it may enable him to contribute to the defence of the country.[7]

It is for purposes of argument that complete coincidence is assumed (1) between wage income and reconstitution of that part of the product consumed by the worker and (2) between net product and the capitalist's income. But economic science has no rational motive to authenticate this twofold coincidence. It makes a clear-cut distinction between wage and net product, but here too its analysis relates to products, not men. The term *net produce* is applied to everything that is produced over and above what is necessary to replace the sum of goods that "give effect to labor." It does not follow that this classification must necessarily generate the formation of corresponding social classes in society, namely the working class and the capitalist class, the latter having a right to the entirety of the net product and alone, therefore, in a position to accumulate.

Let me add that it is possible and almost inevitable that things should be this way, but this is for sociological reasons for which political economy provides no justification of its own but which it can help to change. Indeed it opens up a wide range of possibilities, since in the last chapter of his book Ricardo writes this:

> Suppose that all the commodities in the country, all the corn, raw produce, manufactured goods, etc., which could be brought to market in the course of the year, were of the value of 20 millions, and that in order to obtain this value the labour of a certain number of men was necessary, and that the absolute necessaries of these labourers required an expenditure of 10 millions. I should say that the gross revenue of such society was 20 millions, and its net revenue 10 millions. It does not follow from this supposition that the labourers should receive only 10 millions for their labour; they might receive 12, 14 or 15 millions, and in that case they would have 2, 4 or 5 millions of the net income. The rest would be divided between landlords and capitalists; but the whole net income would not exceed 10 millions (*Principles*, chap. 32).

This passage and what comes after tell one a great deal about how the founder of British pure political economy (which was how Walras described Ricardo) saw the distribution of gross income.

1. What criterion should be used to determine net income? For each individual business the whole of the wage bill is regarded as a "production expenditure." Does this mean that the entirety of the working population's consumption expenditure[8] is reproductive consumption? If this were so, the concepts of reproductive consumption and nonproductive consumption, the importance of which I have stressed along the way, would have no substance since they would be infinitely elastic, as we have already seen from the brief review of the wage earner's bookkeeping (Chapter 3, p. 55 ff.). There one sees that it is the purpose to which the product is put that enables it to be called "net" or not (i.e., an ex post classification). All new investment expenditure, together with public expenditure, therefore has by definition to come out of net product.

2. Is it desirable that workers should receive part of the net product? A little further on in the same chapter Ricardo considers an eventuality in which progress in production techniques results not in higher profits but in higher wages, the latter now including a portion of the net product. He writes: "Be it so . . . it will only prove what is still more desirable, that the situation of another class, and by far the most important class in society, is the one which is chiefly benefited by the new distribution." Ricardo then admits that the distribution of net income is in any case a matter of choice to some extent. "Distribute, then, the net income as you please. Give a little more to one class and a little less to another, yet you do not thereby diminish it" (*Principles,* chap. 32).

3. To whom, then, falls the task of effecting the transfers of income? The answer is, to the government: "If," Ricardo writes, "they [the stockholders] are unjustly benefited, let the degree in which they are so be accurately ascertained, and then it is for the legislature to devise a remedy" (*Principles,* chap. 32).

The conclusion to be drawn from these few, probably overgeneral observations is that in a nonimaginary world the only way to abolish wage labor is to give the workers, individually or collectively, access to the net product. They will then be able to participate in the accumulation process and in the power of last resort which belongs to the owner of capital and can belong to no other.

## The Businessman's Motivation and Business Rationale

When a second-rate economist says one thing right, that is as far as it goes. Having observed that big modern firms were being run by people who were not shareholders, certain authors concluded that "economic power" had changed hands, with the manager taking the place of the capitalist.

This was the theory put forward just after World War II by the U.S. economist James Burnham in his book *The Managerial Era*. The idea was then taken up by Galbraith and developed with all the latter's writing skill, and afterwards it was almost universally acknowledged that the "technostructure" had definitely ousted the owning class from the privileged position it used to hold. For some years, though, this theory, which found extraordinary favor both with right-wing neoliberals and with the modern left and "humanist" circles, has been in doubt.

In essence, the power of capitalists is not to interfere with the management and running of businesses in which they have invested their savings but to demand an account of that management, including the right to dismiss those in charge and to appoint others. No more, no less, but it is enough to ensure the fundamental precedence of the owner over his agent.

Whether an owner be a private individual or a public body, ownership is a *right,* not a function. Consequently, the owner's natural tendency is to relinquish the duty of vigilance over his asset and the effort this calls for, to which his use of the asset does not incline him.[9] The manager's natural inclination, on the other hand, is to fill the vacant place this leaves and to be accountable to nobody but himself. History is full of examples of these two types of behavior. In every era, under every regime, the clever steward has taken advantage of his master's absence. But there nearly always comes a time when the master reminds him that he has his powers on trust from him, the master, alone and withdraws them abruptly, either to give them to someone else or to exercise them, for a while, himself. The recent history of the leading capitalist firms abounds with such cases where company heads who thought they could never be removed are summarily dismissed.

The most surprising thing about the theory set before us is that the emergence of the technostructure corroborates an analysis made long ago by classical political economy, whereas minds as shrewd as Galbraith's see the same development as proof instead that political economy is no longer capable of explaining the driving forces of modern society. From the very beginning, political economy distinguished, at any rate conceptually, between capitalist and entrepreneur. This is one of the few points on which French economists have shown themselves to be more systematic than their British counterparts, of whom the greatest (Ricardo included) made that distinction only by incidence. Today it is axiomatic, having become a fact of life, but it was no mean achievement for Jean-Baptiste Say to observe in 1803 that the entrepreneur as such had to be regarded as a "worker" paid to administer the "work of production." His observation shows the insight of a discerning analyst who was capable of differentiating mentally between two states which in the practice of his day were, more often than not, still merged. There can have been very few entrepreneurs in the Napoleonic era, when Say was writing, who were not at the same time the owners of the factories or business houses they ran. But as the economic system progressed, its components diversified.[10] In the last quarter of the nineteenth century Alfred Marshall, already the most famous British economist of that era, made the following observation which, literary style apart, might have been penned by one of today's writers:

> The ultimate undertakers of the risks incurred by a joint-stock company are the shareholders; but as a rule they do not take much active part in engineering the buisness and controlling its general policy. . . . In the modern world, the employer, who may have but little capital of his own, acts as the boss of the great industrial wheel. The interests of owners of capital and of workers radiate towards him and from him: and he holds them all together in a firm grip.[11]

The argument most often put forward by those who see the advent of the managerial era as belying the execrated principles of "capitalism" finally comes down to this: Today's managers, not being owners of the business, are no longer primarily motivated by the urge to make the maximum profit to go into someone else's pocket. They have other motivations, foremost of which are the desire for power as evidenced by the turnover fixation, wanting to have control for its own sake, and so on.

It is difficult to believe that sensible people can accept this jumble of ideas as a line of reasoning. To bring a modicum of order and clarity, two areas have to be differentiated which are completely alien to each other: (1) the specific motivations of the manager and also of all the people who, at whatever level, hold a position of responsibility in the business; and (2) the rules of the game that the business must obey if it is to hold its own in the economic system. The motivations of the manager and his executives differ with temperaments: enjoying that kind of work, the desire to make money, wanting to "be somebody," and—in the case of the top man, who is often (but not always) the most ambitious of all—the need to impose his "ego" on others. These are probably some of the many subjective factors that impel the members of a business to get into the driver's seat and then stay there. But though they may explain individual behavior, they only partly explain a firm's policy. That policy will admittedly be influenced by the personalities of its managers, and the image it has will depend, say, on whether they are basically go-ahead or basically conservative. But to have any image at all, the firm must exist and stay in existence; and to do that, it must be a successful member of the exchange circuit. And, as I think I have already shown, success here rests entirely on the ability to make a profit—which, as economic life progresses, requires an ever-increasing degree of rationality in decision making all along the line (that is, from the choice of what good or service to supply, to its sale).

## Notes

1. The competition model described by Ricardo allows the rate of profit to be higher in some particularly unattractive activities, otherwise nobody would engage in them. Similarly, equality of profit applies only to one economic territory. From one area to another the rate of profit may differ even if capital can circulate freely, because Ricardo assumes that an Englishman will as a ruler prefer to invest in England, where the rate of profit is lower, rather than in Portugal, where it is higher. In today's world, where investment decisions are taken in the head offices of big multinational corporations, the argument of national preference applies less often or has even ceased to apply; and this is why the world market, at any rate for certain product categories, is becoming progressively more integrated. This movement, however tentative as yet, illustrates the real economy's tendency to conform to the theoretical model.

2. The distinction between necessary price and market price was made by Smith, but it was Ricardo who developed it fully and made it a cornerstone of

his reasoning. It may be of more than passing interest to note that, according to several reliable sources, Ricardo's father, an orthodox Jew who emigrated from Holland to England, sent the young David to the Talmud Tora, a famous school in Amsterdam. It is possible that there he learned to reason according to the method he was to use so brilliantly later in life. His conception of economic law is similar in many respects to the Jewish conception of the law—a goal which is forever inaccessible but toward which man ceaselessly strives.

3. Ricardo, *Principles,* chap. 6. And in chapter 22 we read: "It may be laid down as a principle uniformly true that the only great encouragement to the increased production of a commodity is its market value exceeding its natural or necessary value."

4. Or because of the time taken to run down inventories, if supply is being adjusted downward.

5. It may happen for production to continue to increase after this point has been passed. This would be the case if demand rose. The above definition is subject to the ceteris paribus proviso.

6. It is in practice possible, by means of a better turnover of capital, to maintain a satisfactory rate of return on capital, while reducing the profit margin in relation to gross product. This applies to both the individual business and the economy as a whole.

7. The fact that Ricardo places this passage in a footnote does not mean that it is unimportant. After all, the famous theory of comparative costs, which still serves as the basic principle for free trade and for the charter of the GATT, is set out in a few lines, several of them footnotes.

8. The wage is production expenditure for the business and consumption expenditure for the wage earner.

9. "Ownership is the right to have the use and disposal of things," states the French *Code Civil.* The "disposal of *things,*" not of people.

10. This does not mean that the day will come when there is no owner-entrepreneur. There is no law against a capitalist having the mind and talents of a manager, and if he has he will almost certainly choose to run his own business rather than someone else's. But today's owner-entrepreneur will differentiate carefully between that part of his earnings which represents profit on his capital and that part which represents his wage as a manager and the distinction will be apparent in the firm's accounts.

11. Alfred Marshall, *Elements of Economic Industry,* 1st ed., 1892; reprinted in London by Macmillan in 1964.

*Part Two*

# The Role of the Market in Economics

*9*

# The Objective Value Theory Defines the Subject of Economics

## The So-called "Law" of Supply and Demand

A "free-marketer" should resist with all his might the idea that there is a "law" of supply and demand whereby the price of goods is set objectively in a free market. To claim there was such a "law" would be to consign economics to the realm of the arbitrary and, at bottom, to misunderstand the meaning given to the word *law* in science.

What does this so-called law, predicated by practically all contemporary economists under the influence of writers like Walras, Jevons, and Böhm-Bawerk, the founders of modern economics, tell us? It says that, in a nonregulated market, if there is a strong demand for a particular product—tomatoes, say—then its price will go up, whereas if supply increases, the price will go down. Any street seller of fruit and vegetables knows this and does not need an economist to prove it to him. Neither did the world have to wait for Newton to tell it that when a fruit is ripe its weight will make it fall and land on the head of anyone careless enough to be in the way.

Newton was able to found modern physics because he discovered that the fall of the apple was governed by a more general principle, gravity, which was also the explanation of the movement of the heavenly bodies. Far from being an accident, the fall of the apple was clearly governed by a law and the velocity at which it traveled toward the earth could even be expressed algebraically, with the friction of the air being discounted as negligible.

With regard to prices, the question is whether, over and above their incessant fluctuation on the market through the interaction of supply and demand, which are themselves in constant movement, there is a regulating principle capable of accounting for their long-term trend. We know that the classicists believed they had found this regulating principle in the cost of production (itself proportional to the quantity of labor applied and allowing for the incidence of profit), for which they used the rather strange expression, "natural price." Because of the competition among producers in response to the pressure of demand, the market price will tend to fall in line with this natural price. The factor that determines price, according to this way of thinking, is supply. Demand affects price only for the period during which production has not had time to adjust to the new market conditions. If strong demand arises for a particular good or service the price will rise, but it would be wrong to see the process as confirmation of the so-called law of supply and demand. Competition among producers will quickly put an end to the anomaly known as "overpricing," an expression which has meaning only in relation to production cost. If, conversely, customers no longer want a product, its price will fall (below its "natural price") until the capitalists, because of their declining profit, reduce their investment in that branch of activity, or at least stop increasing their investment at the same rate as in other activities. In the long term—an expression which relates more to the "economic model" than to the world as it is—demand is not a determinant of price. The objective value theory rests on this axiom. It is, however, clear that there is a whole category of goods the value of which is determined solely by the demand for them. These are the scarce goods: in other words, those which are not reproducible at will, either because they are the product of nonstandardized labor (a work of art) or because they exist in limited quantities in nature. In those cases, it is impossible to explain market price in terms of production cost.

This is why Ricardo (after Smith) divided goods into two main categories.

The first is that of goods obtained by standardized labor. These are by far the most numerous. Whenever there is a reference to "laws" governing their value, says Ricardo, these are the goods involved. In other words, they are the only subject of economics, the objective value theory applying solely to them. These goods are reproducible more or less at will. Many of them, Ricardo further states, "may be multiplied . . . almost without any assignable limit, if we are disposed to bestow the labour necessary to obtain them.'' This statement, heavily criticized by Walras, appears prophetic today, for modern industry would be capable of producing most current articles "without any assignable limit."

The second category is that of goods which derive their value from their "scarcity alone." Among these, Ricardo lists pictures and statues, "wines of a peculiar quality," rare books, and coins. "Their value is wholly independent of the quantity of labour originally necessary to produce them, and varies with the varying wealth and inclinations of those who are desirous to possess them." Their characteristic is that "no labour can increase the quantity of such goods and therefore their value cannot be lowered by an increased supply." This is why, says Ricardo, they "form a very small part of the mass of commodities daily exchanged in the market" (*Principles,* chap. 1, sect. 1). After referring to these goods in the first pages of his book, Ricardo decides—a decision the full importance of which has not been realized— not to refer to them again in the rest of his work. By their nature, they are not subject to the labor theory of value and their prices are not, therefore, subject to any regulation. No "law" may be formulated for them.

On the face of it, there is something disconcerting in this dichotomy between some economic goods that are amenable to the theory and others that are not. What sort of a theory is it that, to hold good, has to exclude from its field of application a whole part of the economic life it is supposed to account for? It is not surprising that Ricardo's successors could not rest until they had found a unifying principle enabling them to explain all economic phenomena without allowing for certain more or less arbitrary exceptions. It is this search for an (impossible) unity that, to my mind, has made the deepest mark on the history of economics since the late nineteenth century, and the crisis that economics is currently going through is also caused by this fundamental question—even though this is not always apparent.

As to the unifying principle that Ricardo's successors found, or rather rediscovered, it was hardly a discovery. Linking an automobile (reproducible good) with a Van Gogh (nonreproducible good), or wheat (reproducible good) with a plot of land on the Côte d'Azur (nonreproducible good), there is at least one common denominator: They are all wanted. It is because there is a demand for them that they are on the market. I would add that economists were all the more encouraged to reinstate demand as the determinant of value in that Ricardo, with his uncompromising logic, had mentioned a further exclusion from the field of application of the labor theory of value. This exclusion was so large that it covered the whole of the market. This category of goods, the value of which also depended on scarcity, in other words on demand exceeding supply,[1] was that of monopolized goods and this is true, adds Ricardo, "of all other commodities for a limited period" (*Principles,* chap. 31).

So it is monopoly that frustrates, in all possible cases, the determination of value by labor and the process of accumulation. A monopoly exists whenever, for whatever reason, it is impossible to increase the output of a good for which demand is higher than present supply. Monopoly is definitive for "statues and pictures" and for "wines of a peculiar quality." The same applies to a large number of goods that Ricardo does not list but that play a far more important part in the life of society, with building land (in densely populated areas) at the top of the list.

Alongside these various monopoly situations that arise because it is impossible to increase the quantity supplied, there are others the origin of which is quite different. These are the monopolies created artificially by producers who come to an arrangement. Thus the simplest form of monopoly, namely the control of a market by a single producer, is in reality an extreme case. Between that extreme case and a competitive market there is every possible level of quasi-monopoly and oligopoly, and here the comment of Ricardo that I have just quoted is again relevant. *In the short term, all markets are to a greater or lesser degree in this state because a certain time is always needed for supply to adjust to demand* and a producer is often in a position to make his customer believe that the brand he is selling has special qualities (and is therefore "scarce"). This is why the "effective price" is never the same as the "natural price" but, on a market governed by the principle of competition, the former is constantly being brought down toward the latter. The effect of competition among producers, as markets merge and become more fluid, is to reduce the time it takes for supply to react to demand pressure. Considered from the standpoint we are concerned with here, the inventory policy of the distributive trades is generally a powerful instrument of adjustment which helps to limit the fluctuation of effective prices around the natural price.

The classical analysis also enables us to understand the special situation of most agricultural foodstuffs. The reason a special system of protection can be envisaged for them is that they are at the mercy of the interaction of supply and demand which will sometimes be excessively favorable to them (during periods of shortage) and sometimes disastrously unfavorable (when there is a glut). Intelligently framed measures to stabilize agricultural prices are aimed at keeping the market price close to a "guide price" which should express the average cost of production (including profit). But this latter average is itself bound to change under many influences including the changes of consumption habit on the side of demand and the improvement of production method on the side of supply. That explains why what may be theoretically justified is in practice likely to bring many adverse effects.

The example of farm goods is particularly meaningful because it enables us to understand the place that the market mechanism should in principle have in an organized economy. From what has been said, one might be tempted to conclude that the role of the authorities should be to restrict the free play of supply and demand by acting, depending on the circumstances, either on the latter (buying stocks) or on the former (selling stocks). This is true only for markets where supply is slow to respond to demand (farm goods, raw materials whose production requires heavy investment, etc.) or uncertain (foodstuffs whose production depends as much on weather conditions as on personal effort). In the very many cases where the adjustment is less difficult, it is practically always via the free play of market forces that there is the best chance of arriving at the right price.

In Ricardo's work, the word that recurs most frequently is "regulate." Authentically liberal (in the European sense) classical economic science is both explanatory and normative. Its aim is, as far as possible, to shield economic activity from the arbitrary and the indeterminate. By deliberately forgoing the regulating principle consisting of reference to the necessary labor time (and to profit on accumulated capital), neoliberal economics is caught in an impasse because no law can be derived from an economic model based on the primacy of demand. Thus, many of the constructs it has built over nearly a hundred years, beginning with the famous supply and demand curves—plotted for the first time by Alfred Marshall, who tried to reconcile the irreconcilable (Ricardian theory and the psychological theory of value)—are dubious construction. As to our society, based on this ideology, it is the reflection of that ideology: pseudoscientific, in thrall to the arbitrary.

In the history of modern Western civilization, the objective value theory has so far been no more than a brief intrusion. Its authors sought to put it in place of the psychological ("or utility") theory of value advanced by the economists of the eighteenth century who already believed in the "law of supply and demand." It was too exacting, and the avenue its authors had opened up was quickly sealed off again. The law of supply and demand was re-enthroned about 1870 and has reigned supreme ever since.

The classicists were keenly aware of the fact that this was the most important point on which economists would ever be divided.

Ricardo, for example, wrote: "The opinion that the price of commodities depends solely on the proportion of supply to demand, or demand to supply, has become almost an axiom in political economy, and has been the source of much error in that science" (*Principles*, chap. 30).

The term "law of supply and demand" was used by Adam Smith and then by Malthus, but Smith was the inventor of the labor theory of value, in which Malthus also believed. Appearances notwithstanding, this does not contradict the case I have just made, because the original contribution made by Ricardo, true to his critical approach, was to show that explaining value by labor and at the same time maintaining that there is a law of supply and demand is a contradiction in terms. It is this "law" that modern economists have reinstated for good, or so they believe. In *Value and Capital,* first published in 1937 and, together with two or three other works, the basis of present university doctrine, John Hicks, 1972 Nobel prizewinner in economics, sets out his "theory of exchange," based wholly on demand behavior and ends with the words: "This concludes all I have to say on the theory of exchange. Indeed, I doubt if there is much more, on a similar plane of generality, which can be added." There is indeed nothing to be added to the "law of consumer's demand" or to the "working of the general equilibrium system" developed by Hicks, but—one fears—much to be taken away from it.

## The "Water and Diamond Paradox"

At the source of the modern theory of demand is the "solution" found for the famous water and diamond paradox whereby the Vienna economists a century ago believed they had completely renovated the utility theory of value. Since then, their construct has been "perfected" by, among others, John Hicks who, in pushing wide a door half opened by Vilfredo Pareto, thought he had stripped the theory of its most troublesome subjective aspects, but in fact left the fundamentals intact. Adam Smith, followed by David Ricardo, had noted that water and air, infinitely useful to life, had "under ordinary circumstances" no market value whereas gold or diamonds, though of very little utility by comparison, were highly valuable. Was this not evidence that the basis of value had to be sought elsewhere than in utility?

To show that this was not so, the Vienna economists asked themselves whether there could not be circumstances in which more would be paid for a glass of water than for a diamond. Yes, they decided, whenever there is an urgent need for the water. And they dreamed up the following example. A man is lost in the desert and has used up all his provisions. The only thing left in the bag on his back is a diamond of great value. Surely such a traveller would be prepared to give up his precious stone in exchange for a drink of water that would help him to survive. To make their brilliant deduction applicable to any eventuality, these same economists framed their concept of marginal utility, defined not as the utility of the marginal unit (the utility of the last glass of water) but as the change made to total utility by the addition of one more unit. Here is an example. Jacques has, say, ten liters of water, sufficient to meet his daily needs for drinking, washing himself and his clothes, and so on. If one deciliter is added to this amount, the increase in utility will be hardly perceptible. The situation would be completely different if Jacques' initial stock was only five deciliters of water: in other words, just enough to save him from dying of thirst and to damp his forehead once a day. One additional deciliter would increase total utility considerably. So—the mathematics-obsessed Austrian economists pointed out—marginal utility is a *decreasing* function of quantity. The more water Jacques has, the smaller the marginal utility of one deciliter will become until it is finally imperceptible. In that seemingly harmless conclusion, the Vienna economists thought they had finally found what they had long been looking for: the decisive argument that would confound British classical political economy and its master, Ricardo. Did not diminishing marginal utility prove that utility, like value, is a function of scarcity?

Through reasoning on the basis of want, scarcity became the universal principle to explain value. Ricardo's annoying dichotomy was disposed of. A more general theory had at last been found that applied to all economic goods.

Even though it was admitted that, in the case of reproducible goods, the production cost did play a part in price determination, this was now no more than a secondary cause that could, if necessary, be dispensed with. And even this last concession to the Ricardian theory of value was more apparent than real because the cost of production was now defined as the sum of the costs of the various factors of production: cost of raw materials + wages + depreciation of capital = total cost of production, to which was then applied a rate of profit the origin of which could no longer be explained. In other words, the new school saw the cost of production from the subjective standpoint of the enterprise. Ricardo's production cost had a social character *and was inherently understood* as being proportional to the quantity of labor that had to be expended in producing a commodity.[2] From this standpoint it is absurd to make the cost of production depend on the wage rate. It is the reverse that is true: The number of hours of labor determines the value produced, and the wage rate the distribution of this value among the various parties concerned.

Making scarcity the determinant of value for *all* goods was a complete reversal of perspective. For Ricardo, scarce goods were an exception to the rule. For the new school, the exception became the rule.

It remains to be seen whether the assumptions from which the new school argued were compatible with the problems of exchange as such. The case of the traveller in the desert ready to exchange a precious diamond for a glass of water is an illustration that it is not so. I would not dwell on this fabrication, which could just about serve as the plot for a "B" movie, but for the fact that it is still being taught to economics students in all the capitalist countries as an introduction to marginalist theory.

Let us suppose, therefore, that the man with the diamond, already half-dying of thirst, meets another man in the middle of the desert carrying a goatskin with just a little water left in it. "Please give me a drink of water and I'll give you this magnificent stone," he pleads. Following which, many different situations could arise, *none of them constituting an act of exchange.*

1. The man with the water—let us call him W—will not accept the deal. What use would a diamond be when he has hardly enough water to keep him alive for more than a few days?
2. W, whom I assume for the purposes of this alternative to have the gambling instinct, accepts the offer, telling himself: "Either the oasis is nearer than we think, in which case once we are there I shall be rich, or else I am going to die of thirst and a day sooner or later makes no odds." This is not an exchange for like value; it is a gamble.
3. W, a charitable soul in this case, takes pity on D (the man with

the diamond) and offers him half of his water with no strings attached. Let us assume that our two travellers are fortunate enough to reach the oasis. D then offers the diamond to W in gratitude for sharing his water. In this case there have been two successive gifts: the water given by W to D and the diamond given by D to W.

4. The story could have a less edifying ending, like this: The parched traveller offers his diamond purely to distract the attention of the man he has chanced upon, whom he then attacks suddenly to steal his water. The two men fight savagely using up their remaining strength but neither wins. Meantime the water is spilt upon the sand whilst they are locked in their fruitless struggle. This situation, too, is wholly removed from the world of economics.

Let us try to get back there by changing the circumstances of the example. The two men *know* that they have a reasonable chance of reaching the oasis. The deal proposed is no longer wholly absurd, but it is crooked. W knows he has enough water to save both their lives and if, in spite of this knowledge, he demands a diamond in return, he is behaving like a blackmailer. (Incidentally, if W is the only one to know, then he can be considered as indulging in insider trading.)

Probably the charming professors who were the economists of late nineteenth century Vienna must have been unaware of the enormity of the conclusions that could be drawn from what they thought to be a rigorously argued case. Not for a moment did they stop to consider what it would cost to ship a drink of water to the middle of the desert.

To tackle correctly the problem they set themselves, they should have devised another example. Let us imagine a firm has to establish an outpost in the middle of the desert. What, for such a firm, would be the value of the water it has to bring there at high cost? Those are the terms in which NASA worked on the problem in the early 1970s. To provide a modicum of comfort for Charles Conrad, Pierre Weitz, and Joseph Kervin (the three members of the crew of Skylab in May 1973), NASA did not stint: It installed a washbasin and a shower on board. It worked out that putting one liter of water into orbit cost $2000. That expressed the value of water in space in the current state of the art. If we were to reason like the founders of marginalism we would try to estimate the value on the basis of hypotheses as absurd as they are improbable. It would be imagined that Skylab was forced to prolong its stay in space because of the malfunction of an engine. What sum of money, how big a diamond, would Charles Conrad be prepared to give

Pierre Weitz in exchange for one extra drink of water? To an absurd question like that, no intelligible reply is possible.

In his lecture notes on prices published under the title of *Price Theory* (already quoted in Chapter 3), Milton Friedman writes: "The solution of the diamond–water paradox enables the neo-classicists to bring in demand as determinant of price." It is true that he immediately adds: "However, the triumph of marginal and diminishing marginal utility has, in a sense, been carried too far." Unfortunately, Mr. Friedman drew no conclusions from this latter remark and remained a prisoner of the old theory.

Unable to say at what stage exchange takes place, the psychological school gets the explanation wrong. In the water-in-the-desert case, the exchange takes place in the accounts of enterprise X (the firm establishing an outpost in the desert, or NASA, etc.). This first exchange, relative to the production process, *may* be followed by a second—the sale of the drink of water—provided there is a market. The existence of a market is conceivable neither in the desert where D and W meet nor in the cabin of Skylab.

## Impossibility of Explaining the Functioning of the Market on the Basis of Barter

It is here that the error the psychological school was bound to commit because of its premises comes fully to light. If the exchange value of any good (or service) derives from its utility, it has to be possible to explain the formation of that value on the basis of barter between two persons, each of whom feels the need to own what belongs to the other. That is what the marginalists tried to do, but they solved nothing because it is impossible to reconstitute the functioning of a market by arguing from the premise of elementary barter dealing. Why? The reason is that to form a market at least one other condition is necessary, which is that none of the participants shall have the *power* to impose his solution. The modern theory of games brings out this condition. A game with two participants is distinguished from a game with *n* participants in the degree of *power* that each of them has to affect the outcome of the game.

It is in the light of game theory that the market has to be studied, as is proposed by the mathematician John von Neumann and the economist Oskar Morgenstern in their book *Theory of Games and Economic Behavior* (New York, 1944), a major source of economic thinking over the last twenty-five years. An Austrian by birth, Morgenstern remained faithful to the Viennese school's psychological approach. Nonetheless, the path that von Neumann traced with him may also lead to a return to the objective value theory. For that to come about, economists would first need to escape from the realm, to use Michel Foucault's language, of the episteme established at the end of the nineteenth century by the "neoliberal" school.

The reader may be tempted to see a contradiction between the conditions set here for constructing a competitive market model and what I wrote in Chapter 8, page 211, specifically that the existence of such market could be conceived, at a pinch, with just one producer. But for that to be so, it has to be supposed, as the reader will remember, that the single supplier is not allowed the *power* to fix the quantity supplied as he wishes. Similarly, there could be a competitive market over a lasting period with only two (or three . . .) participants if the law prohibited them from agreeing on prices, quantities produced, and so on. In other words, if, by strictly limiting the choice of their respective *strategies*, the law artificially reestablished the conditions of a game with *n* players.

If we argue the familiar example of the deer hunter and the salmon fisher we come to the same conclusion. Since ten hours of labor are necessary for the fisherman to catch three salmon and for the huntsman to kill one deer, then the exchange has to take place on that basis. But what happens, if the fisherman has no stomach for fish? Is he going to prove that Aristotle was right to maintain that exchange is a relation of equality, and starve to death? More probably, he will finally accept an unfair bargain imposed on him by the huntsman—six salmon, say, for one deer, or the output of twenty hours of labor for the output of ten. Is not the labor theory of value immediately negated by the first transaction between the two men? The answer is no, because this transaction is not an exchange for the reason that the huntsman is wholly in control of the game.

It could be imagined that the huntsman is just as allergic to meat as the fisherman to fish and that each knows the preference of the other, in which case the equivalence of exchange principle stands a very good chance of prevailing. In that eventuality, the isolated couple formed by our two primitives would meet the condition postulated for there to be perfect competition—in other words, that none of the players in the game shall have more influence on the outcome than any other. *In such a game no one loses if he plays rationally.* But for this to be so, it would be necessary in our example to assume that the huntsman's preference for fish and the fisherman's preference for meat are equal—in other words, to introduce into the explanatory model a psychological element that has no place in objective economics. Similarly, a moment ago, it was necessary to introduce the intervention of the government to *impose* the rules of the game on the single producer or the two or three producers involved. That is the deep-lying reason why the perfect competition model has to have *n* competitors assumed to be perfectly *informed* at all times of the rates of exchange obtaining on the market. It is the reciprocal information of the players that here constitutes the decisive factor for neutralizing the effect of preference (Pierre would be ready to hand over four salmon for one deer, but he would not be prepared to pay more than his neighbor who is unwilling to part with more than three salmon).

To explain why perfect competition is so difficult to maintain, the point is that the less control a player has on the outcome of the game the more complicated it is for him to decide on a rational policy. Thus, on the one hand perfect competition, ensuring quality of exchange, is a game in which no player should lose—in contrast with what happens in the aggressive world of the monopolies—provided he plays rationally, whereas on the other it is a game requiring such exceptional qualities that de facto inequality is back again once the first hands in the game are played. Seen in this light, perfect competition is an extreme hypothesis relating to a world of the future that is both rational and more peaceful.

Let us take another look at the inextricable situation in which the holders of the psychological theory of value landed themselves. When I assumed that the huntsman fed solely on fish and the fisherman solely on meat I selected a particularly favorable hypothesis enabling the two preferences to be treated as equivalent because they are absolute in both cases.[3] Since they are equal and of opposite signs they may be disregarded. But in general, a preference is not so clear-cut. The huntsman may like fish more than meat, but from what point on will he consider the marginal utility of fish (for him) to be equal to the marginal utility of meat? According to the psychological theory, this point of equality is determined by the rate at which he will be prepared to exchange his deer for salmon (we may note in passing that the marginalists reasoned on the hypothesis, out of place in a modern economy, that the producer produces both for his own personal consumption and for the market). What will happen if the fisherman, whose preference for meat has a different intensity from the huntsman's preference for fish, therefore applies a different rate of exchange from that of his partner? The marginalists' way out of this dilemma was to introduce the "information" relevant to the market—but that takes us back to the classical model—and the labored arguments they added seem useless in accounting for the phenomenon. In short, the want consideration may, at a pinch, explain what would happen between isolated pairs of producers, each wishing to acquire the goods supplied by the other, but if all those pairs were brought together in the form of a market, the objective value theory would come into its own again. That is what Malthus already failed to understand. In the comments he makes to Malthus, Ricardo refutes in advance the approach taken fifty years later by the Vienna economists:

> In all that Mr. Malthus has yet said about exchangeable value, it appears to depend a great deal on the wants of mankind, and the relative estimation in which they hold commodities. This would be true if men from various countries were to meet in a fair with a variety of productions, and each with a separate commodity, undisturbed by the competition of any other seller. Commodities, under such circumstances, would be bought and sold according to the relative wants of those attending the fair. But, when the wants of society are well known, when there are hundreds of competitors who are willing to satisfy those wants, on the condition only that they shall have the known and usual profits, there can be no such rule for regulating the value of commodities.
>
> In such a fair, as I have supposed, a man might be willing to give a pound of gold for a pound of iron, knowing the use of the latter metal; but when competition freely operated, he could not give that value for iron, and why? Because iron would infallibly sink to its cost of production—cost of production being the pivot about which all the market price moves. (*Notes on Malthus*, p. 24)

This is the place for the critique of the demand curves devised by the neoliberal economists in an attempt to explain the determination of what they called the "equilibrium price" by demand. Modern economists are at last beginning to suspect that these curves are an artificial construction with no scientific significance. The only way of *demonstrating* why this is so is by reference to the labor theory of value.

## Critique of the Demand Curve

In a country where everyone eats his fill, bread is not scarce but not free either. Bakers sell it for more or less what it costs to produce (including profit). The same applies to salt and all the low-priced necessaries. The fact that the cost of production of these goods is very low explains why effective demand for them is more or less the same as total wants, because no one is so poor as not to be able to buy the amount of bread or salt he or she needs. In fact, scarcity does not generate value for any reproducible good *on a free market*.

In its most general form, a demand curve is a graphic representation of a functional relationship between price and quantity. Here is an example. At a price of F.11,000, the annual demand for automobiles will be, say, 1,350,000 units. At a price of F.10,000, it will be 1,500,000 and at F.9000 it will be 1,700,000, and so on. Almost invariably (this is merely a broad outline of the theory) the curve slopes downward from left to right because the quantity of demand increases, in most cases, if the price falls and vice versa. This, in the terminology of modern economists, is the "law of demand" (Hicks, ch. 2). But, as Milton Friedman casually remarks, the function that links quantity with price "cannot be used to analyse a concrete problem." No great effort of thought is necessary to recognize that demand curves are unable to account for reality. It is sufficient to realize the arbitrariness with which they are necessarily constructed. What is their purpose? It is to show on a curve the quantities that *would be* demanded at different prices over the same period of time. But for each period of time there is only one price and only one quantity demanded. French people bought 2,000,000 automobiles in 1973. How many would they have bought if the price had been one-third lower? The most sophisticated market research could never give more than a hypothetical answer to this kind of question. Why, in such conditions, do economists insist on bringing such a function into their reasoning? Because, to justify the existence of a "law" of supply and demand, it is essential to conceive of a supply curve and a demand curve simultaneously.

The first indicates the minimum price at which producers will be prepared to manufacture a particular quantity and the second indicates the maximum quantity that will be bought at a particular price. The point at which the two curves are supposed to intersect is the market equilibrium price. In the classical theory, this point of equilibrium is the cost of production as determined objectively by reference to the quantity of labor (it therefore depends solely on the production conditions). In the neoliberal theory, no such determination is possible because the cost of production is conceived as the sum of a number of costs (wages, raw materials, and so on) the level of which also depends on the relation between supply and demand.

To plot the supply curve, therefore, one has to start from existing prices and reason as follows. At current prices of manpower, raw materials, and so on, the cost price of an automobile is, say, F.10,000 for an output of 1,350,000 vehicles. F.10,000 is therefore the minimum price at which manufacturers will be prepared to produce that quantity (as I have already pointed out, the marginalists are unable to tell us whether the F.10,000 includes profit or not or, if it does, where that profit comes from, but no matter . . .). This being so, it is impossible, in the "neoliberal" model, for the supply curve to tell us the relative values of goods because, to construct it, use has to be made of the scale of prices as already *given* by the market. This is why the demand function is so important. On it rests the entire responsibility for the explanation of the scale of prices. But surely the demand curve, as conceived by the modern economists, also takes the scale of prices as given. If that is so, as I now propose to show, then the famous theory, even in the "perfected" form given to it by John Hicks, is tautological.

This is not the place for a detailed description of the theory revised and corrected by Hicks. Instead I shall concentrate on a few of the problems it raises.

The objection directed at the first-generation marginalists was that their theory assumed it was possible to quantify as vague and subjective a notion as utility. According to them, market equilibirum was reached when the prices of any two goods (let us call them $x$ and $y$) were in the same relation to each other as their marginal utilities:

$$\frac{U_x}{U_y} = \frac{P_x}{P_y}$$

To plot a demand curve it was necessary, at least in principle, to know by how much the utility of a given quantity of $x$ exceeded that of a given quantity of $y$. It was to eliminate this condition, which threw a veil of suspicion over the whole argument of the marginalists, that John Hicks strove, in *Value and Capital,* to present the idea afresh using, among other things, a "discovery" by Vilfredo Pareto. Suffice it to recall here that this innovation consisted in plotting demand curves from "indifference" curves, the simplest model of which relates to a consumer having to choose between two goods, $x$ and $y$.

If M and M' are on the same indifference curve, it means that the consumer derives as much "utility" from having quantity AM of $x$

plus quantity BM of *y* as from having quantity CM' of *x* plus quantity DM' of *y*.

Since it is supposed that greater satisfaction is derived from having more than from having less, the indifference curves to the left of MM' represent less advantageous combinations and the curves to the right represent more advantageous combinations.

A comparison of indifference curves therefore tells us that one combination is held to be preferable to another but there is no need to know by how much (see Figure 9.1). This is why Hicks saw these curves as a major stepping-stone. How did he move on from indifference curves to the demand curve that links price with quantity? Here I refer the curious reader to the reputable textbooks. In principle, the process consists in saying that the consumer has a money income I and reasoning as follows. If the consumer used all I to buy *x*, the unit price of which is $P_x$, he could buy $I/P_x$ units of *x*. If instead he bought only units of *y*, he would obtain $I/P_y$ units. The point $I/P_y$ on the vertical axis is then joined to point $I/P_x$ on the horizontal axis by a straight line.

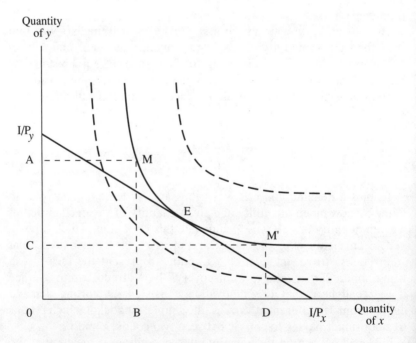

**Figure 9.1** How one is supposed to move from indifference curves to the so-called demand curve.

Any point on that line represents a combination of $x$ and $y$ which the consumer can acquire with his income I. The point of equilibrium is reached at E where the line is tangent to an indifference curve.[4] Demand curves (there are several kinds depending on whether income or prices are assumed constant) are constructed on the basis of a series of indifference curves and a series of income lines.

What criticisms can legitimately be made of the demand curve which, I would repeat, was entirely concocted by the marginalists in order to reassert the "law" of supply and demand?

1.  The purpose of indifference curves is to express the scale of preferences of consumers *in dissociation from prices on the market.* That, however, is impossible except by chance, and here is the reason. One does not need to be a great mathematician to realize that the slope of an indifference curve measures at the margin the rate of substitution of $x$ for $y$ (quantity of $y$ the utility of which compensates the consumer for his forgoing a marginal unit of $x$). But is it possible to define this rate of substitution for products that we *buy* without reference to what they cost? Suppose we were suddenly plunged into a world where everything was free. Our scale of preferences would be completely changed. A large number of goods that we presently consume because they cost less than others would cease to interest us. For many French people, for example, the rate of substitution of margarine for butter is a matter of price. Margarine would disappear from the kitchen if butter were cheaper. The same applies to industrial products. Who would prefer, except for financial reasons, to buy a black-and-white television set? In other words, the demand curve, derived from indifference curves, is a prisoner of the system of prices the formation of which it is supposed to help explain. I would add that the income line joining $I/P_x$ to $I/P_y$ is intrinsically dependent on the system of prices.

2.  According to the tenets of the marginalists, point E is that where the rate of substitution (in terms of utility) of $x$ for $y$ is equal to the ratio between their prices. It was admitted that utility U is not quantifiable but $U_x/U_y$ (which measures the slope of the indifference curve) is, at least indirectly, since this ratio is, by assumption, equal to $P_x/P_y$ (the ratio measuring the slope of the income line). Here we are in pure fantasyland: The so-called equation $U_x/U_y = P_x/P_y$ is meaningless since, at the market equilibrium point, exchange values (prices) are roughly proportional to the cost of production, not to utility. This relation of equality is worthy of the schoolmen in its supposition that the notion of utility corresponds to a quantifiable substance.

Let me digress here for a moment. The masters of the psychological school were clearly not unaware of the objection. We have seen the legerdemain, borrowed from Pareto, that Hicks used to get round it. A more interesting approach is that of Walras, who simply assumed the problem to be resolved. This is what he wrote:

> At first sight, it seems impossible to take the analysis any further because of the fact that absolute utility of intensity escapes us, not being in any direct and measurable relation to time or space as is utility of extension and quantity owned. Well, this difficulty is not insurmountable. *Let us suppose that* such a relation exists; we shall then be able to account exactly and mathematically for the respective influences of utility of extension, utility of intensity and quantity owned on prices.
>
> *I therefore suppose* a standard to exist for measuring the intensity of wants or intensive utility.[5]

This cavalier approach is not prima facie nonscientific. Scientists often find themselves having to assume to be quantifiable things that are not at the start and that become so later after having been used in the theory (an example is mass in physics). But this is certainly not the case with "intensive utility." Ricardo, too, assumes the existence of a universal standard of value (which he, for more convenience, calls gold but which has nothing to do with that metal),[6] at the same time warning us that we do not have, and never shall have, such an invariable standard. Even so, in his sytem, value depends on something that is theoretically quantifiable: the number of hours of labor.

3. With no objective foundation, analysis based on so-called "demand functions" tends to lead to pseudoscientific sophistication. Students are familiar with the "income effect" and the "substitution effect" attributed to changes in the price of a particular good. If the price of something falls, then the consumer will tend to buy more and to reduce his purchases of other goods which are now relatively more expensive. So much for the substitution effect. The income effect, which attracted more attention from the economists, stems from the fact that a fall in the price of a good increases the consumer's purchasing power although his nominal income is unchanged. Here I would like to say a word about the difference in interpretation, much emphasized in textbooks, between Slutsky, the Russian economist, and John Hicks. Here is what the difference is all about. Pierre has an income of $100. The price of $x$ is $1 and so is that of $y$. Pierre buys 50 units of $x$ and 50 of $y$. The price of $x$ falls by half. Pierre then buys 80

units of $x$ (at 50 cents) and 60 of $y$ (at \$1). His total purchase is therefore \$100 but his lot is improved. It is therefore supposed that, to compensate this "income effect," \$25 is taken from him. With his new income of \$75, Pierre can now purchase the same quantity of the two goods as before (50 units of $x$ and 50 units of $y$). For Slutsky, the "apparent real income" (sic) has still not changed. His argument is that with \$75 it is possible, if one so desires, to buy as much as with \$100 regardless of the other possible combinations. But Hicks thinks that the \$75 constitutes a higher "real income" than the previous \$100. Why? Because Pierre, at the new price, has been able to place himself on a higher indifference curve. If, for example, he buys 60 $x$ and 45 $y$ instead of 50 $x$ and 50 $y$, it is because he prefers the former bundle. Hicks argues that, for the "real income" to be kept equal, a few dollars must be taken away from Pierre to bring him back to the old indifference curve (but clearly not to the old 50/50 combination).

This kind of hairsplitting is not evidence of the subtlety of economics—it is a sign of its decadence. To what sort of "real income" is the winner of the 1972 Nobel Prize for economics referring? To what Pierre *imagines* his income to be on the basis of his tastes, preferences, and so on. True subtlety is to be found in Ricardo who, it will be remembered (see Chapters 3 and 6), defined "real" income objectively, without regard to the quantity of products that can be purchased with it. For Ricardo, an income of \$100 represents the value of the product of, say, thirty hours' labor.[7] Pierre should therefore receive in exchange as much of $x$ and $y$ as is produced in thirty hours of labor.[8] If the price of $x$ falls it is because $x$ costs less to make, a fortunate circumstance enabling Pierre to buy more goods but having no effect on the "real" value of his income.

What is the alternative to the crumbling edifice of psychological economics? The explanation of price formation on a competitive market has no room for demand curves, which in essence equate the satisfaction of consuming a certain quantity of good $x$ with a sum of money. The volume of demand is really determined by the *ability to supply* a product of equal value. To account for the functioning of the market as a whole it is sufficient to know the supply available, on the principle that demand is the supply of one good in exchange for another. For example, I would say that the *effective demand* on the market of Citroen, or rather the employees and shareholders of that corporation, is represented by the supply of Citroen automobiles. Citroen sells (supplies) its automobiles. Out of the proceeds, the

Citroen employees and shareholders obtain goods and services the value of which (in the classical sense of the word) has to correspond approximately, if the exchange has not been seriously distorted, to that of the vehicles supplied during the year. These goods and services that are demanded represent what other producers supply.

Doing away with demand curves does not mean ignoring the role of demand in an economy. It is quite obvious that goods are not produced just for the sake of producing and that production is geared to needs. That is why Citroen today makes automobiles rather than railway carriages and will make railway carriages tomorrow if it becomes more economical to travel by rail than by road. The need for automobiles is expressed by the automobile manufacturers' sales.

A little earlier it was seen that demand curves have no practical use for business. Now we see that they are superfluous even theoretically. In the former case the information they are supposed to furnish can never be verified. In the latter they suppose already known what has to be explained. Science rejects useless constructs. As we shall now see, it has all the more reason for doing so.

Demand curves, as I mentioned earlier in passing, show the *maximum* quantities purchased during the time unit (here one year) at a given price. In this way, they turn the problem inside out. If Pierre is in a position to buy something it is because he has something else to supply, say a sum of $100. Logically, Pierre will refuse to pay that amount for any product *valued* at less than $100, but he will buy a product *valued* at more if by chance someone is ready to sell something worth, say, $130 or $150 for $100. The buyer will therefore decide on the *minimum* quantity he wishes to buy for the sum at his disposal. Admittedly, in so deciding, Pierre will compare the satisfaction he hopes to get from his purchase to the money sacrifice he will have to make. That seems to strengthen the case for the psychological school and its demand curves. But exactly what will the comparison relate to? To two comparable things: the value of what is parted with—and an income earner is generally the best person to know that value has some connection with labor—and the value of what is desired. Unless he is overpowered by an irresistible urge, the insidious influence of advertising, or the winning professional smile of the saleswoman, it is unlikely that Pierre will, of himself, agree to hand over more value than he receives. Realizing when he gets back home that he has not been given his "money's worth" (an expression that leads straight back to Ricardo's *Principles*), he will quite rightly conclude that he has been "robbed" or "ripped off" even if he has never read Aristotle's dictum that exchange has to be based on equality.

The critique of the demand curve leads into the critique of the general equilibrium theory, which is the subject of Chapter 10. The notion of general equilibrium is again an invention of the economists of the psychological school and more particularly Walras, the most famous of them all. Recently, this notion has met with the same misfortune as the overvaunted demand curves. Its logical inconsistency is beginning to be realized, to say nothing of its inability to account for the functioning of the market or markets in real life. But here again, modern economists do not (yet) have the conceptual tools to match their intuition. They certainly have the feeling that "general equilibrium" *does not exist* even theoretically but, by turning their backs on the objective value theory, they are incapable of proving this is so.

## The Normative Character of the Objective Value Theory

In basing exchange value on utility, economics is unable to establish any confines for the market other than those imposed from *outside,* by law or habit. Since it knows no law but the "law of supply and demand,"[9] neoliberal economics cannot find any principle in itself to demarcate the marketplace. The market is a place where people buy and sell both goods that are reproducible through human labor (such as automobiles and the factories that make them) and goods that are not reproducible, either because nature does not supply them in plenty (land) or because they are the product of nonstandardized labor (works of art). In addition there are the goods that are artificially nonreproducible, that is, those the scarcity of which stems from the fact that their production is controlled by a monopoly. As the neoliberal economist sees it, the heterogeneity of all these goods is not an obstacle to the unity of economic science—better still, he does not even see this heterogeneity because he finds a common denominator of all these "goods," that of being "wanted," which is enough to give them an exchange value. Prostitutes are wanted. Their rates depend wholly on the "law" of supply and demand. Neoliberal economics, which is concerned solely with "relations of exchange" without defining what these relations relate to, is powerless of itself to exclude from its infinitely expandable market this particular "merchandise." Most economists would probably refuse to take prostitutes into consideration but this would be in the name of "moral principle," "public decency," "human dignity," "respect for the law" (in countries where prostitution is illegal), and so on, all undoubtedly most worthy reasons but all marred by the common defect of having no relevance whatever to economic argument.

A further point I would make is that the heterogeneity of the goods supplied and demanded on the market of the neoliberals does not end there. Not only are the products of human labor bought and sold on it but so is this labor itself. Admittedly, our economists do not pretend that labor is "wanted," but they get round the difficulty by arguing that the demand is indirect. Labor is not demanded just for the sake of the act of labor but because the products of labor are wanted.

The field of investigation of biology was first defined by extension as all the phenomena of life, but theories induced by the observation of those phenomena later made it possible to understand what distinguishes the animate realm from the inanimate realm. In the same way, all sciences supply, be it ex post, the definition of their subject. Till now, economics is the only exception, at least in its "modern" version. In that version, exchange value is determined by utility. "Useful" means "wanted." Want varies from one country to the next and, in a given country, from one period to another, depending on mores, themselves influenced by the dominant ideas, prejudices, and interests. Far from being determined by "human nature," want is in reality governed by that vague and nevertheless all-powerful complex known to philosophers as ideology.

More than all the arguments I have already set forth, the essential reason that seems to me to predestine an early return to the objective value theory, for which a rigorous mathematical formulation could be produced, is this need for an economic science worthy of the name to define the field of its research. Here, the intellectual issue joins with the political issue, namely that of the organization of society. It is not just a matter of nominally restoring economic research to the status of a science (something that it has to earn on the strength of its results). It is a matter of pulling our society out of the rut in which it could well rot away altogether. The "law" that governs the consumer society is precisely that which the late nineteenth century economists of the psychological school, turning their backs on David Ricardo's heroic effort, brought back to reign over economics: the law of supply and demand, which divests the market of any regulatory principle and readmits the merchants to the temple because, according to that law, a thing merely has to be "demanded" for one to be able to sell it.

The question remains of how to put value back on an "objective" basis. To take the path of Marxism would be to replace one ideology by another—likewise leading to the economics of want. To believe Althusser, "the great mistake of Smith and Ricardo is, in Marx's eyes, to have sacrificed the analysis of value-form to the sole consideration of the *quantity* of value: '*value as quantity absorbs their attention.*' " This is why, again according to Althusser, "modern economists are, on this point, on the side of the classicists when they charge Marx with producing in his theory 'non-operational' concepts, i.e. excluding measurement of the subject: surplus-value, for example. But this criticism boomerangs because Marx allows and employs measurement—for the 'specific forms' of surplus-value (profit, rent, and interest). If surplus-value is not measurable it is precisely because it is the *concept* of its forms, which for their part are measurable. Naturally, this simple deduction changes everything."

It changes nothing, because Ricardo had made this (incidentally elementary) distinction by never confusing (among the many examples that could be given), value ("non-operational" concept) with price, a measurable form of value, whereas Marx was not bothered by this epistemological scruple when he identified the concept of exchange value with the measurable magnitude, money capital. The only thing that changes, as the result of a really critical reading of *Principles of Political Economy* and *Capital,* is the respective positions of Ricardo and Marx as regards the discipline of their thinking.

The criticism one would be tempted to make of Ricardo is, in contrast to what Althusser thinks, that of being too exclusively attached to the definition and interplay of concepts. The reaction of his successors was to concern themselves solely with measurable phenomena; but economics quickly gave up identifying phenomena in the light of concepts, and the age of confusion began.

Althusser maintains that Marx accomplished an "immense theoretical revolution" by decoding the classicists. His case, which he presents with an air of great profundity, loses much of that profundity because he brackets classical political economy with modern, empirical economics. He believes he is attacking the former when he accuses the latter of inconsistency, whereas nothing of the Ricardian edifice, except perhaps its accusing shade, remains in the modern construction erected on the shaky foundations of the work of the Austrian school and Walras.

Having lumped the two together, Althusser can say that "political economy relates economic facts to wants" and that "it therefore tends to reduce exchange-value to use-values and the latter ('riches,' to use the term of classical economics) to the wants of men."[10] These criticisms are unanswerable if applied to neoliberal economics. The reason they do not settle the issue is that they are aimed at the wrong target. Althusser feigns ignorance of the fact that Ricardo wrote a whole chapter in his book (chap. 20, entitled "Value and Riches, Their Distinctive Properties") for the specific purpose of showing that value could not be equated with "riches" and with the utility derived from them. If one is going to read *Capital*, subtitled *A Critique of Political Economy*, in a truly scientific spirit, one should also reread the political economy concerned—not the one which emerged after Marx but the one at which Marx directed his critique. The difference between Ricardo's *Principles* (400 pages) and Marx's *Capital* (over 2000) is that between a handbook of geometry and a prodigious historical thesis whose real low point is where the reader is told in all seriousness that "the general formula for capital" is M–C–M', where M' is greater than M".[11] If Althusser had as much concern for geometry as for history, he would not have permitted himself to write the following words about political economy, which apply solely to the "hedonist" doctrine of the neoliberals.

> It is want (on the part of the human subject) that defines the "*economic-ness*" of economics. The *given* of that homogeneous field of economic phenomena is therefore [that "therefore" is wonderful!] given us as economic by this silent anthropology. But then, if we look closely, it is this "giving" anthropology which is the absolute given. (vol. 2, p. 29)

Here, briefly, are the reasons why the two categories of goods that Ricardo distinguishes—reproducible goods and scarce goods—cannot be expressed in terms of each other, since only the former can be a subject of economic science.

1.  If it is accepted that value derives from scarcity, there can be no objective criterion with which to demarcate economics. Everything—regardless of its nature—the price of which can be identified in a market with no boundaries has a "value" for the economist interested only in "relations of exchange." Walras and his successors, our contemporaries, have defined the concept of value in terms of its symptoms. What, then, is the point of having a concept? The correct epistemological approach is the reverse of theirs. It consists in creating a concept of value that can then serve to demarcate the market, which is the subject of economics.

Unlike the economists of the psychological school, for whom every-thing that is wanted is eligible to be a commodity, the classical school, making labor the source of value, homogenized the market more completely than has so far been realized. The suggestion was that the accumulated product of labor, or capital, buys "labor" in the market as though it were possible to equate two things as unlike as the product of labor and the labor that produces it (as I think I have shown). But this anomaly stemmed from the imprecise vocabulary, not the theory, for which the only things that are bought and sold are the products, accumulated or not, of labor.

2. If it is accepted that value derives from scarcity, the system of prices ceases to be determinable. In contradistinction to this funda-mental indeterminacy stands the classical conception that (1) only goods having an exchange value defined according to the labor theory of value have a price roughly equal to their cost and (2) objects not produced by labor have no definable exchange value and therefore no determinable price, since the latter may be zero (the air we breathe) or have no assignable limit (Vermeer's *View of Delft*). With the exchange value criterion, it is possible for the prices actually paid on the market to be analyzed critically. If the economist notes that the "ex-works" selling price of a hair lotion includes a profit the rate of which far exceeds the normal rate of profit, he may attempt to discover the objective reasons for this (monopolistic pattern of the market, etc.). But how about a Holbein? Suppose a masterpiece fetches £500,000 at Christie's in London. Surely that is just as much a fact as the price of a "reproducible" automobile or shampoo? It is a fact, but of a different kind. In a competitive market, the price of an automobile conforms with the principle of equivalence of exchange. In the art market, that principle no longer holds. If I buy a Holbein for £500,000 it is because there is no one to outbid me on that particular day. Its "value" is indeterminate. A picture like this is called "priceless" and price-less is literally what it is, even if a very high price is paid for it. True, art experts "price" pictures, but not by the objective method an accoun-tant would use; they just trust to their flair for divining the trends of fashion and appreciating all the factors, from snobbery to inflation hedging, which constantly influence demand for those things. This fundamental indeterminacy is characteristic of all goods that are not products of standardized labor.

As a social science, economics does more than define its subject; it creates it in the sense that only in a society organized according to the principles it prescribes—equivalence of exchange being by far the most important—are prices determinable.

## Marxist Socialism Has to Be Defined Negatively

What "political" consequences are to be drawn from the theory of exchange? There is no question here of arguing in favor of anything remotely resembling a program or of trying to tilt economics to right or left. As I have already had occasion to point out, the desirability of bending reality to theory will be stronger or weaker depending on whether one is progressive or conservative.

In economics, exchange in the strict sense can take place only between products of standardized—that is, interchangeable—labor. If the practical applications of this analysis are taken to their limit, the confines of the market are reduced to reproducible products only, these naturally including capital goods which are the accumulated products of labor. In its purest form, liberal capitalism (in the European sense) would exclude all scarce goods from the market.

Marx exposed the contradiction, as he found it, between the social character of production and private appropriation of the means of production.

However, no prima facie contradiction exists because, as we have seen (in Chapter 4), not only is accumulation no obstacle to the principle of the equivalence of exchange, it is its most remarkable result. Socialism, in that it defines itself as the collective appropriation of the means of production, has to be defined negatively as a system that withdraws from the exchange process the most important category of products of labor.

From the standpoint of correct economic analysis, the truth is exactly the opposite of what Marx asserts. The "social" character of production guarantees the interchangeability of products. It is the products of individualized labor that are not amenable to the law of exchange. If I were forced to use the language of dialectic, I would say that the "contradiction" lies between the individual character of artistic production and the private appropriation of works of art for the reason that there is no objective rule to determine the value at which the latter should be purchased. For the relation of equivalence that characterizes exchange to exist there has to be a common denominator between the two products exchanged, which is that both have to be the product of a certain amount of labor. In addition, this labor itself has to be interchangeable, at least theoretically. How is it possible to determine in gold—the product of social labor—the price of a statue—the product of the kind of labor of which no one but the sculptor would have been capable?

Is one then to conclude that all works of art should be reserved for the public museums? From the standpoint of economics, the power to obtain by exchange a good that is unique of its kind, or at least not reproducible at will, is always a privilege in the sense that the law of exchange does not justify it. But the law of equivalence of exchange, by definition, applies only to the production and distribution of the products of labor. It does not concern the *use* made of these riches that are produced. This is why human society is not governed by economics alone. A world in which the market no longer went beyond its bounds into fields which are not legitimately its own would have other defects, beginning with that of being deadly dull. But here it is I who am going beyond the bounds of my subject by exhibiting a "preference" that could be contradicted by a contrary preference.

Similarly, the market value of the scarce goods supplied by nature, and first and foremost land, results solely from the interaction of supply and demand. One important exception is agricultural land the price of which, except for high quality vineyards or soil with particular properties, generally does not exceed the cost of the work necessary to prepare it for cropping. In this case, therefore, payment is being made for a product of labor. That would be an argument justifying, to the economist, the private ownership of arable land. But the purchase of farmland to sell it as building land is less defensible. Here again, it would be rash to conclude that the land should be nationalized without more ado just because that fits into the logic of economics. Private ownership can be justified in the modern world by other reasons, perhaps the most important being that—in spite of some examples to the contrary—it provides the best protection of the environment possible at the present time (what would it cost the public purse for the state to do the maintenance that owners do unpaid?).

Let me conclude these somewhat subjective remarks with the comment that the cautiousness of these findings is not solely due to my mistrust of oversudden changes in the legal order. The neutrality of economics in these fields is greater than at first appears. There can be no doubt that, for economics, the market is a logical system only where the interplay of supply and demand is not subject to the whims of the latter but, on the contrary, is *regulated,* so to speak, by the law of value which ensures the objectivity of prices. But that does not

imply that economics "condemns" the market where these regulating
mechanisms cannot exist, as in the case of all nonreproducible goods.
It simply ceases to justify the market "scientifically." After all, society
is free to use the market as a way of distributing these goods if it feels
that other methods would be less convenient and, ultimately, little
fairer. If it is true that economics must try to be something more than
just a collection of empirical recipes if it is to rank as a science, it is
equally true that it is not for economics to rule out the presence of a
certain empiricism in the organization of society.

The fact remains that progress, the advance toward greater rationality, requires that the field of empiricism be gradually reduced. Objectivity of economics implies the building of a world where in principle
artistic and intellectual life in all its forms would lie outside the market,
as was the case in the great ages of civilization, and where the state,
directly or otherwise, would own an increasing share of the land,
though with generalized legal arrangements that would guarantee private individuals long and peaceful enjoyment of their "little plot of
land."

Lastly, as we have seen, economics, in order to ensure the equivalence of exchange, predicates equality in the rate of profit. From this
theoretical requirement, the legislator (see Chapter 8) is able to draw
important conclusions with regard to the distribution of income that
could conceivably have far-reaching effects on the spread of ownership
of capital. A little earlier I said that, in principle, all products of labor,
including therefore the tools of production, were the proper objects of
exchange. Does that mean that economics "condemns" the nationalization of businesses in every case? Here everything depends, once
again, on the circumstances. It is contrary to the principles of economics that excess profit (monopoly rents) should be accumulated purely
for the benefit of capitalists. The government may therefore find itself
having to institute controls over companies in a monopoly situation.
Rather than nationalize them, the most satisfactory answer, in theory,
is to restore freedom of competition whenever that is possible.

The above comments are probably very oversimplified but the purpose of this book is not to "remake society." It is to present a critique
of the reigning economic doctrine and to show some of the paths that
need to be taken so that it may gradually be replaced by a science.
Instead of demonstrating, as I have done, the negative nature of
socialism with regard to the theory of exchange, other writers would,
instead, have stressed all that is positive in this same theory for a
socialist.

I said that socialism has to be defined negatively because its purpose is to withdraw from the market the tools of production that are the accumulated products of labor (if the word "capital" is taken in its broadest acceptance this would mean socializing practically all existing goods).

But, tackling the problem from the opposite standpoint, could I not just as well have said that the theory of exchange, by suggesting that the products of individualized labor and all other scarce goods should be socialized, justifies a practically unlimited extension of the public sector because, as we know, the boundary between reproducible and scarce goods is not in practice very clear-cut? With things put this way, the products belonging to the market economy would constitute the exception to the general rule, which would be socialization. The whole problem would then be to agree on the category of goods to socialize. Because of his erroneous interpretation of the objective value theory, Marx thought this category to be the tools of production. If that theory is interpreted correctly, socialism finds a different area of aim. The preeminently "social" goods are not the riches produced by social labor, but all those which man cannot reproduce at will. Facts seem to show that this is the direction in which the political aspirations of modern societies are tending. The idea that seems to be more or less generally held is that the market economy should be left to develop industry, commerce, and agriculture (subject to the reservations—but not the exclusion—I made regarding agricultural prices), in short everything that it does better than the state, with the latter responsible, first, for controlling all the goods hitherto (and wrongly) allowed to be buyable and sellable and, second, for defining other rules than those of the market for activities such as artistic production, information of the public, and so on.

That having been said, it seems to me that if (with Ricardo) economics expressly makes its sole subject of investigation the production of wealth of goods produced by social labor, then it is in relation to them that the positive or negative character of a doctrine or a program of action should be defined.

## Commodity Fetishism According to Marx

What is at issue goes far beyond the collective—or private—appropriation of the means of production. Marxist socialism aims at nothing less than freeing man from the "law of value" the objectivity of which is allegedly only sham. It was to expose what he considered a self-interested attempt at deception that Marx wrote his "critique of political economy."

We know Marx's argument: The "economic laws" are in reality only the reflection of the relations of production—in other words, the relations between those who exploit the labor of others and those whose labor is exploited. In the "capitalist" economy, producers enter into relation with one another only through the market, where commodities are exchanged. It is only on the market that the equality of the different kinds of human labor appears, but this equality is never perceived directly—it appears in the form of the equality of the exchange values of the commodities. This is what Marx calls the fetishism of the commodity: "the definite social relation between men themselves which assumes here, for them, the fantastic form of a relation between things" (*Capital,* vol. 1, chap. 1, sect. 4).

Socialism would open the way to a new form of production in which men would once again establish between themselves "simple and transparent" (in other words, direct) relations. Capitalist production was concerned solely with abstract labor—what I just called interchangeable labor—being interested only in the exchange value of man-produced articles which, once put on the market, become commodities. In order to compare quantities of labor, the market must constantly reduce concrete labor, which relates to the use value of objects, to abstract labor, a pure expenditure of energy, the quantity of which determines exchange value. And yet, as Marx further pointed out, making a table is not the same thing as weaving a piece of fabric, even if the time and energy devoted to the two tasks are identical. The ultimate goal of the Revolution was to put concrete labor before abstract labor, to make exchange value secondary to use value, which, let it be noted, shows the affinity between Marxism and hedonism (here is the common substance of the modern critique, by Marx and by Walras, of Ricardian political economy).

To free himself from the "fetishism of the commodity," it is not sufficient for man to realize that exchange value reflects the relations of production.

> The belated scientific discovery that the products of labour, in so far as they are values, are merely the material expressions of the human labor expended to produce them, marks an epoch in the history of mankind's development, but by no means banishes the semblance of objectivity possessed by the social characteristics of labour. Something which is

only valid for this particular form of production, the production of commodities, namely the fact that the specific social character of private labours carried on independently of each other consists in their equality as human labour, and, in the product, assumes the form of the existence of value, appears to those caught up in the relations of commodity production (and this is true both before and after the above-mentioned scientific discovery) to be just as ultimately valid as the fact that the scientific dissection of the air into its component parts left the atmosphere itself unaltered in its physical configuration.[12]

This impressive criticism, which seems to reopen the debate just when it might have been thought closed, introduces two arguments.

The first I have, in the course of this book, already answered. Marx asserts that exchange value expresses a social relation specific to capitalist production. This proposition would be acceptable only if the Marxist surplus value theory were right, but the correct interpretation of the labor theory of value has enabled us to establish that exchange is indeed founded on a relation of equality. *In its principle*, therefore, exchange implies no distortion in the relations of production. It is Marx who falls victim to commodity fetishism when he attributes "substance" to value. For Ricardo, value is not labor (he writes, as the reader will remember, that it is "essentially different from the labour itself"), but proportional to it. Hence, labor lies outside the market. Where is the reification of human relations?

The other argument on which Marx's criticism is based is that, as it develops, capitalist production makes labor uniform: "This abstraction of labour in general is not solely the mental result of a concrete totality of effort. Indifference to the work of the individual corresponds to a form of society in which people move easily from one job to another and in which the particular kind of work seems fortuitous and therefore of no concern to them." Here we cannot, I feel, blame Marx[13] for not having seen the way in which modern capitalism would develop. It is a fact that increasing mobility of labor, demanded by the acceleration of trade, implies the interchangeability of labor on which the classical theory of value rests and in which Marx sees another form of man's alienation by capitalist production. The question remains of whether absolute interchangeability of workers—which would be the ultimate point—would reflect a kind of contempt for man on the part of "capitalist production"? Surely this interchangeability, which would mean that the highly skilled workman could replace the engineer and the engineer the workman after a short period of adjustment, would in its way be a mark of the absolute dignity of labor, enshrined in the idea of abstract labor, which is that all kinds of human effort, wherever and however applied (in designing a computer or growing potatoes) are reducible one to another.

Breaking with the Ricardian tradition, which bases the economic system on the dynamics of supply—in other words, on labor—Marx makes the objective of his system "to each according to his need." But needs are unlimited and indeterminate. To found an economy on need or want is to put off forever the day when plenty will reign.[14] To found it on labor is to ask society to adjust demand to supply. But since gains in labor productivity are constantly bringing down the cost of all goods and routine services, the supply will constantly increase. In other words, the road that offers hope to society of becoming what will be recognized as a society of plenty is the opposite of that taken by Marx and, after him, modern society. At bottom, it is a question of standpoint. There is no limit to wants but there is always a limit to what can be supplied. This is why it is easier to be satisfied with what is supplied if one thinks of the labor it costs rather than the want one feels. That is the reply of objective economics to the subjectivism of wants.

It is true that the supreme form of labor is that which is a manifestation of personal expression and therefore not interchangeable. It is also true that political economy's model of social organization is one in which men, or the vast majority of them, do impersonal work. But this standardization of labor considerably increases its productivity. If the ceaseless quest for wants satisfaction, which political economy wisely endeavored to control by giving precedence to supply, did not get in the way, there might be a hope of freeing mankind from the need to devote most of its time to work of a social order, so that it could spend more on personal tasks and other activities.

Let me also say that objective economics engenders its own negation but in a very different way from that imagined by Marx. In society founded on primacy of demand, the spirit of competition that is so vaunted brings about a leveling of minds and tastes. This is because of the continual stimulation of "consumption." In a society closer to the classical model, the spirit of competition would motivate each producer to supply what he is best able to supply (goods or services). His incentive would be to perfect his own capabilities, not to imitate others. In other words, the system would induce every supplier to offer a product of labor that would tend to become "individual." Through the logic of the system it establishes, objective political economy constantly encourages producers to rise above the standardized plane of labor value and develop their activities beyond the "economic" dimension. None of this is as utopian as might at first be believed. The most fundamental characteristic of an economy based on supply is the pride (*conscience professionnelle*) that it causes each of its participants to take in his work. And what is this pride in one's work if not the triumph of "concrete labor" over "abstract labor"? Political economy contains the seeds of its own transcendence. Marx thought it had to be overturned in order to free man from the slavery in which it held him. In reality, the best hope for that freedom lies in carrying the application of its laws to the ultimate.

It is at this precise point, where labor escapes from the uniformity imposed by the market, that we are suddenly faced with the contradiction that proves the undoing of any economic system based on wants satisfaction, be it of Marxist or of neoliberal inspiration. In such a system, wants cannot really be satisfied. A simply way of understanding the logic of this apparent paradox is to see the producer-consumer relationship in terms of the person preparing a meal and the person eating it. The meal will be good or even excellent if the cook, without worrying about the tastes he thinks his customer has (it is up to him as a cook to educate those tastes), simply does his job. The meal will be poor if the cook produces dishes to match what he thinks—even after the relevant "market research"[15]—is his customer's average pattern of tastes. In other words, the diner will be the better served the more the economic system is conceived in terms of the cook.

The reader may be surprised that I should direct this criticism both at the consumer society and at Marxism, since everyone knows that the latter, even though its watchword is the satisfaction of human needs, has not, in practice, been able to live up to its ambitions. The "socialist" countries make one think more of an austere society of producers than a carnival of consumers. And yet, in their way, socialist societies are based even more on want than on labor to the extent that there the redistribution of income is taken further than elsewhere. Conversely, every successful economic reform—witness the case of Hungary—consists in returning to the "to each according to his labor"[16] principle. As to the pride in one's work to which I referred earlier, this tends to disappear both in socialist countries and in those where the methods of the consumer society hold sway.

The deep-lying reason in both cases is exactly the same: The only chance that concrete labor has of reasserting—and modestly at that—

its rights over abstract labor is in a society where emulation among producers is the supreme driving force. In the modern world, the countries that come closest to this model and therefore hold the key to the future of liberal capitalism are probably the countries of the Far East.

Finally, to return to the Marxist theory of the relations of production in capitalist society, let me add that the most conclusive objection to that theory is in fact the solution that Marx advocates to liberate mankind from the "fetishism of the commodity."

"Let us finally imagine, for a change," he writes,

> an association of free men, working with the means of production held in common, and expending their many different forms of labour-power in full self-awareness as one single social labour force. All the characteristics of Robinson's labour are repeated here, but with the difference that they are social instead of individual. All Robinson's products were exclusively the result of his own personal labour and they were therefore directly objects of utility for him personally. The total product of our imagined association is a social product. One part of this product serves as fresh means of production and remains social. But another part is consumed by the members of the association as means of subsistence. This part must therefore be divided amongst them. The way this division is made will vary with the particular kind of social organisation of production and the corresponding level of social development attained by the producers. We shall assume, but only for the sake of a parallel with the production of commodities, that the share of each individual producer in the means of subsistence is determined by his labour-time. Labour-time would in that case play a double part. Its apportionment in accordance with a definite social plan maintains the correct proportion between the different functions of labour and the various needs of the associations. On the other. . . .[17]

The idea of "an association of free men" inevitably begs the question: What happens to those who freely refuse to join it? As for the "definite social plan," this means that here again, but in another form, we shall find the bonds of legal dependence that were implicit in all economic systems prior to the generalization of exchange. Another key question is how the product will be divided among the producers. In a sophisticated economy, it would be impossible to do it *in kind*. But if the division is made in value, will not the "free men" ask for a fair assessment of the value of the products that have to be divided among them? In order not to be objectionable, fairness will have to be grounded on logic and logic will bring the "free men" to rediscover exchange and the laws through which exchange value is determined (including the necessity to include profit accumulated).

In a market operating in satisfactory conditions, the subjectivity of the countless exchange partners is constantly kept in check by the objectiveness of production costs. But in the assembly where the "social plan" is hammered out, who will be the watchdog of cost objectiveness? Marx is not concerned because, as we have seen, the value of things is for him something already established before goods go into circulation. How can the various subjectivities in the forums where the plan is discussed be reconciled? How can some be prevented from imposing their will on the others? "The Cuban regime has become a Fidel Castro monologue," wrote a former French Marxist. This monstrous result of the revolution is not an accident; its seed is already there in Marxist thought, subjective because it is empirical and empirical because it is subjective.

## Notes

1. The reverse is also true. If supply exceeds demand, value is low. In that case one could speak of "negative scarcity."

2. Allowing for the mechanism of the exchange of capital (accumulation). Note again that, as rightly pointed out by John Eatwell (in an article published in *Economica,* May 1975), the "adding-up theory of value" has to be found first in Adam Smith and that Ricardo did oppose to that theory his own analysis (the "deductive relationship between wages and profits" in John Eatwell's words). In *Principles,* chap. 1, sect. 6, Ricardo wrote: "Adam Smith, and all the writers who have followed him, have, without one exception that I know of, maintained that a rise in the price of labour would be uniformly followed by a rise in the price of all commodities. I hope I have succeeded in showing, that there are no grounds for such an opinion. . . ." Obviously, Ricardo failed on that score, since, after him, all economists I know of have been following the paths of Smith! That is still truer today than ever. (Note added to the original French edition of this book published for the first time in 1974.)

3. The equality is even clearer if the huntsman's zero liking for meat is compared with the fisherman's zero liking for fish.

4. This is because the indifference curves are convex. If our consumer shifts to the right or to the left of E on the line linking $I/P_y$ to $I/P_x$, he must necessarily come to a point that is on an indifference curve of a lower order. This can be shown mathematically, provided one accepts the premises of

marginalist reasoning. Here again, I refer the reader to the specialized literature, but that is not necessary to follow the critique of those premises that I set out here.

5. Walras, *Elements of Pure Economics (Abrégé des éléments d'économie politique pure)*, 8th lesson. My italics.

6. Ricardo warns us of the difference between his hypothetical standard and gold. The characteristic of his standard is that it never varies in value because its cost of production is constant over time, which is obviously not so with gold. Sraffa strove to solve the problem in *Production of Commodities by Means of Commodities*.

7. Allowing for the impact of the rate of profit explained in Chapter 5, which introduces an element of indeterminateness (negligible here) in the amount of this value.

8. Ibid.

9. The formulation is sometimes more subtle as expressed by the best commentators of neoliberalism. Raymond Aron writes that "modern economics disregards the 'substance' of value and is concerned only with relations of exchange" (*D'une Sainte Famille à l'autre*). It should be noted that, when he refers to the labor theory of value, Raymond Aron means the Marxist interpretation of the theory and so all he needs to do in order to dismiss it is to speak of the "substance" of value. But we have seen that the authentic labor theory of value expressly rejects the idea of substance of value. Exchange value, as we have seen, tends to be proportionate to the quantum of labor (allowing for accumulation). It does not follow that this quantum of labor has to be regarded as the substance of value.

10. Althusser, *Lire le Capital*, vol. 2, p. 28.

11. Jules Renard said, more or less, that a great writer is a writer who writes a lot, a remark in which there is probably more truth than would appear at first sight. One might understandably have the sneaking feeling that Marx is considered a great economist for that reason.

12. As Raymond Aron does in *D'une Sainte Famille à l'autre* where these words of Marx are quoted.

13. Marx, *Capital*, vol. 1, part 1, chap. 1.4, "The Fetishism of the Commodity."

14. Let us assume that, in the future, everyone wanted to travel in space. The cost of meeting this want would be so high that it would put off indefinitely the moment when the want could be met, and so on and so forth.

15. It is not a question of condemning market research and marketing techniques, whose useful and even essential function in providing proper guidance for the production system I have already pointed out. Misuse begins when the attempt is made to replace the producer's creativeness by the feelings of the consumer. The consumer does not *know* the type of automobile that suits him any more than the public knows in advance what modern painting is. It is the painter who invents the art of his period and, more modestly, it is the producer who invents the kind of automobile that will meet the needs of motorists.

16. Needless to say, every living economic system is necessarily the result of finding the right mix of the two principles "to each according to his labor" and "to each according to his needs." The whole problem is which of the two principles to adopt as the basis of social organization.

17. Marx, *Capital,* vol. 1, part 1, chap. 1.4, "The Fetishism of the Commodity."

*10*

# Outlines of a Critique of General Equilibrium

## Origins of the Notion of "Perfect" or General Equilibrium of the Market

The theory of "perfect" or general market equilibrium devised by Léon Walras is vulnerable to a number of arguments that might dispose of it. Fewer and fewer economists nowadays give credence to this artificial construct, but none seems able to produce final and conclusive reasons for his doubt. This is because the idea of general equilibrium is linked with the psychological theory of value, which makes scarcity "the cause of exchange value" (Walras), and because it is consequently necessary to disprove that theory to reveal the confusion of concepts implied by the "perfect equilibrium of the market" attained (according to Walras) when the effective aggregate demand for each commodity equals its effective aggregate supply. When the market is thus in equilibrium all prices there are determined, Walras says, by one another, and most economists see this "discovery" as a great contribution to the science. Finally, the state of equilibrium is further supposed to be that in which maximum satisfaction is achieved, which stems from the fact (see Chapter 9, regarding the demand curves) that the prices of any two goods are in equilibrium when they are in the same relationship one to another as their marginal utilities. As long as this state of equality does not exist, consumers find it to their advantage to change the pattern of their purchases, which in turn changes the quantities produced. Other definitions of general equilibrium have been proposed, but they all boil down to the idea that, in a market assumed to be perfectly competitive, prices and quantities are established at a level such that optimum satisfaction is obtained.

From what was said in Chapter 7 about the nature of the economic system, we can already gather that the idea of "equilibrium" is ill-suited to an exchange economy. The only things "in equilibrium" are closed systems, like a chemical compound in a test tube. The economic system, however, is a system open to nature, from which it borrows energy, giving it back in the form of labor. The way the system operates precludes equilibrium in the sense understood by traditional physics. The neoliberal economists, enmeshed though they were in their inadequate conceptualization, finally realized this more or less clearly. To get out of their dilemma they tried, though without really succeeding, to progress from what they called "static" equilibrium to "dynamic" equilibrium. But what kind of an economic model is it that introduces movement ex post facto? This will be the central line of criticism to be developed here against Walras' model. The model is permanently stalled on both the demand and supply sides: first, because it rests on an imaginary conception of "effective demand" (see the critique of the demand curve) and, second, because this so-called perfect competition model is in fact based on a monopolistic organization of the market, which is the inevitable result of the link with which Walras first—and all his successors after him—joined value to scarcity.

### The Mobility of Ricardo's Model of the Competition-based Economy

Before reviewing the Walrasian model to which official economics teaching still (alas) refers, a brief outline is necessary of the model it was constructed to refute, the individual features of which have been mentioned in the course of this book.

The essential feature of the Ricardian model of the competitive market is its built-in mobility, ensured by the fact that the desire to consume, or want, is not confined in a "demand curve." Let us take a closer look at how the model works.

1. *In a competitive market, competition is entirely on the supply side*. Producers will increase their output until such time as the market

price is brought down to roughly the level of the cost of production (profit included) by a process that has been discussed many times in this book (see Chapters 1, 8, and 9, for example). At that level, all effective demand (i.e., where there is the means to pay) is satisfied. If it were not, supply would be increased again. Economists have endlessly discussed the conditions that have to be met for a market to be considered competitive. Logically there is only one: that profit-yielding supply should be limitless in the sense that it can always meet a supplementary effective demand.[1]

As soon as a good becomes scarce, for one reason or another, competition moves over to the demand side. The effects here are the exact reverse of those of competition among producers. Competition among producers *always* causes prices to fall (to roughly the level of the production cost). Competition among consumers *always* causes prices to rise *to the point where the quantities demanded equal the quantities supplied*. Thus, it is in relation to supply, not want, that scarcity is defined. There is no scarcity when a commodity is available, provided that one is prepared to pay its cost. Thus, in our societies, automobiles and TV sets are not scarce, although not everyone who wants them has them yet. This brings us to the second characteristic of the Ricardian model.

2. The scale of prices is *regulated* by the scale of values (or costs of production). For this to be the case, it is sufficient and necessary for there to be no restriction on the supply side. To be absolutely faithful to the inadequate vocabulary used by economists since Walras, we would have to say that prices are "in equilibrium" when the exchange ratio between, say, a TV set and a car, or between a car and a trip to the Bahamas, as determined by the scale of prices on the market, reflects fairly accurately the relative quantities of labor expended on the production of those goods and services (allowing for the impact of the rate of profit, as pointed out in Chapter 5). Rather than "equilibrium price," Ricardo, as we know, spoke of "necessary" prices—in other words, rational prices.

3. Consequently the scale of prices, even if it is the most rational possible, *does not predicate any equilibrium as between the different consumer desires, or wants, to be met*. Apart from the fact that such "equilibrium" is impossible to define (in view of the subjective nature of wants), the point is that in a competitive market the degree of wants satisfaction depends on the cost of producing the commodity wanted, and on nothing else. Thus the desire to consume salt is, in our

societies, just about completely satisfied because salt costs very little to produce and, *at the price at which it is offered,* the quantity desired roughly coincides with the quantity actually demanded. Yet, as I pointed out a little earlier, TV sets are not, from the supply standpoint, any scarcer than salt in our industrialized societies, inasmuch as no one has ever been denied a TV set if he agrees to pay its price, which corresponds roughly—as in the case of salt—to the production cost, average profit included. The scarcity effect occurs intermittently, for certain brands and models, in the form of unusually long delivery times, but in ordinary circumstances it can be said to be negligible.

How could it ever occur to anyone that the respective prices of salt and a TV set stand in the same relationship to each other as the want for salt and the want for a TV set (as measured by their respective marginal utilities)? Yet that is what the "master" of modern political economy asserted when he wrote: "In the state of maximum satisfaction, scarcities[2] are proportional to prices," a proposition from which the marginalists derived the equation $P_x/P_y = U_x/U_y$ (in spite of the fact that marginal utility is not the same thing as intensity of the last want satisfied), the untruth of which I have pointed out elsewhere (Chapter 9).

The truth is that the "want" for a TV set can be satisfied as completely as the want for salt the day the cost of producing a TV set, and hence its price, is so low that anybody who wants one can afford one.

The only thing that can be said for certain is that, in the Ricardian model, competition among producers is constantly pushing the selling price down toward its lowest possible level, depending on the current state of production technology. At that price, wants are therefore better satisfied than they would be in a monopolistic economy. It is in this limited sense that the competition model can be called "optimal," but once again the "necessary" price toward which the "market price" will tend *in no way implies that the distribution of wants satisfaction is optimal.* Not only does the model fail to imply it but, as we shall now see, it postulates that this "optimal distribution" is never achieved.

4. Since the consumption want is not a definable magnitude, it is useless to try to define to what *extent* this or that want is satisfied. All that can be said is that complete satisfaction is not reached as long as the price is sufficiently high to deter a number of potential buyers (a circumstance which, as I pointed out a little earlier, *has nothing to do*

*with* scarcity defined by reference to supply). The fact is, therefore, that the majority of wants are not completely satisfied. Since the scale of prices reflects no equilibrium as between these different wants that are not wholly met, it can be readily seen that the desire to consume is in no way *fixed* by the existing price system, even if it were the nearest thing possible to the system of *necessary* or *rational* prices. It could even be said that, far from being stabilized by the existing price system, the desire to consume draws additional factors of instability from that system, whatever it may be. Thus, the desire to possess usually focuses on the most expensive goods, as though it were whetted by their relative inaccessibility.

In the Ricardian model the desire to consume (want) is not linked to effective demand by any utility value theory. It depends on countless constantly shifting factors—biological, sociological, ideological, political, and so on—but the economic system recognizes only effective demand, which we have seen is not an independent variable since the "effective demand" for product A is nothing other than the *effective supply* of products B, C, D, and so on, which are exchanged for A. Let us assume that the desire to consume suddenly focuses on woolen garments. This will produce a situation in which supply is temporarily unable to keep pace with demand, with the result that prices of woolens will rise relative to their production cost (average profit included). What does this mean other than that the exchange of woolens (which I shall call product A) for products B, C, D, and so on, ceases to be an exchange of value for like value? To obtain the same quantity of A, the suppliers of B, C, D, and so on, will now have to hand over more of their products. What the equivocal expression "demand outstrips supply" really means is that equivalence of exchange has ceased. The product received by those wanting woolens is of less value than the products they hand over in return. The producers of woolens will therefore receive extra value which represents a "surplus profit." *If those producers are competing with one another,* each will try to turn the situation to maximum account by increasing his output, which he will have no trouble in doing since the high profits will attract capital to the woolen goods industry. The increase in supply should, after a while, reestablish equivalence of exchange, that is to say equivalence between the aggregate value of effective demand and the aggregate value of supply.

5.  The medium through which the impulses transmitted to the market by the desire to consume affect the way in which production

resources are allocated is therefore (see also Chapter 8) the inequality of the rate of profit between industries and between enterprises. This inequality implies that supply has not had time to adjust to the new demand—in other words, *it implies imperfect competition*. In the Ricardian model the switch from so-called "static" to "dynamic" equilibrium is pointless, since movement of capital from one use to another is built into the system at the outset. The system is a dynamic one because the action of competition cannot be instantaneous, even if all the institutional obstacles have been removed. *In this model the market is and cannot but be imperfect* at each moment of time. Ricardo says this in so many words when he writes that the market price is always to a greater or lesser degree a monopoly price (see Chapter 9, p. 228). If someone bothers—at long last—to make on that score a careful reading of Ricardo, generally portrayed as the theoretician of a perfectly competitive and atomistic market (consisting of an infinite number of small producers), he will discover two things. The first is that Ricardo never regarded so-called "perfect competition" as a *state* but as an organizational principle. If the market is organized according to that principle, *then* the reaction of the independent producers will *necessarily* have the effect of bringing the market price down *toward* the production cost (average profit included). But—and this is the second thing—neither does Ricardo say anywhere in his work that the existence of a large number of production units is a sine qua non of competition. His only stipulation is that profitable supply should not be limited, since this will ensure that the selling price will tend to conform to the production cost. Even if there were only one supplier of product A in the market as I have envisaged (Chapters 8 and 9), provided it were impossible for him to fix the volume of supply as he wanted, the result would be the same as if there were several suppliers: Equivalence of exchange would be reestablished, once the time had elapsed that was necessary for this single but not monopolist producer to adapt his production lines to match the impulses transmitted by the desire to consume.[3]

### The "Perfect Market" à la Walras Is Not Competitive

Having thus outlined the basic assumptions of the Ricardian model of the competitive market, I now propose to consider those of the Walrasian "perfect market equilibrium" model.

We know enough about it to challenge right away the claim to construct, even hypothetically, a "perfect equilibrium" for the market. Walras took as his premise the idea that perfect competition could be a *state*—and that is impossible. His model is irremediably ill-constructed, resting as it does on a conceptual error that prevents him from seeing that the market around which he builds his argument is not competitive. This is due to his conception of exchange value. For Walras exchange value is caused in every case by scarcity. "We have shown," he writes, "that all scarce things, and those things only, have value and are exchangeable."[4] This proposition runs counter to the logic of a competitive market as defined here. The only things that "have value and are exchangeable" from the standpoint of "objective" economics are precisely those things that are not scarce, because they are reproducible at will "almost without assignable limit," to use Ricardo's expression (see Chapter 9, pp. 226–27).

As I shall show in a moment, out of Walras' own mouth, his so-called "competitive market" is one in which supply is indeed limited. In other words, it is really a monopolistic market. In a monopoly situation, prices are, by definition, indeterminate since the regulating action of production costs no longer exists. How did Walras, reasoning from the premise of scarcity, arrive at the idea of an "equilibrium price" or, as he also calls it, a "stationary price"? There is only one way to get there and it is (sad to say) the path on which he set economics and which it has since followed. In a monopolistic system, price is stable assuming that the volume of desired consumption is knowable. And the only way it is possible to determine that volume is to presume that the quantity demanded corresponds to the maximum degree of satisfaction. That, in a nutshell, is the thought process which, reversing the order of the factors, began by stating the axiom that "In the phenomenon of exchange . . . demand has to be regarded as the principal fact, and supply as a subordinate fact" (see Chapter 1, p. 8).

The very first example that Walras cites in support of his "demonstration" undoes him from the start. For him, stock markets constitute the archetype of a competitive market,[5] whereas the exact opposite is true since, on the stock exchange, supply is necessarily limited to the number of shares currently on offer. Share prices depend solely on the interaction of supply and demand; they are not subject to any *law*. This is probably the fundamental reason why there is no sure way of "beating the market," even for the most skilled professionals.

But Walras did not think so. For him there was a "law of effective supply and demand,"[6] in which—a relevant point at this juncture—

Ricardo detected the source of most of the errors of economics past and present (see Chapter 9, page 230). Walras phrased this law in the following terms:

> Given two commodities, for there to be equilibrium of the market for them, or a stationary price of one relative to the other, it is necessary and sufficient that the effective demand for each of the two commodities be equal to the effective supply of each. When this equality does not exist, there must be, in order to arrive at the equilibrium price, a rise in the price of the commodity for which the effective demand exceeds the effective supply, and a fall in the price of the commodity for which the effective supply exceeds the effective demand.

Having said that, Walras drives the point home by adding: "The law is such that we would have been tempted to formulate it immediately after the study of the stock market but a scientific demonstration was necessary."

Let us look at a few important points and try to find this "scientific demonstration." Walras is describing the exchange phenomenon "after the study of the stock market." But the latter is no model for the way markets of reproducible goods and services work. The reason is that the stock market represents available productive units at a certain moment of time. So the exchange phenomenon, as described by Walras, is the reverse of how it occurs in real markets. He assures us that when "effective demand exceeds effective supply," there has to be, "in order to arrive at an equilibrium price, a rise in the price of the commodity." In a real market, on the contrary, this price rise occurs when the situation changes from one of equilibrium to one of shortage—say, because of a poor harvest, an embargo, or any other circumstance which it would be difficult to regard as characteristic of a "general equilibrium" and which Walras nevertheless includes in his idea of that state. In a competitive market—that is to say, let it be repeated, in a market where supply increases when orders exceed the quantities available—it is hard to see how the price could *rise,* as Walras would have it do, since this would mean that the producers, for some strange reason, had set their prices at the lowest possible level when their supply was still insufficient to meet their customers' demand.

The route by which Walras gets us back to "equilibrium" in the converse hypothesis, where "effective supply exceeds effective demand," is just as incompatible, except in a few cases and for very short periods, with the existence of a competitive market. In this hypothesis, Walras says, return to the point of equilibrium is by way of a fall in price. But Walras did not realize that it was an erroneous assumption of symmetry that made him regard as opposites the two hypotheses he examined in turn.[7] In a *competitive* market it is impossible, *barring accidents,* for producers to go on producing more than the quantity demanded.[8] Let us suppose, however, that this has in fact happened because of an error in marketing. This will have lowered the price. If the price has fallen below the production cost, there can be no question of the "point of equilibrium," as Walras would have said, being reached by means of a further fall. The situation will redress itself after the producers have rectified their error by reducing supply, which will have the effect of making prices rise. No wonder Walrasian models are of no use in explaining the real functioning of markets.

The proof that Walras expressly constructed his model on the assumption that quantity was a predetermined magnitude is provided by his text and the equations he constructed: "The utility curves and the *quantities possessed* are, *therefore,* in the last analysis, the necessary and sufficient elements to establish current equilibrium-prices" (my italics). The fact that, ever since, neoliberal economists have remained trapped within this insoluble contradiction is similarly attested by their writings. For instance, in his *Theory of Value* published in 1959, the French economist G. Debreu, presenting his general equilibrium model, wrote that "the number *n* of producers is a given positive integer." Maurice Allais, who quotes Debreu,[9] added this comment: "The free entry of enterprises into an industry is envisaged [by Debreu] but this possibility is not in fact admitted in the demonstrations of the three fundamental theorems of the existence of an equilibrium." How is it possible to go on speaking of *market* equilibrium if the *sole* criterion by which competition is defined—namely the infinite expandability[10] of profitable supply—is excluded from the demonstration?

The misinterpretation by Walras and his followers of the meaning of the principle of competition, which they took to be a state, is the basic reason for another unrealistic element in their model. To account for "perfect equilibrium" as they conceive it, they more often than not have to resort to the assumption that the production units are as small as they can possibly be, which they never would be in real life. Even the economists of our day have launched off into endless discussion about the "optimum size" of these production units.[11] These discussions—let's face it—are pointless since the necessary and sufficient condition for a market to be competitive is that supply should not be limited. As we have seen (Chapter 9, p. 234), this condition can be achieved whatever the number of suppliers, even if there is only one, provided the law compels that supplier to supply the goods he produces, in the quantity demanded, at a price equal to the production cost plus average market profit.

If the necessary and sufficient condition for a competitive market is to be achieved in practice, the producer(s) must not have the *power* to influence the volume of supply. In the case I have just envisaged, I have assumed that this power has been denied the producer by law, but in ordinary circumstances it is understandably difficult to prevent a sole producer, or a small number of producers, from imposing his (or their) will on the market. This is why, in most cases, the market can be considered to become increasingly competitive as the number of producers rises (see Chapter 9, p. 235, the *n* person game). In other words, the optimum size of competing enterprises is determined by *practical* or, if preferred, *policy* considerations: It varies according to the circumstances, the nature of the product, the legal status of the producer(s), and so on. It is not determined by considerations of *logic*. A conceptual model designed to explain the general workings of a market economy need not be concerned with it.

## The Apparent Determination of General Market Equilibrium

In the Ricardian model or supply-based model, as I have just said, the long-run price depends solely on production cost. A market is competitive when competition is on the supply side. Accordingly the model denies the existence of a "law" of supply and demand. The formulation of this alleged law (see Chapter 9, p. 230) is misleading in that it seems to put supply and demand on the same footing, which is impossible. There are two kinds of market, the market for goods producible at will and the market for scarce goods, namely, goods that are monopolized for one reason or another, where competition is between demanders. In the first case the cause of exchange value lies on the supply side, in the second on the demand side.

Since Walras constructed his "perfect market" model on the assumption of limited supply, it follows that in his model demand, and demand only, is the determinant of what he calls the "equilibrium price." Moreover, this is just what he intended. To arrive at that result, Walras made effective demand a variable independent of supply, in contradiction to a supply-based model in which, *on a competitive market,* the effective demand for A is nothing other than the supply of B, C, D, and so on, exchanged for A. In the Ricardian model what is independent of supply is the desire to consume, which, as we have seen, is constantly shifting and which finds an additional spur in the "necessary" system of prices as established by competition among producers. The most expensive products are what generally whet the appetites of consumers, with the result that there is constant pressure on the productive system to lower, by improving its technology, the cost price of the articles desired (motor cars and refrigerators were once luxury items; now they have become mass consumption goods).

To establish the "independence" of effective demand, it was necessary for the latter to depend ultimately on the desire to consume (and not as it should on the capacity to offer something else in exchange), and this is what is expressed by Walras' equations, in which it is hardly an exaggeration to say that modern economics, a hundred years after, is still hopelessly entangled. Walras invents this formula for the demand function $D_a = F_a(P_a)$, and it is on this that the demand curve is based (at a given price of A, there will be a given demand quantity of A, and so on). However, as we have seen, in a competitive market there is only *one* price at which equivalence of exchange exists. At any higher price, demanders lose on the deal since to obtain A they have to hand over products worth more than A. It is unlikely that they will let this state of affairs continue very long. To consider, as Walras does, that there is a "direct and immediate relation" between effective demand and price is tantamount to plotting a curve that determines how much Pierre is prepared to lose in order to obtain A, which is to negate the idea of a competitive market.

The demand equation presupposes that supply is fixed and it describes what happens in a market where this is so. If the supply of *all* products is limited, what will ultimately determine the price ratios of these different goods? Answer: the degree of *intensity* of desire to possess one good rather than another. Thus, at a public auction a Louis XV commode will fetch more than a French Regency fauteuil if such commodes happen to be in vogue. This is the meaning of the equation $P_x/P_y = U_x/U_y$ quoted earlier. According to neoliberal theory, *price is determined by the intensity of the desire to consume and the volume of "effective demand" is a function of that price.*

As to equilibrium, this is achieved when, the prices of the different products being proportional to their marginal utilities, consumers in the aggregate would be in a less satisfying situation if they bought a little less of product A in order to buy a little more of product B or vice versa. In that state, the "situation of maximum efficiency in terms of wants satisfaction" is attained. Already stalled on the supply side by definition, the system is equally so on the demand side by deduction since, with equilibrium achieved, there is no reason why, other things being equal, the transactors in the market would want things to change.

### Prices Are Not Determined by One Another

The interaction of supply and demand is such that prices will change as long as arbitrage is possible between one part of the market and another. If, for example, one Louis XV commode is worth two French Regency fauteuils or one hundred candlesticks and a Regency fauteuil is worth forty candlesticks, it will be to my advantage to begin by acquiring a commode and then trade it for one hundred candlesticks, of which eighty will suffice to obtain two fauteuils (thus gaining 20 candlesticks). The market will not be in equilibrium until the demand for fauteuils has made the rate of exchange rise to the point where the commode/fauteuil price ratio, in terms of fauteuils (2 fauteuils/1 fauteuil = 2), is equal to the commode/fauteuil price ratio in terms of candlesticks (100 candlesticks/50 candlesticks = 2).

This is what Walras expresses in his "theorem" of perfect equilibrium, which we shall encounter again in Chapter 11, p. 296, on the accounting unit: "Perfect or general market equilibrium occurs only if the ratio of the prices of two goods one to another is the same as the ratio of the prices of those two goods in terms of any other."

It is hard at first glance to see why this condition is so important to Walras, since basically it is surely no more than the solution of a very simple arithmetical problem. The reason why it is of such decisive importance in the eyes of neoliberal economists is that, when demand is the principal determinant of prices, *all prices are determined by one another*.[12] If they are to be expressed conveniently by means of an accounting unit (which Walras called *numéraire*) it is necessary, in the Walrasian scheme, to have an additional good as that unit. But is there any reason why the accounting unit should be a good, as Walras seems to suggest? There is nothing in his model that demands the accounting unit have this character. This is why the decision of Western finance ministers in 1973 to give the monetary system an abstract unit of account can be regarded as a consummation, a definitive anointment of the Walrasian model. In that model the unit of account in the form of a commodity is there for form's sake only, since it too derives its value solely from the demand for it. So by implication there is nothing against replacing it by an abstract unit and in considering, for example, that henceforth the unit will be the dollar or the SDR, or any monetary token with no reference whatever to gold.

In an economy governed by the "law" of supply and demand, there is no good the price of which is directly determined by what it cost to produce. There is no need for a currency in the form of a commodity. The rate of exchange of the abstract accounting unit is, like that of all other goods and services, determined by all the rates of exchange of the other goods and services traded on the market. Since the accounting unit serves to define currencies' exchange rates, it follows that it is itself defined by reference to these different currencies,[13] any other reference being in fact without point on a market subject to the "law" of supply and demand. The severing of the link between the accounting unit and gold—in other words, between all the currencies (whose rates are expressed by reference to the accounting unit) and a commodity standard—is the logical outcome of the definition given by Walras a century ago of what he called "perfect market equilibrium." Far from representing a "new rationality," as some maintain, this break with gold is the culmination of an irrational construct.

Contrasting with this construct is the model of a rational market in which the alleged "law" of supply and demand is replaced by competition among producers only. In such a market the prices or rates of exchange of products are proportional to the quantity of labor (allowing for the impact, analyzed in Chapters 4 and 5, of the rate of profit) which has gone into producing them. In other words, the concept of "general equilibrium" is replaced by that of "equivalence of exchange." If the effort required to make a TV set is only a third of that needed to manufacture a motor car, one car will tend to be worth three TV sets, but this rate of exchange will in no way depend on that between, say, a motor car and a plough or a TV set and a trip to the Bahamas, or between the wage and a machine (except for the effect a change in the wage will have on the rate of profit).

If a monetary unit (1 dollar, 1 franc, etc.) is used for convenience to express the rate of exchange between goods and services, the monetary unit must likewise represent the value of a product of labor (a weight of gold mined and refined, for example). This product of labor, chosen by agreement as a value standard, is the *accounting unit* of the system. Value is not determined, as it is with the "abstract" accounting unit, by that of the set of goods the exchange ratios of which are expressed by the unit. Value is determined objectively: A motor car is exchanged for F.10,000 if the quantity of labor (subject to what was said in Chapters 4 and 5 about the impact of the rate of profit) necessary to mine and refine the weight of gold defining the value of one franc is roughly equal to one ten-thousandth of the quantity of labor expended on making a car.

In the neoliberal model, prices are determined by one another in yet a further sense: The price of a motor car results from the *summing* of the price of "labor" (wage), the price of the raw materials, and so on. This is not the case in a rational economic model, where the price of a car in terms of TV sets is three units and where the wage is defined as the percentage of gross receipts that will be paid to the workers.

To make quite clear the difference between the neoliberals' production cost and Ricardo's objectively determined production cost, let us return to our example of the deer and the salmon. For Ricardo, a deer is worth three salmon if it has taken the same quantity of labor to hunt the former as to catch the latter (subject to what has been said about the impact of the rate of profit on value). If the exchange is not distorted, the hunter will receive three salmon in return for his deer. It is these three salmon which he will share with his helpers (employees) and nothing more. If the rate of profit (in this case, as a proportion of gross product) is 33.33 percent, say, the hunter-capitalist will receive one salmon and his employees will share the other two. If the wage is raised, the rate of profit will necessarily be lower: If, say, the employees get two and a half salmon, the capitalist will keep only half a salmon for himself (new rate of profit: 16.66%).

One might be tempted to think that the reasoning holds good only if the principle of equivalence of exchange is complied with. But this is not so *at the level of the economy as a whole*. Let us suppose that our hunter manages to tilt the exchange in his favor and somehow persuades the fisherman to pay him six salmon for one deer. In that event, the hunter's profit and his helpers' earnings can both be increased in absolute terms. If the rate of profit is 33.33 percent, the hunter will get two salmon (instead of 1 as before) and his helpers four (instead of 2); if the rate of profit is 16.66 percent, the hunter will get one salmon (instead of half of one) and the helpers five salmon (instead of two and a half). But anyone can see by looking at the full account of the exchange between Pierre and Paul (see Appendix 1 to Chapter 4), that the simultaneous increase in the hunter's wealth and in that of his helpers will be "paid for" by the decrease in the wealth of the fisherman and his helpers since, at the new rate of exchange (1 deer =

6 salmon), the fisherman and his helpers will have only half a deer to share among themselves, whereas before they had a whole deer.

But the modern subjectivist school, incapable of seeing the act of exchange as a whole, calculates the production cost as it *appears* to each of the parties to the exchange, who obviously are unaware of the objective conditions that determine the rate of exchange in a competitive market. Our hunter, for example, simply notes (first hypothesis, in which the exchange is not distorted and his share of the gross product is 33.33%) that his expenditure on wages is two salmon. To that expenditure he adds his profit in order to determine the selling price. If the hunter manages to find a buyer in the market who, in return for the deer, will pay him not only the two salmon needed as wages but also one extra salmon (2 + 1 = 3 salmon), all is well. Let us now suppose the hunter's assistants get another half-salmon out of their employer. He will try to hold onto his former profit and offer the deer at the price of 2.5 + 1 = 3.5 salmon, but if the market is competitive he will soon have to bring his price down because at that rate he will find no takers.

Since the subjectivist school is unaware of the law of value, it holds that prices are always determined by simply summing the different cost items. Let us assume that the exchange has been distorted, and that in the situation I have just imagined the hunter is able to talk the fisherman into paying him 3.5 salmon for one deer until further notice. The psychological school will conclude that the value, or price, of one deer is 3.5 salmon and on that basis it will draw up its accounts, whereas in this particular instance there is quite obviously a glaring misalignment between the market price and the value or social cost of production. This last example shows again that a competitive market, where ultimately the principle of equivalence of exchange always prevails, and a market where demand remains supreme are of different natures. Yet the idea that there is only one market is what constitutes the foundation of the 'theorem'' of general equilibrium.

## Notes

1. This fundamental proposition raises the following question: Other things being equal, is there competition only if supply can be increased without any change in unit production cost? In other words, does competition, in the strict meaning of the term, imply a constant return? Such an assumption is not necessary here.

2. Walras warns us (*Elements of Pure Economics,* lesson 12) that he uses the word *rareté* (scarcity) to denote the intensity of the last want satisfied.

3. For the reasons explained in Chapter 9 and on page 272 of the present chapter, the *n* person game is nevertheless still the most plausible model of the competitive market.

4. Walras, *Elements of Pure Economics*, lesson 5.

5. Ibid., lessons 5 and 6.

6. Ibid., lesson 6.

7. Once again Walras' description holds good for a stock market but is irrelevant in the case of a market of goods and services.

8. Though this often happens in agricultural markets since farmers cannot control sunshine or rain.

9. "Les Théories de l'équilibre économique général et de l'efficacité maximale—impasses récentes et nouvelles perspectives," *Revue d'économie politique,* May 1971. In this article Maurice Allais presents a critique of the modern theories of general equilibrium, but continues to refer to a subjective conception of exchange by saying that "there is equilibrium if, in the situation concerned, no surplus is possible in respect of any good." For him, the concept of a "distributable surplus" represents "the quantity of a given good that can be released in a change of the economy which leaves all the indicators of preference unchanged." This conception of surplus is a refinement of the notion of the "optimum." Finally, Allais concludes that "any model which, either in its intrinsic hypotheses, or in its results, contradicts observed facts has to be rejected as wrong, however aesthetically satisfying the mathematical reasonings used in the phase of logical deduction may be." There can be no disagreeing with that conclusion, but the mere fact that it has to be made shows how far astray economics had gone. I would just add that there is no real aesthetic satisfaction in the reasonings, mathematical or otherwise, which lead to the formulation of the general equilibrium theory, since those reasonings stem from what appears as an error of conceptualization.

10. "Infinite expandability" means that, at the point where production ceases to increase, no additional orders are placed on the market.

11. According to Allais, the model studied by Debreu implies that "production units are homogeneous—in other words, that returns are assumed constant—and in that case, in a given industry, the output of each production unit *is no longer determinate*" (my italics). But, as we know, this indeterminateness, stemming from the assumption of constant return, establishes the conditions of a competitive market in the strict sense (subject to the ceteris paribus clause).

12. Because of the equation $P_x/P_y = U_x/U_y$ or its alternatives.

13. Since 1976, SDRs have been defined by reference to a "basket" of currencies.

*11*

# The Best Monetary System for Getting Rid of Gold Is the Gold Standard

The psychological conception of value sanctions another form of commodity fetishism, gold providing the most consistent example down the centuries. According to that conception, the commodity which has the most value is the one that is most wanted in the market. Since economic "science" cannot, by definition, analyze the reasons for this want, to accuse subjective economics of justifying the base craving for gold would be unjust. On the other hand, it contains no inherent principle with which this "precious metal" could be toppled from its pedestal.

### How to Make Gold a Commodity Like Any Other

The opponents of the gold standard had their way when the "gold pool" was abolished in March 1968. The pool was a grouping of the principal central banks of the Western world which intervened in the open market for gold in order to keep the latter's price within a very narrow band of fluctuation (no lower than $34.80 per ounce and no higher than $35.20). The opponents of the system maintained that gold should become "a commodity like any other," which for them meant that its price should be determined freely on the market by the "law" of supply and demand. Yet because of the circumstances in which it is produced and the main factors that influence demand for it, gold is the perfect example of a commodity whose "market price" is unlikely to align itself with its "necessary price," equal to production cost. This is because the gold-mining industry has to the $n$th degree the characteristics of all mining industries, and more generally all activities that exploit natural resources, such as agriculture: In a nutshell, output is slow to adjust to any pronounced fluctuation in demand.

In the case of gold there are relatively few workable deposits and the cost of investment is very high. At the same time speculative demand for gold is practically limitless. There are a number of reasons for this, of which the most important are that (1) gold is indestructible and takes up very little room (a double incentive to store it) and (2) gold has no or virtually no utility, which makes it a commodity the value of which tends to be indistinguishable from its exchange value. This last point needs to be emphasized since it explains why it will doubtless never be possible to get rid of gold altogether as an official or unofficial means of payment. Since there is only a small quantity of gold in existence, it is reasonable to think that there will always be enough people wanting to possess it and that consequently it will not be difficult to exchange it. Having no utility of its own, its principal attraction is that it can be converted into any other good. Thus, while possession of this most inert of commodities procures no immediate satisfaction, the commodity itself has every potentiality, all the more in that it defies time.

For objective political economy has Ricardo founded it, gold is also a "commodity like any other" but the problem is fundamentally resolved. A commodity like any other signifies in the classical theory that its value is exclusively a function of its cost of production. The whole mystique of gold is thus dispelled at the very outset: The value of gold is governed by the same principle as that of a humble product like iron, or a bicycle, or chewing gum. It is determined in the last analysis by the labor time necessary to mine and refine it. But how is this revolution of theory to be accomplished in practice? What is needed for the possession of gold to cease being desired for itself? Another way of putting the same question is to ask what must be done in order to divest gold, in the marketplace, of the characteristic of being a "scarce good," that is to say—to make the point again—a good the value of which depends solely on the "caprice" of demand, given that producers are unable to adjust supply rapidly and continually to a demand subject to particularly violent fluctuations.

## What Is the Gold Standard?

If we put preconceived ideas to one side and just think objectively about this question we can see that the gold standard, in its basic principle, provides the most rational answer that can be devised (a monetary system being, by its purpose, of an empirical nature, it can never be entirely rational). What is a monetary system governed by the gold standard? It is worth restating the definition of such a system at a time when there is much confusion of ideas on the subject and when it is a fact that the negotiators of monetary reform, with but few exceptions, do not know what the real subject of their discussion is. The definition is as follows: The monetary system is governed by the gold standard when the value of the currency unit—one franc, one dollar, one pound sterling, and so on—is kept constantly equal to a certain weight of gold (determined by convention, in most cases by reference to a state of fact that has existed for some time). Here we have to remember what used to happen in the past. A tradesman or a private individual would deposit the gold he possessed with a bank, which would issue him a certificate in return. That certificate naturally entitled him to recover the same quantity of gold. Thus, the original function of the system is that *a person rids himself of the actual metal* and obtains in its place a negotiable receipt much easier to handle. Nothing could be further from fetishism. Let me add that the standard could have been something other than gold, provided that this other commodity had at least some of the characteristics that explain why gold has imposed itself over the years as a standard—history is at least as intelligent as the international monetary experts. One of these characteristics is the one I mentioned earlier, namely, the lack or virtual lack of intrinsic utility. Only then might it be hoped that the supply of and demand for the commodity would be determined by primarily monetary causes. If copper, say, were chosen as the standard, the system would be continually disrupted by fluctuations in demand from the industries that use copper. If the industrial uses of gold took up a large share of the amount produced—which is not yet the case, though there are those who for their own reasons would have us think it is—gold would cease to be a satisfactory standard.

The most remarkable effect of the gold standard mechanism, if

allowed to operate freely, is that the scale of gold transactions is kept
to the minimum. The certainty that fluctuations in the value of the
currency unit against the gold standard will be held within tight limits,
through continuous regulation of money issue, means that there is
virtually no motive for gold speculation. Such speculation is then
confined to a few specialized establishments whose gains as a percentage of turnover are very small (as in currency trading when the market
is quiet).

Private transactors may even withdraw completely from a market in
which the opportunities for profit are so small and uncertain. The
central banks are then practically the only buyers or sellers of gold.
The gold standard's underlying logic is thus apparent: Since the
monetary system's need for additional liquidity varies only within
narrow limits, gold production is able to adjust easily to a demand that
emanates chiefly from the banks of issue. Scarcity being an eminently
relative notion, gold by the same token ceases to be scarce.

To sum up, the gold standard can function only in countries where
the desire for gold is not so strong as to thwart the rational arguments
for not possessing gold. History appears to corroborate this interpretation. The gold standard was first adopted by the British, who have
never cared much for gold. In India and China, where the desire for
gold is the most widespread, there has never been a gold standard
(China did adopt it belatedly—in 1931—for a few years, but the country
then went through the most appalling crises due to deflation caused by
exports of silver, which had served as a standard before). In France,
by contrast with what happened in Great Britain, the adoption of the
gold standard resulted in some sterilization of resources owing to the
fact that the bank of issue had to maintain gold reserves on an
economically unwarrantable scale for fear of having to meet sudden
conversion requests from a gold-hungry public.

It would be wrong to think that the general pattern of a gold standard
dates back fifty years and has nothing to do with contemporary
monetary history. The mechanism of the gold standard—just the
mechanism, not the substance—was *technically* reinstated in large part
with the creation of the gold pool in 1961, and on a much wider scale
than in the nineteenth century. (The gold pool operated until March
1968.) Through the pool the central banks of the major countries
bought and sold gold on the free market so as to keep its price at
between $34.80 and $35.20 per ounce. In other words, the dollar (and
through the dollar the other currencies of the pool's member countries)
was *convertible into gold at a fixed price for private individuals.*

Interestingly enough, from 1961 to 1965, a period that saw great stability of the dollar's purchasing power and a remarkable strengthening of the currencies of the Common Market countries, private purchasers showed very little interest in gold, conforming with the pattern I have just described. The consequence was that the pool's transactions showed an aggregate net purchase of gold by the member central banks. From 1965 the pendulum swung the other way, with private transactors considering (and subsequent events were to prove them right) that inflationary policies in the United States and elsewhere would cause currencies to depreciate against gold—a depreciation which, technically, resulted in a rise in the nominal value (or price) of gold expressed in those currencies.

Although the gold standard mechanisms were partly reinstated in a more modern form during the period from 1961 to 1968—which saw the return to free trade and the beginnings of economic unification of Europe—the reinstatement, needless to say, was more formal than real. It is worth considering why. We shall then see that the curtailment of gold's function is not an advance but a colossal retreat from monetary and, by extension, economic rationality.

The real rationality of the gold standard is not in keeping fluctuations in the currency unit's value within the narrow bounds set by the gold points. That is just the means to the end, which is to maintain an organic link between the scale of prices actually paid in the market and the scale of production costs in terms of labor. To measure the objective value of commodities it is necessary to have a standard which itself has a value. The only difference between the commodity standard and other commodities is that it is the only one supplied and demanded on the market to have a fixed price. Here I refer the reader to what I said at the beginning of Chapter 4: a fixed price does not mean a fixed value since the relative production cost of gold, like that of all other products of human labor, varies over time (and space). When the production cost of gold falls relative to other commodities, the gold prices of those commodities rise. When the production cost of gold rises relative to other commodities, their gold prices fall. These price fluctuations due to changes in gold's position in the scale of values take place imperceptibly. History offers many illustrations. The steady rise in prices (2–3% a year) between 1896 and 1913, for instance, is generally attributed—and rightly, I think—to the influx of gold from the end of the nineteenth century onward due to the mining of the South African deposits and the discovery of the cyanide process, which made refining very much easier. Even so, the explanation given in all the university textbooks seems to me faulty in its logic. Those textbooks, drawing on an oversimplified interpretation of the Quantity Theory of Money, give the increase in the *quantity* of gold—itself the origin of an increase in the issue of paper money—as the cause of the rise in prices. The increase in the quantity of gold ranks only second in the chain of cause and effect, since it is simply a result of the relative fall in the value (or cost) of gold, by virtue of the principle that when a commodity costs less to produce, more of it is generally demanded.

Yet it would be wrong to conclude from the above that to bring in the gold standard it is necessary and sufficient for gold to have a fixed price. It is also necessary for the issue of money to be regulated over time by imperceptible changes in the value of gold relative to other goods and services (changes that will be translated into slight variations in the quantities supplied). This was, roughly speaking, the case during the heyday of the gold standard, from 1870 (when the German Reich in turn adopted the system) to the outbreak of World War I. The reason was, as very rightly pointed out by Sir Dennis Robertson in a remarkable little book called *Money* (first published in 1930, with at least ten other editions thereafter), that no country at that time was able to regulate money issue as it liked, not even Great Britain—for Britain, despite being the financial center of the world, still had to reckon with economic powers of equal or greater weight, like the German Empire and the United States—or of almost equal weight, like France. Those other countries held no, or only very small, sterling balances in their respective exchange reserves. On the other hand, India, the Latin American countries, and the minor European powers held part of their reserves in sterling, proof of the specifically colonial nature of the gold exchange standard.

Everything changed after World War I when a single country, the United States, began to exert a dominant influence in international affairs. In the 1920s the world began to live under the regime of the dollar standard—in other words, as Robertson had already noted with rare insight, under the regime of an arbitrary standard. Admittedly gold had a fixed dollar price, but this was more a façade than anything else. The FED's issuing policy was not governed by the subtle shifts in relative costs as between gold and other goods or services. It was governed by sovereign decisions of the U.S. monetary authorities reacting as best they could to the impulses of domestic demand or to internal policy considerations.

Objectivity of the monetary standard is difficult to attain. Among other things, it demands that no power be strong enough to manipulate the money-issuing mechanism at will. The existence of a fixed price for the commodity standard does not guarantee that the commodity concerned really acts as a standard. Throughout the period from the end of World War I to August 1971 during which, with one exception (1933–34), there was a fixed price in dollars for gold, it was not the value of the leading currency unit, the dollar, which was defined by a given weight of gold but the value of gold which was, up to a certain point, defined by its dollar price. Only up to a certain point, because the objectivity of exchange relations will not bow indefinitely to the discretion of politicians, even those of the world's greatest power. On August 15, 1971, the United States in the person of President Nixon severed any formal link between the value of the dollar and that of a certain weight of gold, thus implicitly acknowledging that the real value of gold had nothing to do with its official price. As a result, the world jumped out of the frying pan of an arbitrary dollar standard, posing as a gold standard, into the fire of the arbitrary "law" of supply and demand that now governs both the price of gold and that of the dollar, which "float" more or less freely in the exchange market. However, this last arbitrary influence probably has a built-in limit since it is likely that eventually the free market price will roughly reflect the position of gold in the scale of values. That will be the time to reintroduce a fixed price if the world is to have a rational monetary system again.

## A Crucial Issue

For the time being we are further than ever from that rationality. What makes the monetary reform that was finally adopted such a vital issue is that it will, in all likelihood, seal the ultimate victory of subjective economics over objective theory just at a time when the subjective approach is in all other areas revealing its inability to solve the problems of our time.[1]

There is no longer a fixed price for gold, which has ceased to be considered a standard. Since the role gold was being made to play was in large part fictional, this does not constitute a real innovation. The same goes for the Special Drawing Rights (SDRs), which are the new *numéraire* and the value of which has ceased to be defined in terms of gold. Since this definition was purely formal in that SDRs never were convertible into gold, this other "reform" simply matches the letter to the spirit that has already prevailed for many years in the functioning of the international monetary pseudo-system (a real system has its own

built-in regulators). However, as we have already seen with the experience of the gold pool, the form always affects—in part at least—the
essence. As long as the leading currency unit was formally linked to
gold, this fiction placed certain obligations on the central banks, one
of which was to keep the price of gold within a very narrow band. But
there was nothing fictional about those obligations, their ultimate effect
being to take some of the subjectivity out of the system and give it
back an element of reality. Since they have been relinquished, the
system has gone wrong and the world is falling prey to inflation[2] which
has become impossible to contain because the mechanisms for that
purpose are no longer there.

What is being done today, in the name of the reigning ideology, is
purely and simply to do away with every element in the Bretton Woods
system that still linked money with the objective conception of value.
Instead of those elements we now have the absolute ascendancy of the
alleged "law" of supply and demand, which finds expression in a
system of exchange rates that are floating or semi-floating, since
countries can choose to make parities "fixed but adjustable," an
expression which testifies to the lack of rigor of thinking that shifts
position with the changing impulses of the market. Yet if there is one
market virtually without any *built-in* regulator, it is the foreign exchange market—for the very good reason that it costs nothing to issue
currency.[3] We have seen that market mechanisms do not operate—or
operate very badly—for nonreproducible goods, because for those
goods the notion of production cost has no defined sense. They operate
just as badly in the case of reproducible goods without any directly
appreciable cost, like money. *But it is possible to set a conventional
cost for money by undertaking to maintain its value constantly equal
to a certain weight of gold,* or, more generally, to a certain quantum
of the commodity (product of labor) used as a standard. In that case,
and in that case only, an objective and constant factor of regulation is
reintroduced into the "production" of money. It would be possible for
this factor to operate in the absence of a specified convention. Let us
assume that once the reform has been put through, the central banks
progressively acquire the habit of buying and selling gold in the market:
Their interventions will have the effect of durably stabilizing the price
of gold only if their money-issuing policy is, over a long period, partly
determined by the changes in their gold reserves positions. If one day
the subtle mechanism of the gold standard is reestablished, it will
probably be by this pragmatic line of approach.

Meanwhile the proponents of the reform made no secret of their doctrine. Both France and the United States emphasized that the new "system" would have to be managed by a "political body."[4] In practical terms this means institutionalizing the conferences that have had to be hurriedly convened once or twice a year since the summer of 1971 to try to rebuild ever-waning confidence. In theoretical terms, this continual intervention can be interpreted as the disappearance of any self-regulating mechanism, the substitution of an arbitrary system for an objective system (or at any rate one that tends toward objectivity), and ultimately, appearances notwithstanding, a vast step backwards in the management of monetary affairs. The objective conception of value having ceased to be taught or even understood, the plan put into effect can be likened to a coup de force perpetrated by the government on a public that has been kept in ignorance of the issue. The determination and the passion of the most radical advocates of demonetization of gold, the symbol of objective value, denote the real hatred that economic law has bred and that for a century and a half has driven the best minds to try to prove its basic principles wrong instead of seeking to discover their implications.

## Old Ideas Back in Vogue

Forgetfulness of the law of value is resurrecting ideas about the value standard which, though they may appear modern, actually belong to the preclassical era.

One of these ideas is to have as a monetary standard a range of raw materials that is as wide as possible.[5] It falls foul of at least two objections (from which other arguments could be derived that would have their place in a study of money).

1. The value of raw materials relative to one another is constantly changing according to their respective costs of production. So it seems difficult to set a price for them over a sufficiently long period of time (the necessary if not sufficient condition for a commodity to be a standard of value being, as we know, that its price should be stable). That is why "bimetallism"—with two standards, gold and silver—which operated in several continental European countries in the nineteenth century, never really worked. It is true that Pierre Mendès France proposes an index of the prices of these different raw materials (prices that would remain free to fluctuate against one another), but this in turn is faulty logic. How can the value of the standard, in terms

of which prices of goods and services are expressed, be itself expressed by a price index?

2. The less utility a commodity has, the more chance it has of being a good monetary standard, its use value being, as it were, absorbed into its exchange value. Only then can the demand for and the supply of that commodity be governed by primarily monetary factors (see above).

Another idea, which in a way is a generalization of the preceding one, is that the value standard should be the sum total of commodities supplied in the market. This system, often presented in modern dress (with a computer to calculate the weight at any moment of each of the constituents of the composite standard), is even more fundamentally at odds with logic in that the value standard becomes the sum total of the goods the value of which it is supposed to measure. (We are not discussing here the very theoretical construct proposed by Sraffa of a composite standard commodity, the purpose of which is to neutralize the variations in the value of the standard arising from the fact that different proportions of capital and labor from those used for the production of other commodities are applied in the production of that standard.)

A third idea, on which I shall dwell a little longer because it is the culmination of the subjective theory of value and underlies the monetary reform (finally adopted at the Jamaica Conference of January 7–8, 1976), is to have a purely abstract standard of value. This idea is no newer than the preceding one, as will be seen from the following passage from Ricardo which deals with both:

It was said, too . . . that a pound note did not and ought not to vary with a given quantity of gold, more than with a given quantity of any other commodity. *This idea of a currency without a specific standard* [my italics] was, I believe, first advanced by Sir James Steuart,[6] but no one has yet been able to offer any test by which we could ascertain the uniformity in the value of a money so constituted. Those who supported this opinion did not see that such a currency, instead of being invariable, was subject to the greatest variations—that the only use of a standard is to regulate the quantity, and by the quantity the value of the currency[7]— and that without a standard it would be exposed to all the fluctuations to which the ignorance of the interests of the issuers might subject it.

*It has indeed been said that we might judge of its value by its relation, not to one, but to the mass of commodities* [my italics]. If it should be conceded, which it cannot be, that the issuers of paper money would be willing to regulate the amount of their circulation by such a test, they would have no means of so doing; for when we consider that commodities are continually varying in value, as compared with each other; and that when such variation takes place, it is impossible to ascertain which commodity has increased, which diminished in value, it must be allowed that such a test would be of no use whatever.[8]

In our day, the idea that reference to gold is a relic of the past is firmly rooted in most minds. Those who hold that idea are reasoning erroneously, the error—though difficult to detect—being that from an indisputable fact they are drawing an inference alien to it. I shall call this reasoning "the Professor Triffin illusion," since it was the famous Yale University professor of that name who made the most systematic exposition of it, designed to "prove" that gold will be phased out of the international monetary system in the same way and for the same reasons that it has already been eliminated from the domestic money circulation of each country. The undisputed fact on which Professor Triffin founds his argument is that men are using increasingly abstract means of payment. Metal money has been gradually replaced by bank notes, and these in turn have been largely superseded by demand deposits with everyone beginning to pay by check or transfer and, for current spending, by credit card. It is clear evidence of an advance in economic rationality. But economic rationality demands—as I hope I have shown throughout this book—that the principle of equivalence of exchange should be respected. Yet how can exchange of value for like value possibly take place if the medium of exchange does not have an objectively determined value? In real life, the terms of the problem do not imply any contradiction. The process whereby money assumes increasingly nonmaterial forms in no way precludes the possibility of the monetary unit being constantly maintained at the value of a certain quantum of the commodity chosen as a standard.[9] This derives from the objective value theory: The only thing that can have value, as far as objective economics is concerned, is a product of human labor. Since the use value of the commodity money—gold in our example— is entirely contained in its exchange value, nothing but good will result from replacing it in circulation by *tokens* whose point of consummation is reached when, no longer having any material medium, they are the purely abstract representation of that exchange value. *In a rational monetary system the token is as abstract as possible, but the value it represents is as real as possible.*

I think this interpretation is confirmed by an impartial examination of the course of events cited in argument by all the advocates of standard-less money. If one looks closely, one sees that all the periods in which there was the steadiest expansion of credit were those in which the currency unit was linked most closely to gold. On the other hand, whenever money has severed its ties with gold, individuals have switched from money to "real goods." These then serve as commodity money and are bought for their exchange value without regard for their use value, as was the case with gold. As for states, they revert to protectionism or even to the most primitive forms of exchange: "I'll buy your textiles if you buy my machinery," and so on. A more or less thinly disguised return to barter—that is the price which the irrational aversion to gold is liable to cost the community of nations. None of these outcomes is surprising for the simple reason that the only real way, in a free market economy to rid ourselves of gold, or at any rate to limit its use (and the amount bought and sold by the public) to the minimum, is to apply the gold standard! I have already shown that regulation of money issue by pegging to gold has the effect of virtually eliminating public demand for gold in the economically civilized nations. I need not remind the reader here of how the gold standard—or at any rate a gold standard–inspired monetary system—technically ensures countries' balance-of-payments equilibrium, *which has the effect of reducing gold movements between countries to a minimum.* (These movements have been very considerable in recent times in spite of all the devices tried in order to limit them.)[10]

## Conditions for a Rational Demonetization of Gold

The fact remains, as I said earlier, that although the gold standard is the most rational possible monetary system, its rationality is not perfect. The element of absurdity in it is best demonstrated by Keynes's definition to the effect that the gold standard is that system which causes gold to be dug up out of the ground in South Africa and Siberia only to be reburied forthwith in the vaults of the banks of issue in London, New York, and Paris. And that is what you get from classical political economy and its concern to establish the value of money on an objective basis!

What is one to answer? A first reply is of a pragmatic kind and therefore only half-satisfactory. To banish gold from the monetary scene it is not enough to declare that currencies are neither defined in terms of gold nor convertible into it any longer. Nor is announcing the progressive demonetization of gold sufficient to cause the latter actually to take place. Too many motives, both psychological and rational, conspire to make gold the blue chip of exchange value, and these same motives are all the more influential in that money issue is no longer pegged to gold quantity. We are now seeing the price of gold, which under the gold standard fluctuated by no more than about one-hundredth of a percentage point per day noted only by the specialists, become the plaything of the "law" of supply and demand. That price, now the cynosure of a large public, is published almost every day on the front pages of the financial newspapers, and even the others. So would it not be better officially to acknowledge the monetary role of gold? To make the gold standard operate would be like cutting down trees in the path of a forest fire. You can't put the fire out, so you confine it. Instead of falling victim to a predator, you try to tame it.

But it is also possible to offer a more theoretical justification of the gold standard, by taking the premise that, from the standpoint of the labor theory of value, money is a convenience but not a necessity. Let us pause a while to consider this point. The immense advantage of money is that it is a *practical* way of progressing from barter to the market, for the simple reason that use of money permits *information* of suppliers and demanders, which, as we established in the preceding chapter, is the key element in competition. But let us assume for the sake of argument that each exchange partner is, by means of an ultra-sophisticated electronic system, informed at all times of the rate of exchange for every commodity against every other commodity. Instead of knowing that a TV set is *worth* 1000 francs, an automobile 15,000 francs, an electric razor 100 francs, and a small apartment 60,000 francs, he knows that a TV set is worth ⅟₁₅th of an automobile or ten electric razors, and that the apartment is worth sixty TV sets or four automobiles, and so on and so forth. In that kind of market, the transactors would exchange the products of labor direct for other products of labor, either spot or forward, or again on credit (the apartment purchased on credit would be worth 5 automobiles instead of 4, and so on).

There can be no doubt that this was the way the classicists pictured the workings of the theoretical market.[11] To express the idea that money is, conceptually at least, a dispensable medium, they employed a metaphor that has remained famous among economists. Money, they said, is a veil. By this they meant that the monetary system is in its perfect state if it can be supposed that things would go on exactly as before *were it possible* to do without it. This idea that money had to be as neutral as possible applied to domestic and international trade alike. Ricardo wrote that "the money of each country is apportioned to it in such quantities only as may be necessary to regulate a profitable trade of barter" (*Principles,* chap. 7). In radical opposition to the classical conception stands Walras, for whom "perfect or general market equilibrium" presupposed the existence of some *numéraire* (not necessarily of metal). But the idea of perfect market equilibrium, as I tried to show in the previous chapter, does not correspond to anything intelligible.[12]

To sum up, the sorely vexed question of demonetization of gold has nothing to do with sophistication of credit techniques and the increasingly abstract nature of means of payment. On the contrary, there are good reasons for thinking, as I have pointed out, that the instruments of payment will be all the more sophisticated if their value is guaranteed by reference to a commodity standard. But demonetization of gold would be rational in a world where the market was perfectly transparent, with each transactor being directly informed of the value of each commodity relative to the values of all the others determined by reference to the quantities of labor involved, directly or indirectly, in the production of each and to the average rate of profit. In such a world there would be no need for a standard because there would no longer be any need for money.[13] Hence a monetary system, however perfect, is always in the nature of an excrescence—like the police, whose reason for being would cease in an entirely orderly society.

## The Scatological Undertones of the Gold Standard

So it is by reference to the empirical world in which we live that we have to judge the rationality of the gold standard. The operation of that system, as we have seen, causes the central banks to buy up nearly all the gold produced. Stored in their vaults and strong rooms, gold, which still holds a fascination for the masses,[14] is kept out of sight.

The ultimate raison d'être of the gold standard would be to remove from the surface of the earth a commodity which for practical purposes is useless. Hidden from the gaze of men, no longer having any existence for them except as an entry in the books of the bank of issue, it would now seem like the token of its own value. Approaching even closer to complete abstraction, one could imagine the banks secretly dumping all their gold into the sea but continuing to record its value in their books, but this would be as unreal as a high command secretly destroying all its strategic weapons while continuing to let the world think that its silos and submarines were bulging with nuclear deterrents.

For the justification of Keynes's ironic remark it is therefore necessary to stay with *pure* objective political economy. The theoretical model it proposes precludes money—all money. In a society sufficiently evolved to do without money, just enough gold would be mined to make jewelry and to meet industrial uses. Man would be spared the absurdity of having to dig gold out of the bowels of the earth only for it to be reburied a few hundred miles away. Let it be noted that money is absent from two kinds of economic regime: The primitive economy of barter and the ultra-evolved economy, where *instant knowledge by all the exchange partners of all the commodities supplied and demanded on the markets of the entire world,* and (a) the quantity of labor directly and indirectly involved in the production of each and (b) the average rate of profit, would make it possible in theory to do without money. But as long as society has not attained that degree of perfection, money will be necessary, and the rationality of the labor theory of value will continue to require that the issue of increasingly nonmaterial money tokens be regulated by reference to a commodity chosen as a standard, the value of which ultimately depends on the labor necessary to produce it. Nothing can prevent some degree of fetishism developing for that commodity—today gold, tomorrow maybe some utterly useless substance discovered on Mars—that is regarded as the store of all value and possession of which, itself incapable of procuring the slightest material satisfaction, is virtual possession of all the commodities supplied on the market now and in the future.[15] To hold this fetishism in check, gold, despite its qualities, *must not be allowed to be worth more than it costs to produce.*

By keeping the value of the currency unit equal to a given weight of gold by means of compliance with certain rules of money issue, the gold standard regime makes it impossible for any incremental value to accrue to gold holdings. That is why almost all the world's gold would end up in the vaults of the central banks, the public having in principle lost all interest in the one commodity from which no monetary gain is to be had.[16] Thus gold, the object of desire whenever society yields to the caprices of the alleged "law" of supply and demand—as it has in our time when the price of gold rises in a single day's dealing by $10 or more an ounce—virtually disappears from circulation whenever society consents to conform to the authentic law of value.

Reinterred at Fort Knox and in other strongholds, gold, the unalloyed time-defying substance, suffers the same fate as the vilest refuse. It is removed from sight, and from man's covetousness, as if it too were one of nature's necessary evils. The supreme justification of the gold standard would appear to be that its logic confirms this equivalence between gold and excrement which psychoanalysis claims to have discovered—for entirely different reasons, I need hardly add. At some stretch of the imagination, a central bank governor with the soul of a poet could be pictured melting down the gold ingots in his charge to make a receptacle for what tiny tots and Salvador Dali chatter about with such relish. But let us leave this plane where pure subjectivity and pure objectivity perhaps meet, and return to that of economics. Choosing as a standard a commodity which, in principle, has no use value, and which simply represents a production cost, eliminates utility as the foundation of exchange value.

## MV = PQ

The objective value theory alone is capable of explaining the mechanism that regulates money issue. This is because the system it proposes is determinate. First equation: Value standard $= x$ grams of gold. Second equation: The value of $x$ grams of gold $=$ its cost of production. Hence:

value standard $=$ cost of producing $x$ grams of gold

It is not for me to show how, under the gold standard system, money issue takes place through the interplay of (very slight) changes in the amount of reserves and the rate of interest applicable to the claims held in the central bank's portfolio. My purpose is simply to show that, under such a system, the volume of money in circulation is an objectively determinable magnitude, which is not the case under other monetary systems.

Neoliberal economists proposed a formula for determining the amount of money—a formula that has recently been brought back into favor by Milton Friedman and the economists of the Chicago school who, like him, are supporters of the modern Quantity Theory of Money. According to this formula, the amount of money is deduced from the equation MV = PQ, where V is the velocity of circulation of money, Q the quantity of goods and services produced, and P the level of prices. The amount of money is $M = PQ/V$. The unfortunate thing is that the relation of equality presented thus is of no help at all, whatever Friedman and his disciples may think, for the simple reason, as Jacques Rueff pointed out more than thirty years ago, that it is tautological. The quantity of goods traded in the market multiplied by their price cannot but be equal, over a given period of time, to the quantity of money that is used to settle the corresponding transactions multiplied by the number of times that money turns over during the same period. So here again is the insurmountable contradiction in which the theoreticians of money are trapped by the subjective theory of value: The amount of money depends on the general level of prices, while prices are expressed in money the amount of which is being sought.

The $MV = PQ$ equation is meaningful, on the other hand, if one realizes that the labor theory of value makes it possible, in principle, to calculate PQ independently of MV (by way of the cost of production of Q, estimated as proportional to a quantity of labor, compared with the cost of production of the commodity standard). Here again it would be a mistake to think that this is nothing more than a controversy among theoreticians. Depending on whether the conception of money is objective or subjective, monetary policy will differ as day from night. The "objectivists" think, to use Jacques Rueff's telling expression, that money is "in bondage," in the sense that demand for it is and must be governed by the impulses of economic life. The "subjectivists," following the example of Keynes, are inclined to see money as "the drink which stimulates the system to activity" and which has to be forced down its throat. When Germany carried out its monetary reform in 1948, the source of inspiration was the classical school. At the same time the Bank of England, in systematically issuing money with the aim of bringing interest rates down, was applying the teachings of the psychological school.

For the psychological school, value equals satisfaction of wants. It is not possible to derive any general principle of money issue regulation from this equation since wants are by nature limitless. To express this fundamental indeterminacy, it would be necessary to write a new equation denoting the fact that money (M) is a function of the wants (W) to be satisfied: $M = f(W)$.

On this basis it is impossible to determine in advance the magnitude of M: first, because W is left to the discretion of the system's users; and second, because those users, by their own admission, do not know in what proportions money has to be created in order to meet the needs of the economy—in other words, they are unable to specify the function $f$ quantitatively. As one can see, the equation $M = f(W)$ really denotes the absence of any guiding principle in money issue policy. The finance ministers of the Committee of Twenty who in 1972–74 negotiated a reform of the international monetary system wanted to write a device of this kind into the articles of the "remodelled" International Monetary Fund (IMF). With the idea of limiting the issue of SDRs (Special Drawing Rights), some of them advocated introducing a rule whereby growth of SDRs from year to year would be kept in the same proportions as the increase in international trade (a concept underlying many other reasonings of the same type). This proportionality has no precise significance from the economic standpoint. It would suggest that world trade needs to be financed by additional reserves creation for the benefit of central banks, when basically it finances itself on the foreign exchange market where exporters sell their claims on abroad—commonly called "foreign currency holdings"—to the importers needing them to pay for their purchases (which is an illustration of the "law of markets").

The reform (adopted since this book first appeared) takes the consequences of the subjective conception of value to their utmost limit. The value of nations' currencies is defined no longer in terms of gold but of SDRs elevated to the status of an abstract unit of account. There has been much discussion on this unit of account question which is not, in fact, very interesting. There is no doubt that if one dollar is worth five francs and one franc 0.50 deutschemark, it is possible to express the value of these different currencies relative to one another by a middle term that is defined "abstractly." If, for example, one SDR is declared to be conventionally worth $\$\frac{1}{3} + DM\frac{1}{2} + FF\frac{2}{3} + \pounds\frac{1}{10}$, and so on, it will be easy to deduce from this formula the SDR value of each currency quoted on the market. It is not proposed here to enter into a discussion of the relative merits of the different devices for defining the abstract standard of reckoning. Suffice it to note that the definition of that standard, by nature a technicality, raises no particular difficulty.

But what have we obtained by creating an abstract unit of account? No more than a way of expressing the worths of currencies relative to one another. Why is this innovation presented as a decisive step toward a more "rational" monetary system that has no link with gold? Because the monetary experts of our time, and the ministers who heed them, are still captives of the myth of "perfect market equilibrium" invented by Walras: "Perfect or general market equilibrium is achieved only if the ratio of the price of one commodity to that of another is equal to the ratio of their two prices to that of a third commodity" (cf p. 274). A foreign exchange market is the place of transaction for the buying and selling of foreign holdings, which are nonmaterial goods. (A currency is a claim on a bank.) There is nothing illogical in the prices of these nonmaterial goods being expressed in terms of another nonmaterial good like the SDR; but, as we have seen, the most important question that is posed for a monetary system, however abstract, is the relationship it bears to the *real* world of the goods and services the value of which it is supposed to express. For the Walrasians this question does not arise, for the simple reason that they leave "equilibrium" in the foreign exchange market, as in the market for goods and services, to the "law" of supply and demand.

For objective economics, the "law" of supply and demand does not exist: The monetary system floats—or, more accurately, it is completely adrift—in unreality if the value of the currency unit is not objectively defined by reference to a standard. The experts and the ministers who studied the monetary reform proposals[17] of the Committee of Twenty believed they were in search of "a new monetary rationality." In fact they were but the prisoners of one of economics' most artificial constructs.

Since the gold standard no longer operates, the value of each currency is largely indeterminate. How is it estimated in practice? By reference to a general index of prices.

Consequently, the basket of commodities and services on which the consumer price index is computed tends to fulfill the role of a commodities standard. By so doing, we compound the already mentioned difficulties inherent in the former bimetallic standard.

Abolition of the gold standard has the effect of making it still more difficult to interpret facts. Every general movement of prices is termed inflationary if it tends upward, and deflationary if it tends downward. Yet this is not always true. If prices rise, this may be due to two different causes (or to a combination of the two): Either the value of the money required to express them has itself fallen (this is the most frequent case), or the value (cost of production) of the products whose prices are climbing has risen against the value of the money. For example, it is very probable that the steady rise in prices of 2–3 percent a year between 1896 and 1913, to which I referred earlier, was in no way the result of money issue[18] that had got out of control. On the contrary, it was almost certainly proof that money issue was being meticulously regulated, reflecting a relative decline of gold in the scale of costs, due to the discovery of deposits that were easier to mine, coupled with the invention of more economical refining techniques (the cyanide process). The essential thing is to be able to measure as accurately as possible the relative movements of production costs.

Monetary systems that are forced to base themselves solely on price indexes are incomparably cruder than those that link the currency unit with a commodity chosen as a standard.

The opponents of the gold standard object to the linkage of money issue with gold output. The system's most serious shortcoming, they say, is that it makes no provision for a shortfall in that output. I do not propose to go into that argument. Its proponents take it as read that economic and social development necessitate permanently rising prices. I think that enough examples could be adduced from history to show that a very slight downtrend in prices is most conducive to human well-being.[19] But let us leave that subject, or rather polemic, to one side and observe that, deep down, the refusal to peg money issue to the slow increase of gold stocks is kindred in spirit to the obsession with all-out economic growth without regard for the subtle equivalence that should exist between rational exploitation of natural resources and the development of human activity.

## Notes

1. This is precisely the significance of the reform adopted at the Jamaica Conference on January 7–8, 1976, and brought into operation in 1978 (as the 2nd amendment to the Articles of Agreement on the IMF).

2. And inflation (over-expansion of credit) does necessarily wind up in deflation.

3. If a country's currency falls steeply in the exchange market, the government of that country may take corrective measures, but the market itself will not have redressed the balance, which it would have if there were a mechanism to regulate currency issue by reference to the value-standard.

4. The Interim Committee, set up in 1978.

5. Championed in France by Pierre Mendès France, and in England by Nicholas Kaldor.

6. In a work published in London in 1767 entitled *Inquiry into the Principles of Political Economy*. In *Capital* Marx several times quoted Steuart, whom he regarded as one of the founders of bourgeois economics.

7. In writing "the only use of a standard," Ricardo acknowledges implicitly that the actual payments in gold can be reduced to a minimum, if not to nothing, which is consistent with the logic of the gold standard.

8. Quoted from a pamphlet by Ricardo published in 1816 under the title *Proposals for an economical and secure Currency*. At that time it was a question of whether the gold standard, suspended by the Bank of England in 1797 on the eve of the Napoleonic wars, would be reinstated when peace returned. A great many theoreticians and experts maintained that the pound sterling could well manage without linkage to a specific standard.

9. Ricardo wrote (*Principles,* chap. 27): "A currency is in its most perfect state when it consists wholly of paper money, but of paper money of an equal value with the gold which it professes to represent." Elsewhere Ricardo writes that the use of metal money is "pure caprice." His penchant for paper money was quite remarkable for his time.

10. During the period from 1870 to 1914 temporary balance-of-payments deficits were financed by private loans. Movements of gold were kept to a minimum. By contrast, gold movements have been on a large scale for the past fifty years or more, including the period from 1945 to 1968. More generally, *progress,* in regard to monetary management, consists in having the least possible need for liquid funds. A firm that manages its finances rationally keeps its sight deposits or cash holdings to a minimum, since these by definition earn nothing. It could even reduce that minimum to zero if it managed to make the maturity of its short-term debts coincide exactly with that of its claims. But certain contingencies always have to be allowed for. By the same token, a well-managed international monetary system would function with a small reserves total.

11. The classical or near-classical economists always imagine a moneyless world. It is not by chance that the only contemporary author to have remained true to this tradition is Jacques Rueff (in *L'Ordre Social*), who is probably one of the economists having the closest spiritual kinship with the classical school.

12. The idea acknowledged by economists since Walras that in order to construct an *n* market model it is necessary to have *n* + 1 commodities ceases to be justified if value is determined objectively by the quantity of labor (see pp. 274 and 296–97).

13. Though money would still retain its function as a store of value.

14. A survey conducted at the time of the Tutankhamen exhibition in Paris revealed that what had attracted so many visitors was the fact that the young king's statue was made of gold.

15. This fetishism dies all the harder in that the market always tends to reach beyond commodities, as such, so that everything is for sale: an uninhabited island in the Adriatic, the soul of a corrupt civil servant, and so on and so forth.

16. Naturally, people may still want to hold gold as an insurance against war, revolution, and so on. But this desire lies outside the bounds of economics. There is an even more radical way of preventing capital gains on gold, and that is to prevent its being held by private individuals (where a ban of this kind has a chance of being applied, as in the United States). But prohibition is a

crude method. The gold standard's superiority over all other monetary systems is that it induces the public to turn away from gold on rational grounds.

17. Which paved the way for the Jamaica agreement adopted in January 1976 on the reform of the monetary system (see note 1 above).

18. For conceptual reasons I have preferred not to use the term "money supply," which in my view would be better named "money demand."

19. The last quarter of the nineteenth century, marked by the industrial growth of Germany, Japan, and Russia and also by the introduction of the first social legislation in Great Britain and the German Reich was a period of steadily declining prices but just as steadily rising wages.

*12*

# Are We Rich?

If throughout this book I have argued the case for a complete renewal of economics, the real founding principles of which were established a century and a half ago by Ricardo and afterwards partly forgotten or else misinterpreted, it is first and foremost for the following reason: The principles of (Ricardian) political economy point the way out of the maze into which the fantasies of our time had led us. Then we should be able to see more clearly how to tackle the political issues associated with the economic organization of society. Economics will help us to put "socialism" in its true perspective, both from the standpoint of theory and as regards what is desirable in order to organize human society more rationally. Were it more rational, society would be easier to manage and at the same time more resistant to arbitrary or despotic forms of power.

## The Construction of Socialism or the Mutilation of Political Economy

In the last analysis, all that socialism retains of political economy is the foundation on which the latter is based, namely the fact that the origin of all wealth is human labor. But after the *creation* of wealth comes the circulation of that wealth and the greatest theoretical contribution from classical economics is its discovery that in an economy

301

based on the labor theory of value, that is, where exchange value is proportional to cost of production, exchange is the *rational* way of organizing wealth circulation since it is based on a relationship of equivalence. The organization of exchange presupposes a transition from product to value, for the very good reason that if there is no such transition there is no way of guaranteeing, when Pierre hands over one deer to Jacques in return for one salmon, that one of the two transactors will not be the loser.

The only way round this danger is via the quantity of labor expended allowing, where appropriate (which is always the case), for the effect of accumulation. This makes it possible to establish at *what rate* products can be exchanged for one another so that neither Pierre nor Jacques loses by the *terms of the exchange.* The problem would be easy to resolve if products resulted solely from the application of a certain quantity of labor to resources supplied free of charge by nature: 1 kg of shrimps is *worth* 3 kg of fruit if, in the space of one hour and with the same amount of physical and mental effort, 1 kg of shrimps can be caught at the seaside or 3 kg of apples gathered in the country. But nearly all products of labor are obtained with the aid of other products resulting from labor already performed (the shrimping net, fruit-picking cane, and so on). The involvement of these *accumulated* products of labor that form "capital" complicates the exchange mechanism considerably and, as we have seen in this book, it takes all the resources of classical political economy to explain why the principle that labor is the basis of value *logically* implies that many products having necessitated the same quantity of labor will have different values, whereas others having necessitated different quantities of labor will have the same value. The key to the puzzle is provided in every case by the mechanism of exchange between existing capital and future profit, this mechanism operating throughout the entire period during which the capital is immobilized (see Chapters 4, 5, and 6).

In distinguishing as I have just done between the two stages represented by production and circulation of wealth, I have sought to expose the inherent weakness of Marxist socialism in withdrawing the accumulated products of labor (capital) from the exchange circuit on the contention that the intervention of capital contradicts the labor theory of value which, in the simplistic Marxist version, postulates that value must always be proportional to the quantity of labor *effectively* expended on the production of commodities. However, my distinction is arbitrary since exchange makes its appearance at the outset, that is, at the production stage—buying a net to catch the shrimps.[1] Consequently, in the fullness of its rejection of classical political economy, so-called scientific socialism robs itself of a *rational* organization of production. By necessity, the rejection is more doctrinal than real, since in fact the socialists use the categories of political economy by surreptitiously reintroducing the notion of interest rates (profit on employed capital). Thus the end result of the construction of socialism will not be socialism but the exchange economy, or, to give it its usual name, "capitalism." Yet it would be wrong to say that the transition via socialism will have had no redeeming feature. There is no scientific reason for taking capital out of the exchange circuit, but socialism applied to the letter does more than abolish the market for the tools of production: It also withdraws from the exchange circuit a whole category of goods—"scarce goods"—for which there is no prima facie reason why they should be circulated through the market. In this way, socialism would pave the way for an exchange economy shorn of its excrescences. In its own fashion it might help society to sort itself out.

## The Socialist Dream Is the Transposition of the *Theoretical* Conclusions of Political Economy to an *Imaginary* Future

The socialist dream, in its extreme form, is actually the transposition, to a future and imaginary world, of the theoretical universe built by the economists of the classical era for the purposes of reasoning. But while it draws deeply on political economy, Marxism simultaneously assigns itself the aim of freeing man from the latter's laws. These two approaches are mutually exclusive and that is why the revolutionary program is bedeviled by an irremediable ambiguity. On the one hand, it has "scientific" credentials, but that is because it takes its components from the hypothetical world conceived by genuinely scientific minds, the greatest being Ricardo. On the other, it has no real content, because in rejecting political economy Marxists forget the conditions it had postulated for the realization of its assumptions. We have seen several examples of this strange use of science to nurture political make-believe. Here are a few of the most significant.

### Abolition of wage labor through elimination of profit

Do away with capitalism and you do away with the alienating system of wage labor. That is what Marx says in so many words. But the abolition of wage labor would be possible theoretically only on exactly the opposite assumption from the one he envisages. National product is *necessarily* shared between profit—understood as income from capital—and wages.[2] To make wages disappear, the whole of national income would have to be absorbed by profit! Is that conceivable? Theoretically, yes. That is what would happen if all output were produced with machines capable of working indefinitely (an hypothesis that generalizes the one on which Ricardo first reasoned, back in 1815, in order to reveal the nature of profit!) or of replacing themselves without the agency of new human labor. Then there would be no more workers, only *rentiers* living on the product of capital, consisting of the stock of automatic machines, accumulated by their predecessors (see Chapters 4 and 5 and Appendix 1 to Chapter 4). Thus, the abolition of wage labor could result only from the triumph of capitalism, not from its demise.

**A Moneyless World**

Ricardo reasoned on the assumption of a transparent economy in which goods and services were traded proportionately to the real cost of producing them. At first glance it would seem that the disappearance of money, far from being logically linked with the disappearance of "market relations," as Marx would have said, would be conceivable only if there were such a thing as a perfectly competitive market. There are two reasons for thinking this—one practical, the other substantive.

1.  The competition model (see Chapters 7, 9, and 10) presupposes, among other things, that each competitor is *fully informed*. In practice it would be impossible to do without money unless each transactor in the market were constantly kept informed of the rate of exchange at which *all* commodity transactions are effected at any one time. What is more, each transactor would have to have a computer that would memorize all that information.[3]

2.  It is only on the assumption of a competitive market that commodities will tend to be traded according to their relative real costs of production. In other words, competition is necessary if the principle of equivalence of exchange is to be complied with, but that equivalence relates to the value of the *products exchanged:* It does not relate to men. Among men, on the contrary, free exchange engenders inequality

since it is sufficient for one man to accumulate the product of his labor, instead of consuming it immediately, for equality of income—given equal quantities of labor expended—to cease immediately (because of the profit that capital will bring). Which is why, we shall be told, socialism could not care less about the principle of equivalence of exchange since exchange creates an unequal distribution of national product! Yet how is this national product, comprising an infinite number of individual products, to be distributed according to criteria that are considered more "just" *if one does not know what the respective values of those products are?* "According to needs" is the answer that springs instantly to mind. And that indeed is socialism's answer; if that is as far as it goes, then there is no point in pursuing the discussion since we are entirely in the realm of the arbitrary (needs, or wants, do not lend themselves to any kind of measurement once elementary needs have been satisfied). But if we assume that socialism, too, recognizes the need to measure the value of products in order to be able to distribute them (its position on this point is not clear, certain Marxist theoreticians maintaining—and others not—that the labor value principle still obtains in the socialist economy), how does socialism reconcile this logical requirement with its repudiation of the laws of economics?

**The Plan**

In France the intelligentsia are only just beginning to realize that the market, not only in practice but also in principle, might be a better system of resource allocation than centralized planning.[4] Even so, most commentators and politicians remain convinced that a plan is necessary in order to secure long-term investments which, they contend, would in the ordinary way not have been accommodated by the market. In fact it is inflation which reduces the market's horizon to only a few years. Capitalism, if it has a monetary system good enough to keep value more or less constant over time, is by its nature a system that encourages capital formation in all its forms.

This does not mean that a plan's only use is to make good the inflation-induced shortcomings of the economic system. The market's true domain is all *directly productive* activities, regardless of the duration of investment.

But in an evolved society an increasing proportion of *net product*—yielded by growth—is not and must not be reinvested in productive uses: It has to be used by central and local government for various purposes ranging from community needs like education to major scientific projects like Apollo or other vast enterprises. Needless to say, in many cases the expenditures have to be *programed* over several years by government. Since it is not the purpose of those expenditures to earn an income, it is only logical that they should be financed by taxation rather than by borrowing, another argument for having a monetary system that is as noninflationary as possible, for only then will it be possible to know really what share of national income is preempted by taxation.

In socialist countries it is not only the use of wealth but its production that is subject in principle to a plan. Looked at closely, this kind of planned economy is a caricature of a free market economy, since the market is simply a permanent opportunity for the different producers to adjust their own plans and programs in terms of one another. The central planners, too, have to adjust investment programs to match available resources, but for that to be really possible they would have to know all the data in advance for the whole of the period of the plan. Taking things to the extreme, one could say that the plan, instead of foreseeing the future, either abolishes it in the event of being implemented to the letter (what is a future predetermined by legislation?), or obscures it should the forecasts be wrong. This probably accounts for the dispiritedness of the people in the centrally planned economies: Without a future there can be no real life in the present. In an attempt to remedy this inherent failing, the central planners revise their plans at closer and closer intervals, striving—with no hope of achieving it— for the formal perfection of their model, namely the market with its continual adjustment to the changing data.

I think that one could go even further and see the abolition of the market, the rejection of the almost biological principle of competition that acts as a constant test determining the survival of each enterprise and the position of each individual, as the deep-lying reason for the fact that socialists, when they are to remain socialist, are the whole time exposed to the temptation of nonstop revolution, the only way, under their system, to restore the future to the present as they have to live it.

Here I would again draw attention to the close inspirational kinship of the doctrines, whether socialist or neocapitalist, constructed *in opposition to* Ricardian political economy. Keynes, for example, wrote these mind-boggling words: "Best of all that we should know the future."[5] Here we have a remark that could not be more egregiously unscientific, yet reflects a concern similar to that of the planners who think they can "reduce the unknowns" by projecting their image of the future, as it were, onto a document—the French Plan was until 1986 put to the vote in parliament, which was taking the preposterous to its extreme. In reality, the only intelligent approach that can be taken in order to come to terms with the uncertainty of the future is to create a system that will serve to eliminate those variables *which depend on our will*. In this regard, classical political economy proposes the most "deliberate" organization of society it is possible to have. Take, for example, its preference for the gold standard monetary system, which superficial minds ("those who do no more than repeat what they have learned," as a famous economist of our time has remarked) unfailingly describe as the rule of blind mechanisms, when its deep-lying purpose is to eliminate, as far as that is possible, the uncertainty caused by changes in the value of money, an uncertainty that in any case is impossible to eliminate entirely since the value of the money standard depends on the cost of production of gold, which varies over time.

### The withering away of the state

For the economy, to be able to dispense with the corrective action of government, an imaginary situation would have to exist in which, first, nothing ever disturbed economic life—no wars, no strikes, no climatic upsets, no population boom, no drought—and, second, all economic agents meekly obeyed all the "rules of the game" as laid down by the economics textbooks. In short, here again, the demise of the interventionist state could come about only through the outright triumph of the liberal economy (in the European sense) as ideally conceived by the theoreticians, not through its overthrow.

## Zero Growth and the System's Inherent Logic

Suppose for a moment that the exchange economy had really asserted itself throughout the world. In such a world there might be less interventionism on the part of the state—though it must be remembered that the management of free exchange and a stable monetary system that that world would ultimately necessitate would be a very complex task, requiring constant vigilance by government—but the withering away of the state would not, automatically, follow, for the simple reason (see above) that while, on the one hand, there would be production of wealth—a task we shall assume is left entirely to market forces—on the other hand, there is the use of the wealth produced, and as wealth increases, so do needs like education, health care, safety, and so on—all of them impossible to satisfy on a national scale other than through government or with government help. It is for this latter reason that the state finds itself under increasing pressure to take an ever thicker slice of the product of growth as the only way to meet its mounting expenditure.

Over the long term the central government budget share of national product rises by stages. In the United States, for instance, federal civilian expenditure as a proportion of GNP remained remarkably stable from the end of the Civil War in 1865 until 1933. Throughout that period it was about 2 percent; then, with Roosevelt's New Deal, it jumped to 6 percent. From 1933–34 to 1964–65 it held steady again, notwithstanding World War II. But between 1963 (the end of Kennedy's presidency and the early years of Johnson's) and 1966 it doubled.[6] Since then it has stabilized (one wonders for how long) at around 12 percent.

In the system they were studying, the classical economists revealed one of the laws that govern the evolution of a whole category of systems (including that of living organisms), namely the tendency toward a stationary state, by which they did not mean immobility but cessation of growth.

This book's analysis of the rate of growth as it relates to the rate of profit opens up a by no means hopeless path to the state of zero growth, from which we are still a long way off in any case (if we ever do reach it). The big question is how to use the "overplus" or surplus. It can be reinvested entirely or almost entirely in the productive system. In this way the nation's "capital" is increased and the highest possible rate of growth is ensured. That is what Japan, in particular, has been doing since the end of World War II, and in general all the countries that have made the most rapid economic progress—though this progress has not been so rapid as was thought at first, when the reckoning of the consumption necessary to production did not include the destruction of certain goods, like pure water or air, which now have a "value" since restoring them to their original state costs something. But it is also possible to channel a growing share of the surplus into nonproductive uses—"nonproductive" is not synonymous with "useless"—and thus draw closer to zero growth in increasing comfort, since population ceases to grow, at least in the advanced countries, as capital ceases to accumulate (see Chapters 4 and 6).

Now, classical theory—and this is where again it demonstrates its superiority over Marxist theory as a tool of social analysis—regards this development as *intrinsic to the internal logic of the system.* "Long indeed before this period" (the end of accumulation), wrote Ricardo, ". . . almost the whole produce of the country after paying the labourers will be the property of the owners of land" (though it may be supposed that meanwhile ownership of part of the land such as mines, oilfields, etc., will have passed to the state) "and the receivers of titles and taxes" (*Principles,* chap. 6).[7]

Why is the economic system destined to move (slowly) toward a stationary state? Ricardo's answer on this point is, as we have seen, unequivocal. He categorically rejects the contention of Malthus and, later, Keynes that since capital accumulation is by nature a phenomenon of exponential growth (introducing the idea of compound or *accumulated* interest), there will come a time when *demand* for capital is no longer sufficient to absorb this continually expanding supply—hence the alleged tendency for the rate of profit to fall.

In fact accumulation of goods is not per se a factor of declining profit. To convince oneself of this, it is better to forget about price in money terms and concentrate on exchange ratio. The manufacture of a color TV set, say, requires roughly one-fourth of the accumulated products (capital) and new products of labor required in the manufacture of a car. Hence the approximate ratio: One car equals four color TV sets. If, as a result of increased capital accumulation, the output of both cars and TVs rises steeply, nothing will change the fact that one car is exchanged for four color TVs. But if labor productivity increases faster in the electronics industry than in the motor industry, the exchange ratio will also change: It may be necessary to "pay" five TV sets for a car, although the new exchange ratio does not of itself imply any fall in the rate of profit of TV manufacturers, since it has been assumed that a color TV set now costs less to produce. For things to be different, it would have to be supposed that the decline in the exchange ratio was caused by another factor, namely that all households are equipped with TV sets, that foreign markets are similarly "saturated" and that the number of sets supplied exceeds the normal requirements of the replacement market. In that case, and in that case only, the exchange ratio will fall below the production cost and this will cause profit to decline or even disappear. But it is likely that electronics manufacturers will meanwhile have realized that their markets are shrinking and switched their investment to other activities. If the penny has not dropped, that is their loss, but their error of judgment does nothing to impair the laws of classical political economy, of which the "law of markets" (according to which commodities are paid for with other commodities) remains fundamental. That law implies, let it be stressed, infinite plasticity of human wants, which are considered to be by nature infinitely expandable and liable to take the most diverse forms and in some cases those least expected by the futurologists (if tomorrow, for example, people feel that they need to eat and drink fresh produce only, this will open up a new and virtually limitless field for rapid transportation of farm products and for their marketing by a system that will have to improve in consequence, since simply distributing canned goods will no longer suffice). The indeterminate nature of human wants alone should serve as a warning against any economic system that bases value—as ours does—on so subjective a notion or makes its goal the complete satisfaction of those wants. The socialist dictum "to each according to his needs" has no real meaning whatever.

Ricardo never linked the economic system's slow drifting to the "stationary state" with the idea that demand would one day become insufficient to sustain activity. As to productive potential, this too, in his view, is virtually limitless. On the second page of *The Principles of Political Economy and Taxation,* first published in 1816, and to my knowledge the only wholly consistent theory of capitalism formulated to date, he writes that manufactured commodities "may be multiplied . . . almost without any assignable limit." But, he adds, there is one category of goods for which there is a natural limit to production, and that is food.

Thus, the exchange-based economic system is put together in such a way that is has no built-in brake on its own development: In principle it can go on and on accumulating a capital that will meet the growing needs of a likewise growing population. But the system is "open." What does *open* mean in this context? It means that exchange involves not only the components of the economic system, but also the system's relationship with the outside world. The production units that form that system are constantly trading with one another the products of human labor. But what is this labor applied to? To the materials of every sort supplied by the natural environment, with which the economic system can be regarded as maintaining a constant process of exchange (just as the cells of a living organism exchange with one another the oxygen they borrow from the atmosphere). Sometimes this exchange works in nature's favor (e.g., when the economic system "borrows" iron, clay, and limestone from it and "returns" them in the form of a dam that will serve to irrigate a desert) and sometimes—more and more frequently, alas—it works very much in nature's disfavor (as when the system "borrows" oil and "returns" wastes that pollute rivers and oceans). Ricardo, who speaks of the "original and indestructible powers of the soil" does later argue on the following hypothesis:

> If air, water, the elasticity of steam, and the pressure of the atmosphere were of various qualities; if they could be appropriated, and each quality existed only in moderate abundance, they, as well as the land, would afford a rent, as the successive qualities were brought into use. With every worse quality employed, the value of the commodities in the manufacture of which they were used would rise, because equal quantities of labour would be less productive. Man would do more by sweat of his brow and nature perform less; and the land would be no longer preeminent for its limited powers. (*Principles,* chap. 2)

On the other hand, Ricardo dwells at length on the hypothesis that with a large population it will become more and more difficult to increase agricultural production, given that arable acreage is limited. Logically (he did not say historically) there will come a moment when production will cease to yield a "surplus," being completely swallowed up by current consumption. When that moment comes, net product will have fallen to zero and "growth" will therefore have ceased.

### Malthus, Ricardo, and the Club of Rome's Conclusions

Let me say here and now that it would be misunderstanding Ricardian theory to see in it a first blueprint of the report of the Club of Rome which created such a stir some years ago. The "economists" (if they can be dignified with that name) of the Massachusetts Institute of Technology simply fed into a computer a series of figures which they had interpreted beforehand—computers never say anything that they are not programed to say—as a confirmation of the theories of Malthus, the arch-opponent of Ricardian political economy. A series of statistics on the "soaring" growth of the world's population (in truth, it was the paucity of thought of the MIT experts which plumbed new depths) was accompanied by another on the steady depletion of natural resources, given current rates of consumption in the rich countries. The report concluded with a set of recommendations, *all* of them deriving from a crudely degenerated utilitarian doctrine which has become the main current of thought in our century and which is largely responsible for today's wastage.

Yet as Ricardo saw it, population was not fated to grow faster than the resources necessary or considered necessary to support it. The purpose of political economy was to define the conditions allowing these two variables to evolve in harmony with each other (see Chapters 3, 4, and 6). Once a society is organized on the model proposed by political economy, the causal relationship is reversed: Population grows *because* economic wealth increases. The MIT experts, incapable of imagining a growth model other than that of the so-called consumer society, simply gave up and advocated a halt to expansion. In fact, what the situation demands is the opposite. The first thing to do in order to avert the twin dangers of overpopulation and deterioration of the environment is to understand and apply everywhere, in industrialized and nonindustrialized countries alike, the laws of economic development, laws that the consumer society and the three theoretical models expressed in it (the Keynesian model, the neoclassical model, the Friedmanian model) are trying to break away from, the first ignoring the role of the capital "saving" function (in both meanings of the word), and all three ignoring the value function. But since it is impossible to eliminate those functions, the practical outcome is today's extraordinary wastage and—the intellectual outcome—the stagnation of economic thought.

The fact remains that mankind will always be subject to the constraint of production of staple foodstuffs. The great undertaking of future generations will perhaps be to phase in zero growth in such a way that it will not be caused by the end of accumulation due to the "inevitable" limits to the earth's resources—in fact, those resources will prove to be virtually limitless if rationally used—but will result from the allocation of net product to uses that are not directly productive but are designed to increase the well-being of society.

## Relative Impoverishment

Since value is proportional to a quantity of labor, the idea of "well-being" or "wealth" is clearly associated with a fall and not a rise in value. This is what today's national accounting experts have the greatest trouble in understanding and in making understood, for the very good reason that their system is directly descended from the psychological theory of value formulated by the economists of the late nineteenth century. According to that theory, the exchange value of goods and services derives from their "utility." Will mankind therefore become richer because the value of national product increases owing to the need to install costly antipollution equipment to give us back pure and increasingly "useful" air and water? The truth is that mankind will have become poorer to the same extent as it has to work harder to obtain resources that were previously a "no charge loan" from nature. A land of milk and honey, where the majority of necessary or enjoyable goods were to be had without effort, would have a near-zero GNP and yet could be considered the richest country on earth. Whereas a country where the inhabitants went about in space helmets because the air was unbreathable and, more generally, nothing could be obtained without labor, could have the highest per capita GNP in the world and yet rightly be regarded as the country with the lowest standard of living of all. In an attempt to break out of the contradictions in which modern economics has become ensnared because of the inadequacy of its concepts, its critics are devising new yardsticks like "gross national happiness" (as if happiness could ever be gross, as opposed to net, or measurable), "social well-being," and so on. In doing so, they are actually working themselves deeper still into the indeterminacy and arbitrariness of the psychological school, whose subtlety of subtleties was Vilfredo Pareto's invention, at the turn of the century, of the "social optimum."

### Scarce and Pseudo-scarce Goods

What about the value of "scarce goods"?

On this question, I have pointed out (see Chapter 9) that classical political economy introduced a distinction the importance of which has not, in my opinion, been sufficiently appreciated, inasmuch as it has major implications not only for theoretical thinking but also for the organization of society. To be absolutely rigorous, the only goods that can be called scarce are those of which the quantity is *once and for all* limited for natural reasons: for example, building sites in the heart of a city (although a site can be "enlarged," up to a point, by building upward), works of art, and so on. For this category of goods, value depends solely on the caprice of demand, to quote Ricardo, who *expressly* excludes them from the field of investigation of economics. From this one should conclude, in my opinion, that keeping such goods in the exchange circuit is not of itself justified by economic science. It may be decided, for convenience sake or to take account of vested interests and not to disrupt the habits of society, to let the market determine their price, but the resulting market price is not a *necessary* price, since by definition there is no "cost of production": This price is purely a matter of the luck of the deal in the unpredictable poker game of supply and demand. But that chance, let it be repeated in opposition to the demagogues, is often preferable to a rigid system of allocation, because it is one of the forms in which life manifests itself. So much so that another argument can be added to the case I set out in Chapter 9 for leaving the market to determine the price of certain goods: The market, even without inbuilt regulating mechanisms, is often a better interpreter of the driving forces of economic life than the "will" of the state. That having been said, the lawmakers may, if they consider it advisable, decide to withdraw some or all scarce goods from exchange by "socializing" them without thereby "violating" the laws of economics (provided that the owners of those goods are adequately compensated, though the basic criteria for such compensation would often be difficult to define).

As to the other category of goods sometimes also referred to as "scarce"—though the term is wrongly used (Ricardo never makes this mistake)—it consists of products of labor the alleged scarcity of which derives from the fact that more and more labor is required to produce them, with the result that they cost more and more to obtain. This is true of agricultural production if the most fertile lands are already being used to the full and therefore either poorer land has to be cultivated or the land currently under cultivation has to be made to "yield" more, which means "working" it harder and increasing the injection of capital (e.g., fertilizer, etc.). The harvest will be abundant, but returns will diminish. A similar case is that of ore mining when the rich veins are becoming depleted and deposits have to be worked where mining costs are higher.

What distinguishes the economics of these products and others which we shall discuss in a moment is that the best-placed producer, the one who farms the most fertile land or works the opencast mine located close to consumption outlets, is able to sell his output with "excess profit," because the selling price will necessarily align itself with the cost price of the enterprise producing under the worst conditions. This is inevitable for an obvious reason: If this *marginal* enterprise is in business, it is because, *at the lowest price they are in a position to charge,* the output of the better-placed enterprises is insufficient to meet the demand in the market.[8] At this juncture the (too often misused) concept of scarcity reenters, but not for long. The pressure of demand will force up the price, but only until effective demand is met as a result of the market being entered by producers with lower and lower productivity. From this it follows that *at the margin* the *value* of the products in question will be determined by the objective factors revealed by the labor theory of value. *It will be a function of production cost as meant in that theory.* Incidentally, the mechanism I have just outlined shows us the true role, in a competitive market, of the interaction of supply and demand, which is to make the "law of value" prevail. Whenever price ceases to be a function of production cost and depends solely on excess of demand over supply, competition has in fact ceased.

In classical theory the "extra profit" accruing to enterprises whose productivity exceeds that of the marginal enterprise is called *rent*. In the case of agriculture, and mines (on which Ricardo based his argument),[9] the rent is in principle paid by the farmer or miner to the landowner. The fact that this excess profit is transferred from the "capitalist"—in this case, the farmer[10] or mine exploiter—to the landowner produces a remarkable result. It destroys the *scarcity effect* on the earnings of the well-placed producer. These earnings are brought back within the purview of "common law," as it were, namely the law of value, since they now depend solely on the cost of production. As to the marginal enterprise, it is by definition the one that pays no rent because, in current market conditions, it earns no more than enough to obtain the average rate of profit.[11]

## Marginalist Economics Mistakes Profit for Rent

In this book I have criticized—conclusively, I hope—the "marginalist" theory of the neoliberals (see, in particular, Chapters 3, 4, and 6) but championed the Ricardian theory of rent based on marginal cost (Chapters 3 and 8) because I believe that it alone poses the problem of scarcity correctly. Appearance notwithstanding, there is no contradiction between these two positions, and the reason there is none needs to be stressed because, in my view, it offers a weighty argument in favor of the relevancy today of the classical theory, due to the aptness of its concepts to economic phenomena.

In the Ricardian model, the aggregate that does not fall into any defined category is rent, because it is simply a residual. Rent is the excess profit represented by the difference between the production cost of the most efficient enterprises and that of the least efficient, whose contribution is nonetheless necessary in order to make scarcity cease in the market.[12] That contribution is understandable only because the sector of activity concerned is operating with diminishing returns; in other words, if the most efficient enterprises increased their output, their efficiency would decrease.[13]

Scarcity is therefore always linked with monopoly in the view of classical political economy: Just as the owners of the most fertile land have a monopoly because fertile land exists in limited quantity, so the best-run and the most technologically advanced firms have a certain monopoly, as long as market prices mirror the production cost of less efficient firms.

This has far-reaching implications theoretically, since it follows conversely that, in all cases where there is no monopoly, the assumption regarded as normal by classical political economy is that of constant if not increasing returns, the idea of increasing returns certainly seeming to be implied in the assertion that manufactured goods can be "multiplied . . . almost without any assignable limit."

It follows also that the principle of competition transcends the market. In a business that is operating with constant costs, all its products are competing with one another, inasmuch as there is no reason to prefer the first unit off the assembly line to those that follow. The same would hold true in terms of an entire country, supposing that all the commodities it produced came from one integrated enterprise.

In an article published in 1926 (in the *Economic Journal*), which has remained a milestone in the history of modern economic thought, Piero Sraffa voiced his view that the diminishing returns hypothesis on which the marginalist theory is founded does not square with the conditions in which industrial firms actually operate. Sraffa's critique, it seems to me, was incomplete and sometimes used the wrong arguments.[14] But it was enough to rock the pillars of the temple. Since that time, marginalist doctrine, which still serves as the foundation of economics teaching, has been insecure. One good heave and it should all collapse.

There is a simple explanation and it is that in essence the doctrine is an extension of the theory of rent, misinterpreted. The economists of the late nineteenth century, incapable of explaining profit in the general model of exchange, which necessitates, as we have seen in Chapter 4, reference to an objective basis of value, saw it as a "residual," namely the difference between the average cost and the marginal cost. To get there they had to say that, in all cases, human industry, wherever applied (in agriculture or in manufacturing), operated at the margin in conditions of diminishing returns, this being necessarily so for the cost of producing the last unit of output to be higher than the average cost of production (in which case, it will be to the advantage of the enterprise to increase its output to the point where the cost of production of the last unit is equal to the market price). This turns the exception into the rule.

The irony is that the "modern" economists have criticized Ricardo for having, in the early years of the nineteenth century, devised a system patterned on the agricultural economy; instead it is they who have extended to all enterprises the hypothesis which their illustrious predecessor had conceived for agricultural (and mine) undertakings only (and even then he took care to specify that advances in farming would constantly push back the moment at which their returns would begin to diminish!). In this way the "marginalists" contrived a theory which has no explanatory value because most modern businesses would be able to avoid increasing or even lower their cost price if they could increase their output. But what proves that the marginalists' theory is false is that it will not work, either, in the context of its basic hypothesis. In the marginalist schema the capital used in producing the last unit of output would bring no profit. This books' analysis of the origin of profit (Chapter 4 and its Appendix 1, and Chapter 6) entirely refutes this interpretation for which, incidentally, there has never been a shred of proof in terms of practical experience. A well-run business expects to get a profit from *all* the capital it has invested. And we have seen that in his treatment of "rent" Ricardo did not make this appalling blunder. For him, the "marginal" agricultural undertaking *did* make a profit, so much so that it was that profit which governed the rate of profit of the other undertakings, with "rent" as the leveler. So, for a whole century, capitalism has indulged in the extravagance of teaching an economic doctrine in which profit is no more than a by-product of the system!

## The Three "Scarcities"

In its various aspects, classical theory is able to explain the three principal phenomena filed, often a little too precipitately, under the heading of "scarcity."

1. *Indiscriminate use of natural resources or preempted growth*

There is the "scarcity" that comes from the indiscriminate use of natural resources, as often happens in the case of, say, air or water pollution, soil deterioration, and so on. The rule suggested by political economy would be to restore natural resources to their former state whenever the powers of nature prove not to be "indestructible" (see page 311). Moreover, technological progress should be directed primarily toward the development of new, "cleaner" manufacturing processes.

This book's analysis of value has made it possible to show why our economic growth is partly (if not wholly) preempted—without its being necessary to resort to airy theories about well-being, quality of life, and so on. The reason is that we make no allowance for the consumption of resources that we wrongly believe to be obtainable in plenty *without labor*. If industry, for example, endangers the supply of pure water, this means in economic terms that pure water henceforth has a certain exchange value, equal to the cost of installing water treatment plant or replacing polluting with nonpolluting technologies. Earlier I defined profit or net product as the excess of output over the consumption necessary to produce it. Needless to say, the calculation of the rate of profit—from which the rate of economic growth is calculated in turn—is distorted if consumption is not made to include the cost, as I have just defined it, of maintaining natural resources in their proper state. Probably the only course in some cases would be purely and simply to discontinue the production activity concerned, such as the shipment of oil in huge quantities, understanding that the wreck of a supertanker will cause ecological disaster. This would commensurately reduce the value of the gross product supposed to be a gauge of a nation's wealth.

2. *Scarcity caused by inflation*

In most cases scarcity is an illusion, as we saw with the spiraling of raw material and energy prices in 1972 and 1973. The price escalation is not, of course, due to a sudden change in the state of natural resources but to inflation, which creates "excess demand," namely demand independent of potential supply.

The situation in the market for scarce goods in this second category is liable to reverse itself dramatically. Following a period of prosperity in conditions of inflation, an economic recession could cause a collapse of raw material prices and then one would hear the same commentators who confused the rise in copper and tin prices with the pseudoscientific conclusions in the early 1970s of the Club of Rome on the depletion of natural resources speak once again of the "crisis of overproduction inherent in the capitalist system," or some other such nonsense.

3. *Scarcity due to a "monopolistic" policy*

Is oil a scarce good? No, certainly not, if one reckons with the fact that from present oilfields it is possible to produce as much as is needed, very cheaply. Yes, possibly, if one takes into account this second fact that proven reserves can meet no more than about thirty years' worth of present consumption. It was on this second line of reasoning that the oil-producing states raised taxes and royalties to the point where the market price aligned itself, according to them, with the price of "coal gasification or liquefaction" (a "marginal" source of energy). The corresponding revenues constitute the rent of the land(subsoil)owner, since they represent the difference between the cost of production of one barrel of oil (including the profit of the oil companies, which in this case replace the "farmer" in the Ricardian scheme) and the cost of production of the most expensive "comparable" fuel. In economic terms, however, the justification of rent, and its amount, depends on the *real* state of workable reserves, which is not known.

By raising the price of a resource that is cheap (but liable to become scarce if new reserves are not discovered) to the level of the "marginal replacement cost," a whole chain of events is set off—reduction of the demand previously stimulated by the cheapness of that resource, acceleration of technological progress which lowers the cost of competing resources, and so on and so forth—*the effect of which is to eliminate scarcity.*

## Economic Theory Is Independent of the Legal Order

Let it be noted that the theory of rent has the further advantage of revealing the inevitable opposition of interests between the entrepreneur-capitalist (the oil company, in this instance), whose aim is to sell as much as possible in order to increase his profits (representing a given percentage of the selling price), and the landowner (the oil country) anxious to maximize his rent, which implies a high price itself tending to limit consumption.

But is it in the interest of the entrepreneur-capitalist, too, to prolong the lifespan of the land (oilfields) from which he derives his profits? If we look back to what was said earlier about the nature of capital (see Chapter 3 and 6)—a permanent advance for its owner until such time as it is withdrawn from the productive process (or lost owing to adverse business circumstances)—we see that the capitalist is relatively independent of the activity in which he has invested his capital. When the oil is exhausted or has no more use, the oil company will invest its capital—incremented meanwhile by retained earnings—in other industries: nuclear power (if the company finds it more convenient to stay in the energy sector it already knows), making chewing gum, or any other activity that shows itself to be profitable at the time. Exhaustion of the oilfields per se would be a serious misfortune for the oil company only if it mismanaged the changeover, which would cause it to lose part of its capital (as we saw in Chapter 6, concerning equipment that has become obsolete). For the company, it is a question of expediency: choosing the right moment at which to switch its capital to another line of activity. For the landowner, the problem is very different: Exhaustion of the oilfield—or oil's replacement by other, cheaper fuels—means that his rent will cease. Thus it will be seen that it is in the oil company's interests to produce as much as possible, while oil is still in demand, so as to earn the maximum profit. Meanwhile it is in the oil country's interests not to make a gift of its rent to consumers, or to the oil companies, as long as oil is less expensive and easier to use than any other form of energy. Nor should it raise its rent, in the form of taxes, too high lest this hasten oil's replacement by any other competing energy form, the latter risk being lessened, incidentally, by the fact that oil and natural gas are used not only as fuel but also as feedstocks and raw materials for the chemicals and textile industries, among others.

It is a delusion—one dispelled by classical theory—to believe that the conflict of interest between landowner and capital-owner would vanish with a change in the system of capital ownership. Let us suppose that an oil state becomes, as is now happening, the owner of the capital of the oil companies (the latter possibly retaining their role of entrepreneur). This would not negate economic theory since its concepts are very much independent—possibly even totally independent—of the legal order of society. Having become the owner not only of the land (and what lies beneath) but also of the tools of production, the state would have to make a trade-off between its inevitably conflicting interests of landowner and capitalist. To date, only classical political economy has formulated the problem clearly. But for the last century or so economists have turned their backs to the door opened by Ricardo. Today's changed circumstances will probably force them to take up the line of reasoning where he left off. Arguing by reference to quantitative examples, which he himself admitted were simplified to the extreme, the greatest exponent of classical economics formulated the first rudiments of a complete theory of the divergent paths of rent and profit. According to that theory, rent is by force of circumstance destined to take an increasing share of net product away from capitalists, a tendency that is constantly being checked by technological progress, which has the effect of reducing the relative advantage of fertile over unfertile land and, mutatis mutandis, of oil over nuclear power and other energy sources.

## Putting Economic Science Back on Its Feet
## So As to Change the World

It is not difficult to see how the idea of "autonomous" demand can creep into the reasoning: The scheme by which supply necessarily precedes demand *seems* to condemn to starvation all those who, for one reason or another, are unable to produce. So, to prevent this dire outcome, should not demand be regarded as a force that has to be sustained for its own sake, or even to be created from nothing? Such an idea stems, in the last analysis, from the confusion of two viewpoints: the macroeconomic and that of the individual. At the macroeconomic level it is impossible to conceive of satisfied (effective) demand exceeding supply. At the level of the individual—and voter—there may be demand without supply because of income transfers, that is, redistribution of a part of production. The unfortunate thing is that demand-side policies are conceived on the macroeconomic scale. What they do is to create income artificially by pretending to give to some what is not (at least overtly) taken from others. The result is a permanent state of inflation, which by definition is impossible to bring under control because the only solid basis on which to govern an economy is equality (and inflation destroys that equality) between the total value of goods and services supplied and the total value of the income generated by that supply.

The precedence given to demand leads to constant overstimulation of wants, the most inevitable result of which is to disadvantage the consumer. This is something I have tried to show in this book, especially in my story of the man who prepares a meal and the man who eats it (Chapter 9). For the diner to be served the best possible meal, there clearly has to be an economic system built entirely around the idea of the customer getting "his money's worth," in other words, the principle of equivalence of exchange. The chef, however honest, will surely be tempted to charge as much as possible for a meal that has cost him as little as possible. The surest way of allowing him to do this is to establish an economic system that is demand biased. This will have the effect of making the chef summon all his ingenuity and talent to arouse in the diner "wants" that apparently are more and more sophisticated, but the common characteristic of which will be that they cost the chef (relatively) little to meet and the diner a great deal to assuage.

In a way, society has played at being rich, whereas if it had tried to keep our consumption proportionate to our ability to produce without harming the environment, we would probably have had to reduce that consumption significantly, until such time as progress in technology and organization of labor made it possible to put our available resources to better use. Mass production, which has enabled a large section of the population to acquire a certain material affluence, has in some cases simply replaced one form of poverty by another. In preindustrial societies a small minority were really well-off (exquisitely crafted objects for the home, as well as services of every sort from trained domestics, and more). But this sublime luxury was "paid for" by the poverty in which the great majority of the population lived. Today, many people enjoy a comfortable standard of living, but this (relative) well-being for a large segment of society has to be paid for, too. It is all very well to say that everyone can have a car, but this means producing ever greater quantities of pollution-emitting internal combustion engines. If we are marketing products that are harmful in one way or another, it is in fact because we are not rich enough to produce sufficient quantities of others that would meet our needs better and at the same time do no harm.

But it is pretty certain that things will change soon. Even before economists have had time to rediscover the labor theory of value, circumstances are again demanding that cost be given precedence over want. In business, production technologies are again becoming a more important consideration than sales techniques, because of the need to save energy and to bring down production costs often pushed up by pollution control.

At the same time mankind is discovering that it will not be "rich" until it is able to produce sufficient food for everyone (that is without resorting to crop-farming methods that could sooner or later exhaust the soil). Here again, success will largely depend on our ability to adapt the organization of the economy to the long-term needs of the population. When we are less obsessed with the idea of instant returns we can probably develop an agricultural system that will produce more, without perceptible harm to the natural environment.

A parallel development under way will take place in consumer habits, which will change radically. There will be less wastage, less pointless sophistication in the range of goods and services supplied. Greater preference will be given to better quality and durability. However, the necessary redirection of demand and the means of satisfying it is liable to be inhibited if not prevented by the economic system as it is now organized. It is completely locked into the short term and that is one of the main impediments. To resolve the problems that beset our society, business must extend not only its geographical horizon (which the exchange economy has managed to do fairly well up till now) but also its time horizon. But with the consumer-society demand-propelled economy and the inflation (which shows up through high interest rates) it inevitably breeds, the time span that calculations and forecasts are able to cover is no more than a few years or even months.

However, for economic activity to be able, through exchange, to redeploy itself in space (to the benefit of the poorest countries) and time (to the benefit of long-term investment), it is necessary among other things—as we have seen in Chapter 11—to reestablish something that today seems totally out of reach: namely, a general system of payments based on an objective conception of the value of money. This represents a reversal of thinking for which minds schooled in the neoliberal and hedonist doctrines bequeathed by the late nineteenth century economists are wholly unprepared. And it is here that we may perhaps begin to realize the vital need to reintroduce into economic science its true foundations by reverting to analysis of the objective value theory: Production costs are not determined independently of the market. In the absence of competition they would be higher. Another irreplaceable function of the market is to adjust the volume of output—and the cost of production will vary according to the quantity produced—to the changing volume of demand. Notwithstanding this circumstance, from the standpoint of classical economic theory the market ranks second to economic "law." Translated into political sociology terms, this means that in a society governed by really liberal principles (in the European sense), the marketers would not lay down the law. This is a far cry from the vulgar utilitarianism of the consumer society that would happily make "business schools" the highest form of university education and in whose view astute marketing is the foremost of human activities.

## An Extremely Serious Issue: Guaranteeing a Minimum Income for All

The sort of more or less leftward-leaning economics—and economic policy—inspired by this doctrine of "want," as Marxism may be defined, is not alone in its ignorance of the equations of economic science. The most modern neoclassical economic doctrines, descended from the psychological conception of value fabricated at the end of the last century, are suggesting to the politicians of Western Europe and North America programs the realization of which would almost certainly set their countries on a downward path.[15] This applies to the schemes in Britain, and elsewhere, to guarantee each taxpayer and ultimately each citizen a minimum income by means of an ingenious— or rather, overingenious—reform of taxation. At first glance, these schemes seem to provide an answer—neat in theory and efficient in practice—to the problem of poverty. If it is not easy to say why they are liable in the long run to exhaust the economic system, it is because the principle they flout is at once fundamental and definitionally imprecise. The principle is that income is linked with labor.

Since labor, as such, is excluded from the exchange circuit, it is impossible to say there is a determinate relation between the quantity of labor supplied by the worker and the quantity of goods and services he gets back in the form of wages. This is the central proposition of the Ricardian theory, as has been brought fully to light in this book (see Chapter 5). From that proposition the important conclusion follows that, contrary to what Taylorism maintains, there is no real correlation between wage and labor productivity. If productivity falls by 10 percent, say, there is no reason why wages should automatically be docked by 10 percent. Similarly, if productivity increases—which is more frequently the case—the system's logic does not imply that wages should increase by exactly the same proportion (they may do so, but they may also increase by more or by less, depending on the circumstances).

As Ricardo thought (and Marx after him), the level of the wage is largely a matter of judgment. It depends on how, at each moment of time and in each country, the "needs" of this or that category of wage earners are rated. In fact, as I have shown in Chapter 6, the wage in the strict sense is a resultant of the rate of profit; this is the key variable of economic science which is so difficult for *political* economy to "sell"! But its amount, thus objectively determined, is increased by the inclusion of a certain share of the net product. So the wage-versus-profit notion is not so clear-cut as might appear at first glance. Since the actual amount of the wage, currently designated by the nonscientific expression "payment for labor," is, within certain limits, determined by the habits and customs of the moment, why should not our "brave new world" venture further? In particular, why should the fact that income is linked with labor be regarded as sacred dogma? Does not the way forward consist, among other things, in determining, given all the facts we now know, the "minimum needs" of a man living in a developed society in the late twentieth century and guaranteeing this minimum standard of living to every citizen, whether employed or not?

It is significant that this tempting and seemingly revolutionary project is currently advocated, in the English-speaking countries, by dedicated free-marketers like Milton Friedman. In the area of incomes policy this might be termed the culminating point of the want-based economic doctrine. But the characteristic of a false doctrine is that it fails to achieve its object. Schemes providing a guaranteed income for everyone are probably the surest way to swell the ranks of the poor. I am aware that I am probably taking a risk in spelling out this inconsistency since, among free-marketers, the idea of a guaranteed minimum income is gaining ground and the leftists will probably accuse me of succumbing to the blind belief in work (of others).

Let us first examine the principle of the many minimum-income schemes now under study.

In its simplest form, the system is structured like this: The government estimates that each individual should receive a minimum of, say, 600 francs a month—a figure chosen at random and bearing no relation to present reality—to bring him above the "poverty line." Each citizen, therefore, whether employed or not, will have *the right* to receive this sum.

Let us suppose, then, that Pierre, hitherto unemployed, has managed to find a job that will bring him a monthly income of F.500. If the system is applied absolutely strictly, all the state will pay him is the difference between the "statutory minimum" and his wage, in other words, F.600 − F.500 = F.100. For Pierre this is virtually the same thing as having his wages taxed at the rate of 100 percent, so there is no incentive for him to work.

To get round this drawback, the legislature has no alternative but, so to speak, to apply a lower rate of tax, say 30 percent. In our example the result would be this: The state will pay Pierre, who is now earning F.500, the difference between F.600 and F.150 [(500 × 30)/100], that is, F.450. His total monthly income will now be F.500 + F.450 = F.950. In other words, if he goes out to work and earns F.500, Pierre will increase his income by F.950 − F.600[16] = F.350.

Let us suppose that Pierre still wants to better himself and therefore works harder and earns F.600 a month. The state will now pay him F.600 − F.180 [(600 × 30)/100] = F.420, giving him a total income of F.600 + F.420 = F.1,020. So Pierre increases his income by F.1,020 − F.600 = F.420.

One can therefore say that, below a certain income threshold, the system in its extreme form completely destroys the incentive to work, and in its more moderate form blunts that incentive to a greater or lesser degree, because its effect is to introduce steep progressivity of taxation at the lower end of the income ladder. The schemes that have been devised are inevitably more complex than the rudimentary one outlined here, since they have to take into account a great number of factors (of which size of family is one), but all of them have at least one consequence in common, and that is to weaken the incentive to work. It was because of this that in the summer of 1969 the U.S. Senate shelved, sine die, the White House plan for guaranteed minimum incomes. Had it been adopted, the plan would in some cases have had really astonishing results. One case quoted was that of a family which, if no one worked, could have received an annual allowance of $6,000, whereas if some members of the family were foolish enough to earn the greater part of that sum themselves, about $20 would automatically be lost.

By and large, the plans proposed are less ambitious. Most of them are linked—another idea of Milton Friedman's—with a reform of the traditional tax system.

The negative income tax schemes seem to be designed in such a way as not to interfere with the exchange mechanism. Their originality, it can be argued, is that the minimum income level they are intended to guarantee is not an obligation on businesses since, if the latter are unable to pay the equivalent minimum wage, it is the "new-style" tax regime which will make up the income difference by means of the tax credit. But the "system" is neutral only at the level of each individual business. At the level of the national economy, this neutrality is a pretense, since what the system does is to disconnect demand from supply by making the amount of distributed income depend on discretionary policy and on nothing else.

Under the parliamentary system of government, the nation's elected representatives decide by vote the amount of tax to be deducted from incomes formed entirely without their intervention. Under the scheme proposed, a political decision would determine the minimum income level *independently* of the forces of the market. What is to prevent Parliament from raising that level at any time for the benefit of all citizens, whether taxpayers or not? Some will trust in "commonsense" and "a sense of proportion" to keep demands within acceptable limits. But both experience and reason show that appeals to "popular consensus" are never *by themselves* capable of taking the place of a regulatory mechanism that does not exist or exists no longer (governments which rely on the "goodwill" of employers and workers to bring inflation under control daily demonstrate the ineffectiveness of such appeals).

The reader may object that such schemes, if applied strictly, are simply a more highly developed system of redistributing existing income. To condemn it would therefore be just as retrograde as the arguments advanced half a century ago by those who claimed to see in progressive income tax a death blow to capitalism. (Though sooner or later the time will come for a serious discussion of tax progressivity, which has been regarded, wrongly, as the perfection of fiscal justice.) In answer, I would say that what the system of negative income tax does in effect is to introduce progressivity of taxation into the lower earning brackets—in other words, where the "disincentive to work" will be strongest. It allocates, as supplementary income, a share of net product to the lowest-paid workers. When the production effort has been slowed—as it inevitably will be—by the "work disincentive" that the scheme causes, the surplus that will then more than ever be needed to finance capital/labor substitution will decrease, at least in relative terms. This slower growth of production will affect the entire population. To remedy this state of affairs, Parliament will have to increase tax credits again, and so on and so forth.

To avoid this chain of events, there would have to be fantastic advances in technology, and, even then, technology seems hardly likely ever to be able to replace man's labor in services, where the manpower shortage is liable to be particularly serious.

It is only too easy to imagine the hypocrisy with which such a system would have to be implemented so as to alleviate the inevitable consequences. Newly arrived foreign workers, if not all foreign workers, would have to be made ineligible since, if this "precaution" were not taken, it would soon be necessary to close the frontiers—a measure as unjustifiable, in its *principle,* as the system dictating it.

The idea that a regular and sufficient income can be guaranteed to anyone in return for *not* working would never occur to a worker. In fact, it is typically the idea of a wealthy man "of private means" incapable of thinking in terms other than his own. Automatically giving the lowest-paid worker an income increment is a disincentive to self-improvement, through training, and so on. The personal development process implicit in any progressive society is thus balked at the first step.

In such circumstances there can be hardly any doubt that middle-income earners, seeing low-paid workers benefit from the tax credit, will try to win pay increases in order to restore the differentials that have been squeezed by unearned advantages. But the reappearance of those differentials will make the lower wage levels seem too low by comparison. So there will be renewed pressure on the government to increase the tax credit, and so on and so forth. This is another reason for thinking that the system, far from having its own built-in brake, is put together in such a way that it will siphon off a growing share of the state's income as it increases the number of the nation's "poor."

If one compares the negative income tax schemes with the system recently applied in France and elsewhere to guarantee all workers a minimum wage, one sees that the latter, provided it is managed sufficiently flexibly,[17] is much the superior from the economic standpoint. First, because it assigns a limit to the discretionary action of government: Since the minimum wage is paid direct by employers, its amount must be decided in the light of the ability of businesses to meet this imposed wage cost. Second, because a raising of the minimum wage encourages the most progressive businesses to modernize their equipment and management methods, which is something the negative tax system does not do; if anything it encourages employers to pay very low wages in the knowledge that the state will augment them.

That having been said, it is right and proper that society should extend a helping hand to the neediest of its members. The whole question is how to avoid setting up a social system leaving permanently open the question of whether man is to be allowed to exploit society in idleness or is to be exploited by society in dignity!

## Political Economy and the "Poor Laws"

What helps to give negative tax its "cachet" is its seeming newness. It is seen as the response of the conservatives of our time to the question posed by socialism.

History tells a very different story. Guaranteeing a minimum income for all is a replica, nearly two centuries later, of the Poor Laws enacted in England in the eighteenth century with the purpose of guaranteeing a minimum income for the poverty-stricken and supplementing the incomes of the lowest-paid workers.

Just as the negative tax system is intended to do today, the Poor Laws gave a *right* to the needy. But whether enshrined in law or not, the fact remains that systems of this kind belong to the domain of public charity. Even Maoist China knew that. The people's commune of Tatchai was often held up as an example in those times. The 300 or so inhabitants of this little Chinese village used to, we were told, reject help from the state when misfortune struck. Even if their gesture was no more than compliance with orders from an all-powerful party, it had the merit of reminding one that, no matter what the regime, charity cannot be substituted for exchange, however thwarted the latter may be (as in Maoist China), as the *general principle* of society's organization, except at the cost of man's dignity.

Because their introduction was followed by an unbroken increase in the number of assisted persons, the Poor Laws gave rise to great controversy in the late eighteenth and early nineteenth centuries. William Pitt, who led Britain to victory against Napoleon, was an ardent supporter. Ricardo, on the other hand, wrote this:

> If by law every human being wanting support could be sure to obtain it, and obtain it in such a degree as to make life tolerably comfortable, theory would lead us to expect that all other taxes together would be light compared with the single one of poor rates. The principle of gravitation is not more certain than the tendency of such laws to change wealth and power into misery and weakness; to call away the exertions of labour from every object, except that of providing mere subsistence.

But then Ricardo added:

> Happily these laws have been in operation during a period of progressive prosperity, when the funds for the maintenance of labour have regularly increased, and when an increase of population would be naturally called

for. But if our progress should become more slow; if we should attain the stationary state, from which I trust we are yet far distant, then will the pernicious nature of these laws become more manifest and alarming; and then, too, will their removal be obstructed by many additional difficulties. (*Principles*, chap. 5)

There can be no doubt that Ricardo's critique was just as shocking to his contemporaries as it would be to ours. But the question here is not whether it is unseemly to criticize the Poor Laws in their original or in their present version; it is whether they are capable of fulfilling their purpose, which is to reduce or even eradicate poverty in our "rich societies."

But the problem goes far beyond assistance grants as such. The big countries of the Western world have let their social welfare expenditure as a whole get out of control. If that expenditure continues to grow at its present rate, it is hard to see what can prevent it from swallowing up all the proceeds of growth (*net* national product) in the relatively near future, a possibility that British classical economics foresaw.[18]

The quantitative studies done several years ago in France by the National Plan experts were particularly significant in this regard. Their conclusions were so disturbing that the file was hurriedly closed almost as soon as it had been opened. By now, bleak prospects of this kind can hold nothing surprising for the reader. They follow logically from our finding that *an economic system with want as its sole guide has no built-in regulator.* I would point out that the few measures which were taken in France to try to bring the nation's welfare budget back into balance consisted in reintroducing the consideration of cost alongside that of need. In its way, the "reform" of the French social security system, promised a long time ago but continually postponed, is one episode in the struggle between psychological economics and objective economics. It illustrates the need to return to the latter if society is not to be condemned to stagnation and the proliferation of useless expenditures.

### Individual Insecurity and Collective Security

Up to what point should the material security of the individual be guaranteed? Today, as at the dawn of the industrial revolution, this is probably the biggest issue of all. It is likely to become increasingly central to economic and political thinking, especially if we are to enter a period of more or less pronounced recession [written in 1973]. It is not an issue that can be settled by across-the-board solutions, since two dimensions are involved, each with its own different principle. On the one hand, there is the production of wealth (goods and services), which is governed by the laws of exchange; on the other, there is the use of part of that wealth for purposes other than production, or at any rate purposes which are not directly productive, such as education, health care, and so on.

Unfortunately, national accounts do not sufficiently clearly differentiate between the two, and this compounds the confusion since they do not—or should not—answer to the same principles of organization.

As far as exchange is concerned, theory and experience show that the better form of organization is that provided by a market operating in conditions of maximum competition, and competition does not allow "protection" of competitors. Once a business or a social group arrogates a monopoly to itself, the "monopolists" inhibit the development of other businesses and other groups. One could say of a society governed by the principle of competition that the security of its collective future is in direct ratio to the insecurity of each of its constituent members. The biologist would not disagree with the economist on this point.

The redistribution of wealth proceeds, by nature, from an entirely different principle, since its primary objective is to redress the inequality of income distribution that occurs in a market economy (mainly because of the capital accumulation mechanism). The exchange economy is based on a relationship of equality that concerns *products* (which should be traded value for like value), whereas income redistribution is based—or should be—on a relationship of equality between people: Everyone is entitled to the same health care, the same education, the same police protection, the same guarantees from the courts of law, and so on. Exchange is no guarantee of justice, but how can justice be sought in ignorance of the law of exchange?

## Notes

1. And we have also shown (see Chapter 4 and its Appendix 1) that there is likewise "exchange" if I make the net myself.
2. To these two categories the classicists, rightly, added rent, but rent can be regarded as profit in another guise.
3. On the theoretical absence of the need to have a unit of account, see pages 274 and 291–92.

4. In the late 1950s, most opinion leaders in France (several of whom have since been completely won over to American-style capitalism) still believed so implicitly in the superiority of the planning method that for them it was only a matter of time before the Soviet Union overtook the United States. The newspapers and magazine articles of the time tell us that the "pessimists" predicted Soviet GNP would catch up with U.S. GNP by about 1970, whereas the "optimists" gave the United States a few more years in the lead. It was to disgrace the idea that the East would outpace the West that in 1961 the OECD proposed as a target for its member countries that their combined GNP should double in the decade of the 1960s. The present obsession with growth for growth's sake, the equation of civilization with a high output of steel tonnage, can be traced straight to socialism. Capitalism in effect has done no more than to play follow-the-leader, only it has had the wherewithal to come out in front!

5. Keynes, *General Theory,* chap. 13. Similarly, in *Theory of Value* (1959) the French economist Debreu considers two equilibrium models of a "perfect market," one of which is defined by the fact that the future in it is known with absolute certainty. This assumption alone would be enough to discredit the concept of market equilibrium, since it is founded on an indefensible conception of determinism (see Chapter 10).

6. The best-remembered feature of this period was the growth of military expenditure due to the Vietnam War. But from the economist's standpoint it was even more marked by the steepest rise ever in U.S. nondefense spending (the Great Society).

7. My parenthesis.

8. I am excluding, for the time being, the all too frequent case where supply is intentionally limited.

9. As did Malthus. For once the two opponents are in agreement.

10. The farmer or the mine exploiter here is both entrepreneur and owner of "capital" (farm implements, fertilizer). But for the purposes of the argument, he is considered solely as a capitalist.

11. Inevitably Ricardo's thesis drew the objection that the farmer of even the most unfertile land still has to pay "rent" to his landlord. Ricardo's answer was that this "rent" has nothing to do with the rent that is the subject of the theory discussed here. The first kind of rent represents interest on capital, since almost invariably the landowner has invested some capital in his land, if only in the form of access tracks, hedges, and so on—all "accumulated products of labor." Furthermore, Ricardo does not usually reason on the difference in returns to capital and labor on land of varying fertility, but on the difference in returns as between successive and equal applications of capital and labor to the same land. This is why rent, with the meaning it has in classical political economy (see Chapter 3), is payable on almost all land.

12. Rent is only a form of profit. That is why it does not constitute a category apart.

13. An idea that is very easy to understand on reading Ricardo's hypotheti-

cal account of successive applications of capital and labor to *the same plot of land* (see note 11, page 332).

14. See in particular "Notes on Piero Sraffa's 'Prelude,' " p. 335.

15. The French socialist government has introduced a *salaire minimum d'insertion* at the end of 1988, in order to "tackle the problem of poverty."

16. The sum he would receive from the authorities if he decided not to work.

17. If the system of compulsory payment of a minimum wage is applied indiscriminately (which is often the case), this may prevent the hiring of some persons capable of doing only very rudimentary—which is not the same as "useless"—work.

18. In the same chapter Ricardo wrote: "whilst the present laws are in force, it is quite in the natural order of things that the fund for the maintenance of the poor should progressively increase till it has absorbed all the net revenue of the country, or at least so much of it as the state shall leave to us, after satisfying its own never-failing demands for the public expenditure."

# Notes on Piero Sraffa's "Prelude"

With regard to Piero Sraffa's key work, *Production of Commodities by Means of Commodities*, I shall confine myself to a few comments on the subjects dealt with specifically in my book. Sraffa's book, which he presents as a *Prelude to a Critique of Economic Theory*, constituted the point of departure for a return (as yet incomplete) to the classical approach, in that it restated the problems of profit and value (price) with no reference to the pseudoanalyses of the marginalists but in terms of cost of production. However, the weak point of Sraffa's analysis is that he does not show how price and profit interrelate with exchange, and the reason is that he has to some extent remained a prisoner of Marxist vocabulary and hence of Marxist interpretation.

I can give several examples of this Marxist taint. In chapter 9 of his book Sraffa writes that "the conclusion about the quantity of labour 'contained' [his quotation marks] in a commodity and its proportionality to value at zero profits can also, without any straining of the ordinary meaning of words, be extended to commodities jointly produced." The beginning of the sentence is Marxist and the rest (from "its proportionality" onward) is Ricardian. Sraffa's manner of formulation is even more confused (thus marring a work admirable in the rigor of its reasoning) in chapter 10, paragraph 80, where he writes: "Since in the case of zero profits the original value represents the quantity of labour that has been required to produce the machine, it is

335

natural to extend this notion to the subsequent years and say that its value at any given age represents the quantity of labour which it 'embodies' [Sraffa's quotation marks], that is to say the quantity which has gone to produce it, minus such quantities as year by year have passed into its product." For Sraffa, therefore, value "represents" a quantity of labor (in spite of the fact that labor is essentially different from "value," as we have seen) which, as for Marx, is "embodied" in the commodity. However, Sraffa's use of quotation marks may denote a certain distrust of this vocabulary which, to use Marxist language, makes labor the "substance" of value, especially since in a number of instances Sraffa speaks, correctly, of the "proportionality" of value to the quantity of labor. I shall return a little later to Sraffa's machine.

Sraffa states the problem of distribution correctly when he says that if the wage rises, profit decreases and vice versa. But he abides by the Marxist interpretation, the erroneousness of which I have demonstrated, when he describes (chap. 1, paragraphs 15 ff.) the process in the event of a change in the rate of profit. In that event, he sees "deficit industries," those with the lowest proportion of labor to means of production, and "surplus industries," those with the highest proportion of labor to means of production. In the deficit industries, a fall in the wage will not release enough to pay the profit on capital (means of production), whereas in the surplus industries a wage reduction will release more than is necessary for the payment of profit to the owners of means of production.

To reason in this way is implicitly to admit the Marxist distinction between exchange value and *price of production* (i.e., selling price), the former being converted into the latter by the workings of the market, which redistributes surplus value equally among all owners of capital in order to achieve a uniform rate of profit. I have already shown (in Chapters 4 and 5) that this manner of presenting things, derived from volume 3 of *Capital*, is not justified. In a free market, prices are determined by the laws of exchange of which a built-in element, as I think I have shown, is the inclusion of profit (whatever the nature of the capital committed) and therefore exchange value is a notion directly related to market price. One might say that the apportionment of gross product between profit and wage is determined for the entire economy and, through the workings of the market, that rate of apportionment is imposed on all the enterprises participating in the market (in countries where the market is not unified, i.e. the "dual economy," there can be more than one rate of apportionment).

The market is in fact the place of greatest *transparency*, whereas for

Marx—and in this case for Sraffa, too—it is that obscure place where the surplus industries cede their surplus to the deficit industries, the result of which is to distort somewhat the "true" prices which would correspond to each industry's particular mix of labor and means of production. This conception is pointless and false inasmuch as it seems to imply that exchange value can be independent of exchange. Sraffa assumes that between time $t_1$ and $t_2$ the rate of profit rises from, say, 10 to 20 percent of the gross product (and wages in consequence fall from 90 to 80% of gross product). Like Ricardo (and like Marx), he shows that this change will determine changes in price reflecting the different proportions of labor to means of production used by different industries. Like Marx, Sraffa sees the purpose of these price changes as being to redress the balance of the rate of profit between industries. This vision of things presupposes that, conceptually, between $t_1$ and $t_2$ everything takes place first in the account books of enterprises (Sraffa wrongly assumes that a change in the rate of profit leaves the same competitors on the market), inasmuch as they have to pay less in wages in order to pay out more in profits, and second in the market-place, where the surplus of certain industries is ceded to the so-called deficit industries; whereas everything takes place first in the market (with consequent repercussions on the account books of enterprises), where the exchange phenomenon may have the further effect of eliminating from competition a certain number of enterprises or a certain number of items of capital equipment which, as I have shown in my ultrasimplified example of the machine which has the same yield as a man, cease to be usable at a higher rate of profit.

On the other hand, Sraffa parts company with both Ricardo and Marx when he assumes that the sums paid in wages bring no profit in the current year, this being postulated in the equation he writes in chapter 6:

$$L_a w + L_{a_1} w (1 + r) + \ldots + L_{a_n} w (1 + r)^n + \ldots = A p_a$$

This is a wrong way of writing the production equation, though admittedly it is consistent with all modern analyses and in particular with all the analyses based on the concept of "value added."

The ambiguity of Sraffa's thinking is again strikingly apparent when, after ingeniously constructing a standard capable of infallibly indicating the origin of price movements (by neutralizing those caused by changes in the value of the standard itself), he writes that the best measure of value is "the quantity of labour that can be purchased by the Standard net product" (chap. 3, paragraph 43).

Despite his immense merit, Sraffa has indeed come no further than a "prelude" to the "critique of political economy," since he too continues to regard the quantity of labor as a commodity.

Sraffa might have also remained on the surface of Ricardian theory without being able to get to the heart of it when he says that the rate of profit can be determined by "the level of the money rates of interest," whereas Ricardo was right, in contradistinction to neoclassical theoreticians, when he said that the rate of interest is determined by the rate of profit and not the other way around. Was Straffa fully able to reintroduce profit into the general mechanism of exchange?

Sraffa also assumes (chap. 10) that the profit yielded by a machine diminishes with the years because the price of the machine diminishes with wear and tear. In fact, as we have seen, profit is the remuneration of the saving and not of the particular asset that has been purchased with that saving.

# Selected Bibliography

Allais, Maurice. "Les théories de l'équilibre économique général et l'efficacité maximale—Impasses récentes et nouvelles perspectives." *Revue d'économie politique,* Paris, June 1971.

Althusser, Louis. *Pour Marx.* Paris: François Maspéro, n.d.

——. *Lire le Capital.* Vols. 1 and 2. Paris: François Maspéro, 1970.

Aron, Raymond. *D'une Sainte Famille à l'autre.* Paris: Gallimard, 1969.

Barkai, Haim. "The Labour Theory of Value as an Operational Proposition." *Economica,* London School of Economics, May 1970.

Barre, Raymond. *Economie politique* (2 vols.). Paris: Presses Universitaires de France, 1955.

Blaug, Mark. *Economic Theory in Retrospect.* 3d ed. Irwin, 1978.

de Marchi, N. B. "The Empirical Content and Longevity of Ricardian Economics." *Economica,* London School of Economics, August 1970.

Eatwell, John. "The Interpretation of Ricardo's *Essay on Profits.*" *Economica,* London School of Economics, May 1975.

Engels, Friedrich. *Anti-Dühring.* Paris: Editions Sociales, 1955.

Fisher, Irving. *The Nature of Capital and Income.* New York: Augustus M. Kelley ("reprints of Economic Classics"), 1965.

Friedman, Milton. *Price Theory.* Chicago: Aldine, 1962.

Harcourt, G. C. *Some Cambridge Controversies in the Theory of Capital.* London: Cambridge University Press, 1972.

Hicks, J. R. *Value and Capital*. 2d ed. London: Oxford University Press, ElyHouse, 1968.

Keynes, John Maynard. *A Treatise on Money: The Pure Theory of Money*. London: Macmillan for the Royal Economic Society, n.d.

———. *The General Theory*. London: Macmillan for the Royal Economic Society, 1973.

———. *Essays in Biography*. New York: Norton, 1963.

———. "The Balance of Payments of the United States." *Economic Journal*, London, June 1946.

———. *The End of Laisser-faire*. London: Hogarth Press, 1926.

Konüs, A. A. "The Empirical Assumption of Ricardo's 93% Labour Theory of Value. A Comment." *Economica*, London School of Economics.

Leijonhufvud, Axel. *On Keynesian Economics and the Economics of Keynes. A Study in Monetary Theory*. New York: Oxford University Press, 1968.

Malthus, Thomas Robert. *Principles of Political Economy Considered with a View to Their Practical Applications*. Published in the second volume of Ricardo's works with the *Notes* on Malthus' *Principles*.

Marshall, Alfred. *Elements of Economic Industry*. London: Macmillan, 1964.

Marx, Karl. *Capital* (6 vols.). Translation by Joseph Roy, revised by Karl Marx. Paris: Editions Sociales, 1950.

———. The English version *Capital*. Introduced by Ernest Mandel, translated by Ben Fowkes. Harmondsworth, U.K.: Pelican Marx Library, Penguin Books, 1976.

———. *Oeuvres*. *Economie* (2 vols.). New translation and editing. Paris: Bibliothèque de la Pléiade, Gallimard.

Von Neumann, John, and Morgenstern, Oskar. *Theory of Games and Economic Behavior*. New York: Wiley, 1967.

Ricardo, David. *Complete Works* (10 vols.). Edited by Piero Sraffa. Cambridge, U.K.: Cambridge University Press, 1966.

Robinson, Joan. *The Rate of Interest and Other Essays*. London: Macmillan, 1979.

Say, Jean-Baptiste. *Traité d'économie politique*. Paris: Calmann Levy, 1972.

Smith, Adam. *The Wealth of Nations*. Edited by Edwin Cannan. New York: Modern Library, 1965.

Sraffa, Piero. *Production of Commodities by Means of Commodities: Prelude to a Critique of Economic Theory*. Cambridge, U.K.: Cambridge University Press, 1977.

Walker, Argus. "Karl Marx. The Declining Rate of Profit and British Political Economy." *Economica*, London School of Economics, November 1971.

Walras, Léon. *Abrégé des éléments d'économie politique pure ou théorie de la richesse sociale*. Paris: R. Pichon et Durand-Auzias, 1952.

# Index